EIKON BASILIKE

with selections from
EIKONOKLASTES

broadview editions
series editor: L.W. Conolly

EIKON BASILIKE

The Portraiture of
His Sacred Majesty
in His Solitudes and Sufferings

with selections from
EIKONOKLASTES

John Milton

edited by Jim Daems and Holly Faith Nelson

broadview editions

Library and Archives Canada Cataloguing in Publication

Eikon basilike : the portraiture of His Sacred Majesty in his solitudes and sufferings : with selections from Eikonoklastes, John Milton / edited by Jim Daems and Holly Faith Nelson.

(Broadview editions)
First published soon after the execution of King Charles I in 1649, this work purports to be his autobiography, although John Gauden claimed authorship later.
Includes bibliographical references.
ISBN 1-55111-594-8

1. Charles I, King of England, 1600-1649. 2. Great Britain—History—Civil War, 1642-1649—Sources. 3. Spiritual biography—Great Britain—Early works to 1800. 4. Charles I, King of England, 1600-1649—Portraits. I. Charles I, King of England, 1600-1649. II. Daems, Jim, 1966- III. Nelson, Holly Faith, 1966- IV. Gauden, John, 1605-1662. V. Milton, John, 1608-1674. Eikonoklastes. VI. Title.

Portraiture of His Sacred Majesty in his solitudes and sufferings.

DA400.E49 2005   941.06′2   C2005-904478-0

Broadview Editions

The Broadview Editions series represents the ever-changing canon of literature in English by bringing together texts long regarded as classics with valuable lesser-known works.
Advisory editor for this volume: Jennie Rubio

Broadview Press Ltd. is an independent, international publishing house, incorporated in 1985. Broadview believes in shared ownership, both with its employees and with the general public; since the year 2000 Broadview shares have traded publicly on the Toronto Venture Exchange under the symbol BDP.

North America
Post Office Box 1243, Peterborough, Ontario, Canada K9J 7H5
3576 California Road, Post Office Box 1015, Orchard Park, NY, USA 14127
Tel: (705) 743-8990; Fax: (705) 743-8353;
email: customerservice@broadviewpress.com

UK, Ireland, and continental Europe
NBN Plymbridge, Estover Road, Plymouth PL6 7PY UK
Tel: 44 (0) 1752 202301;   Fax: 44 (0) 1752 202331
Fax Order Line: 44 (0) 1752 202333
Customer Service: cservs@nbnplymbridge.com Orders: orders@nbnplymbridge.com

Australia and New Zealand
UNIREPS, University of New South Wales
Sydney, NSW, 2052 Australia
Tel: 61 2 9664 0999; Fax: 61 2 9664 5420
email: info.press@unsw.edu.au

www.broadviewpress.com

Broadview Press Ltd. gratefully acknowledges the financial support of the Government of Canada through the Book Publishing Industry Development Program for our publishing activities.

Typesetting and assembly: True to Type Inc., Mississauga, Canada.

PRINTED IN CANADA

For Willy Daems and Marion Paterson Wilson Dunn
and in memory of
Elisabeth Daems (1934–2003) and
James Campbell Henderson (1936–1993)

Contents

Acknowledgements

In preparing this edition for publication, we have incurred many debts. We acknowledge the SSHRC funding granted to us by Trinity Western University, which ensured the timely completion of this project. We are indebted to Alan Rudrum and W. Speed Hill, teachers who have greatly contributed to our understanding of the editorial process. We wish to acknowledge Robert Wilcher, whose conversations and scholarship on *Eikon Basilike* have greatly benefited this volume, and Thomas N. Corns, for his advice early in the project on our selections from *Eikonoklastes*. We want to express our appreciation to our research assistant, Elizabeth Anne Roosien, and to the librarians and staff at the British Library, Simon Fraser University Library, and the Norma Marion Alloway Library, particularly Ted Goshulak and Sharon Vose, whose able assistance was inestimable. We also wish to recognize Kent Clarke for his advice on Greek translation, Carl Peters for sharing his editorial experience, and Randy Radney for his counsel on early-modern philology. We are most grateful to Kevin Sharpe, whose monumental research on Charles I and his writings significantly informed this project. We wish to express our deepest thanks to Sheila Roberts—teacher, humanitarian, and friend—for her willingness to impart her expertise on early-modern literature and for her unwavering encouragement. Our greatest debt is to our parents, to whom this volume is dedicated; and to Russell, Caleb, and Faith Nelson, who lovingly supported a much absent wife and mother.

List of Illustrations

Introduction

Vota dabunt, quæ bella negârunt.[1]
— *Eikon Basilike*

"In a word, it [*Eikon Basilike*] was an army and did vanquish more than any sword could."
—Bishop John Gauden

"Thy book [*Eikon Basilike*] is our best language."
—Francis Gregory

"There was in it [*Eikon Basilike*] a nobleness and a justness of thought, with a greatness of style, that made it to be looked on as the best writ book in the English language."
—Bishop Gilbert Burnet

The Royal Resurrection

Soon after the execution of Charles I outside the Banqueting House of Whitehall Palace, *Eikon Basilike: the Portraiture of His Sacred Majesty in His Solitudes and Sufferings* made its appearance. Decapitated on the afternoon of 30 January 1649, Charles I was resurrected in print in this portrait of the king. The regicides had taken every precaution to prevent the scene on the scaffold becoming a spectacle of martyrdom: "Divers Companies of Foot and Troops of Horse were placed on each side of the Street, which hindred the Approach of the very numerous Spectators, and the King from speaking what he had premeditated, and prepared for them to hear" (Nalson 113). The troops served to thwart rescue attempts, to muffle the voice of the king, and to prevent, for the most part, the collection of relics. Only moments after the axe fell, the troops forced the spectators from the site of the execution. However, despite the carefully crafted directives of Parliament, the words of Charles I were indelibly recorded on the pages of *Eikon Basilike*, "the King's Book." Though most copies of *Eikon Basilike* were seized and destroyed in London, the royalist pub-

---

1 "What we could not get by our Treaties, we may gain by our Prayers."

lisher Richard Royston moved a press outside of the city and ensured that *Eikon Basilike* made its appearance on the day of the king's death. The book's profound effect on its royalist readers, therefore, foiled the attempts of Parliament to prevent the birth of the Cult of the Royal Martyr.

Eikon Basilike was an immediate commercial success in Britain and, soon after, on the Continent: thirty-five editions of the book were published in England and twenty-five elsewhere in Europe in 1649 alone (Madan 2). In the *History of His Own Time*, Bishop Burnet recalls that the volume "had the greatest run in many impressions that any book has had in our age" (I.50). Though his political and ecclesiastical policies were often unpopular during his reign, this professed final testament of Charles I proved a rhetorical tour de force whose influence and popularity were undiminished even by the polemical prose of John Milton, one of the most brilliant prose controversialists of his age. A political and financial triumph, its publishing success and the pamphlet debate it provoked bears out that it was, indeed, as Elizabeth Skerpan claims, "the most popular and influential tract of the English Revolution" ("Rhetorical Genres" 101).[1]

In life, Charles I had been careful to control the production and reproduction of his image. John Peacock has demonstrated Charles' attentiveness to the politics of portraiture in multiple media, for Charles oversaw the circulation of his sacred image on coinage, medals, prints, sculpture, paintings, and masques. Charles was variously fashioned by his admirers and himself an imperial cavalier, Protestant hero, sacred monarch, chivalric lover, victorious Hercules, guardian of the people, and forgiving patriarch. However, the portrait of Charles in *Eikon Basilike* is unsurpassed, for in this work the king is transformed into "*the Martyr of the People*," a title he grants himself in his scaffold speech (Appendix B.3).

Kevin Sharpe notes the irony of the post-mortem popularity of the king when he remarks, "there can be little doubt that his man-

---

1   Its commercial success is all the more impressive when we consider the cost of *Eikon Basilike* in 1649: copies sold for as much as fifteen shillings. In *The Cult of King Charles the Martyr*, Andrew Lacey cites a letter written in 1649 from Richard Holdsworth to William Sancroft, later Archbishop of Canterbury, to advise him that the volume was "excessively dear," particularly those printed by Richard Royston, which were "above six shillings"(85).

ner of dying was the most popular thing Charles I ever did" ("Image Doting" 32). A mythology surrounded Charles I soon after his execution, which gave rise to the Cult of the Royal Martyr. This mythology was perhaps aided by an odd coincidence, revealed to the king on the morning of his death:

> That Morning, before his Majesty was brought thence, the Bishop of *London* (who with much ado was permitted to wait upon him a day or two before, and to assist him in that sad Instant) read Divine Service in his Presence; in which the 27th of St. *Matt.* (the History of our Saviours Crucifixion) proved the Second Lesson. The King supposing it to have been selected on purpose, thank'd him afterwards for his seasonable Choice: But the Bishop modestly declining that, undue Thanks, told him that it was the *Lesson* appointed by the *Calendar* for that day, He also then and there received of the Bishop the *Holy Sacrament*, and performed his Devotions in preparation to his Passion. (Nalson 112)

Charles' identity as a martyred saint was also fostered by the additional material included in later editions of *Eikon Basilike*: emotive prayers attributed to the king, dramatic accounts of his final encounters with two of his youngest children, and fervent elegies on the slain king (205-16).[1]

In the royalist literature of mourning published after the execution, Charles I was heralded "A Butcher'd Martyr King," a "Princely Proto-Martyr" whose spilt blood was capable of healing the sick of scrofula and blindness (qtd in Raymond 65). Elegies abounded on the executed king, whom poets often identified with the suffering and slain Christ.[2] Thomas Pierce predicted,

> *Posterity will say, he should have died*
> *No other Death,* than by being *Crucified.*

---

1 All quotations from *Eikon Basilike* and the supplementary material published in later editions are taken from this Broadview edition.
2 For a discussion of poems on Charles' execution, see Chapter 5 ("The Unprecedented Future") in Gerald M. MacLean's *Time's Witness: Historical Representation in English Poetry, 1603–1660*, and Chapter 11 ("Lamenting the King, 1649") in Robert Wilcher's *The Writing of Royalism 1628–1660*.

And their renownedst *Epocha* will be
Great Charles his Death, next *Christ's Nativity*. (qtd in MacLean
216)

Eikon Basilike participated in this mythology, encouraging
readers to view Charles as a neotype of the crucified Christ.
Though, as Andrew Lacey has demonstrated, the fundamental
themes and imagery of the cult of the Royal Martyr "were identified and made available before Charles went to his death" (48), it
was in *Eikon Basilike* that Charles allegedly voiced his own political and moral innocence in the face of a most brutal martyrdom
at the hands of his disloyal subjects.[1]

Faced, however, with kingly absence, *Eikon Basilike* served as
an incarnational text, for it provided a revered, material textual
body for Charles I. Many early-modern readers experienced the
volume as the sacred, authoritative Word. In an elegy to Charles I,
Alexander Brome transparently compares *Eikon Basilike* to Holy
Writ: "Whose leafs shall like the Sibyls be adored, / When time
shall open each prophetic word: / And shall like scripture be the
rule of good / To those that shall survive the flaming flood" ("On
the Death of King Charles" I.296). The inclusion of the iconic
frontispiece in which the godly Charles reaches for the crown of
glory further sanctifies the monarch. The fusion of the verbal and
the visual rendered his word flesh, and provided Charles, like
Christ, a resurrected body.

The Authorship Controversy

The majority of early-modern readers accepted Charles I as the
author of *Eikon Basilike*. The king, after all, voices his thoughts,
actions, and prayers in the first person throughout the volume,
although the chapter headings refer to him in the third person.
The work, therefore, was not merely perceived as a partisan royalist account of the Civil Wars, but as the sacred, authorized utter-

---

1   Edward Symmons, for example, wrote of Charles I prior to his trial and
    execution, "I will set him [Charles I] forth in Christ's *Robes*, as clothed
    with *sorrows*, and show what a perfect similitude there hath been and is,
    between our *Saviour* and our *Sovereign* in the four last years of both their
    sufferings." Symmons, *A Vindication of King Charles: Or, A Loyal Subject's
    Duty* (London, 1648) 241.

ance of a slain saint. Pierre Bourdieu has shown that "the social position of the speaker ... governs the access he can have to the language of the institution, that is, to the official, orthodox and legitimate speech" (109). As monarch, Charles I had access to the legitimate instruments of expression and his social position increased the authority and force of his words. Bourdieu further explains that "a performative utterance is destined to fail each time that it is not pronounced by a person who has the 'power' to pronounce it" (111). It is quite possible, therefore, that *Eikon Basilike* would not have affected social reality as it did had the majority of its readers questioned its royal origins.

Aware of this possibility, Parliamentarians immediately sought to cast doubt on the king's authorship in order to deconstruct and demystify *Eikon Basilike*. In the frontispiece to *Eikon Alethine*, published in August 1649 to expose "the falsities and hypocrisies" of the King's Book, a curtain is drawn to reveal the true clerical author of *Eikon Basilike*—a "Presumptuous Priest" who would make "his King his Bastard Issue own" (see Appendix A.1). However, while many Parliamentarians questioned the work's autobiographical status, they were unable to identify its true author. In *Eikonoklastes* (October 1649), Milton also casts aspersions on *Eikon Basilike*'s authorship, triumphing in his discovery of the true author of one of the king's prayers, "stolen word for word from the mouth of a Heathen Woman" in Sir Philip Sidney's *Arcadia* (*Eikonoklastes* 236).[1] Yet, Milton ultimately declares authorial identity irrelevant. Readers, Milton asserts, must focus on the substance of the text rather than its source: "But as to the Author of these Soliloquies, whether it were the late King, as is Vulgarly believed, or any secret *Coadjutor*, and some stick not to name him, it can add nothing, nor shall take from the weight, if any be, or reason which he brings" (*Eikonoklastes* 227). The most pressing danger posed by *Eikon Basilike* is that the "factious and defeated" Royalists have made "the Book their own rather than the King's" in order to promote "their own future designs" (*Eikonoklastes* 221).

The authorship debate did not end with the flurry of attacks on and defences of *Eikon Basilike* in 1649. In 1690, a possible ghostwriter emerged: Dr. John Gauden, Dean of Bocking, later Bishop of Exeter and, shortly before his death, Bishop of Worcester. The

---

1 All quotations from *Eikonoklastes* are from this Broadview edition, unless otherwise noted.

rumour of his authorship had circulated in certain communities since the Restoration, which Gauden relied upon to rise through the ecclesiastical ranks from a royal chaplaincy to the bishopric of Worcester. These ecclesiastical preferments suggest that Gauden's claim to authorship had some validity. As early as 1661, Gauden felt he deserved no less, for he averred in a letter to Edward Hyde, Earl of Clarendon that "the book and figure [frontispiece] was wholly and only my invention, making and design, in order to vindicate the King's wisdom, honour and piety" (qtd in Wordsworth 15-17). Clarendon's response points to Royalist anxieties about the authorship of the King's Book following the Restoration. In a letter dated 13 March 1661, Clarendon states that if a ghostwriter is revealed, it "will please none but Mr Milton" (qtd in Madan 143). The Duke of Somerset and the Earl of Southampton attested to Gauden's authorship of *Eikon Basilike* in the presence of Charles II and the Duke of York, later James II. So too did the Duke of York inform Bishop Burnet in 1673 that Dr. Gauden, not his father, had written *Eikon Basilike*. While Gauden's claim to authorship was known and rewarded in court society, H.A. Beecham speculates that this information circulated within another community: one of Gauden's sons apparently boasted of his father's authorship of *Eikon Basilike* to members of the dissenting community in or about 1678 (143).

Gauden's role in the authorship of *Eikon Basilike*, however, remained largely hidden from view until the publication of the Anglesey Memorandum in 1690 (Appendix C.2). In 1686, the auctioneer selling the library of Arthur Annesley, first Earl of Anglesey, noted on the leaf of the Earl's copy of *Eikon Basilike* a handwritten memorandum indicating that in 1675 Charles II and the Duke of York had informed Anglesey that Gauden had composed the book. Although Millington, the auctioneer, tore out the memorandum and sent it to Whitehall as a state document, it appears that William Ashurst, a London alderman and Whig sympathizer, had seen the memorandum at the auction and had copied it. After the Glorious Revolution (1688), Ashurst, now a Whig member of Parliament, made it available to the public. The memorandum was soon pasted into new editions of Milton's *Eikonoklastes* (Trevor-Roper 211-20).[1]

---

1 Madan initially exposed the role of Ashurst in the revelation of the contents of the Anglesey Memorandum in his letter to *The Times Literary Supplement*, 31 August 1956. The edition of *Eikonoklastes* containing the Anglesey Memorandum was first published in Amsterdam in 1690 (Madan 139-140).

Although there is no doubt that Gauden was involved in the composition and production of *Eikon Basilike*, it is difficult to determine the extent to which he can be viewed as its author. There is evidence to suggest that the work is based, at least in part, on papers written by Charles I to vindicate his policies and actions in the 1640s. In *The Princely Pelican*, an intimate of the king tells his readers that in 1642 Charles I announced at Theobald's that he would write an *apologia* for his handling of Parliament and his agreement to Strafford's execution. Perhaps some of his papers captured at the Battle of Naseby in the summer of 1645 (and eventually restored to him) contained such a vindication of his political decisions. While imprisoned at Holmby in 1647, the king was clearly engaged in literary activity, for Major Huntingdon and other witnesses reported viewing several pages of his royal "meditations." Whatever the nature of his writings, the king desired to have the substance of his "loose papers" systematized and sought a sympathetic and skilled friend to undertake such a task; he found such an assistant in the father of Sir John Brattle, or so Richard Hollingworth, incumbent of St. Botolph Aldgate in London, later testified:

> That in the year [16]47. King *Charles*, having drawn up the most considerable part of this Book, and having writ it in some loose papers, at different times, desired Bishop *Juxon* to get some Friend of his (whom he could commend to him as a trusty person) to look it over, and to put it into an exact method; the Bishop pitch'd upon Sir *John's* Father, whom he had been acquainted withal for many years, who undertaking the Task, was assisted by this his Son, who declares, he sate up with his Father some nights, to assist him in methodizing these Papers, all writ with the King's own Hand: Thanks be to God, Sir *John* is yet alive, and is ready to give the same Account to any man that asks him. (*A Defence* 39)

It appears that Gauden had the opportunity to view the royal papers "methodized" by the father of Sir John Brattle when the manuscript was lent to him by the Reverend Edward Simmons, the author of *A Vindication of King Charles* (1647), who had joined the king at Hampton Court in the latter months of 1647. Simmons had been Gauden's clerical neighbour in Essex and they were like-minded in their defence of their "Sovereign Lord the

King."[1] Gauden, according to his servant William Allen, "sat up one whole night to transcribe" the manuscript before returning it to the king, where it was observed by Colonel Hammond, the king's keeper at Carisbrooke Castle on the Isle of Wight, in March 1648.[2] F.F. Madan is convinced that the king's "authentic materials" formed the basis of Gauden's work, which Gauden originally entitled *Suprisia Regalia*, the *Sighs of a King*, later renaming it *Eikon Basilike* on the advice, it is speculated, of Jeremy Taylor (Madan 130).

The testimony of Gauden's wife suggests that her husband completed *Suprisia Regalia* in May 1648, for it was then seen by Sir Arthur, Lord Capel, who suggested that the king have the opportunity to review the text and consent to its publication. The Marquis of Hertford acted as intermediary, delivering Gauden's manuscript to Charles I on the Isle of Wight. Mrs. Gauden recalled that Bishop Duppa read out passages of Gauden's text to the king, who "did exceedingly approve of them" but felt that it should not be published in his name (Madan 130). However, after some persuasion, Charles I consented to have the work published in his name, though he first, according to Bishop Symon Patrick, a Gauden family friend, "both corrected and heightened" the text. Charles I, therefore, appears to have engaged in revising and editing the text.

Eikon Basilike is, therefore, a product of authorial cooperation. This fact has frustrated modern readers of the work who demand a single and singular author for the volume. In the nineteenth and early twentieth centuries, scholars attempted to prove through comparative analysis that the textual voice of *Eikon Basilike* was either that of Gauden or Charles I. Charles Edward Doble and James Anson Farrer compared the known works of Gauden to the text of *Eikon Basilike* and claim to find a remarkable similarity in style. In the introduction to his edition of *Eikon Basilike*, however, Edward Almack just as convincingly compares extracts from Gauden's *Stratoste Aiteutikon: A just invective against those of the*

---

1 A phrase from the subtitle of Gauden's *The Religious & Loyal Protestation, of John Gauden Dr in Divinity* (London, 1649).
2 William Allen's account of Gauden's activities was published in *A Vindication of King Charles the Martyr, Proving that His Majesty was the Author of Eikon Basilike. Against a Memorandum said to be Written by the Earl of Anglesey: and Against the Exceptions of Dr. Walker, and Others* (London, 1697) 31-33.

army and their abettors, who murdered King Charles I (London, 1661) to extracts from *Eikon Basilike* and concludes that there is a remarkable dissimilarity of expression and style (xii-xvi). In the preface of his 1880 edition of *Eikon Basilike*, Edward Scott also confidently asserts that the King's Book "bears on every page the peculiar stamp of Charles's mind and habit of thought" (xliii). As there is substantial historical and stylistic evidence to support both the authorship of Charles I and John Gauden, we are best served to read the King's Book as a heteroglossic, collaborative royalist effort.

The Rhetorical Power of *Eikon Basilike*

Despite its contested origins, *Eikon Basilike* participated in the reclamation of "the divine for Charles I and his son" (Sharpe, "Image Doting" 35). Indeed, the association of Charles I and Christ—of monarchy and divinity—in *Eikon Basilike* and subsequent royalist publications helped to facilitate the smooth transition back to Stuart rule after eleven years of the Commonwealth and Protectorate. Kevin Sharpe convincingly argues that the failure of republican culture is attributable to its inability to foster a new discourse for the Commonwealth. The discourse of popular sovereignty espoused by those on the margins was too radical for the newly emerging government that desperately sought, as Sharpe explains, "to speak and write a new discourse that would utter and inscribe its own authority" and "supplant the image of monarchy" ("Image Doting" 29-30). But the discourse of kingship could not be easily supplanted, as the Rump and Oliver Cromwell soon discovered, particularly during the Protectorate, for it had been long embedded in the cultural consciousness. Soon after he rejected the offer of the crown and was invested as Lord Protector, Cromwell was fashioned in monarchical rather than military or republican terms.[1] Cromwell, as Sharpe explains, "increasingly adopted the rhetoric and style of a king" for he rec-

---

1 On the regal symbolism associated with Cromwell, see Sean Kelsey, *Inventing a Republic: the Political Culture of the English Commonwealth, 1649-1653*; Laura Lunger Knoppers, *Constructing Cromwell: Ceremony, Portrait, and Print, 1645-1661;* Roy Sherwood, *The Court of Oliver Cromwell.*

ognized that he could not at this moment in history replace "the symbols and images of kingship" ("Image Doting" 54).

Even during the trial of the king (Appendix B.2), regal symbols and images prompted certain difficulties that reflected Parliament's struggle to authorize itself.[1] A new Great Seal, for instance, was needed to replace the current one, which bore the image of the accused. The king's attire during his trial also caused some consternation: in a closed meeting in the Painted Chamber on January 20th, the Commissioners decided, "But to the Prisoner's putting off his Hat, the Court will not insist upon it" (Nalson 25). The court found itself deferring here, if only symbolically, to the royal defendant. Three days later, however, the royal coat of arms, which hung behind the judges, was suddenly replaced with the cross of St. George. This was a particularly important symbolic moment, not only because it replaced the royal arms, but also because it directly challenged the George worn by the king, the insignia of the Order of the Garter, the "chivalric order with which the king had long sought so firmly to identify himself" (Kelsey "Staging the Trial" 84). There is one additional significance to this change of symbolism. On 22 January, the Scots had once again lodged a protest against the trial:

> By erecting the George, someone was proclaiming not only the distinction and supremacy of the national interest over the regal, but also the impending dissolution of the triple crown of Great Britain and Ireland. On 23 January, the High Court ... was herewith branded unmistakeably as an English tribunal. (Kelsey, "Staging the Trial" 84)

These symbolic moments during the trial mocked, but did not wholly undermine, the sacred authority of kingship.

Eikon Basilike attempts to counter such symbolic attacks on royalty and Royalism. It endeavours to embed the rhetoric of kingship into the minds of its early-modern readers, despite the physical absence of the king. The work not only reaffirms the sacred roots of kingship but also anticipates its restoration, for its penultimate chapter sets forth policies for the future Charles II to implement on his restoration. While Parliamentarians were successfully dismantling his military forces and attempting to frac-

---

1 The line engraving, the *Trial of King Charles* (Appendix B.1), presents iconographically this struggle for symbolic capital.

ture his political networks, Charles I and his supporters were engaged in linguistic renovation, for the author of *Eikon Basilike* is concerned to build a rhetorical citadel around the concept of divine kingship. The King's Book, that is, is engaged in symbolic manipulation, the ultimate goal of which is to retain the established social order. *Eikon Basilike* does not merely wish to describe historical facts regarding the king's treatment of Parliament and the people; it is self-consciously a performative utterance, a political pre-vision, or "a pre-diction which aims to bring about what it utters" (Bourdieu 128).

Eikon Basilike's rhetorical arsenal in this urgent defence of the monarch, and linguistic restructuring of monarchy, is varied and complex.[1] It includes the absorption and transformation of a variety of popular secular and religious forms. The King's Book is, in fact, a curious hybrid of genres: political memoir, *apologia*, spiritual autobiography, martyrology, hagiography, meditation, and Psalter. The book's strength lies in its ability to manipulate this range of representational codes, which paradoxically merge into a unitary image or iconic "portrait" of the suffering Charles I.

Eikon Basilike is clearly a political memoir, for it traces the political events that led up to the Civil War and the imprisonment of Charles I, beginning with the king's calling of the Long Parliament in November 1640, and concluding with his imprisonment in Carisbrooke Castle in November 1647. It is also decidedly a political *apologia*, for historical incidents are introduced for the sole purpose of defending the policies and practices of the king. In accordance with Aristotle's three modes of persuasion, *Eikon Basilike* crafts the personal character of the speaker, presenting him as a reasonable man of conscience "resolved to reform" what he should "by free and full advice in Parliament, be convinced to be amiss" (*Eikon Basilike* 52); stirs emotions in its readers, thereby placing them in a receptive frame of mind; and provides apparent proof to support the royalist version of historical events (Aristotle, *Rhetoric* 17).

The political memoir and apologia, however, were often viewed as self-serving documents. The authors of *Eikon Basilike*, therefore, grafted devotional genres onto political ones to render the portrait of the king a sacred, transcendent text or, as Steven N. Zwicker puts it, to transform it into "the holy book of royalist pol-

---

1 For a discussion of genres in *Eikon Basilike* see Elizabeth P. Skerpan, "Rhetorical Genres and the *Eikon Basilike*."

itics" (37). While early-modern political memoirs are generally "not rich in personal revelation" (Delany 120), *Eikon Basilike* presents the spiritual musings of a king who guards his conscience despite the brutal onslaughts of his enemies. Charles I, in the King's Book, moves as a sort of regal Everyman through the events of the Civil Wars, repenting of his sins and attempting to conform himself to the Divine Will. Charles I admits his fallen state and cries out to God for mercy: *"Forgive, I beseech thee, my Personal, and my People's sins; which are so far mine, as I have not improved the power thou gavest me, to thy glory, and my Subjects' good: Thou hast now brought me from the glory and freedom of a King, to be a Prisoner to my own Subjects: Justify, O Lord, as to thy over-ruling hand, because in many things I have rebelled against thee"* (*Eikon Basilike* 176). The king, however, carefully selects the sins of which he repents, and those sins tend to indict his enemies rather than himself. His greatest sin, he declares, was permitting himself to be persuaded by members of Parliament to allow the execution of the Earl of Strafford, whom he knew to be an innocent man. By repenting of such a sin, Charles I appears less concerned with his own complicity than with the conduct of his political opponents, who destroyed an innocent man and wounded the king's conscience.

In fact, although *Eikon Basilike* often relies upon the language of spiritual autobiography, it functions less as an indictment of the sins of the speaker than as a sustained condemnation of his political enemies. The king, unlike John Bunyan in *Grace Abounding to the Chief of Sinners*, is not a victim of a tortured conscience; he is God's servant, a victim of those who persecute him *"under the colour of Religion"* (*Eikon Basilike* 106). Identified with Job, King David, and the crucified Christ, Charles I is a figure of innocence afflicted and heroic suffering. He is presented as a Protestant martyr, not unlike those described by John Foxe in his *Acts and Monuments*, a book read by the king during his imprisonment.

However, in order to present himself as a Protestant autobiographer and martyr, Charles I must substantially transform the genres of spiritual autobiography and martyrology. In early-modern England, those who challenged the state chiefly composed such devotional works. As Paul Delany explains, "imprisonment for religious dissent was often a stimulus to the autobiographical urge" (63). In Caroline England, both literary forms functioned primarily as oppositional genres against the king and his support of the unpopular ecclesiastical innovations of Archbishop Laud—

it asserted a transcendent order against that which the autobiographer felt to be a corrupt worldly order. The genres were effective in justifying the individual conscience, the inner light of the believer, in the face of established religious forms of worship. *Eikon Basilike* accomplishes something quite different in that it asserts the fixity of the king's conscience through his defence of his established duties and obligations against over-zealous innovations. Whereas the genres normally recounted an individual's successive confrontations with a corrupt worldly regime in order to bring about the spiritual regeneration of Protestantism, *Eikon Basilike* presents the king as the fixed rock of established authority, a still point buffeted by various forms of social chaos that threaten order.

This renovation of devotional genres in *Eikon Basilike* serves to present Charles I as central to religio-political order. He is figured as the defender of both Church and State, the guardian of the British Church and Parliament. His enemies, on the other hand, are fashioned as fanatical zealots intent on subduing the conscience of the king and obliterating the biblically based ecclesiastical body:

> I must now be urged with an Army, and constrained either to hazard My own, and My Kingdom's ruin, by my Defence; or prostrate My Conscience to the blind obedience of those men, whose zealous superstition thinks, or pretends, they cannot do God and the Church a greater service, than utterly to destroy that Primitive, Apostolical, and anciently Universal Government of the Church by Bishops. (*Eikon Basilike* 83-84)

The fixed conscience of the king compels him, the reader is told, to express his "modest and sober desires" for the public good. He highlights the affective bonds of duty and obligation—the "generous constancy and cautiousness" (*Eikon Basilike* 51)—of Royalism, of which the king is exemplary. Charles I always retains decorum and dignity in response to affronts, as is evident in the account of his treatment at Hull:

> no disdain, or emotion of passion transported Me ... to do or say anything, unbeseeming My self, or unsuitable to that temper, which, in greatest injuries, I think, best becomes a Christian, as coming nearest to the great example of Christ. And indeed, I desire always more to remember I am a Christian, than a King. (*Eikon Basilike* 77)

Charles I, therefore, is not caught up in the unruly and misguided movement of the rarely identified challengers of his authority—"some men" and "they"—who have misled the people "into the most desperate precipices of actions" (*Eikon Basilike* 122).

The text often affirms this political stance through biblically based nautical imagery, providing another link between the king's fixity and the divine order. Reflecting on the need to restrain "the violent designs and motions" in his kingdoms, Charles I declares: "As it is one of the most convincing Arguments that there is a God, while his power sets bounds to the raging of the Sea: so 'tis no less, that he restrains the madness of the people" (*Eikon Basilike* 60). The nautical imagery evokes the Psalms, specifically Psalm 89, as well as the creation story of Genesis 1. Charles I is God's viceregent, a worldly buttress who maintains the divinely ordained bounds of the social order, imploring God to make his heir "an Anchor, or Harbour rather, to these tossed and weather-beaten Kingdoms" (*Eikon Basilike* 193).

Charles I layers such biblical allusions throughout the narrative, assimilating scriptural fragments in prayers at the conclusion of all but one chapter of *Eikon Basilike*. The king often merges his own text and the biblical text in these Davidic prayers or meditations to create a seamless text. However, by italicizing the concluding section as a whole, the entire prayer—a composite of the biblical and kingly word—appears biblical in origin. The king's political reflections in these prayers are, as a result, presented as universal and eternal truths in light of this prestigious affiliation with Scripture. The use of the Psalms as a model for Charles I's penitence in these meditations "further reinforces the link between Charles and the biblical line of kingship represented by David and Christ, while highlighting the pathos of the royal martyr, a king more sinned against than sinning" (Loewenstein 54). The familiarity of this biblical model enables Charles I to assume the figure of the persecuted yet patient sufferer, unwilling to avenge the usurpation of his authority.

Eikon Basilike: Frontispiece

The impact of *Eikon Basilike* on its readers was rooted not merely in its masterly logocentrism—its ability to identify the words of Charles I with the Word—but also in the iconographic authority of the book's frontispiece. The frontispiece by William Marshall

Figure 1: William Marshall, Frontispiece, *Eikon Basilike. The Portraiture of His Sacred Majesty in His Solitudes and Sufferings*. London: Reprinted for James Young, 1648 [1649]. Madan 24, Second Issue. This item is reproduced by permission of The British Library.

was not the original design. Royston had, apparently, received his manuscript of *Eikon Basilike* on 23 December 1648 which included a frontispiece of three crowns (representing the three Stuart kingdoms) indented on a crown of thorns, a motif which is reworked in the frontispiece as we have it. Royston claims to have received the Marshall frontispiece shortly after obtaining the original manuscript. Based on Gauden's claim that the frontispiece design was his own invention, Madan concludes: "It appears therefore that Marshall designed the frontispiece, under Gauden's direction, in the second half of December 1648" (175).

The reader of the book is first confronted with an image of the king in an emblematic landscape, accompanied in later editions with a poetic "Explanation of the Emblem" (Figure 1). In Marshall's illustration, Charles I, though "Palm-like Depressed," transcends chaos "as th'unmoved Rock out brave's / The boisterous Winds and raging waves." It was, as Sharpe argues, the "visual evocation and the power of its emblematic frontispiece" that "most dismayed the critics of *Eikon Basilike*" ("Image Doting" 33). Its figuration of Charles I as a humble, steadfast, and triumphant imitator of Christ who cast aside his crown of glory to wear a crown of thorns was viewed as idolatrous.[1] That concern is evident in the published attacks on King's Book. The author of *The Pseudo-Martyr Discovered*, for example, accuses royalists of "canonizing him [Charles I] for a saint, and idolizing his memory for an innocent martyr"; indeed, Charles I is depicted "in a posture of devotion, in imitation of *David* in his ejaculations to Heaven ... the better to stir up the People and vain beholders to pity him" (Appendix A.2). Milton, too, scorns "the conceited portraiture before his Book, drawn out to the full measure of a Masquing Scene, and set there to catch fools and silly gazers" (*Eikonoklastes* 224).

The narrative that follows in *Eikon Basilike*, however, brilliantly performs that emblem, merging text and image into "an object to be revered" (Corns, *Uncloistered Virtue* 209). And at the end of the text, we meet with the epithet, "*Vota dabunt, quæ bella negârunt,*" bringing us full circle, back to the image which both confirms and strengthens "the vein of piety developed throughout

---

1 For a variation of the Marshall frontispiece (of which there were many), see Figure 2, the frontispiece engraved by Thomas Rawlins for *Eikon Basilike. Le Portrait du Roy de la Grand Bretagne* (Rouen, 1649), a continental edition of the King's Book.

the text" (Loewenstein 53). The process and time spent reading, even meditating upon the King's Book, reassuringly returns the reader to that image of stability; it leaves the royalist "better assured, what I may join My heart unto" (*Eikon Basilike* 171). The book itself becomes a prefiguration of royalist devotion for the dark days of the Interregnum.

Eikonoklastes

Milton, as well as other polemicists, was clearly faced with a difficult task when he sought to shatter the iconic representation of martyrdom that *Eikon Basilike* had so successfully created in its fusion of image and text. As Thomas N. Corns writes,

> *Eikon Basilike* is the cleverest of propaganda initiatives, and it offers a very elusive target to his enemies. The apparent author is dead, and the book itself seems not to be a work of controversy but variously a psalter, an act of devotion, and—most tellingly—an object to be revered, not a text to be read. Milton must transmute it into forms tractable to attack and confutation. Two principal but curiously contradictory tactics obtain, one accepting but distorting the *Eikon Basilike*'s claim to be judged as something other than polemic, the other transforming the text into an exercise in controversial prose which can be met by the methods of political controversy. (*Uncloistered Virtue* 209)

Milton drew on years of experience as a prose controversialist in his response to the King's Book. He quite possibly accepted an offer to do so from the Council of State around the time of his appointment as Secretary of Foreign Tongues to that body in March 1649. *Eikonoklastes* was, for Milton, a "work assigned" (*Eikonoklastes* 222). He would soon after be requested by the Council of State to respond to the Earl of Ormonde's "Articles of Peace" with the Irish rebels, as well as Salmasius' *Defensio Regia*. Milton does not seem to have been the first choice for an "authorized" response to *Eikon Basilike*; however, his prose career made him a very capable second choice. Since 1641, Milton had engaged in polemical debates, including several anti-prelatical tracts and four divorce tracts. In the middle of February 1649, he had published *The Tenure of Kings and Magistrates* which argued the justness of the trial and execution of the king, while attacking the Scots for their hypocrisy and newfound royalist sentiments:

> He [Charles] who but erewhile in the Pulpits was a cursed Tyrant, an enemie to God and Saints, lad'n with all the innocent blood spilt in three Kingdoms, and so to be fought against, is now, though nothing penitent or alter'd from his first principles, a lawful Magistrate, a Sovran Lord, the Lords anointed, not to be touch'd, though by themselves imprison'd. As if this onely were obedience, to preserve the meere useless bulke of his person, and that onely in prison, not in the field, and to disobey his commands, deny him his dignity and office, every where to resist his power but where they thinke it onely surviving in thir own faction. (*CPW* 3:197)

Milton makes a similar argument in *Eikonoklastes*, demonstrating that *Eikon Basilike* is "stuffed with naught else but the common grounds of Tyranny and Popery" (222), in order to demolish any budding political alliances prompted by the King's Book. *Eikon Basilike* is not a kingly incarnation, Milton pronounces, but rather a posthumous "useless bulk" of monarchy and royalism.

Eikon Basilike was not the first tract that Milton refuted in a point-by-point deconstruction. This fact is significant for two reasons. First, Milton need not have been aware of *Eikon Alethine* (Appendix A.1), an earlier systematic attack on *Eikon Basilike* published on 26 August 1649, to adopt this strategy. In 1923, Warren B. Lowenhaupt argued that Milton was indebted to *Eikon Alethine*; however, the editors of the *Yale Complete Prose Works of John Milton* firmly state: "As a 'source' for *Eikonoklastes*, *Eikon Alethine* is negligible" (CPW 3:149). Second, Milton's use of this rhetorical strategy in *Eikonoklastes* differs significantly from his earlier employment of point-by-point refutation of an opponent's argument, reflecting perhaps a degree of deference to the king in *Eikonoklastes*. In earlier polemical pamphlets, Milton had launched *ad hominem* attacks, using this rhetorical tactic to identify a weakness in his opponent's argument, a disparity between his words and deeds, or a personal failing.

Such a strategy would be inappropriate in *Eikonoklastes*, which had probably been authorized by the Council of State, because the fledgling Commonwealth did not wish to alienate any support it had secured. A comparison with *Eikon Alethine* is instructive. That text is abusively sarcastic primarily because it assumes that

Figure 2: Thomas Rawlins, Frontispiece, *Eikon Basilike. Le Portrait Du Roy de la Grand Bretagne*. Jean Berthelin: Rouen, 1649. Madan 54. This item is reproduced by permission of The British Library.

a clergyman, not the king, authored *Eikon Basilike*. Certainly, this is one way to attack the text. However, as was previously noted, Milton takes the king's authorship of *Eikon Basilike* as a moot point:

But since he himself, making new appeal to Truth and the World, hath left behind him this Book as the best advocate and interpreter of his own actions, and that his Friends by publishing, dispersing, commending, and almost adoring it, seem to place therein the chief strength and nerves of their cause, it would argue doubtless in the other party great deficience and distrust of themselves, not to meet the force of his reason in any field whatsoever, the force and equipage of whose Arms they have so often met victoriously. (*Eikonoklastes* 222)

Royalists, and the newly royalist Presbyterians, have made the book their own, Milton tells his readers. This is a key premise of Milton's argument in *Eikonoklastes*, and thus his attack on the King's Book must be more "subtly subversive," as Corns explains:

The avoidance of eager and gloating triumphalism is profoundly politic.... Milton's text works to kill emotion, and by foregoing celebration of the victory of his faction he simultaneously avoids stimulating pity or anger.... But he scrupulously avoids outraging an unsympathetic or neutral readership.... It [*Eikonoklastes*] shows a determined politeness that is abandoned only carefully, preparedly, and temporarily. (*Uncloistered Virtue* 204-5)

Milton constantly measures the king's words against his deeds, even his narrative against his prayers, and in order to avoid alienating readers, he frequently appeals to their memory and cognition. His readers, "by only remembering them the truth of what they themselves know to be here [in *Eikon Basilike*] misaffirmed" (*Eikonoklastes* 222), will dismiss the king's historical revisionism.

Admittedly, there are awkward moments in which Milton challenges the king's sense of decorum. Jane Hiles argues that Milton demonstrates a "royalist reflex" because he tends to "follow the royalist pattern of shifting the blame for the king's crimes to advisors or others, minimizing the king's offenses by failing to elaborate on them, and focussing on the literary aspects of the conflict to the near exclusion of larger ideological issues" (87). Milton does stumble at times when attempting to counter royalist symbolism. In the second chapter of *Eikon Basilike*, for example, commonplace regal symbolism is applied to the Earl of Strafford:

For those were prone to create in him great confidence of undertakings, and this was like enough to betray him to great errors, and many enemies: Whereof he could not but contract good store, while moving in so high a sphere, and with so vigorous a lustre, he must needs (as the Sun) raise many envious exhalations, which condensed by a popular *odium*, were capable to cast a cloud upon the brightest merit, and integrity. (54)

For Milton, the imagery here is indecorous, as Charles praises Strafford's "great *Abilities*; and with Scholastic flourishes beneath the decency of a King, compares him to *the Sun*, which in all figurative use, and significance bears allusion to a King, not to a Subject" (*Eikonoklastes* 239). Milton, however, while seeming to uphold traditional royalist decorum, does so in order to turn it against Charles. The king has enacted his own "fall," he suggests, by undermining royalist symbolism. One might suggest, contra Hiles, that even in a curious passage like this, Milton is upholding a sense of rhetoric in the service of civic responsibility against courtly artifice.

Indeed, in his comments on the rational weaknesses of "courtly adversaries" in the Preface, Milton is playing with the notion of the duel in this contest between icon and iconoclast. Milton's suggestive analogy, however, is quickly dropped. *Eikon Basilike* "casts down no gauntlet. In its avoidance of specificity and its pietistic tone it avoids direct challenge to anyone" (Corns 210). Rather than engage in a ritualized form of combat, Milton will approach the King's Book as he hopes any of its readers should: rationally. In so doing, he unravels the rhetorical fabric of the text. This is evident even in Milton's choice not to respect the typographical layout of *Eikon Basilike*—he moves through the book chapter-by-chapter, even, at times, sentence-by-sentence, but Milton does not distinguish between the roman type of the king's narratives and the italic type of the king's prayers, the "privileged" insights into his motivations. Charles' conscience, Milton intimates, cannot be separated so neatly from his actions.

Stripping *Eikon Basilike* of its artful representation of privilege, of its tyrannical grip on the imagination of its readers, Milton highlights both the way the book is composed as well as how it should be read: "Milton battered *Eikon Basilike* not only for being an image and a performance, but also for *not* being a book—or at least a solid one.... He, unlike the King, does not pretend to be doing anything other than writing a book" (Helgerson 12). The rhetorical artifice of the King's Book masks the truth, and it is a small step from this claim for Milton to argue for the similarities

between *Eikon Basilike* and the elaborate courtly theatrical enter-
tainments which had been so central to Caroline political culture—the masque. In the Preface to *Eikonoklastes*, Milton sees the
title, frontispiece, and closing Latin motto in theatrical terms,
reading *Eikon Basilike* as a courtly performance:

> And here may be well observed the loose and negligent curios-
> ity of those who took upon them to adorn the setting out of this
> Book; for though the Picture set in Front would Martyr him
> and Saint him to befool the people, yet the Latin Motto in the
> end, which they understand not, leaves him, as it were, a politic
> contriver to bring about that interest by fair and plausible
> words, which the force of Arms denied him. But quaint
> Emblems and devices begged from the old Pageantry of some
> Twelfth-night's entertainment at *Whitehall*, will do but ill to
> make a Saint or Martyr. (224)

While some critics might fault Milton for this approach as being
overly concerned with the style of *Eikon Basilike*, he is quite effectively demonstrating rhetorical abuses in order to transform the
martyred king into an artfully constructed icon of tyranny.

Early-Modern Governance: Monarchy, Absolutism, Tyranny, and Republicanism

What lies at the core of *Eikon Basilike*, *Eikonoklastes*, and other
texts in this pamphlet debate, as well as in the trial of Charles I, is
the nature of governance and the foundation of political authority. As with Thomas Hobbes' *Leviathan*, the King's Book, and the
royalist and republican pamphlets written in response to it,
address and defend political formations. In *Eikon Basilike*, Charles
defends monarchical sovereignty by appealing to a patriarchal
notion of kingship, which is seamlessly linked to his "hopeful Posterity" (*Eikon Basilike* 74), and the promise of a somewhat providential restoration. Such patriarchal notions are political com-
monplaces of the period. James I made extensive use of
father/king analogies in both his speeches and writings, proclaim-
ing, for instance, in *The True Law of Free Monarchies*: "By the Law
of Nature the King becomes a natural Father to all his Lieges at
his Coronation: And as the Father of his fatherly duty is bound to
care for the nourishing, education, and virtuous government of

his children; even so is the king bound to care for all his subjects" (65). The analogy continues in the works of royalist political theorists of the Caroline period. Sir Robert Filmer finds the origins of monarchy in the Old Testament patriarchs and traces their authority back through the dominion granted Adam in the Garden of Eden. Filmer succinctly states his views in a passage from *Patriarcha*:

> If we compare the natural duties of a father with those of a king, we find them to be all one, without any difference at all but only in the latitude and extent of them. As the father over the family, so the king, as father over many families, extends his care to preserve, feed, clothe, instruct and defend the whole commonwealth. His wars, his peace, his courts of justice and all his acts of sovereignty tend only to preserve and distribute to every subordinate and inferior father, and to their children, their rights and privileges, so that all the duties of a king are summed up in an universal fatherly care of his people. (12)

The patriarchal family comes to serve as one of the essential anchoring points of monarchical discourse. It effectively joins the king's two bodies—political and natural—as is evident in the advice on governing and deportment given to Prince Henry in James I's *Basilikon Doron* and to the future Charles II in Chapter 27 of *Eikon Basilike*. The king begets heirs and begets laws which ensure the continuance and order of the body politic.[1]

The analogy ultimately rests "upon the *sexual* character of patriarchy, for it is the act of *begetting* that finally unites fatherhood and kingship" (Boehrer 107). *Eikon Basilike* relies upon this analogy. Charles, for example, claims that he "cannot allow their [Parliament's] wisdom ... to exclude My self ... without whose Reason concurrent with theirs (as the Sun's influence is necessary to all nature's productions) they cannot beget, or bring forth any one

---

1 The republican effort to undermine the trope of the king as the nation's benevolent father, and the resilience of that trope after the regicide, altered the cultural landscape in complex ways. In *Crime, Gender and Social Order in Early Modern England*, Garthine Walker, for example, notes that the regicide affected forensic discourse in the trials of women charged with killing their husbands—after the king's execution, women rarely justified such homicides by accusing their late husbands of unnatural, domestic tyranny (previously a commonplace defence).

complete and authoritative Act of public wisdom, which makes the Laws" (*Eikon Basilike* 99). In *Eikonoklastes*, Milton engages with this passage and challenges the king's generative politics in which a feminized parliament requires the king's "masculine coition" to beget an act. Milton writes,

> Yet so farr doth self opinion of fals principles delude and transport him, as to think the *concurrence of his reason* to the Votes of Parlament, not onely Political, but Natural, *and as necessary to the begetting,* or bringing forth of any one *compleat act of public wisdom as the Suns influence is necessary to all natures productions.* So that Parlament, it seems, is but a Female, and without his procreative reason, the Laws which they can produce are but wind-eggs. (*CPW* 3: 467)

Milton's "it seems" categorizes the argument of *Eikon Basilike* in two ways. First, he claims that Charles is transported into a deluded misperception of his political role, countering the fixity of the king's self-representation throughout *Eikon Basilike*. Second, Milton acknowledges the king's argument and language here in order to refute the commonplace generative notion. Milton's rhetorical move is odd. As with Hiles, Bruce Boehrer discovers in Milton's prose a "royalist reflex," for he argues that "Milton's own rhetoric is predetermined ... for in his role of respondent to the royalist arguments he has no choice but to neutralize whatever patterns of representation the royalists find useful" (105). Milton, though perhaps trapped in this rhetoric, turns the analogy on its head by claiming that Charles,

> ought then to have so thought of a Parlament, if he count it not Male, as of his Mother, which, to civil being, created both him, and the Royalty he wore. And if it hath bin anciently interpreted the presaging signe of a future Tyrant, but to dream of copulation with his Mother, what can it be less then actual Tyranny to affirme waking, that the Parlament, which is his Mother, can neither conceive or bring forth any *autoritative Act* without his masculine coition. (*CPW* 3:467)

Milton makes Parliament, and ultimately the people, generatively prior to the king. Boehrer finds the above quoted passage "ludicrous," and, to a certain extent it is: "the king, after all, could act reasonably like a father to his people, but who could believe for a moment that the gentlemen of the Rump might be anyone's mother?" (113).

This was not the first, nor was it the last time, that Milton would directly confront such notions. In his *First Defense*, Milton sought to dismantle the analogy in response to Salmasius' *Defensio Regia Pro Carolo I* (1649). Milton writes,

> you think this metaphor has forced me to apply right off to kings whatever I might admit to fathers. Fathers and kings are very different things: Our fathers begot us, but our kings did not, and it is we, rather, who created the king. It is nature which gave the people fathers, and the people who gave themselves a king; the people therefore do not exist for the king, but the king for the people. (*CPW* 4:326-7)

But even if there are some similarities shared by kings and fathers, Milton asserts,

> We endure a father though he be harsh and strict, and we endure such a king too; but we do not endure even a father who is tyrannical. If a father kill his son he shall pay with his life: shall not then a king too be subject to this same most just of laws if he has destroyed the people who are his sons? (*CPW* 4:327)

Milton proclaims that a king does not have the appeal to natural law that a father does over his children, but, even if a king could appeal to natural law, neither he nor a biological father is above the established laws of the nation.[1] Monarchy, "the meer contingencie of a begetting" (*CPW* 3:487),[2] was rightly and justly swept away in order to enable a "nation of self-architects" (Norbrook 209), where subjection to the father/king is replaced by a fraternal commonwealth.[3]

---

1 Incidentally, Sir Robert Filmer responded to Milton's arguments in the *First Defense*. See, his *Observations Concerning the Originall of Government, upon Mr Hobs 'Leviathan', Mr Milton Against Salmasius, H. Grotius 'De Jure Belli'* in *Patriarcha and Other Writings*.
2 Milton *Eikonoklastes*, *CPW* 3:487. This phrase occurs in a revised passage of the 1650 edition of *Eikonoklastes*.
3 For a concise summary of debates on Milton's republicanism, see Martin Dzelzainis, "Republicanism"; for a comprehensive study of the republican tradition, see J.G.A. Pocock, *The Machiavellian Moment*.

As these debates suggest, and as evident even in the initial responses to *Eikon Basilike*, Parliamentarians attempt to restyle the regal martyr as a tyrannical monarch who rules according to his own will rather than to the laws of the nation. Walter Benjamin sees this as the essential Janus-face of the baroque monarch: "the tyrant and the martyr are but the two faces of the monarch. They are the necessarily extreme incarnations of the princely essence" (62). For Milton, Charles I's tyranny is self-evident; it is apparent in the king's and his supporters' assertion of his martyrdom:

> But Martyrs bear witness to the truth, not to themselves. If I bear witness to my self, saith *Christ*, my witness is not true. He who writes himself *Martyr* by his own inscription, is like an ill Painter, who, by writing on the shapeless Picture which he hath drawn, is feign to tell passengers what shape it is.... [N]o more than how a Martyrdom can belong to him, who therefore dies for his Religion because it is *established*.... Lastly, if to die for *the testimony of his conscience*, be enough to make him Martyr, what Heretic dying for direct blasphemy, as some have done constantly, may not boast a martyrdom? (*Eikonoklastes* 266-67)

Charles I's constancy as represented in *Eikon Basilike* is evidence not of martyrdom, but of the unrepentant, obstinate tyranny of the king's unbridled will. Those that have been duped by the idolatry of the King's Book have consigned their reason and understanding "to a double tyrannie, of Custom from without, and blind affections within" (Milton *Tenure*, *CPW* 3:190). They have alienated themselves, and the Commonwealth, by investing their affective response in a "juncture of hearts" (*Eikon Basilike* 169).

Yet, despite these attacks, *Eikon Basilike*, this most successful piece of royalist propaganda won out, "threatening its readers' self-possession ... [and] the new revolutionary regime's possession of England" (Helgerson 14). *Eikon Basilike* proved to all that the "words of a KING ... [are] *full of power*" (*Eikon Basilike* 164). The King's Book ultimately managed to unify a royalist vision—a remarkable accomplishment, as the breakdown of censorship apparatuses during the Civil Wars had challenged the king's control of his image, particularly in newsbooks, the forerunner of the modern newspaper. The oppositional elements of the commercial printing trade tended to desacrilize and demystify the king by representing his "political career ... as a series of vignettes, decisive or symbolic moments in his personal fortune and the history of his times" (Raymond 48). *Eikon Basilike*, however, manages to reappropriate those moments for Charles and to reincorporate them into a monumental, and authoritative, whole. As Richard Helgerson suggests, the book effectively merges earlier forms of regal self-representation—the physical, yet iconic performativity of Elizabeth I and the absolutist textuality of James I—in an emerging print culture (8-9). In so doing, *Eikon Basilike* accomplished what the regicides had attempted to prevent as well as "what Charles had foreseen his martyrdom would do: it raised the king above the polemical fray, enshrined his memory, and so deprived the fruits of victory to his conquerors" (Sharpe, "Image Doting" 33).

A Brief Historical Chronology

1599   Oliver Cromwell born (April).

1600   Charles born at Dunfermline (19 November), the second son, and third surviving child, of James VI and Anne of Denmark.

1603   Death of Elizabeth I (March) and accession of James VI/I.

1605   Gunpowder Plot discovered (November).

1608   John Milton born in London (9 December).

1612   Death of Henry, Prince of Wales (May); Charles now heir to the throne.

1614   First meeting of George Villiers (later Duke of Buckingham) and James VI/I (August).

1618   Thirty Years' War begins; James VI/I's *Book of Sports*.

1619   Inigo Jones begins work on the Whitehall Banqueting House.

1625   Death of James VI/I (March) and accession of Charles I; marriage of Charles I and the French princess Henrietta Maria (May); Charles' first parliament (June to August); war with Spain marked by the failure of the Cadiz expedition.

1626   Charles' second parliament (February to June), dissolved when it attempts to impeach Buckingham; William Laud created Bishop of Bath and Wells (June).

1627   War with France and notable failure of the La Rochelle expedition; Laud appointed to the Privy Council (April).

1628   Charles' third parliament (1st session, March to June); Cromwell sits as MP for the borough of Huntingdon; Laud created Bishop of London (July); assassination of Buckingham (August).

1629   Second session of Charles' third parliament (January to March). Its dissolution marks the beginning of the "eleven years' personal rule."

1630   Birth of Charles (May), later Charles II.

1632   Thomas Wentworth appointed Lord Deputy of Ireland (January).

1633   William Juxon appointed Bishop of London (October); Charles I's Scottish coronation (June); Laud appointed Archbishop of Canterbury (September); birth of James

(October), later James II; Charles reissues the *Book of Sports* (October).

1634 First writ of Ship Money (October), demanded from maritime counties.

1635 Second writ of Ship Money (August), extending collection to inland counties.

1636 Juxon appointed Lord High Treasurer (March); third writ of Ship Money (October).

1637 Hampden Case, challenging the legality of Ship Money (November to December); papal agent received at court; new Prayer Book imposed on Scotland.

1638 Scottish National Covenant (February); verdict in Hampden Case for the king (June).

1639 First Bishops' War; Pacification of Berwick (June); Wentworth returns from Ireland (September).

1640 Wentworth appointed Lord Lieutenant of Ireland and created Earl of Strafford (January); Short Parliament (April to May); Second Bishops' War, concluded by Treaty of Ripon (October); Long Parliament convenes (November 3); Root and Branch Petition (December); Strafford arrested (November).

1641 Triennial Act (February); Bill of Sitting (May); trial and execution of Strafford (May); courts of High Commission and Star Chamber abolished (July); Irish Rebellion begins (October); Grand Remonstrance (November).

1642 Charles I leaves London after an unsuccessful attempt to arrest five members of the House of Commons and one of the House of Lords (January); the Exclusion Bill (February); the king's repulse by Sir John Hotham (April); King's standard raised at Nottingham (August); first Civil War begins; battle of Edgehill (October).

1643 Westminster Assembly of Divines established (June); first Battle of Newbury (September); Solemn League and Covenant between Parliament and the Scots (September).

1644 Scots' army crosses into England as per the Solemn League and Covenant (January).

1645 Laud executed (January); Directory of Worship replaces abolished Prayer Book (January); Uxbridge negotiations between the king and Parliament (January to February); Self-Denying Ordinance and creation of New Model Army with Sir Thomas Fairfax as commander-in-chief

(April); battle of Naseby (June); Charles I's captured correspondence published by order of Parliament in *The King's Cabinet Opened* (June); the royalist printer Richard Royston is imprisoned for publishing anti-parliament tracts.

1646 Charles I surrenders to the Scots, ending the first Civil War (May); Newcastle Propositions (July); episcopacy abolished (October).

1647 Scots hand Charles I over to Parliament (January); he is seized by the army (June); Levellers become a strong political force through the summer; Charles I escapes army custody to the Isle of Wight (November); Charles I signs the "Engagement" with the Scots (December).

1648 Scots invade England, beginning the second Civil War (July); battle of Preston marks the end of the second Civil War (August); Treaty of Newport (September). Pride's Purge (December); Royston receives the manuscript of *Eikon Basilike* (23 December); Thirty Years' War ends.

1649 Trial and execution of Charles I (January); Charles II proclaimed in Ireland; *Eikon Basilike*, first edition, first issue, published by Richard Royston (January 30); *Eikon Basilike*, first edition, second issue, published (February 4); Charles II proclaimed king in Scotland (February); abolition of the monarchy; Milton appointed Secretary for Foreign Tongues to the Council of State (March); William Dugard's edition of *Eikon Basilike*, including prayers, published (March) Dugard arrested (15 March); Declaration of Commonwealth; Leveller mutiny (May); Cromwell's re-conquest of Ireland begins (August); *Eikon Alethine* published (August 26); *Eikonoklastes* published (c. 6 October).

1650 Dugard re-arrested and imprisoned (February); after recanting his royalism, Dugard appointed printer to the Council of State (April); Charles II takes the Covenant (June); Cromwell succeeds Fairfax as Lord-General of the army (June), and invades Scotland (July); battle of Dunbar (September); second and last English edition of Milton's *Eikonoklastes* published.

1651 Charles II crowned at Scone (January); Dugard publishes Milton's *Pro populo Anglicano Defensio* (February); Scots' army invades England (August); battle of Worcester (September); Charles II escapes to France (October); *The*

Pseudo-Martyr and Joseph Jane's *Eikon Aklastos* published.

1653 The New Model Army, led by Cromwell, expels the Rump of the Long Parliament (April) and assembles the Barebones Parliament (July); Cromwell created Lord Protector (December).

1657 Cromwell declines offer of the crown (May).

1658 Death of Cromwell, succeeded by his son Richard (September).

1659 Richard resigns as Lord Protector; Rump Parliament recalled (May); Rump expelled by army (October) and recalled (December).

1660 General Monck reaches London; readmits M.P.s expelled by Pride's Purge (February); Long Parliament votes to dissolve itself (March); Declaration of Breda (April); Charles II proclaimed king (8 May); royal proclamation calling in *Eikonoklastes* (August); Milton arrested and imprisoned for seven months.

1662 Death of Dugard; Royston publishes the *Works* of Charles I in folio, to which he is given sole rights.

1669 Death of Henrietta Maria.

1673 Royston becomes Master of the Stationers' Company.

1674 Death of Milton (8 November).

1686 Discovery of Anglesey Memorandum; death of Royston.

1690 *Eikonoklastes* published in Amsterdam; some copies include the Anglesey Memorandum.

A Note on the Texts

All of the printed editions of *Eikon Basilike* are identified and categorized in Francis F. Madan's *A New Bibliography of the* Eikon Basilike *of King Charles the First*. This Broadview edition follows the text of the first issue of the first edition of *Eikon Basilike* printed by John Grismond for Richard Royston (British Library, Shelfmark C.118.d.1), the edition available on the day of the king's execution. The copy-text for the supplementary material appended to later editions of *Eikon Basilike*—included in this edition immediately following the main text—is the twenty-second edition of *Eikon Basilike*, printed by William Dugard for Francis Eglesfield (Huntington Library, Rare Books 114348), the first edition to contain this additional matter. The selections from *Eikonoklastes* follow the text of the first edition, first state, of that work, printed by Matthew Simmons (British Library, Shelfmark E.578[5]) on or about 6 October 1649, the day George Thomason received his copy.

In the present volume, we have modernized spelling, added apostrophes where necessary to indicate possession, printed "and" for the ampersand, and corrected obvious misprints. Obsolete usages, such as *then* for *than*, *country* for *county*, *otherways* for *otherwise*, *drave* for *drove*, *shew* for *show*, and *strooken* for *stricken*, have also been modernized. We have left intact the original capitalization, italicization, and punctuation (with the exception of apostrophe usage). In the preparation of footnotes, we have relied primarily on the second edition of the *Oxford English Dictionary*, the *Oxford Classical Dictionary*, and the 1611 edition of *The King James Bible*.

All of the dates in the paratextual matter are given according to the Julian Calendar, or Old Style. However, we have taken the year as beginning on January 1, not on March 25, as did the British in the seventeenth century. We have not altered the dates in the original texts.

EIKON BASILIKE

Εἰκών βασιλική

THE
POVRTRAICTVRE

OF

HIS SACRED
MAIESTIE

IN
HIS SOLITVDES
AND
SVFFERINGS

ROM. 8.
More then Conquerour, &c.

Bona agere, & mala pati, Regium est.

LONDON.
Printed for *R. Royston* in Ivie-lane.

M. DC. XLVIII.

THE CONTENTS

Meditations upon Death, after the Votes of Non-Addresses, and HIS MAJESTY'S *closer Imprisonment in* Carisbrooke-Castle.

1. *Upon His Majesty's calling this last Parliament.*[1]

This last Parliament I called, not more by others' advice, and necessity of My affairs, than by My own choice and inclination; who have always thought the right way of Parliaments most safe for My Crown, and best pleasing to My People: And although I was not forgetful of those sparks, which some men's distempers formerly studied to kindle in Parliaments, (which by forbearing to convene for some years, I hoped to have extinguished) yet resolving with My self to give all just satisfaction to modest and sober desires, and to redress all public grievances in Church and State; I hoped by My (freedom and their moderation) to prevent all misunderstandings, and miscarriages in this: In which as I feared affairs would meet with some passion and prejudice in other men, so I resolved they should find least of them in My self; not doubting, but by the weight of Reason I should counterpoise the over-balancings of any factions.

I was, indeed, sorry to hear, with what partiality and popular heat Elections were carried in many places; yet hoping that the gravity and discretion of other Gentlemen would allay and fix the Commons to a due temperament, (guiding some men's well-meaning zeal by such rules of moderation as are best both to preserve and restore the health of all States and Kingdoms:) No man was better pleased with the convening of this Parliament, than My self; who knowing best the largeness of My own Heart toward My People's good and just contentment, pleased My self most in that good and firm understanding, which would hence grow between Me and My People.

All Jealousies being laid aside, My own and My Children's Interests gave me many obligations to seek and preserve the love and welfare of my Subjects. The only temporal blessing that is left to the ambition of just Monarchs, as their greatest honour and safety, next God's protection; I cared not to lessen My self in some things of My wonted Prerogative; since I knew I could be no loser, if I might gain but a recompense in My Subjects' affections.

---

1   The Long Parliament was called by Charles I (November 1640) in the aftermath of the Second Bishops' War. Prior to this and the Short Parliament of April to May 1640, no parliaments had been called by the king since 1629. The intervening period is known as the eleven years' personal rule.

I intended not only to oblige My friends, but Mine enemies also: exceeding even the desires of those, that were factiously discontented, if they did but pretend to any modest and sober sense.

The *odium*[1] and offences which some men's rigour or remissness in Church, and State, had contracted upon My Government, I resolved to have expiated by such Laws, and regulations for the future, as might not only rectify what was amiss in practice, but supply what was defective in the constitution: No man having a greater zeal to see Religion settled, and preserved in Truth, Unity, and Order, than My self; whom it most concerns both in piety, and policy; as knowing, that, No flames of civil dissentions are more dangerous than those which make Religious pretensions the grounds of Factions.

I resolved to reform, what I should by free and full advice in Parliament be convinced to be amiss; and to grant whatever My Reason and Conscience told Me, was fit to be desired; I wish I had kept My self within those bounds, and not suffered My own Judgement to have been over-borne in some things, more by others' Importunities, than their Arguments; My confidence had less betrayed My self, and My Kingdoms, to those advantages, which some men sought for, who wanted nothing but power, and occasion to do mischief.

But our sins being ripe, there was no preventing of God's Justice, from reaping that glory in our Calamities, which we robbed him of in our Prosperity.

For thou (O Lord) hast made us see, that Resolutions of future Reforming do not always satisfy thy Justice, nor prevent thy Vengeance for former miscarriages.

Our sins have overlaid our hopes; Thou hast taught us to depend on thy mercies to forgive, not on our purpose to amend.

When thou hast vindicated thy glory by thy Judgements, and hast showed us, how unsafe it is to offend thee, upon presumptions afterwards to please thee; Then I trust thy mercies will restore those blessings to us, which we have so much abused, as to force thee to deprive us of them.

For want of timely repentance of our sins, Thou givest us cause to Repent of those Remedies we too late apply.

Yet I do not Repent of My calling this last Parliament; because, O

---

1 Hatred.

Lord, I did it with an upright intention, to Thy glory, and My People's good.

The miseries which have ensued upon Me and My Kingdoms, are the Just effects of thy displeasure upon us; and may be yet (through thy mercy) preparatives of us to future blessings, and better hearts to enjoy them.

O Lord, though thou hast deprived us of many former comforts; yet grant Me and My people the benefit of our afflictions, and thy chastisements; that thy rod as well as thy staff may comfort us:[1] Then shall we dare to account them the strokes not of an Enemy, but a Father: when thou givest us those humble affections, that measure of patience in repentance, which becomes thy Children;[2] I shall have no cause to repent the miseries this Parliament hath occasioned, when by them thou hast brought Me and My People, unfeignedly to repent of the sins we have committed.

Thy Grace is infinitely better with our sufferings, than our Peace could be with Our sins.

O thou sovereign goodness and wisdom, who Over-rulest all our Counsels; over-rule also all our hearts; That the worse things we suffer by thy Justice, the better we may be by thy Mercy.

As our sins have turned our Antidotes into Poison, so let thy Grace turn our Poisons into Antidotes.

As the sins of our Peace disposed us to this unhappy War, so let this War prepare us for thy blessed Peace.

That although I have but troublesome Kingdoms here, yet I may attain to that Kingdom of Peace in My Heart, and in thy Heaven, which Christ hath Purchased, and thou wilt give to thy Servant (though a Sinner) for my Saviour's sake, Amen.

2. *Upon the Earl of* Strafford's *death.*[3]

I looked upon my Lord of *Strafford*, as a Gentleman, whose great abilities might make a Prince rather afraid, than ashamed to employ him, in the greatest affairs of State.

---

1 Psalm 23:4.

2 Hebrews 12:5-11.

3 Thomas Wentworth (1593-1641) served Charles I as president of the Council of the North, Privy Councillor, and Lord Deputy of Ireland. He was created Earl of Strafford in 1640. Seen as one of the prime "evil counsellors" in Charles I's circle, Strafford was impeached, tried, and found guilty of treason early in 1641. After a day of indecision, Charles I signed his death warrant and Strafford was executed on Tower Hill on 12 May 1641.

For those were prone to create in him great confidence of undertakings, and this was like enough to betray him to great errors, and many enemies: Whereof he could not but contract good store, while moving in so high a sphere, and with so vigorous a luster, he must needs (as the Sun) raise many envious exhalations,[1] which condensed by a popular *odium*, were capable to cast a cloud upon the brightest merit, and integrity.

Though I cannot in My Judgement approve all he did, driven (it may be) by the necessities of times, and the Temper of that People, more than led by his own disposition to any height and rigour of actions: yet I could never be convinced of any such criminousness[2] in him, as willingly to expose his life to the stroke of Justice, and malice of his enemies.

I never met with a more unhappy conjuncture of affairs, than in the business of that unfortunate Earl: when between My own unsatisfiedness in Conscience, and a necessity (as some told me) of satisfying the importunities of some people; I was persuaded by those, that I think wished me well, to choose rather what was safe, than what seemed just; preferring the outward peace of My Kingdoms with men, before that inward exactness[3] of Conscience before God.

And indeed I am so far from excusing or denying that compliance on My part (for plenary[4] consent it was not) to his destruction, whom in My Judgement I thought not, by any clear Law, guilty of death: That I never bare any touch of Conscience with greater regret: which, as a sign of My repentance, I have often with sorrow confessed both to God and men, as an act of so sinful frailty, that it discovered more a fear of Man, than of God,[5] whose name and place on Earth no man is worthy to bear, who will avoid inconveniences of State, by acts of so high injustice, as no public convenience[6] can expiate or compensate.

I see it a bad exchange to wound a man's own Conscience, thereby to salve State sores; to calm the storms of popular discontents, by stirring up a tempest in a man's own bosom.

Nor hath God's Justice failed in the event and sad conse-

---

1 Expressions of anger or distrust.
2 Criminal guilt.
3 Rigour.
4 Complete.
5 Proverbs 29:25.
6 Agreement, accommodation.

quences, to show the world the fallacy of that Maxim, *Better one man perish (though unjustly) than the people be displeased, or destroyed.*[1] For,

In all likelihood, I could never have suffered, with My People, greater calamities, (yet with greater comfort) had I vindicated *Strafford's* innocency, at least by denying to Sign that destructive BILL, according to that Justice, which My Conscience suggested to Me, than I have done since I gratified some men's unthankful importunities with so cruel a favour. And I have observed, that those, who counselled Me to sign that Bill, have been so far from receiving the rewards of such ingratiatings with the People, that no men have been harassed and crushed more than they: He only hath been least vexed by them, who counselled Me, not to consent against the vote of My own Conscience; I hope God hath forgiven Me and them, the sinful rashness of that business.

To which being in My soul so fully conscious, those Judgements God hath pleased to send upon Me, are so much the more welcome, as a means (I hope) which his mercy hath sanctified so to Me, as to make Me repent of that unjust Act, (for so it was to Me) and for the future to teach Me, That the best rule of policy is to prefer the doing of Justice, before all enjoyments, and the peace of My Conscience before the preservation of My Kingdoms.

Nor hath any thing more fortified My resolutions against all those violent importunities, which since have sought to gain alike consent from Me, to Acts, wherein my Conscience is unsatisfied, than the sharp touches I have had for what passed Me, in My Lord of *Strafford's* Business.

Not that I resolved to have employed him in My affairs, against the advice of My Parliament, but I would not have had any hand in his Death, of whose Guiltlessness I was better assured, than any man living could be.

Nor were the Crimes objected against him so clear, as after a long and fair hearing to give convincing satisfaction to the Major part of both Houses; especially that of the Lords, of whom scarce a third part were present, when the Bill passed that House: And for the House of Commons, many Gentlemen, disposed enough

---

1 After the arrest of Jesus, the High Priest Caiaphas advises the Jews that it is "expedient that one man should die for the people" (John 18:14). The allusion is developed throughout this chapter and elsewhere in *Eikon Basilike* in regards to Strafford.

to diminish My Lord of *Strafford's* greatness and power, yet unsatisfied of his guilt in Law, durst not Condemn him to die: who for their Integrity in their Votes, were by Posting their Names, exposed to the popular calumny, hatred, and fury; which grew then so exorbitant in their clamours *for Justice*, (that is, to have both My self and the two Houses Vote, and do as they would have us) that many ('tis thought) were rather terrified to concur with the condemning party, than satisfied that of right they ought so to do.

And that after Act vacating the Authority of the precedent, for future imitation, sufficiently tells the world, that some remorse touched even his most implacable enemies, as knowing he had very hard measure, and such as they would be very loath should be repeated to themselves.

This tenderness and regret I find in my soul, for having had any hand (and that very unwillingly God knows) in shedding one man's blood unjustly, (though under the colour[1] and formalities of Justice, and pretences of avoiding public mischiefs) which may (I hope) be some evidence before God and Man, to all Posterity, that I am far from bearing justly the vast load and guilt of all that blood which hath been shed in this unhappy War; which some men will needs charge on *Me*, to ease their own souls, who am, and ever shall be, more afraid to take away any man's life unjustly, than to lose my own.

But thou, O God of infinite mercies, forgive me that act of sinful compliance, which hath greater aggravations upon Me than any man. Since I had not the least temptation of envy, or malice against him, and by my place should, at least so far, have been a preserver of him, as to have denied my consent to his destruction.

O Lord, I acknowledge my transgression, and my sin is ever before me.[2]

Deliver me from blood guiltiness O God, thou God of my salvation, and my tongue shall sing of thy righteousness.

Against thee have I sinned, and done this evil in thy sight, for thou sawest the contradiction between my heart and my hand.

Yet cast me not away from thy presence, purge me with the blood of

---

1 Pretext.
2 Psalm 51:3. This entire prayer is indebted to Psalm 51, much of which it quotes or paraphrases.

my Redeemer, and I shall be clean; wash me with that precious effusion, and I shall be whiter than snow.

Teach me to learn Righteousness by thy Judgements, and to see my frailty in thy Justice: while I was persuaded by shedding one man's blood to prevent after-troubles, thou hast for that, among other sins, brought upon me, and upon my Kingdoms, great, long, and heavy troubles.

Make me to prefer Justice, which is thy will, before all contrary clamours, which are but the discoveries of man's injurious will.

It is too much that they have once overcome me, to please them by displeasing thee: O never suffer me for any reason of State, to go against my Reason of Conscience, which is highly to sin against thee, the God of Reason, and Judge of our Consciences.

What ever, O Lord, thou seest fit to deprive me of, yet restore unto me the joy of thy Salvation, and ever uphold me with thy free Spirit, which subjects my will to none, but thy light of Reason, Justice, and Religion, which shines in my Soul, for Thou desirest Truth in the inward parts, and Integrity in the outward expressions.

Lord hear the voice of thy Son's, and my Saviour's Blood, which speaks better things;[1] *O make me, and my People, to hear the voice of Joy and Gladness, that the bones which thou hast broken, may rejoice in thy salvation.*

3. *Upon His Majesty's going to the House of Commons.*[2]

My going to the House of Commons to demand Justice upon the 5 Members, was an act, which My enemies loaded with all the obloquies and exasperations[3] they could.

It filled indifferent men with great jealousies and fears; yea, and many of My friends resented it as a motion rising rather from

---

1 In Genesis 4:10, Abel's blood is said to cry unto God from the ground. In Hebrews 12:24, the blood of Jesus ("the mediator of the new Covenant") is said to "speaketh better things than that of Abel."

2 On 4 January 1642, Charles attempted to arrest for high treason five members of the House of Commons (John Hampden, Arthur Hazelrige, Denzil Holles, John Pym, and William Strode) and one member of the House of Lords (Edward Montague, Lord Kimbolton). Concerned for his safety after a public outcry against his actions, Charles retreated to Hampton Court and the MPs, who had escaped arrest, returned victoriously to Westminster.

3 *obloquies* Reproaches; *exasperations* Exaggerations; malignant representations.

Passion than Reason, and not guided with such discretion, as the touchiness of those times required.

But these men knew not the just motives, and pregnant grounds, with which I thought my self so furnished, that there needed nothing to such evidence, as I could have produced against those I charged, save only a free and legal Trial, which was all I desired.

Nor had I any temptation of displeasure, or revenge against those men's persons, further than I had discovered those (as I thought) unlawful correspondencies[1] they had used, and engagements they had made, to embroil my Kingdoms: of all which I missed but little to have produced writings under some men's own hands, who were the chief contrivers of the following Innovations.

Providence would not have it so, yet I wanted[2] not such probabilities as were sufficient to raise jealousies in any King's heart, who is not wholly stupid and neglective of the public peace, which to preserve by calling in Question half a dozen men, in a fair and legal way (which God knows was all my design) could have amounted to no worse effect, had it succeeded, than either to do Me, and my Kingdom right, in case they had been found guilty; or else to have cleared their Innocency, and removed my suspicions; which, as they were not raised out of any malice, so neither were they in Reason to be smothered.

What flames of discontent this spark (though I sought by all speedy and possible means to quench it) soon kindled, all the world is witness: The aspersion which some men cast upon that action, as if I had designed by force to assault the House of Commons, and invade their privilege, is so false, that as God best knows, I had no such intent; so none that attended me could justly gather from any thing I then said, or did, the least intimation of any such thoughts.

That I went attended with some Gentlemen, as it was no unwonted[3] thing for the Majesty and safety of a King so to be attended, especially in discontented times; so were my followers at that time short of my ordinary Guard,[4] and no way propor-

---

1 Communications.
2 Lacked.
3 Unusual; unfamiliar.
4 In the *Memoirs of the Life of Colonel Hutchinson*, Lucy Hutchinson (a Parliamentarian) claims that Charles was then attended with his "extraordinary guard, of about four hundred gentlemen and soldiers, armed with swords and pistols...."

tionable to hazard a tumultuary conflict. Nor were they more scared at my coming, than I was un-assured of not having some affronts cast upon me, if I had none with me to preserve a reverence to me; For many people had (at that time) learned to think those hard thoughts, which they have since abundantly vented against Me, both by words and deeds.

The sum of that business was this.

Those men, and their adherents were then looked upon by the affrighted vulgar, as greater protectors of their Laws and Liberties, than my self, and so worthier of their protection. I leave them to God, and their own Consciences, who, if guilty of evil machinations; no present impunity, or popular vindications of them will be subterfuge sufficient to rescue them from those exact Tribunals.

To which, in the obstructions of Justice among men, we must religiously appeal, as being an argument to us Christians of that after un-avoidable judgement, which shall rejudge, what among men is but corruptly decided, or not at all.

I endeavoured to have prevented, if God had seen fit, those future commotions, which I fore-saw, would in all likelihood follow some men's activity (if not restrained) and so now hath done to the undoing of many thousands; the more is the pity.

But to over-awe the freedom of the Houses, or to weaken their just Authority by any violent impressions upon them, was not at all my design: I thought I had so much Justice and Reason on my side, as should not have needed so rough assistance; and I was resolved rather to bear the repulse with patience, than to use such hazardous extremities.

But thou, O Lord, art my witness in heaven, and in my Heart:[1] *If I have purposed any violence or oppression against the Innocent: or if there were any such wickedness in my thoughts.*

Then let the enemy persecute my soul, and tread my life to the ground, and lay mine Honour in the dust.[2]

Thou that seest not as man seeth, but lookest beyond all popular appearances, searching the heart, and trying the reins,[3] *and bringing to light the hidden things of darkness,*[4] *show thy self.*

---

1 Job 16:19.
2 Psalm 7:5.
3 Kidneys, the seat of the affections; following biblical usage in Psalm 26:2, Jeremiah 11:20 and 17:10, and Revelation 2:23.
4 1 Corinthians 4:5.

Let not my afflictions be esteemed (as with wise and godly men they cannot be) any argument of my sin, in that matter: more than their Impunity among good men is any sure token of their Innocency.

But forgive them wherein they have done amiss, though they are not punished for it in this world.

Save thy servant from the privy conspiracies, and open violence of bloody and unreasonable men,[1] according to the uprightness of my heart, and the innocency of my hands in this matter.

Plead my cause, and maintain my right, O thou that sittest in the Throne, judging rightly, that thy servant may ever rejoice in thy salvation.[2]

4. Upon the Insolency of the Tumults.[3]

I never thought any thing (except our sins) more ominously presaging all these mischiefs, which have followed, than those Tumults in *London* and *Westminster*, soon after the Convening of this Parliament; which were not like a storm at Sea, (which yet wants not its terror) but like an Earth-quake, shaking the very foundations of all; than which nothing in the world hath more of horror.

As it is one of the most convincing Arguments that there is a God, while his power sets bounds to the raging of the Sea:[4] so 'tis no less, that he restrains the madness of the people. Nor doth any thing portend more God's displeasure against a Nation, than when he suffers the confluence and clamours of the vulgar, to pass all boundaries of Laws, and reverence to Authority.

Which those Tumults did to so high degrees of Insolence, that they spared not to invade the Honour and Freedom of the two Houses, menacing, reproaching, shaking, yea, and assaulting some Members of both Houses, as they fancied, or disliked them: Nor did they forbear most rude and unseemly deportments both in contemptuous words and actions, to My self and My Court.

---

1 Psalm 59:2.

2 *Plead ... rightly* Psalm 9:4; *rejoice ... salvation* A phrase repeated throughout the Psalms (Psalm 9:14, 13:5, 20:5, 35:9; see also I Samuel 2:1 and Isaiah 25:9).

3 Soon after Charles' failed coup, presentations of popular petitions to king and parliament led to mass demonstrations and popular riots: one occurred in Westminster on 11 January 1642, and another on January 31st in Moor Fields, London.

4 Psalm 89:9.

Nor was this a short fit or two of shaking, as an ague, but a quotidian[1] fever, always increasing to higher inflammations, impatient of any mitigation, restraint, or remission.

First, they must be a guard against those fears, which some men scared themselves and others withall; when indeed nothing was more to be feared and less to be used by wise men, than those tumultuary confluxes of mean and rude people, who are taught first to petition, then to protect, then to dictate, at last to command and overawe the Parliament.

All obstructions in Parliament (that is, all freedom of differing in Votes, and debating matters with reason and candour) must be taken away with these Tumults: By these must the Houses be purged, and all rotten Members (as they pleased to count them) cast out: By these the obstinacy of men resolved to discharge their Consciences must be subdued, by these all factious, seditious, and schismatical proposals against Government Ecclesiastical or Civil, must be backed and abetted, till they prevailed.

Generally, who ever had most mind to bring forth confusion and ruin upon Church and State, used the midwifery of those Tumults: whose riot and impatience was such, that they would not stay the ripening and season of Counsels, or fair production of Acts, in the order, gravity, and deliberateness befitting a Parliament; but ripped up with barbarous cruelty, and forcibly cut out abortive Votes, such as their Inviters and Encouragers most fancied.

Yea, so enormous and detestable were their outrages, that no sober man could be without an infinite shame and sorrow to see them so tolerated, and connived at by some, countenanced, encouraged, and applauded by others.

What good man had not rather want any thing he most desired, for the Public good, than obtain it by such unlawful and irreligious means? But men's passions and God's directions seldom agree; violent designs and motions must have suitable engines,[2] such as too much attend their own ends, seldom confine themselves to God's means. Force must crowd in what Reason will not lead.

Who were the chief Demagogues and Patrons of Tumults, to send for them, to flatter and embolden them, to direct and tune their clamorous importunities, some men yet living are too con-

1 Daily.
2 Instruments.

scious to pretend ignorance: God in his due time will let these see, that those were no fit means to be used for attaining his ends.

But, as it is no strange thing for the Sea to rage, when strong winds blow upon it; so neither for Multitudes to become insolent, when they have Men of some reputation for parts[1] and piety to set them on.

That which made their rudeness most formidable, was, that many Complaints being made, and Messages sent by My self and some of both Houses; yet no order for redress could be obtained with any vigour and efficacy, proportionable to the malignity of that now far-spread disease, and predominant mischief.

Such was some men's stupidity, that they feared no inconvenience; Others' petulancy, that they joyed to see their betters shamefully outraged, and abused, while they knew their only security consisted in vulgar flattery: So insensible were they of Mine, or the two Houses' common safety and Honours.

Nor could ever any order be obtained, impartially to examine, censure, and punish the known Boutefeus,[2] and impudent Incendiaries, who boasted of the influence they had, and used to convoke[3] those Tumults as their advantages served.

Yea, some (who should have been wiser States-men) owned them as friends, commending their Courage, Zeal, and Industry; which to sober men could seem no better than that of the Devil, who *goes about seeking whom he may* deceive, and *devour*.[4]

I confess, when I found such a deafness, that no Declaration from the Bishops, who were first foully insolenced and assaulted; nor yet from other Lords and Gentlemen of Honour; nor yet from My self could take place for the due repression of these Tumults; and securing not only Our freedom in Parliament, but Our very Persons in the streets; I thought My self not bound by My presence, to provoke them to higher boldness and contempts; I hoped by My withdrawing[5] to give time, both for the ebbing of their tumultuous fury, and others regaining some degrees of modesty and sober sense.

Some may interpret it as an effect of Pusillanimity[6] for any

---

1 Personal attributes, especially of an intellectual kind; talents.
2 Firebrands; those who kindle strife and inflame passions.
3 Summon to assemble.
4 1 Peter 5:8.
5 Charles initially withdrew to Hampton Court.
6 Cowardliness.

man for popular terrors to desert his public station. But I think it a hardiness, beyond true valour, for a wise man to set himself against the breaking in of a Sea; which to resist, at present, threatens imminent danger; but to withdraw, gives it space to spend its fury, and gains a fitter time to repair the breach. Certainly a Gallant man had rather fight to great disadvantages for number and place in the field, in an orderly way, than scuffle with an undisciplined rabble.

Some suspected and affirmed that I meditated[1] a War, (when I went from *Whitehall* only to redeem My Person, and Conscience from violence) God knows I did not then think of a War. Nor will any prudent man conceive that I would by so many former, and some after Acts, have so much weakened My self, if I had purposed to engage in a War, which to decline by all means, I denied My self in so many particulars: 'Tis evident I had then no Army to fly unto, for protection, or vindication.

Who can blame Me, or any other, for a withdrawing our selves from the daily baitings of the Tumults, not knowing whether their fury and discontent might not fly so high, as to worry and tear those in pieces, whom as yet they but played with in their paws? God, who is My sole Judge, is My Witness in Heaven, that I never had any thoughts of going from My House at *Whitehall*, if I could have had but any reasonable fair Quarter;[2] I was resolved to bear much, and did so, but I did not think My self bound to prostitute the Majesty of my Place and Person, the safety of My Wife and Children, to those, who are prone to insult most, when they have objects and opportunity most capable of their rudeness and petulancy.

But this business of the Tumults (whereof some have given already an account to God,[3] others yet living know themselves desperately guilty) Time and the guilt of many hath so smothered up, and buried, that I think it best to leave it, as it is; Only I believe the just Avenger of all disorders, will in time make those men, and that City, see their sin in the glass of their punishment. 'Tis more than an even-lay[4] that they may one day see themselves punished by that way they offended.

Had this Parliament, as it was in its first Election and Consti-

---

1 Planned; contemplated.
2 Treatment; terms.
3 Romans 14:12.
4 Even bet.

tution, sat full and free, the Members of both Houses being left to their freedom of Voting, as in all reason, honour, and Religion, they should have been; I doubt not but things would have been so carried, as would have given no less content to all good men, than they wished or expected.

For, I was resolved to hear reason in all things, and to consent to it so far as I could comprehend it: but as Swine are to Gardens and orderly Plantations, so are Tumults to Parliaments, and Plebeian concourses[1] to public Counsels, turning all into disorders and sordid confusions.

I am prone sometimes to think, That had I called this Parliament to any other place in *England* (as I might opportunely enough have done) the sad consequences in all likelihood, with God's blessing, might have been prevented. A Parliament would have been welcome in any place; no place afforded such confluence of various and vicious humours, as that where it was unhappily convened. But we must leave all to God, who orders our disorders, and magnifies his wisdom most, when our follies and miseries are most discovered.

But thou O Lord art My refuge and defence; [2] *to thee I may safely fly, who rulest the raging of the Sea, and the madness of the People.*

The floods, O Lord, the floods are come in upon me, and are ready to overwhelm me. [3]

I look upon My sins, and the sins of My people, (which are the tumults of our souls against thee O Lord) as the just cause of these popular inundations which thou permittest to overbear all the banks of loyalty, modesty, Laws, Justice, and Religion.

But thou that gatheredst the waters into one place, and madest the dry land to appear, and after did'st assuage the flood which drowned the world, by the word of thy power; [4] *Rebuke those beasts of the people, and deliver Me from the rudeness and strivings of the multitude.*

Restore, we beseech thee, unto us, the freedoms of our Councils and Parliaments, make us unpassionately to see the light of Reason, and Religion, and with all order, and gravity to follow it, as it becomes Men and Christians; so shall we praise thy name, who art the God of order and counsel.

---

1 Crowds.
2 Psalm 59:16.
3 Psalm 69:2.
4 *gatheredst ... appear* Genesis 1:9; *assuage the flood* Genesis 8:13.

What man cannot, or will not repress, thy omnipotent Justice can and will.

O Lord, give them that are yet living, a timely sense and sorrow for their great sin, whom thou knowest guilty of raising or not suppressing those disorders: Let shame here, and not suffering hereafter be their punishment.

Set bounds to our passions by Reason, to our errors by Truth, to our seditions by Laws duly executed, and to our schisms by Charity, that we may be, as thy Jerusalem, *a City at unity in it self.*[1]

This grant, O My God, in thy good time for Jesus Christ's sake, Amen.

5. *Upon His Majesty's passing the Bill for the Triennial Parliaments: And after settling this, during the pleasure of the two Houses.*[2]

That the world might be fully confirmed in My purposes at first, to contribute, what in Justice, Reason, Honour, and Conscience, I could, to the Happy success of this Parliament, (which had in Me no other design but the General good of My Kingdoms) I willingly passed the BILL for Triennial Parliaments: which, as gentle and seasonable Physic, might (if well applied) prevent any distempers from getting any head or prevailing; especially, if the remedy proved not a disease beyond all remedy.

I conceived, this Parliament would find work with convenient recesses for the first three Years; But I did not imagine that some men would thereby have occasioned more work than they found to do, by undoing so much as they found well done to their hands. Such is some men's activity that they will needs make work rather than want it; and choose to be doing amiss, rather than do nothing.

When that first Act seemed too scanty to satisfy some men's fears, and compass public affairs; I was persuaded to grant that BILL of Sitting during the pleasure of the Houses, which amounted in some men's sense to as much as the perpetuating this Parliament. By this Act of highest confidence, I hoped for ever to shut out, and lock the door upon all present Jealousies,

---

1 The New Jerusalem, described by John in Revelation 21:2, 10.

2 Passed 16 February 1641, the Triennial Act provided for the automatic election and assembly of a parliament three years after the previous one's dissolution, if the monarch failed to summon one in that period. A later act, the "Bill of Sitting," forbade the dissolution of the Long Parliament without its own consent (10 May 1641).

and future mistakes: I confess I did not thereby intend to shut My self out of doors, as some men have now requited me.

True, It was an Act unparalleled by any of My Predecessors; yet cannot in reason admit of any worse interpretation than this, of an extreme confidence I had, that My Subjects would not make ill use of an Act, by which I declared so much to trust them, as to deny My self in so high a point of My Prerogative.

For good Subjects will never think it just or fit that My condition should be worse by My bettering theirs: Nor indeed would it have been so in the events, if some men had known as well with moderation to use, as with earnestness to desire advantages of doing good, or evil.

A continual Parliament (I thought) would but keep the Common-weal in tune, by preserving Laws in their due execution and vigour, wherein My interest lies more than any man's, since by those Laws, My Rights as a KING, would be preserved no less than My Subjects; which is all I desired. More than the Law gives Me, I would not have, and less the meanest Subject should not.

Some (as I have heard) gave it out, that I soon repented Me of that settling Act: and many would needs persuade Me, I had cause so to do; but I could not easily nor suddenly suspect such ingratitude in Men of Honour. That the more I granted them, the less I should have, and enjoy with them. I still counted My self undiminished by My largest concessions, if by them I might gain and confirm the love of My People.

Of which, I do not yet despair, but that God will still bless Me with increase of it: when Men shall have more leisure, and less prejudice; that so with unpassionate representations they may reflect upon those, (as I think) not more princely than friendly contributions, which I granted towards the perpetuating of their happiness, who are now only miserable in this, That some men's ambition will not give them leave to enjoy what I intended for their good.

Nor do I doubt, but that in God's due time, the Loyal and cleared affections of My people will strive to return such retributions of Honour, and love to Me, or My Posterity, as may fully compensate both the acts of My confidence and My sufferings for them; which (God knows) have been neither few, nor small, nor short; occasioned chiefly by a persuasion I had, that I could not grant too much, or distrust too little, to Men, that being professedly My Subjects, pretended singular piety, and religious strictness.

The Injury of all Injuries is, That which some men will needs load Me withal; as if I were a wilful and resolved Occasioner of My own and My Subjects' miseries; while (as they confidently, but (God knows) falsly divulge) I repining at the establishment of this Parliament, endeavoured by force and open hostility to undo what by My Royal assent I had done. Sure it had argued a very short sight of things, and extreme fatuity[1] of mind in Me, so far to bind My own hands at their request, if I had shortly meant to have used a Sword against them. God knows, though I had then a sense of Injuries; yet not such, as to think them worth vindicating by a War: I was not then compelled, as since, to injure My self by their not using favours, with the same candour wherewith they were conferred. The Tumults indeed threatened to abuse all Acts of Grace, and turn them into wantonness; but I thought at length their own fears, whose black arts first raised up those turbulent Spirits would force them to conjure them down again.

Nor if I had justly resented any indignities put upon Me, or others, was I then in any capacity to have taken just revenge in an Hostile and Warlike way upon those, whom I knew so well fortified in the love of the meaner sort of the people, that I could not have given My enemies greater, and more desired advantages against Me, than by so unprincely Inconstancy, to have assaulted them with Arms, thereby to scatter them, whom but lately I had solemnly settled by an Act of Parliament.

God knows I longed for nothing more than that My self, and My Subjects might quietly enjoy the fruits of My many condescendings.[2]

It had been a Course full of sin, as well as of Hazard, and dishonour for Me to go about the cutting up of that by the Sword, which I had so lately planted, so much (as I thought) to my Subjects' content, and Mine own too, in all probability: If some men had not feared where no fear was, whose security consisted in scaring others.

I thank God I know so well the sincerity and uprightness of My own heart, in passing that great Bill, which exceeded the very thoughts of former times; That although I may seem less a Politician to men, yet I need no secret distinctions or evasions before God. Nor had I any reservations in My own Soul, when I passed it; nor repentings after, till I saw that My letting some men go up

1 Stupidity.
2 Concessions.

to the Pinnacle of the Temple, was a temptation to them to cast Me down head-long.

Concluding, that without a miracle, Monarchy it self, together with Me, could not but be dashed in pieces, by such a precipitious fall as they intended. Whom God in mercy forgive, and make them see at length, That as many Kingdoms as the Devil showed our Saviour, and the glory of them,[1] (if they could be at once enjoyed by them) are not worth the gaining, by ways of sinful ingratitude and dishonour, which hazards a Soul worth more Worlds than this hath Kingdoms.

But God hath hitherto preserved Me, and made Me to see, That it is no strange thing for men, left to their own passions, either to do much evil themselves, or abuse the over-much goodness of others, whereof an ungrateful Surfeit[2] is the most desperate and incurable disease.

I cannot say properly that I repent of that Act, since I have no reflections upon it as a sin of my will, though an error of too charitable a judgement: Only I am sorry other men's eyes should be evil, because mine were good.

To Thee (O my God) do I still appeal, whose All-discerning Justice sees through all the disguises of men's pretensions, and deceitful darknesses of their hearts.

Thou gavest me a heart to grant much to My Subjects; and now I need a Heart fitted to suffer much from some of them.

Thy will be done,[3] though never so much to the crossing of ours, even when we hope to do what might be most conformable to thine and theirs too; who pretended they aimed at nothing else.

Let thy grace teach me wisely to enjoy as well the frustratings, as the fulfillings of My best hopes, and most specious desires.

I see while I thought to allay others' fears, I have raised Mine own; and by settling them, have unsettled My self.

Thus have they requited Me evil for good, and hatred for My good will towards them.[4]

O Lord be thou My Pilot in this dark and dangerous storm, which

---

1 Matthew 4:8-9; Luke 4:5-6.
2 Excess.
3 A phrase from the Lord's Prayer (Matthew 6:10 and Luke 11:2); also spoken by Jesus when faced with his inevitable death (Matthew 26:42).
4 Psalm 109:5.

neither admits My return to the Port whence I set out, nor My making any other, with that safety and honour which I designed.

'Tis easy for Thee to keep Me safe in the love and confidence of My people; nor is it hard for Thee to preserve Me amidst the unjust hatred and jealousies of too many, which thou hast suffered so far to prevail upon Me, as to be able to pervert and abuse My acts of greatest Indulgence to them, and assurance of them.

But no favours from Me can make others more guilty than My self may be, of misusing those many and great ones, which Thou, O Lord, hast conferred on Me.

I beseech Thee give Me and them such Repentance, as thou wilt accept, and such Grace as we may not abuse.

Make Me so far happy as to make a right use of others' abuses, and by their failings of Me, to reflect, with a reforming displeasure, upon My offences against Thee.

So, although for My sins I am by other men's sins deprived of thy temporal blessings, yet I may be happy to enjoy the comfort of thy mercies, which often raise the greatest Sufferers to be the most glorious Saints.

6. *Upon His Majesty's retirement from* Westminster.[1]

With what unwillingness I withdrew from *Westminster*, let them judge, who, unprovided of tackling, and victual, are forced to Sea by a storm, yet better do so, than venture splitting or sinking on a Lee shore.[2]

I stayed at *Whitehall*, till I was driven away by shame more than fear; to see the barbarous rudeness of those Tumults who resolved they would take the boldness to demand any thing, and not leave either My self, or the Members of Parliament the liberty of our Reason, and Conscience to deny them any thing.

Nor was this intolerable oppression My case alone, (though chiefly Mine) For the Lords and Commons might be content to be over-voted by the *major* part of their Houses, when they had used each their own freedom.

Whose agreeing Votes were not by any Law or reason conclusive to My Judgement; nor can they include, or carry with them

---

1 Charles retreated with Henrietta Maria to Hampton Court after his failure to arrest the "Five Members," moving soon after to Windsor Castle. After Henrietta Maria departed for Holland on 23 February 1642, Charles retired to Theobalds.

2 Shore upon which the wind blows.

My consent, whom they represent not in any kind. Nor am I further bound to agree with the Votes of both Houses, than I see them agree with the will of God, with My just Rights, as a King, and the general good of My People. I see that as many men they are seldom of one mind; and I may oft see, that the major part of them are not in the right.

I had formerly declared to sober and moderate minds, how desirous I was to give all just content, when I agreed to so many Bills, which had been enough to secure and satisfy all: If some men's Hydropic insatiableness[1] had not learned to thirst the more by how much more they drank; whom no fountain of Royal bounty was able to overcome; so resolved they seemed, either utterly to exhaust it, or barbarously to obstruct it.

Sure it ceases to be Counsel; when not Reason is used, as to men to persuade; but force and terror as to beasts, to drive and compel men to assent to what ever tumultuary patrons shall project. He deserves to be a slave without pity, or redemption, that is content to have the rational sovereignty of his Soul, and liberty of his will, and words so captivated.

Nor do I think My Kingdoms so considerable as to preserve them with the forfeiture of that freedom; which cannot be denied Me as a King, because it belongs to Me as a Man, and a Christian; owning the dictates of none, but God, to be above Me, as obliging Me to consent. Better for Me to die enjoying this Empire of My Soul, which subjects Me only to God, so far as by Reason or Religion he directs Me, than live with the Title of a King, if it should carry such a vassalage with it, as not to suffer Me to use My Reason and Conscience, in which I declare as a King, to like or dislike.

So far am I from thinking the Majesty of the Crown of *England* to be bound by any Coronation Oath, in a blind and brutish formality, to consent to what ever its subjects in Parliament shall require; as some men will needs infer; while denying Me any power of a Negative voice as King, they are not ashamed to seek to deprive Me of the liberty of using My Reason with a good Conscience, which themselves, and all the Commons of *England* enjoy proportionable to their influence on the public; who would take it very ill to be urged, not to deny, whatever My self, as King, or the House of Peers with Me, should, not so much desire as

---

1 Unquenchable thirst.

enjoin them to pass. I think My Oath fully discharged in that point by My Governing only by such Laws, as My People with the House of Peers have Chosen, and My self have consented to. I shall never think My self conscientiously tied to go as oft against My Conscience, as I should consent to such new Proposals, which My Reason, in Justice, Honour, and Religion bids Me deny.

Yet so tender I see some men are of their being subject to Arbitrary Government, (that is, the Law of another's will, to which themselves give no consent) that they care not with how much dishonour and absurdity they make their King the only man, that must be subject to the will of others, without having power left Him, to use His own Reason, either in Person, or by any Representation.

And if My dissentings at any time were (as some have suspected, and uncharitably avowed) out of error, opinion, activeness, weakness, or wilfulness, and what they call Obstinacy in Me (which not true Judgement of things, but some vehement prejudice or passion hath fixed on My mind;) yet can no man think it other than the Badge and Method of Slavery, by savage rudeness, and importunate obtrusions of violence, to have the mist of His Error and Passion dispelled, which is a shadow of Reason, and must serve those that are destitute of the substance. Sure that man cannot be blameable to God or Man, who seriously endeavours to see the best reason of things, and faithfully follows what he takes for Reason: The uprightness of his intentions will excuse the possible failings of his understandings; If a Pilot at Sea cannot see the Pole-star, it can be no fault in him to steer his course by such stars as do best appear to him. It argues rather those men to be conscious of their defects of Reason, and convincing Arguments, who call in the assistance of mere force to carry on the weakness of their Counsels, and Proposals. I may, in the Truth and uprightness of My heart, protest before God and Men; that I never wilfully opposed, or denied any thing, that was in a fair way, after full and free debates propounded to Me, by the two Houses, Further than I thought in good reason I might, and was bound to do.

Nor did any thing ever please Me more, than when My Judgement so concurred with theirs, that I might with good Conscience consent to them: yea, in many things where not absolute and moral necessity of Reason, but temporary convenience on point of Honour was to be considered. I chose rather to deny My self, than them; as preferring that which they thought necessary for My People's good, before what I saw but convenient for My self.

For I can be content to recede much from My own Interests, and Personal Rights, of which I conceive My self to be Master; but in what concerns Truth, Justice, the Rights of the Church, and My Crown, together with the general good of My Kingdoms; (all which I am bound to preserve as much as morally lies in Me;) here I am, and ever shall be fixed and resolute, nor shall any man gain My consent to that, wherein My Heart gives My tongue or hand the Lie; nor will I be brought to affirm that to Men, which in My Conscience I denied before God. I will rather choose to wear a Crown of Thorns with My Saviour, than to exchange that of Gold[1] (which is due to Me) for one of lead, whose embased[2] flexibleness shall be forced to bend, and comply to the various, and oft contrary dictates of any Factions; when instead of Reason, and Public concernments, they obtrude nothing but what makes for the interest of parties, and flows from the partialities of private wills and passions.

I know no resolutions more worthy a Christian King, than to prefer His Conscience before His Kingdoms.

O my God, preserve thy servant in this Native, Rational and Religious freedom; For this I believe is thy will, that we should maintain: who, though thou dost justly require us, to submit our understandings and wills to thine; whose wisdom and goodness can neither err, nor misguide us, and so far to deny our carnal reason, in order to thy sacred Mysteries, and commands, that we should believe and obey rather than dispute them; yet dost thou expect from us, only such a reasonable service of thee, as not to do any thing for thee, against our consciences; and as to the desires of men, enjoinest us to try all things by the touch-stone of Reason and Laws, which are the rules of Civil Justice; and to declare our consents to that only which our Judgements approve.

Thou knowest, O Lord, how unwilling I was to desert that place, in which thou hast set me, and whereto the affairs of My Kingdoms at present did call me.

---

1 *Crown of Thorns* Worn by Jesus at his crucifixion (Matthew 27:29; Mark 15:17; John 19:2); *that of Gold* Awarded to those who remain faithful (Psalm 21:3; 2 Timothy 4:8; James 1:12; 1 Peter 5:4; Revelation 2:10).
2 Debased.

My People can witness how far I have been content for their good, to deny My self, in what thou hast subjected to My disposal.

O Let not the unthankful importunities, and tumultuary violence of some men's Immoderate demands, ever betray Me to that degenerous[1] and unmanly slavery, which should make Me strengthen them by My consent in those things which I think in My Conscience to be against thy glory, the good of My subjects, and the discharge of My own duty to Reason and Justice.

Make Me willing to suffer the greatest indignities, and injuries they press upon Me, rather than commit the least sin against My Conscience.

Let the just liberties of My people be (as well they may) preserved in fair, and equal ways, without the slavery of My soul.

Thou that hast invested Me by thy favours, in the power of a Christian King, suffer Me not to subject My Reason to other men's passions, and designs, which to Me seems unreasonable, unjust, and irreligious: So shall I serve thee in the truth and uprightness of My heart, though I cannot satisfy these men.

Though I be driven from among them, yet give Me grace to walk always uprightly before thee.

Lead Me in the way of Truth and Justice,[2] for these, I know, will bring Me at last to peace and happiness with thee; though for these I have much trouble among men.

This I beg of thee for My Saviour's sake.

7. *Upon the Queen's departure, and absence out of* England.[3]

Although I have much cause to be troubled at My Wife's departure from Me, and out of My Dominions; yet not Her absence, so much, as the scandal of that necessity, which drives her away, doth afflict Me. That She should be compelled by My own Subjects, and those pretending to be Protestants, to withdraw for Her

---

1 Degenerate.
2 Psalm 25:5.
3 The Commons had impeached Henrietta Maria in May 1643—the Lords assented some months later. The impeachment resulted, in part, from her continental trip (1642-43) during which she pawned some of the crown jewels to support her husband's cause. In April 1644, with Parliamentary forces threatening Oxford, the pregnant Henrietta Maria, accompanied part of the way by Charles I, left for Exeter. After giving birth to Henrietta Anne, she sailed for France on 14 July 1644, not returning to England until the Restoration.

safety: This being the first example of any Protestant Subjects, that have taken up Arms against their King, a Protestant: For I look upon this now done in England, as another Act of the same Tragedy which was lately begun in Scotland;[1] the brands of that fire being ill quenched, have kindled the like flames here. I fear such motions (so little to the adorning of the Protestant profession) may occasion a farther alienation of mind, and divorce of affections in Her, from that Religion, which is the only thing wherein we differ.

Which yet God can, and I pray he would in time take away; and not suffer these practices to be any obstruction to Her judgement; since it is the motion of those men, (for the most part) who are yet to seek and settle their Religion for Doctrine, Government, and good manners, and so not to be imputed to the true English Protestants; who continue firm to their former settled Principles and Laws.

I am sorry My relation to so deserving a Lady, should be any occasion of her danger and affliction; whose merits would have served her for a protection among the savage *Indians*; while their rudeness and barbarity knows not so perfectly to hate all Virtues, as some men's subtilty doth; among whom I yet think few are so malicious as to hate Her for Her self. The fault is, that she is My wife.

All justice then as well as affection commands Me, to study her Security, who is only in danger for My sake; I am content to be tossed, weather-beaten, and shipwrecked, so as she may be in safe Harbour.

This comfort I shall enjoy by her safety in the midst of My Personal dangers, that I can perish but half, if she be preserved: In whose memory, and hopeful Posterity, I may yet survive the malice of My enemies, although they should be satiated with My blood.

I must leave her, and them, to the Love and Loyalty of My good Subjects; and to his protection, who is able to punish the faults of Princes, and no less severely to revenge the injuries done to Them, by those who in all duty and Allegiance, ought to have made good that safety, which the Laws chiefly provide for Princes.

But common civility is in vain expected from those, that dispute their Loyalty: Nor can it be safe (for any relation) to a King,

1   The allusion is to the two Bishops' Wars.

to tarry among them who are shaking hands with their Allegiance, under pretence of laying faster hold on their Religion.

'Tis pity so noble and peaceful a soul should see, much more suffer, the rudeness of those who must make up their want of justice, with inhumanity, and impudence.

Her sympathy with Me in My afflictions, will make her virtues shine with greater lustre, as stars in the darkest nights; and assure the envious world, that she loves Me, not My fortunes.

Neither of us but can easily forgive, since We do not much blame the unkindness of the Generality, and Vulgar; for we see God is pleased to try both our patience, by the most self-punishing sin, the Ingratitude of those, who having eaten of our bread, and being enriched with Our bounty, have Scornfully lifted up themselves against Us; and those of Our own Household are become Our enemies. I pray God lay not their sin to their charge:[1] who think to satisfy all obligations to duty, by their Corban[2] of Religion: and can less endure to see, than to sin against their benefactors as well as their Sovereigns.

But even that policy of my enemies is so far venial, as it was necessary to their designs, by scandalous articles, and all irreverent demeanour, to seek to drive her out of My Kingdoms; lest by the influence of her example, eminent for love as a Wife, and Loyalty, as a Subject, she should have converted to, or retained in their love, and Loyalty, all those whom they had a purpose to pervert.

The less I may be blessed with her company, the more I will retire to God, and My own Heart, whence no malice can banish Her. My enemies may envy, but they can never deprive Me of the enjoyment of her virtues, while I enjoy My self.

Thou O Lord, whose Justice at present sees fit to scatter us, let thy mercy, in thy due time, reunite us, on earth, if it be thy will; however bring us both at last, to thy heavenly Kingdom.

Preserve us from the hands of our despiteful and deadly enemies; and prepare us by our sufferings for thy presence.

Though we differ in some things, as to Religion, (which is my greatest temporal infelicity) yet Lord give, and accept the sincerity of our affections, which desire to seek, to find, to embrace every Truth of thine.

---

1 Stephen, the martyr, cried out these words as he died (Acts 7:60).
2 An offering given to God in performance of a vow.

Let both our Hearts agree in the love of thy self, and Christ cruci-
fied for us.

Teach us both what thou wouldst have us to know, in order to thy
glory, our public relations, and our souls' eternal good, and make us
careful to do what good we know.

Let neither Ignorance of what is necessary to be known, nor unbe-
lief, or disobedience to what we know, be our misery or our wilful
default.

Let not this great Scandal of those my Subjects, which profess the
same Religion with me, be any hindrance to her love of any Truth thou
wouldst have her to learn, nor any hardening of her, in any error thou
wouldst have cleared to her.

Let mine, and other men's constancy be an Antidote against the poi-
son of their example.

Let the Truth of that Religion I profess, be represented to her Judge-
ment, with all the beauties of Humility, Loyalty, Charity, and Peace-
ableness; which are the proper fruits, and ornaments of it: Not in the
odious disguises of Levity, Schism, Heresy, Novelty, Cruelty, and Dis-
loyalty, which some men's practices have lately put upon it.

Let her see thy sacred and saving Truths, as Thine; that she may
believe, love and obey them as Thine, cleared from all rust and dross of
human mixtures.

That in the glass of thy Truth she may see thee, in those mercies
which thou hast offered to us, in thy Son Jesus Christ, our only Sav-
iour, and serve thee in all those Holy duties, which most agree with his
holy doctrine, and most imitable example.

The experience we have of the vanity, and uncertainty of all human
Glory, and greatness in our scatterings and Eclipses, let it make us both
so much the more ambitious to be invested in those durable honours,
and perfections, which are only to be found in thy self, and obtained
through Jesus Christ.

8. *Upon His Majesty's repulse at* Hull, *and the fates of the* Hothams.[1]
My repulse at *Hull* seemed at the first view an act of so rude disloyalty, that My greatest enemies had scarce confidence enough

---

1   Charles attempted to seize control of the garrison at Hull, a strategic
    military post well stocked with ammunition. Sir John Hotham, the par-
    liamentary governor of Hull, refused Charles entry to the town on 23
    April 1642. When Hotham, and his eldest son John, later negotiated the
    betrayal of the post to Royalists, they were arrested by Parliament in
    June 1643, and executed in January 1645.

to abet, or own it: It was the first overt Essay[1] to be made, how patiently I could bear the Loss of My Kingdoms.

God knows, it affected me more with shame and sorrow for others, than with anger for My self; nor did the affront done to Me trouble Me so much as their sin, which admitted no colour or excuse.

I was resolved how to bear this, and much more, with patience: But I foresaw they could hardly contain themselves within the compass of this one unworthy act, who had effrontery enough to commit, or countenance it. This was but the hand of that cloud, which was soon after to overspread the whole Kingdom, and cast all into disorder and darkness.

For 'tis among the wicked Maxims of bold and disloyal undertakers: That bad actions must always be seconded with worse, and rather not be begun than not carried on, for they think the retreat more dangerous than the assault, and hate repentance more than perseverance in a Fault.

This gave Me to see clearly through all the pious disguises, and soft palliations[2] of some men; whose words were sometime smoother than oil, but now I saw they would prove very Swords.[3]

Against which I having (as yet) no defence, but that of a good Conscience, thought it My best policy (with patience) to bear what I could not remedy: And in this (I thank God) I had the better of *Hotham*, that no disdain, or emotion of passion transported Me, by the indignity of his carriage, to do or say any thing, unbeseeming My self, or unsuitable to that temper, which, in greatest injuries, I think, best becomes a Christian, as coming nearest to the great example of Christ.

And indeed, I desire always more to remember I am a Christian, than a King; for what the Majesty of one might justly abhor, the Charity of the other is willing to bear; what the height of a King tempteth to revenge, the humility of a Christian teacheth to forgive. Keeping in compass[4] all those impotent passions, whose excess injures a man, more than his greatest enemies can; for these give their malice a full impression on our souls, which otherwise cannot reach very far, nor do us much hurt.

I cannot but observe how God not long after so pleaded, and

---

1 Trial.
2 Pleasing cloaks.
3 Psalm 55:21; Proverbs 5:3-4.
4 Within the bounds of moderation.

avenged My cause, in the eye of the world, that the most wilfully blind cannot avoid the displeasure to see it, and with some remorse and fear to own it as a notable stroke, and prediction of divine vengeance.

For, Sir *John Hotham* unreproached, unthreatened, uncursed by any language or secret imprecation of Mine, only blasted with the conscience of his own wickedness, and falling from one inconstancy to another, not long after pays his own and his eldest Son's heads, as forfeitures of their disloyalty, to those men, from whom surely he might have expected another reward than thus to divide their heads from their bodies, whose hearts with them were divided from their KING.

Nor is it strange that they who employed them at first in so high a service, and so successful to them, should not find mercy enough to forgive Him, who had so much premerited of them: For, Apostacy unto Loyalty some men account the most unpardonable sin.

Nor did a solitary vengeance serve the turn, the cutting off one head in a Family is not enough to expiate the affront done to the head of the Common-weal. The eldest Son must be involved in the punishment, as he was infected with the sin of the Father,[1] against the Father of his Country: Root and branch God cuts off in one day.

These observations are obvious to every fancy: God knows, I was so far from rejoicing in the *Hothams'* ruin, (though it were such as was able to give the greatest thirst for revenge a full draught, being executed by them who first employed him against Me) that I so far pitied him; as I thought he at first acted more against the light of his Conscience, than I hope many other men do in the same Cause.

For, he was never thought to be of that superstitious sourness, which some men pretend to, in matters of Religion; which so darkens their judgement that they cannot see any thing of Sin and Rebellion in those means, they use, with intents to reform to their Models, of what they call Religion, who think all is gold of piety, which doth but glister[2] with a show of Zeal and fervency.

Sir *John Hotham* was (I think) a man of another temper, and

---

1   In the Old Testament, sons are often said to inherit the sins of the father (e.g., 1 Kings 15:3: "And he walked in all the sins of his father, which he had done before him").

2   Glitter.

so most liable to those downright temptations of ambition, which have no cloak or cheat of Religion to impose upon themselves or others.

That which makes me more pity him is, that after he began to have some inclinations towards a repentance for his sin, and reparation of his duty to Me, He should be so unhappy as to fall into the hands of their Justice, and not My Mercy, who could as willingly have forgiven him, as he could have asked that favour of Me.

For I think clemency a debt, which we ought to pay to those that crave it, when we have cause to believe they would not after abuse it, since God himself suffer us not to pay any thing for his mercy but only prayers and praises.

Poor Gentleman, he is now become a notable monument of unprosperous disloyalty, teaching the world by so sad and unfortunate a spectacle, that the rude carriage of a Subject towards his Sovereign carries always its own vengeance, as an unseparable shadow with it, and those oft prove the most fatal, and implacable Executioners of it, who were the first Employers in the service.

After-times will dispute it, whether *Hotham* were more infamous at *Hull*, or at *Tower-hill*; though 'tis certain that no punishment so stains a man's Honour, as wilful perpetrations of unworthy actions; which besides the conscience of the sin, brands with most indelible characters of infamy, the name and memory to posterity, who not engaged in the Factions of the times, have the most impartial reflections on the actions.

But thou, O Lord, who hast in so remarkable a way avenged thy Servant, suffer me not to take any secret pleasure in it, for as his death hath satisfied the injury he did to me, so let me not by it gratify any passion in me, lest I make thy vengeance to be mine,[1] and consider the affront against me, more than the sin against thee.

Thou indeed, without any desire or endeavour of mine, hast made his mischief to return on his own head, and his violent dealing to come down on his own pate.[2]

Thou hast pleaded my cause,[3] even before the sons of men, and

---

1   Romans 12:19; see also Deuteronomy 32:35.
2   *pate* Head; *his mischief ... pate* Psalm 7:16.
3   Lamentations 3:58; 1 Samuel 25:39.

taken the matter into thine own hands; that men may know it was thy work, and see that thou, Lord, hast done it.[1]

I do not, I dare not say, so let mine enemies perish O Lord![2] *yea Lord, rather give them repentance, pardon, and impunity, if it be thy blessed will.*

Let not thy justice prevent the objects and opportunities of my mercy; yea, let them live and amend who have most offended me in so high a nature; that I may have those to forgive, who bear most proportion in their offences to those trespasses against thy majesty, which I hope thy mercy hath forgiven me.

Lord lay not their sins (who yet live) to their charge for condemnation, but to their consciences for amendment: Let the lighting of this thunderbolt, which hath been so severe a punishment to one, be a terror to all.

Discover to them their sin, who know not they have done amiss, and scare them from their sin, that sin of malicious wickedness.

That preventing thy judgements by their true repentance, they may escape the strokes of thine eternal vengeance.

And do thou, O Lord, establish the Throne of thy servant in mercy, and truth meeting together; let my Crown ever flourish in righteousness, and peace, kissing each other.[3]

Hear my prayer, O Lord, who hast taught us to pray for, to do good to, and to love our enemies, for thy sake;[4] *who hast prevented us with offertures*[5] *of thy love, even when we were thine enemies, and hast sent thy Son Jesus Christ to die for us, when we were disposed to crucify him.*

9. *Upon the listing, and raising Armies against the* KING.[6]

I find that I am at the same point and posture I was, when they forced Me to leave *White-hall*: what Tumults could not do, an

---

1 Psalm 109:27.
2 Charles rejects David's plea in the Psalms that his enemies perish and adopts the New Testament imperative to forgive those who trespass against us (e.g., Matthew 6:14-15).
3 *mercy, and truth ... each other* Psalm 85:10; *Crown ... flourish* Psalm 132:18.
4 *Hear ... O Lord* Psalm 39:12, 102:1, 143:1; *taught us to pray* Luke 11:1; *love our enemies* Matthew 5:44; Luke 6:27, 35.
5 *prevented us* Predisposed our heart to seek God through prevenient grace; *offertures* Offerings.
6 In July 1642 Parliament voted itself an army to be raised under the leadership of Robert Devereux, Earl of Essex; *listing* Enlisting.

Army must; which is but Tumults listed, and enrolled to a better order, but as bad an end: My recess hath given them confidence that I may be conquered.

And so I easily may as to any outward strength, which, God knows, is little or none at all: But I have a Soul invincible through God's grace enabling Me; here I am sure to be Conqueror,[1] if God will give Me such a measure of Constancy, as to fear him more than man: and to love the inward peace of My Conscience, before any outward tranquillity.

And must I be opposed with force, because they have not reason wherewith to convince me? O my Soul! be of good courage,[2] they confess their known weakness, as to truth, and Justice, who chose rather to contend by Armies, than by Arguments.

Is this the reward and thanks that I am to receive for those many Acts of Grace I have lately passed, and for those many Indignities I have endured? Is there no way left to make Me a glorious KING but by My sufferings?

It is a hard and disputable choice for a King, that loves his People, and desires their love, either to kill his own Subjects, or to be killed by them.

Are the hazards and miseries of Civil War in the bowels of My most flourishing Kingdom, the fruits I must now reap after 17 years living and reigning among them, with such a measure of Justice, Peace, Plenty, and Religion, as all Nations about either admired, or envied? notwithstanding some miscarriages in Government, which might escape; rather through ill counsel of some men driving on their private ends, or the peevishness of others envying the public should be managed without them, or the hidden and insuperable necessities of State, than any propensity, I hope, of my self either to injuriousness or oppression.

Whose innocent blood during My Reign have I shed, to satisfy My lust, anger, or covetousness? what Widows' or Orphans' tears can witness against me; the just cry of which must now be avenged with My own blood? For the hazards of War are equal, nor doth the Cannon know any respect of Persons.

---

1 Romans 8:37; this verse is cited on the title page of *Eikon Basilike*, establishing Charles I as a spiritual conqueror (if not a military victor) who overcomes persecution, peril, and the sword.
2 A familiar Old Testament phrase (see, for example, Psalm 27:14, 31:24).

In vain is My Person excepted by a Parenthesis of words,[1] when so many hands are armed against Me with Swords.

God knows how much I have studied to see what Ground of Justice is alleged for this War against Me; that so I might (by giving just satisfaction) either prevent, or soon end so unnatural a motion; which (to many men) seems rather the productions of a surfeit of peace, and wantonness of minds, or of private discontents, Ambition and Faction (which easily find, or make causes of quarrel) than any real obstructions of public Justice, or Parliamentary Privilege.

But this is pretended, and this I must be able to avoid and answer before God in My own Conscience, however some men are not willing to believe Me, lest they should condemn themselves.

When I first withdrew from *White-hall*, to see if I could allay the insolency of the Tumults, (the not suppressing of which, no account in Reason can be given, (where an orderly Guard was granted) but only to oppress both Mine and the Two Houses' freedom of declaring and voting according to every man's Conscience) what obstructions of Justice were there further than this, that what seemed just to one man, might not seem so to another?

Whom did I by power protect against the Justice of Parliament?

That some men withdrew, who feared the partiality of their trial, (warned by My Lord of *Strafford's* death) while the vulgar threatened to be their Oppressors, and Judgers of their Judges, was from that instinct, which is in all creatures to preserve themselves. If any others refused to appear, where they evidently saw the current of Justice and Freedom so stopped and troubled by the Rabble, that their lawful Judges either durst not come to the Houses, or not declare their sense with liberty and safety; it cannot seem strange to any reasonable man when the sole exposing them to public *odium* was enough to ruin them, before their Cause could be heard or tried.

Had not factious Tumults overborne the Freedom and Honour of the two Houses; had they asserted their Justice against them, and made the way open for all the Members quietly to come and declare their Consciences: I know no man so dear to Me, whom I had the least inclination to advise either to withdraw himself, or deny appearing upon their Summons, to whose Sentence according to Law (I think) every Subject bound to stand.

---

1 Excluded in a parenthetical remark.

Distempers (indeed) were risen to so great a height, for want of timely repressing the vulgar insolencies; that the greatest guilt of those which were Voted and demanded as Delinquents[1] was this, That they would not suffer themselves to be over-awed with the Tumults, and their Patrons; nor compelled to abet by their suffrages, or presence; the designs of those men who agitated innovations, and ruin, both in Church and State.

In this point I could not but approve their generous constancy and cautiousness; further than this I did never allow any man's refractoriness against the Privileges and Orders of the Houses; to whom I wished nothing more, than Safety, Fullness, and Freedom.

But the truth is, some men, and those not many, despairing in fair and Parliamentary ways by free deliberations, and Votes to gain the concurrence of the Major part of Lords and Commons, betook themselves (by the desperate activity of factious Tumults) to sift and terrify away all those Members whom they saw to be of contrary minds to their purposes.[2]

How oft was the business of the Bishops' enjoying their Ancient places, and undoubted Privileges in the House of Peers, carried for them by far the Major part of Lords. Yet after five repulses, contrary to all Order and Custom, it was by tumultuary, instigations obtruded again, and by a few carried,[3] when most of the Peers were forced to absent themselves.

In like manner, was the Bill against Root and Branch,[4] brought on by tumultuary Clamours, and schismatical Terrors, which could never pass, till both Houses were sufficiently thinned and over-awed.

To which Partiality, while in all Reason, Justice and Religion, My conscience forbids Me by consenting to make up their Votes to Acts of Parliament; I must now be urged with an Army, and constrained either to hazard My own, and My Kingdom's ruin,

---

1   Those who failed in or neglected their duty; a favourite term of contempt employed by Parliamentarians.
2   Only two bishops, for example, sat in the House of Lords on 28 December 1641, because of popular intimidation.
3   Passed in February 1642, the Bishops' Exclusion Bill banned bishops from the House of Lords.
4   The London Root and Branch Petition (11 December 1640) called for the abolition of episcopacy and the re-organization of the Church. The Root and Branch Bill eventually passed in September 1642.

by my Defence; or prostrate My Conscience to the blind obedience of those men, whose zealous superstition thinks, or pretends, they cannot do God and the Church a greater service, than utterly to destroy that Primitive, Apostolical, and anciently Universal Government of the Church by Bishops.

Which if other men's judgements bind them to maintain, or forbids them to consent to the abolishing of it; Mine much more; who, besides the grounds I have in My judgement, have also a most strict and indispensable Oath upon My Conscience, to preserve that Order, and the Rights of the Church; to which, most Sacrilegious and abhorred Perjury, most un-beseeming a Christian King, should I ever by giving My Consent be betrayed, I should account it infinitely greater misery, than any hath, or can befall Me; in as much as the least sin hath more evil in it than the greatest affliction. Had I gratified their Anti-episcopal Faction at first in this point, with My consent, and sacrificed the Ecclesiastical Government, and Revenues, to the fury of their covetousness, ambition, and revenge, I believe they would then have found no colourable[1] necessity of raising an Army to fetch in, and punish Delinquents.

That I consented to the Bill of putting the Bishops out of the House of Peers, was done with a firm persuasion of their contentedness to suffer a present diminution in their Rights, and Honour for My sake, and the Common-weal's, which I was confident they would readily yield unto, rather than occasion (by the least obstruction on their part) any dangers to Me, or to My Kingdom. That I cannot add My consent for the total extirpation of that Government (which I have often offered to all fit regulations) hath so much further tie upon My Conscience, as what I think Religious and Apostolical; and so very Sacred and Divine, is not to be dispensed with, or destroyed, when what is only of civil Favor, and privilege of Honour granted to men of that Order, may with their consent, who are concerned in it be annulled.

This is the true state of those obstructions pretended to be in point of Justice and Authority of Parliament; when I call God to witness, I knew none of such consequence as was worth speaking of a War, being only such as Justice, Reason, and Religion had made in My own and other men's Consciences.

Afterwards indeed a great show of Delinquents was made;

---

1 Specious.

which were but consequences necessarily following upon Mine, or others' withdrawing from, or defence against violence: but those could not be the first occasion of raising an Army against Me. Wherein I was so far from preventing them, (as they have declared often, that they might seem to have the advantage and Justice of the defensive part, and load Me with all the envy and injuries of first assaulting them) that God knows, I had not so much as any hopes of an Army in My thoughts. Had the Tumults been Honourably and Effectually repressed by exemplary Justice, and the liberty of the Houses so vindicated, that all Members of either House might with Honour and Freedom, becoming such a Senate, have come and discharged their Consciences, I had obtained all that I designed by My withdrawing, and had much more willingly, and speedily returned than I retired; this being My necessity driving, the other My choice desiring.

But some men knew, I was like to[1] bring the same judgement and constancy, which I carried with Me, which would never fit their designs: and so while they invited Me to come, and grievously complained of My absence, yet they could not but be pleased with it: especially when they had found out that plausible and popular pretext of raising an Army to fetch in Delinquents: when all that while they never punished the greatest and most intolerable Delinquency of the Tumults, and their Exciters, which drove My self, and so many of both Houses from their places, by most barbarous indignities, which yet in all Reason and Honour, they were as loath to have deserted, as those others were willing they should, that so they might have occasion to persecute them with the Injuries of an Army, for not suffering more tamely the Injuries of the Tumults.

That this is the true state, and first drift and design in raising an Army against Me, is by the sequel so evident, that all other pretences vanish. For when they declared by Propositions, or Treaties, what they would have to appease them; there was nothing of consequence offered to Me, or demanded of Me, as any original difference in any point of Law, or order of Justice. But among other lesser Innovations, this chiefly was urged, The Abolition of Episcopal, and the Establishment of Presbyterian Government.[2]

---

1 Was likely to.
2 The Episcopal church, governed by bishops, is comprised of three orders: bishops, priests, and deacons. The Presbyterian church is governed by presbyters or presbyteries. No higher order than that of presbyter or elder is recognized, and all elders are ecclesiastically of equal rank.

All other things at any time propounded were either impertinent as to any ground of a War, or easily granted by Me, and only to make up a number, or else they were merely consequential, and accessary, after the War was by them unjustly began.

I cannot hinder other men's thoughts, whom the noise and show of piety, and heat for Reformation and Religion, might easily so fill with prejudice, that all equality and clearness of judgement might be obstructed. But this was, and is, as to my best observation, the true state of affairs between us, when they first raised an Army, with this design, either to stop My mouth, or to force My consent: and in this truth, as to My conscience, (who was (God knows) as far from meditating a War, as I was in the eye of the world from having any preparation for one) I find that comfort, that in the midst of all the unfortunate successes of this War, on My side, I do not think My Innocency any whit prejudiced or darkened; Nor am I without that Integrity, and Peace before God, as with humble confidence to address My Prayer to Him.

For Thou, O Lord, seest clearly through all the cloudings of human affairs; Thou judgest without prejudice: Thy Omniscience eternally guides thy unerrable Judgement.

O my God, the proud are risen against me, and the assemblies of violent men have sought after my soul, and have not set Thee before their eyes.[1]

Consider My enemies, O Lord, for they are many, and they hate me with a deadly hatred without a cause.[2]

For Thou knowest, I had no passion, design or preparation to embroil My Kingdoms in a Civil War; whereto I had least temptation; as knowing I must adventure more than any, and could gain least of any by it.

Thou, O Lord, art my witness how oft I have deplored, and studied to divert the necessity thereof, wherein I cannot well be thought so prodigally thirsty of my Subjects' blood, as to venture my own Life, which I have been oft compelled to do in this unhappy War; and which were better spent to save than to destroy my People.

O Lord, I need much of thy grace, with patience to bear the many afflictions thou hast suffered some men to bring upon me; but much more to bear the unjust reproaches of those, who not content that I suf-

---

1 Psalm 86:14.
2 Psalm 25:19.

fer most by the War, will needs persuade the world that I have raised first, or given just cause to raise it.

The confidence of some men's false tongues is such,[1] that they would make me almost suspect my own innocency:Yea, I could be content (at least by my silence) to take upon me so great a guilt before men, If by that I might allay the malice of my Enemies, and redeem my People from this miserable War; since thou O Lord knowest my Innocency in this thing.

Thou wilt find out bloody and deceitful men; many of whom have not lived out half their days,[2] in which they promised themselves the enjoyment of the fruits of their violent and wicked Counsels.

Save, O Lord, thy servant, as hitherto thou hast, and in thy due time scatter the people that delight in War.[3]

Arise O Lord, lift up thy self, because of the rage of mine Enemies, which increaseth more and more. Behold them that have conceived mischief, travelled with iniquity, and brought forth falsehood.[4]

Thou knowest the chief design of this War is, either to destroy My Person, or force My Judgement, and to make me renege my Conscience and thy Truth.

I am driven to cross David's *choice and desire, rather to fall into the hands of men, by denying them, (though their mercies be cruel) than into thy hands by sinning against My Conscience, and in that against thee, who art a consuming fire;[5] Better they destroy Me, than thou shouldst damn Me.*

Be thou ever the defence of My soul, who wilt save the upright in heart.[6]

If nothing but My blood will satisfy My Enemies, or quench the flames of My Kingdoms, or thy temporal Justice, I am content, if it be thy will, that it be shed by Mine own Subjects' hands.

But O let the blood of Me, though their King, yet a sinner, be washed with the Blood of My Innocent and peace-making Redeemer, for in that thy Justice will find not only a temporary expiation, but an eternal plenary satisfaction; both for my sins, and the sins of my People; whom I beseech thee still own for thine, and when thy wrath is

---

1 Psalm 120:3; in Psalm 120, those with "false tongues" who speak of war are condemned, unlike the Psalmist who is "for peace."
2 Psalm 55:23.
3 *Save ... servant* Psalm 86:2; *scatter ... War* Psalm 68:30.
4 *Arise ... Enemies* Psalm 7:6; *conceived ... falsehood* Isaiah 59:4; *travelled* Laboured.
5 Deuteronomy 4:24; Hebrews 12:29.
6 Psalm 7:10.

appeased by my Death, O Remember thy great mercies toward them,
and forgive them! O my Father, for they know not what they do.[1]

10. *Upon their seizing the King's Magazines, Forts, Navy, and Militia.*[2]

How untruly I am Charged with the first raising of an Army, and beginning this Civil War, the eyes that only pity Me, and the Loyal hearts that durst only pray for Me, at first, might witness which yet appear not so many on My side, as there were men in Arms listed against Me; My unpreparedness for a War may well dishearten those that would help Me; while it argues (truly) My unwillingness to fight; yet it testifies for Me, that I am set on the defensive part; having so little hopes or power to offend others, that I have none to defend My self, or to preserve what is Mine own from their proreption.[3]

No man can doubt but they prevented[4] Me in their purposes, as well as their injuries, who are so much before-hand in their preparations against Me, and surprisals of My strength. Such as are not for Them, yet dare not be for Me; so over-awed is their Loyalty by the others' numbers and terrors. I believe My Innocency, and unpreparedness to assert My Rights and Honour, makes Me the more guilty in their esteem; who would not so easily have declared a War against Me, if I had first assaulted them.

They knew My chiefest Arms left Me, were those only, which the Ancient Christians were wont[5] to use against their Persecutors, Prayers and Tears.[6] These may serve a good man's turn, if not to Conquer as a Soldier, yet to suffer as a Martyr.

---

1 Jesus spoke these words on the cross (Luke 23:34).

2 In December 1641, Arthur Hazelridge introduced the Militia Bill, empowering Parliament to make all military and naval appointments; it was passed by Parliament but rejected by the king. In February 1642, both Houses voted that the nation be put "in a posture of defence" and issued in March the Militia Ordinance, giving Parliament control of the county militia. The Earl of Warwick was appointed commander of the navy and magazines and military posts throughout England were secured. *Magazines* Repositories of arms, ammunition, and other military equipment.

3 Slow advance.

4 Anticipated.

5 Accustomed.

6 Here Charles foreshadows the concluding words of *Eikon Basilike* "Vota dabunt, quae bella negarunt"—"What we could not get by our treaties, we may gain by our prayers."

Their preventing of Me, and surprizing my Castles, Forts, Arms, and Navy, with the Militia, is so far best for me, That it may drive me from putting any trust in the arm of flesh,[1] and wholly to cast my self into the protection of the living God, who can save by few, or none, as well as by many.

He that made the greedy Ravens to be *Elias'* Caterers, and bring him food,[2] may also make their surprisal of outward force and defence, an opportunity to show me the special support of his power and protection.

I thank God I reckon not now the want of the *Militia* so much in reference to My own protection as My People's.

Their many and sore oppressions grieve Me, I am above My own, what I want in the hands of Force and Power, I have in the wings of Faith and Prayer.

But this is the strange method these men will needs take to resolve their riddle of Making Me a glorious King, by taking away my Kingly power: Thus I shall become a support to My Friends, and a Terror to My Enemies by being unable to succour the one, or suppress the other.

For thus have they designed, and proposed to Me, the new modelling of Sovereignty and Kingship, as without any reality of power, or without any necessity of subjection and obedience: That the Majesty of the Kings of *England* might hereafter, hang like *Mahomet's* Tomb, by a magnetic Charm,[3] between the Power and Privileges of the two Houses, in an airy imagination of Regality.

But I believe the surfeit of too much Power, which some men have greedily seized on, and now seek wholly to devour, will ere long make the Common-wealth sick both of it and them, since they cannot well digest it; Sovereign Power in Subjects seldom agreeing with the stomachs of fellow Subjects.

Yet I have even in this point of the constant *Militia* sought, by satisfying their fears, and importunities, both to secure My Friends, and overcome Mine Enemies, to gain the peace of all, by depriving My self of a sole power to help, or hurt any: yielding the

---

1 2 Chronicles 32:8.
2 After informing Ahab, the idolatrous Israelite king, that God would punish the nation by drought, Elijah (Elias) the prophet hid by Cherith brook and was fed by ravens at God's command (1 Kings 17).
3 It was popularly believed that the tomb of Mohammed (Mahomet) was suspended in mid-air.

Militia (which is My undoubted Right no less than the Crown) to be disposed of as the two Houses shall think fit, during My time.

So willing am I to bury all Jealousies in them, of Me, and to live above all Jealousies of them, as to My self; I desire not to be safer than I wish them and My People; If I had the sole actual disposing of the *Militia*, I could not protect My People, further than they protected Me, and themselves: so that the use of the *Militia* is mutual. I would but defend My self so far, as to be able to defend My good Subjects from those men's violence and fraud, who conscious to their own evil merits and designs, will needs persuade the world, that none but Wolves are fit to be trusted with the custody of the Shepherd and his Flock.[1] Miserable experience hath taught My Subjects, since Power hath been wrested from Me, and employed against Me and Them! that neither can be safe if both be not in such a way as the Law hath entrusted the public safety and welfare.

Yet even this Concession of Mine as to the exercise of the *Militia*, so vast and large, is not satisfactory to some men; which seem to be Enemies not to Me only, but to all Monarchy; and are resolved to transmit to posterity such Jealousies of the Crown, as they should never permit it to enjoy its just and necessary Rights, in point of Power; to which (at last) all Law is resolved, while thereby it is best protected.

But here Honour and Justice due to My Successors, forbid Me to yield to such a total alienation of that power from them, which civility and duty (no less than justice and honour) should have forbade them to have asked of Me.

For, although I can be content to Eclipse My own beams, to satisfy their fears; who think they must needs be scorched or blinded, if I should shine in the full lustre of Kingly Power, wherewith God and the Laws have invested Me: yet I will never consent to put out the Sun of Sovereignty to all Posterity, and succeeding Kings; whose just recovery of their Rights from unjust usurpations and extortions, shall never be prejudiced or obstructed by any Act of Mine, which indeed would not be more injurious to succeeding Kings, than to My Subjects; whom I desire to leave in a condition not wholly desperate for the future; so as by a Law to be ever subjected to those many factious distractions,

---

1 Charles associates his enemies with the false prophets of Matthew 7:15, who appear "in sheep's clothing, but inwardly ... are ravening wolves."

which must needs follow the many-headed *Hydra*[1] of Government: which as it makes a show to the People to have more eyes to foresee; so they will find it hath more mouths too, which must[2] be satisfied: and (at best) it hath rather a monstrosity, than any thing of perfection, beyond that of right Monarchy; where counsel may be in many as the senses, but the Supreme Power can be but in One as the Head.

Happily where men have tried the horrors and malignant influence which will certainly follow My enforced darkness and Eclipse, (occasioned by the interposition and shadow of that body, which as the Moon receiveth its chiefest light from Me) they will at length more esteem and welcome the restored glory and blessing of the Sun's light.

And if at present I may seem by My receding so much from the use of My Right in the Power of the *Militia*, to come short of the discharge of that trust to which I am sworn for My People's protection; I conceive those men are guilty of the enforced perjury, (if so it may seem) who compel Me to take this new and strange way of discharging My trust, by seeming to desert it; of protecting My Subjects by exposing My self to danger or dishonour, for their safety and quiet.

Which in the conflicts of Civil War and advantages of Power cannot be effected but by some side yielding; to which the greatest love of the public Peace, and the firmest assurance of God's protection (arising from a good conscience) doth more invite Me, than can be expected from other men's fears; which arising from the injustice of their actions (though never so successful) yet dare not adventure their Authors upon any other way of safety than that of the Sword and *Militia*; which yet are but weak defences against the strokes of divine vengeance, which will overtake; or of men's own Consciences, which always attend injurious perpetrations.

For My self, I do not think that I can want any thing which providential necessity is pleased to take from Me, in order to My People's tranquility and God's glory, whose protection is sufficient for me; and he is able by his being with Me, abundantly to compensate to Me, as he did to *Job*, what ever honour, power, or

---

1 In Greek mythology, a many-headed snake whose heads re-grow as quickly as they are cut off.
2 Emended from "much."

liberty the Chaldeans, the Sabeans, or the Devil himself can deprive Me of.[1]

Although they take from me all defence of Arms and *Militia*, all refuge by land, of Forts, and Castles, all flight by Sea in my Ships, and Navy; yea, though they study to rob me of the Hearts of my Subjects, the greatest Treasure and best ammunition of a King, yet cannot they deprive me of my own innocency, or God's mercy, nor obstruct my way to Heaven.

Therefore, O my God, to thee I fly for help, if thou wilt be on my side, I shall have more with me than can be against me.[2]

There is none in Heaven, or in Earth, that I desire in comparison of thee: In the loss of all, be thou more than all to me: Make haste to succour me, thou that never failest them, that put their trust in thee.[3]

Thou seest I have no power to oppose them that come against me, who are encouraged to fight under the pretence of fighting for me: But my eyes are toward thee.[4]

Thou needest no help, nor shall I, if I may have thine; If not to conquer, yet at least to suffer.

If thou delightest not in my safety, and prosperity, behold here I am willing to be reduced to what thou wilt have me; whose Judgements oft begin with thy own Children.

I am content to be nothing, that thou mayst be all.

Thou hast taught me, That no King can be saved by the multitude of an Host; but yet thou canst save me by the multitude of thy mercies, who art the Lord of Hosts, and the Father of mercies.

Help me, O Lord, who am sore distressed on every side, yet be thou on my side, and I shall not fear what man can do unto me.[5]

I will give thy Justice the glory of my distress.

---

1   In the Book of Job, God permits Job, an upright man, to suffer at the hands of Satan to prove his worthiness. The Sabeans seize Job's oxen and the Chaldeans his camels. His sheep are burned, his servants and children killed, and his body is diseased. When Job continues to bless God, he is rewarded with twice as much as he had before.

2   Romans 8:31.

3   *There is none ... of thee* Psalm 73:25; *put their trust in thee* A common biblical phrase, especially in the Psalms.

4   Psalm 25:15.

5   *sore ... every side* 2 Corinthians 4:8, 7:5; *yet be ... unto me* Psalm 118:6; see also Psalm 56:4 and Hebrews 13:6.

O let thy mercy have the glory of my deliverance from them that persecute my Soul!

By my sins have I fought against thee, and robbed thee of thy glory, who am thy subject, and justly mayest thou, by my own Subjects, strip me of my strength, and eclipse my glory.

But show thy self, O my hope, and only refuge! Let not mine enemies say, There is no help for him in his God.[1]

Hold up my goings in thy paths, that my footsteps slip not.[2]

Keep me as the apple of thine eye, hide me under the shadow of thy wings.[3]

Show thy marvellous loving kindness, O thou that savest by thy right hand them that put their trust in thee, from those that rise up against them.[4]

From the wicked that oppress me, from my deadly enemies that compass me about.[5]

Show me the path of life. In thy presence is fullness of joy, at thy right hand there are pleasures for evermore.[6]

11. *Upon the* 19 *Propositions first sent to the* KING; *and more afterwards.*[7]

Although there be many things, they demand, yet if these be all, I am glad to see at what price they set My own safety, and My People's peace; which I cannot think I buy at too dear a rate save only the parting with My Conscience and Honour. If nothing else will satisfy, I must choose rather to be as miserable, and inglorious, as My enemies can make or wish me.

Some things here propounded to Me have been offered by Me; Others are easily granted; The rest (I think) ought not to be

1 Psalm 3:2.
2 Psalm 17:5.
3 Psalm 17:8.
4 Psalm 17:7.
5 Psalm 17:9.
6 Psalm 16:11.
7 In June 1642, Charles was sent the Nineteen Propositions by Parliament, demanding: control of the armed forces and all fortresses; authority over the nation's "great affairs"; approval of key political appointments and the creation of new peers; reform of the Church; prosecution of Roman Catholics; the military support of Protestants in Europe; and the supervision of the education, upbringing, and marriage of the royal children. Charles rejected these propositions as a threat to monarchy itself.

obtruded[1] upon Me, with the point of the Sword; nor urged with the injuries of a War; when I have already declared that I cannot yield to them, without violating My Conscience: 'tis strange, there can be no method of peace, but by making war upon My soul.

Here are many things required of Me, but I see nothing offered to Me, by the way of grateful exchange of Honour; or any requital for those favours I have, or can yet grant them.

This Honour they do Me, to put Me on the giving part, which is more princely and divine. They cannot ask more than I can give, may I but reserve to My self the Incommunicable Jewel of my Conscience; and not be forced to part with that, whose loss nothing can repair or requite.

Some things (which they are pleased to propound) seem unreasonable to me, and while I have any Mastery of my Reason, how can they think I can consent to them? Who know they are such as are inconsistent with being either a King, or a good Christian. My yielding so much (as I have already) makes some men confident I will deny nothing.

The love I have of my People's peace, hath (indeed) great influence upon me; but the love of Truth, and inward peace hath more.

Should I grant some things they require, I should not so much weaken my outward state of a King; as wound that inward quiet of my Conscience, which ought to be, is, and ever shall be (by God's grace) dearer to me than my Kingdoms.

Some things which a King might approve, yet in Honour and Policy are at some time to be denied, to some men, lest he should seem not to dare to deny any thing; and give too much encouragement to unreasonable demands, or importunities.

But to bind my self to a general and implicit consent, to what ever they shall desire, or propound, (for such is one of their Propositions) were such a latitude of blind obedience, as never was expected from any Free-man, nor fit to be required of any man, much less of a King, by His own Subjects; any of whom he may possibly exceed as much in wisdom, as He doth in place and power.

This were as if *Sampson* should have consented, not only to bind his own hands, and cut off his hair, but to put out his own eyes, that the *Philistines* might with the more safety mock, and

---

1 Thrust forcibly.

abuse him; which they chose rather to do, than quite to destroy him, when he was become so tame an object, and fit occasion for their sport and scorn.[1]

Certainly, to exclude all power of denial, seems an arrogancy, least of all becoming those who pretend to make their addresses in an humble and loyal way of petitioning; who by that sufficiently confess their own inferiority, which obligeth them to rest, if not satisfied, yet quieted with such an answer as the will and reason of their Superior thinks fit to give; who is acknowledged to have a freedom and power of Reason, to Consent, or Dissent, else it were very foolish and absurd to ask, what another having not liberty to deny, neither hath power to grant.

But if this be My Right belonging to Me, in Reason, as a Man, and in Honour as a Sovereign King, (as undoubtedly it doth) how can it be other than extreme injury to confine my Reason to a necessity of granting all they have a mind to ask, whose minds may be as differing from Mine both in Reason and Honour, as their aims may be, and their qualities are; which last God and the Laws have sufficiently distinguished, making me their Sovereign, and them my Subjects: whose Propositions may soon prove violent oppositions, if once they gain to be necessary impositions upon the Regal Authority. Since no man seeks to limit and confine his King, in Reason, who hath not a secret aim to share with him, or usurp upon him in Power and Dominion.

But they would have me trust to their moderation, and abandon mine own discretion; that so I might verify what representations some have made of me to the world, that I am fitter to be their Pupil than their Prince. Truly I am not so confident of my own sufficiency, as not willingly to admit the Counsel of others: But yet I am not so diffident of my self,[2] as brutishly to submit to any men's dictates, and at once to betray the Sovereignty of Reason in my Soul, and the Majesty of my own Crown to any of my Subjects.

Least of all have I any ground of credulity, to induce me fully to submit to all the desires of those men, who will not admit or

---

1 Deceived by his Philistine wife Delilah, Samson allowed his hands to be bound. His hair, the source of his herculean strength, was then shaved off and he was imprisoned and blinded by the Philistines. After making "sport" for his captors, Samson pushed down the pillars of a building in which he and his enemies were housed (Judges 16).

2 Wanting in self-confidence.

do refuse, and neglect to vindicate the freedom of their own and others, sitting and voting in Parliament.

Besides, all men that know them, know this, how young Statesmen (the most part) of these propounders are; so that, till experience of one seven years hath showed me, how well they can Govern themselves, and so much power as is wrested from me, I should be very foolish indeed, and unfaithful, in my Trust, to put the reins of both Reason and Government, wholly out of my own, into their hands, whose driving is already too much like *Jehu's*;[1] and whose forwardness to ascend the throne of Supremacy pretends more of *Phaeton* than of *Phoebus*;[2] God divert the Omen if it be his will.

They may remember, that at best they sit in Parliament, as my Subjects, not my Superiors; called to be my Counsellors, not Dictators: Their Summons extends to recommend their advice, not to command my Duty.

When I first heard of Propositions to be sent Me, I expected either some good Laws, which had been antiquated by the course of time, or overlaid by the corruption of manners, had been desired to a restoration of their vigour and due execution; or some evil customs preterlegal,[3] and abuses personal had been to be removed:[4] or some injuries done by My self, and others, to the Common-weal, were to be repaired: or some equable offertures were to be tendered to Me, wherein the advantages of My Crown being considered by them, might fairly induce Me to condescend, to what tended to My Subjects' good, without any great diminution of My self, whom nature, Law, Reason, and Religion, bind Me (in the first place) to preserve: without which, 'tis impossible to preserve My People according to My Place.

Or (at least) I looked for such moderate desires of due Reformation of what was (indeed) amiss in Church and State, as might still preserve the foundation and essentials of Govern-

---

1 Jehu became King of Israel after he drove his chariot "furiously" to Jezreel to kill the Judaean king Ahaziah and the Israelite Jehoram (2 Kings 9:20).

2 In Greek mythology, Phaeton, the son of Helios, tried to guide the solar chariot. Unable to control the immortal horses, the chariot threatened to set the world on fire until Zeus killed Phaeton with a thunderbolt. Phoebus, god of the Sun, would show no such unruliness.

3 Not in accordance with the law.

4 Were to be.

ment in both; not shake and quite overthrow either of them, without any regard to the Laws in force, the wisdom and piety of former Parliaments, the ancient and universal practice of Christian Churches; the Rights and Privileges of particular men: Nor yet any thing offered in lieu, or in the room of what must be destroyed, which might at once reach the good end of the other's Institution, and also supply its pretended defects, reform its abuses, and satisfy sober and wise men, not with soft and specious words, pretending zeal and special piety, but with pregnant and solid reasons both divine and human, which might justify the abruptness and necessity of such vast alterations.

But in all their Propositions I can observe little of these kinds, or to these ends: Nothing of any Laws dis-jointed, which are to be restored; of any right invaded; of any justice to be un-obstructed; of any compensations to be made; of any impartial reformation to be granted; to all, or any of which, Reason, Religion, true Policy, or any other human motives, might induce me.

But as to the main matters propounded by them at any time, in which is either great novelty, or difficulty. I perceive that what were formerly looked upon as Factions in the State, and Schisms in the Church, and so, punishable by the Laws, have now the confidence, by vulgar clamours, and assistance (chiefly) to demand not only Tolerations of themselves, in their vanity, novelty, and confusion; but also Abolition of the Laws against them: and a total extirpation of that Government, whose Rights they have a mind to invade.

This, as to the main; other Propositions are (for the most part) but as waste paper in which those are wrapped up to present them somewhat more handsomely.

Nor do I so much wonder at the variety, and horrible novelty of some Propositions (there being nothing so monstrous, which some fancies are not prone to long for).

This casts me into, not an admiration, but an ecstasy, how such things should have the fortune to be propounded in the name of the two Houses of the Parliament of *England*, among whom, I am very confident, there was not a fourth part of the Members of either House, whose judgements free, single, and apart did approve or desire such destructive changes in the Government of the Church.

I am persuaded there remains in far the Major part of both Houses, (if free, and full) so much Learning, Reason, Religion, and just moderation, as to know how to sever[1] between the use and the abuse of things; the institution, and the corruption, the Government and the Mis-government, the Primitive Patterns, and the aberrations or blottings of after Copies.

Sure they could not all, upon so little, or no Reason (as yet produced to the contrary) so soon renounce all regard to the Laws in force, to antiquity, to the piety of their reforming Progenitors, to the prosperity of former times in this Church and State, under the present Government of the Church.

Yet, by a strange fatality, these men suffer, either by their absence, or silence, or negligence, or supine[2] credulity (believing that all is good, which is gilded with shows of Zeal and Reformation) their private dissenting in Judgement to be drawn into the common sewer or stream of the present vogue and humour; which hath its chief rise and abetment from those popular clamours and Tumults: which served to give life and strength to the infinite activity of those men, who studied with all diligence, and policy, to improve to their Innovating designs, the present distractions.

Such Armies of Propositions having so little, in My Judgement, of Reason, Justice, and Religion on their side, as they had Tumult and Faction for their rise, must not go alone, but ever be backed and seconded, with Armies of Soldiers: Though the second should prevail against My Person, yet the first shall never overcome Me, further than I see cause; for, I look not at their number and power so much, as I weigh their Reason and Justice.

Had the two Houses first sued out their livery,[3] and once effectually redeemed themselves from the Wardship of the Tumults, (which can be no other than the Hounds that attend the cry, and hollow[4] of those Men, who hunt after Factious, and private Designs, to the ruin of Church and State.)

Did My judgement tell Me, that the Propositions sent to Me were the Results of the Major part of their Votes, who exercise their freedom, as well as they have a right to sit in Parliament: I should then suspect My own judgement, for not speedily and fully concurring with every one of them.

---

1 Make a separation or division.
2 Morally or mentally inactive or inert.
3 Instituted a suit as heir to possess lands held by the court of wards (here used figuratively).
4 Holler.

For, I have charity enough to think, there are wise men among them: and humility to think, that, as in some things I may want; so 'tis fit I should use their advice, which is the end for which I called them to a Parliament. But yet I cannot allow their wisdom such a completeness and inerrability as to exclude My self; since none of them hath that part to Act, that Trust to discharge, nor that Estate and Honour to preserve as My self; without whose Reason concurrent with theirs (as the Sun's influence is necessary in all nature's productions) they cannot beget, or bring forth any one complete and authoritative Act of public wisdom, which makes the Laws.

But the unreasonableness of some Propositions is not more evident to Me than this is, That they are not the joint and free desires of those in their Major number, who are of right to Sit and Vote in Parliament.

For, many of them savour very strong of that old leaven of Innovations, masked under the name of Reformation; (which in My two last famous Predecessors' days, heaved at, and sometime threatened both Prince and Parliaments:) But, I am sure was never wont so far to infect the whole mass of the Nobility and Gentry of this Kingdom; however it dispersed among the Vulgar: Nor was it likely so suddenly to taint the Major part of both Houses, as that they should unanimously desire, and affect so enormous and dangerous innovations in Church and State, contrary to their former education, practice, and judgement.

Not that I am ignorant, how the choice of many Members was carried by much faction in the Counties; some thirsting after nothing more, than a passionate revenge of what ever displeasure they had conceived against me, my Court, or the Clergy.

But all Reason bids me impute these sudden and vast desires of change to those few, who armed themselves with the many-headed, and many-handed Tumults.

No less doth Reason, Honour, and Safety both of Church and State command me, to chew such morsels, before I let them down; If the straitness[1] of my Conscience will not give me leave to swallow down such Camels,[2] as others do of Sacrilege, and injustice both to God and man, they have no more cause to quarrel with me, than for this, that my throat is not so wide as theirs.

---

1 Strictness, rigour.
2 In Matthew 23:24, Jesus criticizes the hypocrisy of the Pharisees, "blind guides, which strain at a gnat, and swallow a camel."

Yet by God's help I am resolved, That nothing of passion, or peevishness, or list[1] to contradict, or vanity to show my negative power, shall have any bias upon my judgement, to make me gratify my will, by denying any thing, which my Reason and Conscience commands me not.

Nor on the other side, will I consent to more than Reason, Justice, Honour, and Religion persuade me, to be for God's glory, the Church's good, my People's welfare, and my own peace.

I will study to satisfy my Parliament, and my People; but I will never, for fear, or flattery, gratify any Faction, how potent soever; for this were to nourish the disease, and oppress the body.

Although many men's loyalty and prudence are terrified from giving me, that free, and faithful counsel, which they are able and willing to impart, and I may want; yet none can hinder me from craving of the counsel of that mighty Counsellor, who can both suggest what is best, and incline my heart steadfastly to follow it.

O thou first and eternal Reason, whose wisdom is fortified with omnipotency, furnish thy Servant, first with clear discoveries of Truth, Reason, and Justice, in My Understanding: then so confirm My will and resolution to adhere to them, that no terrors, injuries, or oppressions of my Enemies may ever enforce me against those rules, which thou by them hast planted in My Conscience.

Thou never madest me a King, that I should be less than a Man; and not dare to say, Yea, or Nay, as I see cause; which freedom is not denied to the meanest creature, that hath the use of Reason, and liberty of speech.

Shall that be blameable in Me, which is commendable veracity and constancy in others?

Thou seest, O Lord, with what partiality, and injustice, they deny that freedom to Me their KING, which Thou hast given to all Men; and which Themselves pertinaciously challenge to themselves; while they are so tender of the least breach of their priveleges.

To Thee I make my supplication, who canst guide us by an unerring rule, through the perplexed Labyrinths of our own thoughts, and other men's proposals; which, I have some cause to suspect, are purposely cast as snares, that by My granting or denying them, I might be more entangled in those difficulties, wherewith they lie in wait to afflict Me.

O Lord, make thy way plain before Me.[2]

---

1 Desire.
2 Psalm 5:8.

Let not My own sinful passions cloud, or divert thy sacred suggestions.

Let thy glory be my end, thy word my rule, and then thy will be done.

I cannot please all, I care not to please some men; If I may be happy to please thee, I need not fear whom I displease.[1]

Thou that makest the wisdom of the world foolishness[2] *and takest in their own devices, such as are wise in their own conceits, make me wise by thy Truth, for thy honour, my Kingdom's general good, and my own soul's salvation, and I shall not much regard the world's opinion, or diminution of me.*

The less wisdom they are willing to impute to me, the more they shall be convinced of thy wisdom directing me, while I deny nothing fit to be granted, out of crossness, or humour; nor grant any thing which is to be denied, out of any fear, or flattery of men.

Suffer me not to be guilty, or unhappy, by willing or inconsiderate advancing any men's designs, which are injurious to the public good, while I confirm them by my consent.

Nor let me be any occasion to hinder or defraud the public of what is best, by any morose or perverse dissentings.

Make me so humbly charitable, as to follow their advice, when it appears to be for the public good, of whose affections to me, I have yet but few evidences to assure Me.

Thou canst as well bless honest errors, as blast fraudulent counsels.

Since we must give an account of every evil and idle word in private, at thy Tribunal;[3] *Lord make me careful of those solemn Declarations of my mind which are like to have the greatest influence upon the Public, either for woe, or weal.*[4]

The less others consider what they ask, make me the more solicitous what I answer.

Though Mine own, and My People's pressures are grievous, and peace would be very pleasing; yet Lord, never suffer Me to avoid the one, or purchase the other, with the least expense or waste of my Conscience; whereof thou O Lord only art deservedly more Master than My self.

---

1 Galatians 1:10.
2 1 Corinthians 3:19.
3 Matthew 12:36.
4 The common good.

12. *Upon the Rebellion, and troubles in* Ireland.[1]

The Commotions in *Ireland* were so sudden, and so violent, that it was hard at first either to discern the rise, or apply a remedy to that precipitant[2] Rebellion.

Indeed, that sea of blood, which hath there been cruelly and barbarously shed, is enough to drown any man in eternal both infamy and misery, whom God shall find the malicious Author or Instigator of its effusion.

It fell out, as a most unhappy advantage to some men's malice against me; that when they had impudence enough to lay any thing to my charge, this bloody opportunity should be offered them, with which I must be aspersed. Although there was nothing which could be more abhorred to me, being so full of sin against God, disloyalty to my self, and destructive to my Subjects.

Some men took it very ill not to be believed, when they affirmed, that what the Irish Rebels did, was done with my privity (at least) if not by my Commission:[3] But these knew too well, that it is no news for some of my Subjects to fight, not only without my Commission, but against my Command, and Person too; yet all the while to pretend, they fight by my Authority, and for my Safety.

I would to God the *Irish* had nothing to allege for their imitation against those, whose blame must needs be the greater, by how much Protestant Principles are more against all Rebellion against Princes, than those of Papists. Nor will the goodness of men's intentions excuse the scandal, and contagion of their Examples.

But who ever fail of their Duty toward me, I must bear the blame; this Honour my Enemies have always done me, to think moderate injuries not proportionate[4] to me, nor competent trials, either of my patience under them, or my pardon of them.

Therefore with exquisite[5] malice they have mixed the gall and vinegar of falsity and contempt, with the cup of my Afflic-

---

1 The Irish Rebellion broke out in October 1641 and a provisional Irish Catholic government, the Kilkenny Confederacy, was later established.
2 Hasty, rash.
3 Some leaders of the Irish Rebellion claimed to have the King's warrant for their actions. The document was a forgery.
4 In due proportion; adequate.
5 Consummate, extreme.

tion;[1] Charging me not only with untruths, but such, as wherein I have the greatest share of loss and dishonour by what is committed; whereby (in all Policy, Reason, and Religion, having least cause to give the least consent, and most grounds of utter detestation) I might be represented by them to the world the more inhumane and barbarous: Like some Cyclopic monster, whom nothing will serve to eat and drink, but the flesh and blood of my own Subjects; in whose common welfare my interest lies as much as some men's doth in their perturbations:[2] who think they cannot do well but in evil times, nor so cunningly as in laying the *odium* of those sad events on others, wherewith themselves are most pleased, and whereof they have been not the least occasion.

And certainly, 'tis thought by many wise men, that the preposterous rigour, and unreasonable severity, which some men carried before them in *England*, was not the least incentive, that kindled, and blew up into those horrid flames, the sparks of discontent, which wanted not pre-disposed fuel for Rebellion in *Ireland*; where despair being added to their former discontents, and the fears of utter extirpation to their wonted oppressions, it was easy to provoke to an open Rebellion, a people prone enough, to break out to all exorbitant violence, both by some Principles of their Religion, and the natural desires of liberty; both to exempt themselves from their present restraints, and to prevent those after rigours, wherewith they saw themselves apparently threatened, by the covetous zeal, and uncharitable fury of some men, who think it a great Argument of the truth of their Religion, to endure no other but their own.

God knows, as I can with Truth wash my hands in Innocency, as to any guilt in that Rebellion; so I might wash them in my Tears, as to the sad apprehensions I had, to see it spread so far, and make such waste. And this in a time, when distractions, and jealousies[3] here in *England*, made most men rather intent to their own safety, or designs they were driving, than to the relief of those, who were every day inhumanely butchered in *Ireland*: Whose tears and blood might, if nothing else, have quenched, or

---

1   The soldiers gave Jesus "vinegar to drink, mingled with gall" shortly before his crucifixion (Matthew 27:34); *cup of my Affliction* Anticipating his death, Jesus prayed that the "cup" of affliction would be taken from him (Matthew 26:39).

2   Commotions.

3   Vehement feelings, zeal.

at least for a time, repressed and smothered those sparks of Civil dissensions, and Jealousies, which in *England* some men most industriously scattered.

I would to God no man had been less affected with *Ireland's* sad estate than my self; I offered to go my self in Person upon that expedition; But some men were either afraid I should have any one Kingdom quieted; or loath they were to shoot at any mark here less than my self; or that any should have the glory of my destruction but themselves.[1] Had my many offers been accepted, I am confident neither the ruin had been so great, nor the calamity so long, nor the remedy so desperate.

So that, next to the sin of those, who began that Rebellion, theirs must needs be: who either hindered the speedy suppressing of it by Domestic dissensions, or diverted the Aids, or exasperated the Rebels to the most desperate resolutions and actions, by threatening all extremities, not only to the known heads, and chief incendiaries, but even to the whole community of that Nation; Resolving to destroy Root and Branch, men, women and children; without any regard to those usual pleas for mercy, which Conquerors, not wholly barbarous, are wont to hear from their own breasts, in behalf of those, whose oppressive fears,[2] rather than their malice, engaged them; or whose imbecility for Sex and Age was such, as they could neither lift up a hand against them, nor distinguish between their right hand and their left: Which preposterous, and (I think) un-evangelical Zeal is too like that of the rebuked Disciples, who would go no lower in their revenge, than to call for fire from Heaven upon whole Cities, for the repulse or neglect of a few;[3] or like that of *Jacob's* sons, which the Father both blamed and cursed: choosing rather to use all extremities, which might drive men to desperate obstinacy, than to apply moderate remedies;[4] such as might punish some with exemplary Justice, yet disarm others, with tenders of mercy upon their sub-

---

1 In April 1642, Charles I offered to go to Ireland to attempt to suppress the rebellion, but Parliament feared that he would garner support for his cause and return with an Irish Catholic army to England.

2 Emended from "faces," a misprint corrected in the second edition.

3 Jesus admonished James and John for their desire to incinerate a village of unreceptive Samaritans (Luke 9:51-56).

4 While blessing his twelve sons, Jacob blamed Simeon and Levi for cruel wrath (Genesis 49) because they slaughtered all the men of Sechem to avenge the rape of their sister Dinah (Genesis 34).

mission, and our protection of them, from the fury of those, who would soon drown them, if they refused to swim down the popular stream with them.

But some kind of Zeal counts all merciful moderation, lukewarmness; and had rather be cruel than counted cold, and is not seldom more greedy to kill the Bear for his skin, than for any harm he hath done. The confiscation of men's estates being more beneficial, than the charity of saving their lives, or reforming their Errors.

When all proportionable succours[1] of the poor Protestants in *Ireland* (who were daily massacred, and overborne with numbers of now desperate Enemies) was diverted and obstructed here; I was earnestly entreated, and generally advised by the chief of the Protestant party there, to get them some respite and breathing by a cessation, without which they saw no probability (unless by miracle) to preserve the remnant that had yet escaped:[2] God knows with how much commiseration and solicitous caution I carried on that business, by persons of Honour and Integrity, that so I might neither encourage the Rebels' Insolence, nor discourage the Protestants' Loyalty and Patience.

Yet when this was effected in the best sort, that the necessity and difficulty of affairs would then permit, I was then to suffer again in my reputation and Honour, because I suffered not the Rebels utterly to devour the remaining handfuls of the Protestants there.

I thought, that in all reason, the gaining of that respite could not be so much to the Rebels' advantages (which some have highly calumniated[3] against me) as it might have been for the Protestants' future, as well as present safety; If during the time of that Cessation, some men had had the grace to have laid *Ireland's* sad condition more to heart; and laid aside those violent motions, which were here carried on by those, that had better skill to let blood than to staunch it.

But in all the misconstructions of my actions, (which are prone to find more credulity in men to what is false, and evil, than love or charity to what is true and good) as I have no Judge but God above me, so I can have comfort to appeal to his omniscience,

---

1 Appropriate assistance.
2 Charles I's Lord Deputy of Ireland, the Duke of Ormonde, negotiated a cessation of arms with the Irish rebels on 15 September 1643.
3 Slandered.

who doth not therefore deny my Innocence, because he is pleased so far to try my patience, as he did his servant *Job's*.

I have enough to do to look to my own Conscience, and the faithful discharge of my Trust as a KING; I have scarce leisure to consider those swarms of reproaches, which issue out of some men's mouths and hearts, as easily as smoke, or sparks do out of a furnace; Much less to make such prolix Apologies, as might give those men satisfaction: who conscious to their own depth of wickedness, are loath to believe any man not to be as bad as themselves.

'Tis Kingly to do well, and hear ill: If I can but act the one, I shall not much regard to bear the other.

I thank God I can hear with patience, as bad as my worst enemies can falsely say. And I hope I shall still do better than they desire, or deserve I should.

I believe it will at last appear, that they who first began to embroil my other Kingdoms, are in great part guilty, if not of the first letting out, yet of the not-timely stopping those horrid effusions of blood in *Ireland*.

Which (whatever my Enemies please to say, or think) I look upon, as that of my other Kingdoms, exhausted out of my own veins; no man being so much weakened by it, as my self; And I hope, though men's insatiable cruelties never will, yet the mercy of God will at length say to his justice, *It is enough*:[1] and command the Sword of Civil Wars to sheathe it self: his merciful justice intending, I trust, not our utter confusion, but our cure: the abatement of our sins, not the desolating of these Nations.

O my God, let those infinite mercies prevent us once again, which I and my Kingdoms have formerly abused, and can never deserve, should be restored.

Thou seest how much cruelty among Christians is acted under the colour of Religion; as if we could not be Christians, unless we crucify one another.

Because we have not more loved thy Truth, and practised in charity, thou hast suffered a Spirit of Error and bitterness,[2] of mutual and mortal hatred to rise among us.

O Lord, forgive wherein we have sinned, and sanctify what we have suffered.

---

1   2 Samuel 24:16; 1 Chronicles 21:15.
2   1 John 4:6.

Let our Repentance be our recovery, as our great sins have been our ruin.

Let not the miseries I and my Kingdoms have hitherto suffered seem small to thee: but make our sins appear to our consciences, as they are represented in the glass of thy judgements; for thou never punishest small failings with so severe afflictions.

O therefore, according to the multitude of thy great mercies, pardon our sins, and remove thy judgements which are very many, and very heavy.

Yet let our sins be ever more grievous to us, than thy judgements; and make us more willing to repent, than to be relieved; first give us the peace of penitent consciences, and then the tranquillity of united Kingdoms.

In the sea of our Saviour's blood drown our sins, and through this red sea of our own blood bring us at last to a state of piety, peace, and plenty.[1]

As my public relations to all, make Me share in all My Subjects' sufferings; so give Me such a pious sense of them, as becomes a Christian King, and a loving Father of My People.

Let the scandalous and unjust reproaches cast upon Me, be as a breath, more to kindle my compassion; Give me grace to heap charitable coals of fire upon their heads to melt them,[2] *whose malice or cruel Zeal hath kindled, or hindered the quenching of those flames, which have so much wasted my three Kingdoms.*

O rescue and assist those poor Protestants in Ireland, whom thou hast hitherto preserved.

And lead those in the ways of thy saving Truths, whose ignorance or errors have filled them with rebellious and destructive principles; which they act under an opinion, That they do thee good service.

Let the hand of thy justice be against those, who maliciously and despitefully have raised, or fomented those cruel and desperate Wars.

Thou that art far from destroying the Innocent with the Guilty, and the Erroneous with the Malicious; Thou that hadst pity on Niniveh for the many Children that were therein,[3] *give not over the whole stock of that populous and seduced Nation, to the wrath of those, whose cov-*

---

1 With divine aid, Moses parted the Red Sea, thereby creating a path to freedom for the Israelites who fled enslavement by the Egyptians (Exodus 14:15-23).

2 Proverbs 25:22; Romans 12:20.

3 Jonah's prophecies of destruction caused the Ninevites to repent of their sins, and God spared them (Jonah 2).

etousness makes them cruel; nor to their anger, which is too fierce, and therefore justly cursed.

Preserve, if it be thy will, in the midst of the furnace of thy severe justice a Posterity, which may praise thee for thy mercy.

And deal with Me, not according to man's unjust reproaches, but according to the Innocency of my hands in thy sight.

If I have desired, or delighted in the woeful day of my Kingdoms' calamities, if I have not earnestly studied, and faithfully endeavoured the preventing and composing of these bloody distractions; then let thy hand be against me, and my Father's house. O Lord, thou seest I have enemies enough of men; as I need not, so I should not dare thus to imprecate thy curse on me and mine, if my Conscience did not witness my integrity, which thou O Lord knowst right well; But I trust not to my own merit, but thy mercies; spare us O Lord, and be not angry with us for ever.

13. *Upon the Calling in of the* Scots, *and their Coming.*[1]

The *Scots* are a Nation, upon whom I have not only common ties of Nature, Sovereignty, and Bounty, with My Father of blessed memory;[2] but also special and late obligations of favours, having gratified the active Spirits among them so far; that I seemed to many, to prefer the desires of that Party, before My own interest and Honour. But, I see, Royal bounty emboldens some men to ask, and act beyond all bounds of modesty and gratitude.

My charity, and Act of Pacification, forbids Me to reflect on former passages;[3] wherein I shall ever be far from letting any man's ingratitude, or inconstancy, make Me repent of what I granted them, for the public good: I pray God it may so prove.

1　Supporters of the Scottish National Covenant (1638), a defence of the Scottish Presbyterian Church against Laudian Anglicanism, were known as Covenantors. The Solemn League and Covenant, signed by Parliament in September 1643, solidified an alliance between Parliament and the Covenantors, and required the preservation of "the reformed religion in the Church of Scotland" and the "reformation of religion" in England and Ireland.

2　Charles I was born on 19 November 1600 at Dumfermline.

3　The Pacification of Berwick (June 1639) ended the uneventful First Bishops' War. Upon his return to London, Charles I ordered the common hangman to burn copies of the treaty which had been authorized for publication by the Scottish Covenanters.

The coming again of that Party into *England*,[1] with an Army, only to conform this Church to their late New model, cannot but seem as unreasonable, as they would have thought the same measure offered from hence to themselves.

Other errand I could never understand, they had, (besides those common and vulgar flourishes for Religion and Liberty) save only to confirm the Presbyterian Copy they had set, by making this Church to write after them, though it were in bloody Characters.

Which design and end, whether it will justify the use of such violent means, before the divine Justice: I leave to their Consciences to judge, who have already felt the misery of the means, but not reaped the benefit of the end, either in this Kingdom, or that.

Such knots and crossness of grain being objected here, as will hardly suffer that form which they cry up, as the only just reformation, and settling of Government and discipline in Churches, to go on so smoothly here, as it might do in *Scotland*; and was by them imagined would have done in *England*, when so many of the *English* Clergy, through levity, or discontent, if no worse passion, suddenly quitted their former engagements to Episcopacy, and faced about to their Presbytery.

It cannot but seem either passion, or some self-seeking, more than true Zeal, and pious Discretion, for any foreign State or Church to prescribe such medicines only for others, which themselves have used, rather successfully than commendably; not considering that the same Physic on different constitutions, will have different operations; That may kill one, which doth but cure another.

Nor do I know any such tough and malignant humours in the constitution of the *English* Church, which gentler applications than those of an Army, might not easily have removed: Nor is it so proper to hew out religious Reformations by the Sword, as to polish them by fair and equal disputations among those that are most concerned in the differences, whom not force, but Reason ought to convince.

But their design now, seemed rather to cut off all disputation here, than to procure a fair and equal one: For, it was concluded

---

1 The Scots previously crossed into England during the Second Bishops' War (1640).

there, that the *English* Clergy must conform to the *Scots'* pattern before ever they could be heard, what they could say for themselves, or against the other's way.

I could have wished fairer proceedings both for their credits, who urge things with such violence; and for other men's Consciences too, who can receive little satisfaction in these points which are maintained rather by Soldiers fighting in the Field, than Scholars disputing in free and learned Synods.

Sure in matters of Religion those truths gain most on men's Judgements and Consciences, which are least urged with secular violence, which weakens Truth with prejudices; and is unreasonable to be used, till such means of rational conviction hath been applied, as leaving no excuse for ignorance, condemns men's obstinacy to deserved penalties.

Which no charity will easily suspect of so many learned and pious Church-men in *England*; who being always bred up, and conformable to the Government of Episcopacy, cannot so soon renounce both their former opinion and practice, only because that Party of the *Scots* will needs, by force assist a like Party here, either to drive all Ministers, as sheep into the common fold of Presbytery, or destroy them; at least fleece them, by depriving them of the benefit of their Flocks. If the *Scotch* sole Presbytery were proved to be the only institution of Jesus Christ, for all Churches' Government; yet I believe it would be hard to prove that Christ had given those *Scots*, or any other of my Subjects, Commission by the Sword to set it up in any of my Kingdoms, without my Consent.[1]

What respect and obedience Christ and his Apostles paid to the chief Governors of States, where they lived is very clear in the Gospel;[2] but that he, or they ever commanded to set up such a parity of Presbyters, and in such a way as those *Scots* endeavour; I think is not very disputable.

If Presbytery in such a supremacy be an institution of Christ; sure it differs from all others; and is the first and only point of Christianity, that was to be planted and watered with so much Christian blood; whose effusions run in a stream so contrary to

---

1 The Long Parliament established the Westminster Assembly in June 1643. In conjunction with Parliament, the Assembly progressively dismantled episcopacy, culminating in the establishment of a Presbyterian church system and the abolition of episcopacy in 1646.

2 Matthew 17:25-27, 22:17-21; Mark 12:14-17; Luke 20:21-25.

that of the Primitive planters, both of Christianity and Episcopacy, which was with patient shedding of their own blood, not violent drawing other men's; sure there is too much of Man in it, to have much of Christ, none of whose institutions were carried on, or begun with the temptations of Covetousness or Ambition; of both which this is vehemently suspected.

Yet was there never any thing upon the point, which those *Scots* had by Army or Commissioners to move me with, by their many Solemn obtestations,[1] and pious threatenings, but only this; to represent to me the wonderful necessity of setting up their Presbytery in *England*, to avoid the further miseries of a War; which some men chiefly on this design at first had begun, and now further engaged themselves to continue.

What hinders that any Sects, Schisms, or Heresies, if they can get but numbers, strength and opportunity, may not, according to this opinion and pattern, set up their ways by the like methods of violence? all which Presbytery seeks to suppress, and render odious under those names; when wise and learned men think, that nothing hath more marks of Schism, and Sectarism, than this Presbyterian way, both as to the Ancient, and still most Universal way of the Church-government, and specially as to the particular Laws and Constitutions of this *English* Church, which are not yet repealed, nor are like to be for me, till I see more Rational and Religious motives, than Soldiers use to carry in their Knapsacks.[2]

But we must leave the success of all to God, who hath many ways (having first taken us off from the folly of our opinions, and fury of our passion) to teach us those rules of true Reason, and peaceable Wisdom, which is from above, tending most to God's glory, and his Church's good; which I think my self so much the more bound in Conscience to attend, with the most judicious Zeal and care, by how much I esteem the Church above the State, the glory of Christ above mine Own; and the salvation of men's Souls above the preservation of their Bodies and Estates.

Nor may any men, I think, without sin and presumption, forcibly endeavour to cast the Churches under my care and tuition, into the moulds they have fancied, and fashioned to their

---

1 Entreaties or protestations which call upon God as witness.
2 To justify its opposition to the king, Parliament ordered various printings of selections from Scripture for its army; for example, *The Soldier's Pocket Bible* (London 1643) and *The Soldier's Catechism: Composed for the Parliament's Army* (London 1644).

designs, till they have first gained my consent, and resolved, both my own and other men's Consciences by the strength of their Reasons.

Other violent motions, which are neither Manly, Christian, nor Loyal, shall never either shake or settle my Religion; nor any man's else, who knows what Religion means: And how far it is removed from all Faction, whose proper engine[1] is force; the arbitrator of beasts, not of reasonable men, much less of humble Christians, and loyal Subjects, in matters of Religion.

But men are prone to have such high conceits of themselves, that they care not what cost they lay out upon their opinions; especially those, that have some temptation of gain, to recompense their losses and hazards.[2]

Yet I was not more scandalised at the *Scots'* Armies coming in against my will, and their forfeiture of so many obligations of duty, and gratitude to me: than I wondered, how those here, could so much distrust God's assistance; who so much pretended God's cause to the People, as if they had the certainty of some divine Revelation; considering they were more than competently furnished with my Subjects' Arms and Ammunition; My Navy by Sea, my Forts, Castles, and Cities by Land.

But I find, that men jealous of the Justifiableness of their doings, and designs before God, never think they have human strength enough to carry their work on, seem it never so plausible to the People; what cannot be justified in Law or Religion, had need be fortified with Power.

And yet such is the inconstancy that attends all minds engaged in violent motion, that whom some of them one will earnestly invite to come into their assistance; others of them soon after are weary of, and with nauseating cast them out: what one Party thought to rivet to a settledness by the strength and influence of the *Scots*, that the other rejects and contemns; at once, despising the Kirk[3] Government, and Discipline of the *Scots*, and frustrating the success of so chargeable,[4] more than charitable assistance: For, sure the Church of *England* might have purchased at a far cheaper rate, the truth and happiness of Reformed government and discipline (if it had been wanting) though it had entertained

---

1 Instrument, means.
2 Risks.
3 Church.
4 Troublesome; also, financially burdensome.

the best Divines of Christendom for their advice in a full and free Synod; which, I was ever willing to, and desirous of, that matters being impartially settled, might be more satisfactory to all, and more durable.

But much of God's justice, and man's folly will at length be discovered, through all the films and pretensions of Religion, in which Politicians wrap up their designs; In vain do men hope to build their piety on the ruins of Loyalty. Nor can those considerations or designs be durable, when Subjects make bankrupt of their Allegiance, under pretence of setting up a quicker trade for Religion.

But, as My best Subjects of *Scotland* never deserted Me, so I cannot think that the most are gone so far from Me, in a prodigality of their love and respects toward Me, as to make Me to despair of their return; when besides the bonds of nature and Conscience, which they have to Me, all Reason and true Policy will teach them, that their chiefest interest consists in their fidelity to the Crown, not in their serviceableness to any Party of the People, to a neglect and betraying of My Safety and Honour for their own advantages: However the less cause I have to trust to men, the more I shall apply My self to God.

The Troubles of My Soul are enlarged, O Lord, bring thou me out of My distress.[1]

Lord direct thy Servant in the ways of that pious simplicity, which is the best policy.

Deliver Me from the combined strength of those, who have so much of the Serpent's subtilty, that they forget the Dove's Innocency.[2]

Though hand join in hand,[3] *yet let them not prevail against My soul, to the betraying of My Conscience, and Honour.*

Thou, O Lord, canst turn the hearts of those Parties in both Nations, as thou didst the men of Judah *and* Israel, *to restore* David *with as much loyal Zeal,*[4] *as they did with inconstancy and eagerness pursue Him.*

---

1 Psalm 25:17.
2 Jesus said to his disciples "be ... wise as serpents, and harmless as doves" (Matthew 10:16).
3 Proverbs 11:21, 16:5.
4 After Saul's death, David was anointed King of Judah and, soon after, King of Israel (2 Samuel 2:4, 5:3).

Preserve the love of thy Truth and uprightness in Me, and I shall not despair of My Subjects' affections returning towards Me.

Thou canst soon cause the overflowing Seas to ebb, and retire back again to the bounds which thou hast appointed for them.

O My God, I trust in thee; let me not be ashamed; let not My enemies triumph over Me.

Let them be ashamed who transgress without a cause;[1] *let them be turned back that persecute My Soul.*[2]

Let integrity and uprightness preserve Me, for I wait on thee O Lord.

Redeem thy Church, O God, out of all its Troubles.[3]

14. *Upon the Covenant.*

The *Presbyterian Scots* are not to be hired at the ordinary rate of Auxiliaries; nothing will induce them to engage, till those that call them in, have pawned their Souls to them, by a Solemn League and Covenant:

Where many engines of religious and fair pretensions are brought chiefly to batter, or raze[4] Episcopacy; This they make the grand evil Spirit, which, with some other Imps purposely added, to make it more odious, and terrible to the Vulgar, must by so solemn a charm and exorcism be cast out of this Church, after more than a thousand years' possession here, from the first plantation of Christianity in this Island, and an universal prescription of time and practice in all other Churches since the Apostles' times till this last Century.

But no Antiquity must plead for it, Presbytery, like a young Heir, thinks the Father hath lived long enough, and impatient not to be in the Bishop's Chair and Authority (though Lay-men go away with the Revenues) all art is used to sink Episcopacy, and launch Presbytery in *England*; which was lately buoyed up in *Scotland* by the like artifice of a Covenant.

Although I am unsatisfied with many passages in that Covenant (some referring to My self with very dubious and dangerous limitations) yet I chiefly wonder at the design and drift touching the Discipline and Government of the Church; and such a manner of carrying them on to new ways, by Oaths and

---

1 Psalm 25:2-3.
2 Psalm 143:3.
3 Psalm 25:21-22.
4 Sweep away or destroy completely.

Covenants, where it is hard for men to be engaged by no less, than swearing for, or against those things, which are of no clear moral necessity; but very disputable, and controverted among learned and godly men: whereto the application of Oaths can hardly be made and enjoined with that judgement, and certainty in one's self, or that charity and candour to others of different opinion, as I think Religion requires, which never refuses fair and equable[1] deliberations; yea, and dissentings too, in matters only probable.

The enjoining of Oaths upon People must needs in things doubtful be dangerous, as in things unlawful, damnable; and no less superfluous, where former religious and legal Engagements, bound men sufficiently, to all necessary duties. Nor can I see how they will reconcile such an Innovating Oath and Covenant, with that former Protestation which was so lately taken, to maintain the Religion established in the Church of *England*: since they count Discipline so great a part of Religion.

But ambitious minds never think they have laid snares and gins[2] enough to catch and hold the Vulgar credulity: for by such politic and seemingly pious stratagems, they think to keep the populacy fast to their Parties under the terror of perjury: Whereas certainly all honest and wise men ever thought themselves sufficiently bound by former ties of Religion, Allegiance, and Laws, to God and man.

Nor can such after-Contracts, devised and imposed by a few men in a declared Party, without My consent, and without any like power or precedent from God's or man's laws, be ever thought by judicious men sufficient either to absolve or slacken those moral and eternal bonds of duty which lie upon all My Subjects' consciences both to God and Me.

Yet as things now stand, good men shall least offend God or Me, by keeping their Covenant in honest and lawful ways; since I have the charity to think, that the chief end of the Covenant in such men's intentions, was, to preserve Religion in purity, and the Kingdoms in peace: To other than such ends and means they cannot think themselves engaged; nor will those, that have any true touches of Conscience endeavour to carry on the best designs, (much less such as are, and will be daily more apparently factious and ambitious) by any unlawful means, under that title of the

---

1 Equitable.
2 Nets; traps.

Covenant: unless they dare prefer ambiguous, dangerous and unauthorized novelties, before their known and sworn duties, which are indispensable, both to God and My self.

I am prone to believe and hope, That many who took the Covenant, are yet firm to this judgement, That such later Vows, Oaths, or Leagues, can never blot out those former gravings,[1] and characters, which by just and lawful Oaths were made upon their Souls.

That which makes such Confederations by way of solemn Leagues and Covenants more to be suspected, is, That they are the common road, used in all factious and powerful perturbations of State or Church: When formalities of extraordinary zeal and piety are never more studied and elaborate, than, when Politicians most agitate desperate designs against all that is settled, or sacred in Religion, and Laws, which by such screws are cunningly, yet forcibly wrested by secret steps, and less sensible degrees, from their known rule and wonted practice, to comply with the humours of those men, who aim to subdue all to their own will and power, under the disguises of Holy Combinations.

Which cords and withes[2] will hold men's Consciences no longer, than force attends and twists them: for every man soon grows his own Pope, and easily absolves himself of those ties, which, not the commands of God's word, or the Laws of the Land, but only the subtlety[3] and terror of a Party casts upon him; either superfluous and vain, when they were sufficiently tied before; or fraudulent and injurious, if by such after-ligaments they find the Imposers really aiming to dissolve, or suspend their former, just, and necessary obligations.

Indeed, such illegal ways seldom, or never, intend[4] the engaging men more to duties, but only to Parties; therefore it is not regarded how they keep their Covenants in point of piety pretended, provided they adhere firmly to the Party and Design intended.

I see the Imposers of it are content to make their Covenant like Manna (not that it came from Heaven, as this did) agreeable to every man's palate and relish, who will but swallow it:[5] They

---

1 Engravings, inscriptions.
2 Flexible twigs used for binding.
3 Craftiness; cunning.
4 Direct.
5 After Moses led the Israelites out of Egypt, they were sustained for forty years in the desert by manna sent from heaven (Exodus 16:15-35).

admit any men's senses of it, the diverse or contrary; with any salvos, cautions, and reservations, so as they cross not their chief Design which is laid against the Church, and Me.

It is enough if they get but the reputation of a seeming increase to their Party; So little do men remember that God is not mocked.[1]

In such latitudes of sense, I believe many that love Me, and the Church well, may have taken the Covenant, who yet are not so fondly and superstitiously taken by it, as now to act clearly against both all piety and loyalty: who first yielded to it, more to prevent that imminent violence and ruin, which hung over their heads in case they wholly refused it, than for any value of it, or devotion to it.

Wherein, the latitude of some general Clauses may (perhaps) serve somewhat to relieve them, as of *Doing and endeavouring what lawfully they may,* in *their Places and Callings,* and *according to the Word of God*: for, these (indeed) carry no man beyond those bounds of good Conscience, which are certain and fixed, either in God's Laws, as to the general; or the Laws of the State and Kingdom, as to the particular regulation and exercise of men's duties.

I would to God such as glory most in the name of *Covenanters,* would keep themselves within those lawful bounds, to which God hath called them: Surely it were the best way to expiate the rashness of taking it: which must needs then appear, when besides the want of a full and lawful Authority at first to enjoin it, it shall actually be carried on beyond and against those ends which were in it specified and pretended. I willingly forgive such men's taking the Covenant, who keep it within such bounds of Piety, Law, and Loyalty, as can never hurt either the Church, My self, or the Public Peace: Against which, no man's lawful Calling can engage him.

As for that Reformation of the Church, which the Covenant pretends, I cannot think it just or comely, that by the partial advice of a few Divines, (of so soft and servile tempers, as disposed them to so sudden acting and compliance, contrary to their former judgements, profession, and practice) such foul scandals and suspicions should be cast upon the Doctrine and Government of the Church of *England,* as was never done (that I have heard) by any that deserved the name of *Reformed Churches*

---

1   Galatians 6:7.

abroad, nor by any men of learning and candour at home: all whose judgements I cannot but prefer before any men's now factiously engaged.

No man can be more forward than My self to carry on all due Reformations, with mature judgement, and a good Conscience, in what things I shall (after impartial advice) be, by God's Word, and right reason, convinced to be amiss, I have offered more than ever the fullest, freest, and wisest Parliaments did desire.

But the sequel of some men's actions makes it evident, that the main Reformation intended, is the abasing of Episcopacy into Presbytery, and the robbing the Church of its Lands and Revenues: For, no men have been more injuriously used, as to their legal Rights, than the Bishops, and Church-men. These, as the fattest Deer, must be destroyed; the other Rascal-herd of Schisms, Heresies, etc. being lean, may enjoy the benefit of a Toleration: Thus *Naboth's* Vineyard made him the only Blasphemer of his City, and fit to die.[1] Still I see, while the breath of Religion fills the Sails, Profit is the Compass, by which Factious men steer their course in all seditious Commotions.

I thank God, as no men lay more open to the sacrilegious temptation of usurping the Church's Lands, and Revenues, (which issuing chiefly from the Crown, are held of it, and legally can revert only to the Crown with My Consent) so I have always had such a perfect abhorrence of it in My Soul, that I never found the least inclination to such sacrilegious Reformings: yet no man hath a greater desire to have Bishops and all Church-men so reformed, that they may best deserve and use, not only what the pious munificence of My Predecessors hath given to God and the Church, but all other additions of Christian bounty.

But no necessity shall ever, I hope, drive Me or Mine to invade or sell the Priests' Lands, which both *Pharaoh's* divinity, and *Joseph's* true piety abhorred to do:[2] So unjust I think it both in the eye of Reason and Religion, to deprive the most sacred employment of all due encouragements; and like that other hardhearted

---

1 When Naboth refused to give his vineyard to King Ahab, Jezebel (Ahab's wife) had him falsely tried and executed. Ahab then seized the vineyard, but repented when the prophet Elijah cursed his family (1 Kings 21:1-9).

2 During the famine, Joseph provided food to the Egyptians in exchange for their land, procured for Pharaoh. The priests were allowed to retain their land, surviving on a food allotment from Pharaoh (Genesis 47:22).

Pharaoh, to withdraw the Straw, and increase the Task;[1] so pursuing the oppressed Church, as some have done, to the red sea of a Civil War, where nothing but a miracle can save either It, or Him, who esteems it His greatest Title to be called, and His chiefest glory to be *The Defender of the Church, both in its true Faith, and its just fruitions; equally abhorring, Sacrilege, and Apostacy.*

I had rather live as my Predecessor Henry 3. sometime did, on the Church's Alms, than violently to take the bread out of Bishops' and Ministers' mouths.[2]

The next work will be *Jeroboam's* reformation, consecrating the meanest of the People to be Priests in *Israel*, to serve those Golden Calves who have enriched themselves with the Church's Patrimony and Dowry; which how it thrived both with Prince, Priests, and People, is well enough known:[3] And so it will be here, when from the tuition of Kings and Queens, which have been nursing Fathers and Mothers of this Church, it shall be at their allowance, who have already discovered, what hard Fathers, and Stepmothers they will be.

If the poverty of *Scotland* might, yet the plenty of *England* cannot excuse the envy and rapine[4] of the Church's Rights and Revenues.

I cannot so much as pray God to prevent those sad consequences, which will inevitably follow the parity and poverty of

---

1   Pharaoh assigned a quota of bricks to be made by the enslaved Israelites, but refused to supply them with straw, a necessary ingredient, insisting that they "gather their own straw" (Exodus 5:6-19). Such oppression caused the Israelites to flee Egypt and cross the Red Sea to freedom (Exodus 13:18).

2   Henry III, whose reign was also troubled by factional politics, religious reform, and civil war, was forced to sell his lands and jewels and eventually to rely upon the hospitality of the Church to survive during the rebellion of the barons. The similarities between the two reigns were elsewhere noted: see Sir William Dugdale's *A short view of the late troubles in England briefly setting forth, their rise, growth, and tragical conclusion, as also, some parallel thereof with the barons-wars in the time of King Henry III* (London, 1681).

3   Jeroboam, the king of ten of the tribes of Israel, erected two golden calves at Bethel and Dan and appointed "priests drawn from the lowest of the people" for his temples. Abijah the prophet declared Divine vengeance upon the house of Jeroboam (1 Kings 12-14).

4   Plunder.

Ministers, both in Church and State; since I think it no less than a mocking and tempting of God, to desire him to hinder those mischiefs whose occasions and remedies are in our own power; it being every man's sin not to avoid the one, and not to use the other.

There are ways enough to repair the breaches of the State without the ruins of the Church; as I would be a Restorer of the one, so I would not be an Oppressor of the other, under the pretence of Public Debts: The occasions contracting them were bad enough, but such a discharging of them would be much worse; I pray God neither I, nor Mine, may be accessary to either.

To thee, O Lord, do I address My prayer, beseeching thee to pardon the rashness of My Subjects' Swearings, and to quicken their sense and observation of those just, moral, and indispensable bonds, which thy Word, and the Laws of this Kingdom have laid upon their Consciences; From which no pretensions of Piety and Reformation are sufficient to absolve them, or to engage them to any contrary practices.

Make them at length seriously to consider, that nothing violent and injurious can be religious.

Thou allowest no man's committing Sacrilege under the Zeal of abhorring Idols.

Suffer not sacrilegious designs to have the countenance of religious ties.

Thou hast taught us by the wisest of Kings, that it is a snare to take things that are holy, and after Vows to make enquiry.[1]

Ever keep thy Servant from consenting to perjurious and sacrilegious rapines, that I may not have the brand and curse to all posterity of robbing Thee and thy Church, of what thy bounty hath given us, and thy clemency hath accepted from us, wherewith to encourage Learning and Religion.

Though My Treasures are Exhausted, My Revenues Diminished, and My Debts Increased, yet never suffer Me to be tempted to use such profane Reparations; lest a coal from thine Altar set such a fire on My Throne and Conscience as will be hardly quenched.[2]

Let not the Debts and Engagements of the Public, which some men's folly and prodigality hath contracted, be an occasion to impoverish thy Church.

---

1   Proverbs 20:25.
2   Isaiah 6:6.

The State may soon recover, by thy blessing of peace upon us; The Church is never likely, in times, where the Charity of most men is grown so cold, and their Religion so illiberal.

Continue to those that serve Thee and thy Church all those encouragements, which by the will of the pious Donors, and the justice of the Laws are due unto them; and give them grace to deserve and use them aright to thy glory, and the relief of the poor; That thy Priests may be clothed with righteousness, and the poor may be satisfied with bread.[1]

Let not holy things be given to Swine; nor the Church's bread to Dogs;[2] *rather let them go about the City, grin like a Dog, and grudge that they are not satisfied.*

Let those sacred morsels, which some men have already by violence devoured never digest with them, nor theirs; Let them be as Naboth's *Vineyard to* Ahab, *gall in their mouths, rottenness to their names, a moth to their Families, and a sting to their Consciences.*

Break in sunder, O Lord, all violent and sacrilegious Confederations, to do wickedly and injuriously.

Divide their hearts and tongues who have bandied together against the Church and State, that the folly of such may be manifest to all men, and proceed no further.

But so favour My righteous dealing, O Lord, that in the mercies of thee, the most High, I may never miscarry.

15. *Upon the many Jealousies raised, and Scandals cast upon the* KING, *to stir up the People against Him.*

If I had not My own Innocency, and God's protection, it were hard for Me to stand out against those stratagems and conflicts of malice, which by Falsities seek to oppress the Truth; and by Jealousies to supply the defect of Real causes, which might seem to justify so unjust Engagements against Me.

And indeed, the worst effects of open Hostility come short of these Designs: For, I can more willingly lose My Crowns, than My Credit; nor are My Kingdoms so dear to Me, as My Reputation and Honour.

Those must have a period[3] with My life; but these may survive to a glorious kind of Immortality, when I am dead and gone: A good name being the embalming of Princes, and a sweet

---

1   Psalm 132:9, 15.
2   Matthew 7:6.
3   End.

consecrating of them to an Eternity of love and gratitude among Posterity.

Those foul and false aspersions were secret engines at first employed against My people's love of Me: that undermining their opinion and value of Me, My enemies, and theirs too, might at once blow up their affections, and batter down their loyalty.

Wherein yet, I thank God, the detriment of My Honour is not so afflictive to Me, as the sin and danger of My people's souls, whose eyes once blinded with such mists of suspicions, they are soon mis-led into the most desperate precipices of actions; wherein they do not only, not consider their sin and danger, but glory in their zealous adventures; while I am rendered to them so fit to be destroyed, that many are ambitious to merit the name of My Destroyers; Imagining they then fear God most, when they least honour their King.

I thank God, I never found but My pity was above My anger; nor have My passions ever so prevailed against Me, as to exclude My most compassionate prayers for them, whom devout errors more than their own malice have betrayed to a most religious Rebellion.

I had the Charity to interpret, that most part of My Subjects fought against My supposed Errors, not My Person; and intended to mend Me, not to end Me: And I hope that God pardoning their Errors, hath so far accepted and answered their good intentions, that as he hath yet preserved Me, so he hath by these afflictions prepared Me, both to do him better service, and My people more good, than hitherto I have done.

I do not more willingly forgive their seductions, which occasioned their loyal injuries, than I am ambitious by all Princely merits to redeem them from their unjust suspicions, and reward them for their good intentions.

I am too conscious to My own Affections toward the generality of My people, to suspect theirs to Me; nor shall the malice of My Enemies ever be able to deprive Me of the comfort, which that confidence gives Me; I shall never gratify the spitefulness of a few with any sinister thoughts of all their Allegiance, whom pious frauds have seduced.

The worst some men's ambition can do, shall never persuade Me, to make so bad interpretations of most of My Subjects' actions; who possibly may be Erroneous, but not Heretical in point of Loyalty.

The sense of the Injuries done to My Subjects is as sharp, as those done to My self; our welfares being inseparable; in this only they suffer more than My self, that they are animated by some seducers to injure at once both themselves and Me.

For this is not enough to the malice of My Enemies, that I be afflicted; but it must be done by such instruments, that My afflictions grieve Me not more, than this doth, that I am afflicted by those, whose prosperity I earnestly desire, and whose seduction I heartily deplore.

If they had been My open and foreign Enemies, I could have borne it; but they must be My own Subjects, who are next to My Children, dear to Me: And for the restoring of whose tranquillity, I could willingly be the *Jonah*;[1] If I did not evidently foresee, that by the divided Interests of their and Mine Enemies, as by contrary winds the storm of their miseries would be rather increased than allayed.

I had rather prevent My people's ruin than Rule over them; nor am I so ambitious of that Dominion which is but My Right, as of their happiness; if it could expiate, or countervail such a way of obtaining it, by the highest injuries of Subjects committed against their Sovereign.

Yet I had rather suffer all the miseries of life, and die many deaths, than shamefully to desert, or dishonourably to betray My own just Rights and Sovereignty; thereby to gratify the ambition, or justify the malice of My Enemies; between whose malice, and other men's mistakes, I put as great a difference, as between an ordinary Ague and the Plague; or the Itch of Novelty, and the Leprosy of Disloyalty.

As Liars need have good memories, so Malicious persons need good inventions; that their calumnies may fit every man's fancy; and what their reproaches want of truth, they may make up with number and show.

My patience (I thank God) will better serve Me to bear, and My charity to forgive, than My leisure to answer the many false Aspersions which some men have cast upon Me.

Did I not more consider My Subjects' Satisfaction, than My own Vindication; I should never have given the malice of some

---

1 Jonah permitted sailors to cast him into the sea to calm a storm sent by God as a punishment for his refusal to prophesy in Ninevah (Jonah 1:9-15).

men that pleasure, as to see Me take notice of, or remember what they say, or object.

I would leave the Authors to be punished by their own evil manners, and seared Consciences, which will, I believe, in a shorter time than they be aware of, both confute and revenge all those black and false Scandals, which they have cast on Me; And make the world see, there is as little truth in them, as there was little worth in the broaching of them, or Civility, (I need not say Loyalty) in the not-suppressing of them; whose credit and reputation, even with the people, shall ere long be quite blasted by the breath of that same furnace of popular obloquy, and detraction, which they have studied to heat and inflame to the highest degree of infamy, and wherein they have sought to cast and consume My Name and Honour.

First, nothing gave Me more cause to suspect, and search My own Innocency; than when I observed so many forward to engage against Me, who had made great professions of singular piety; For this gave to vulgar minds so bad a reflection upon Me, and My Cause, as if it had been impossible to adhere to Me, and not withall part from God; to think or speak well of Me, and not to Blaspheme him; so many were persuaded that these two were utterly inconsistent, to be at once Loyal to Me, and truly Religious toward God.

Not but that I had (I thank God) many with Me, which were both Learned and Religious, (much above that ordinary size, and that vulgar proportion, wherein some men glory so much) who were so well satisfied in the cause of My sufferings, that they chose rather to suffer with Me, than forsake Me.

Nor is it strange that so religious Pretensions as were used against Me, should be to many well-minded men a great temptation to oppose Me; Especially, being urged by such popular Preachers, as think it no sin to lie for God, and what they please to call God's Cause, cursing all that will not curse with them; looking so much at, and crying up the goodness of the end propounded, that they consider not the lawfulness of the means used, nor the depth of the mischief, chiefly plotted and intended.

The weakness of these men's judgements must be made up by their clamours and activity.

It was a great part of some men's Religion to scandalize Me and Mine, they thought theirs could not be true, if they cried not down Mine as false.

I thank God, I have had more trial of his grace, as to the constancy of My Religion in the Protestant profession of the Church of *England*, both abroad, and at home, than ever they are like to have.

Nor do I know any exception, I am so liable to, in their opinion, as too great a fixedness in that Religion, whose judicious and solid grounds, both from Scripture, and Antiquity, will not give My Conscience leave to approve or consent to those many dangerous and divided Innovations, which the bold Ignorance of some men would needs obtrude upon Me, and My People.

Contrary to those well tried foundations both of Truth, and Order, which men of far greater Learning, and clearer Zeal, have settled in the Confession and Constitution of this Church in *England*, which many former Parliaments in the most calm, and unpassionate times, have oft confirmed; In which I shall ever, by God's help, persevere, as believing it hath most of Primitive Truth and Order.

Nor did My using the assistance of some Papists, which were my Subjects, any way fight against My Religion, as some men would needs interpret it: especially those who least of all men cared whom they employed, or what they said, and did, so they might prevail.

'Tis strange that so wise men, as they would be esteemed, should not conceive, That differences of persuasion in matters of Religion may easily fall out, where there is the sameness of duty, Allegiance, and subjection. The first they owe as men, and Christians to God; the second, they owe to Me in Common, as their KING; different professions in point of Religion cannot (any more than in Civil Trades) take away the community of relations either to Parents, or to Princes: And where is there such an *Oglio*[1] or medley of various Religions in the world again, as those men entertain in their service (who find most fault with me) without any scruple, as to the diversity of their Sects and Opinions?

It was, indeed, a foul and indelible shame, for such as would be counted Protestants, to enforce Me, a declared Protestant, their Lord and King, to a necessary use of Papists, or any other, who did but their duty to help Me to defend My self.

Nor did I more than is lawful for any King, in such exigents to use the aid of any [of] his Subjects.

I am sorry the Papists should have a greater sense of their Alle-

---

1 A mixture of heterogenous things.

giance, than many Protestant Professors;[1] who seem to have learned and to practise the worst Principles of the worst Papists.

Indeed, it had been a very impertinent and unseasonable scruple in Me, (and very pleasing no doubt to My Enemies) to have been then disputing the points of different beliefs in My Subjects when I was disputed with by Swords' points: and when I needed the help of My Subjects as men, no less than their prayers as Christians.

The noise of My Evil Counsellors was another useful device for those, who were impatient any men's counsels but their own should be followed in Church or State; who were so eager in giving Me better counsel that they would not give Me leave to take it with freedom, as a Man; or honour, as a King; making their counsels more like a drench that must be poured down, than a draught which might be fairly and leisurely drank, if I liked it.

I will not justify beyond human errors and frailties My self, or My Counsellors: They might be subject to some miscarriages, yet such as were far more reparable by second and better thoughts, than those enormous extravagances, wherewith some men have now even wildered,[2] and almost quite lost both Church and State.

The event of things at last will make it evident to My Subjects, that had I followed the worst Counsels, that My worst Counsellors ever had the boldness to offer to Me, or My self any inclination to use; I could not so soon have brought both Church and State in three flourishing Kingdoms, to such a *Chaos* of confusions, and Hell of miseries, as some have done; out of which they cannot, or will not in the midst of their many great advantages, redeem either Me, or My Subjects.

No men were more willing to complain, than I was to redress what I saw in Reason was either done or advised amiss; and this I thought I had done, even beyond the expectation of moderate men: who were sorry to see Me prone even to injure My self, out of a Zeal to relieve My Subjects.

But other men's insatiable desire of revenge upon Me, My Court, and My Clergy; hath wholly beguiled both Church and State, of the benefit of all My, either Retractations, or Concessions; and withall, hath deprived all those (now so zealous Perse-

---

1 Ones who profess.
2 Strayed from.

cutors) both of the comfort and reward of their former pretended persecutions, wherein they so much gloried among the vulgar; and which, indeed, a truly humble Christian will so highly prize, as rather not be relieved, than be revenged, so as to be bereaved of that Crown of Christian Patience, which attends humble and injured sufferers.

Another artifice used to withdraw My people's affections from Me, to their designs, was, The noise and ostentation of liberty, which men are not more prone to desire, than unapt to bear in the popular sense; which is to do what every man liketh best.

If the Divinest liberty be to will what men should, and to do what they so will, according to Reason, Laws, and Religion; I envy not My Subjects that liberty, which is all I desire to enjoy My self; So far am I from the desire of oppressing theirs: Nor were those Lords and Gentlemen which assisted Me so prodigal[1] of their liberties, as with their Lives and Fortunes to help on the enslaving of themselves and their posterities.

As to Civil Immunities, none but such as desire to drive on their Ambitious and Covetous designs over the ruins of Church and State, Prince, Peers, and People, will ever desire greater Freedoms than the Laws allow; whose bounds good men count their Ornament and Protection; others their Manacles and Oppression.

Nor is it just any man should expect the reward and benefit of the Law, who despiseth his rule and direction; losing justly his safety while he seeks an unreasonable liberty.

Time will best inform My Subjects, that those are the best preservers of their true liberties, who allow themselves the least licentiousness against, or beyond the Laws.

They will feel it at last to their cost, that it is impossible those men should be really tender of their fellow-subjects' liberties, who have the hardiness to use their King with so severe restraints; against all Laws, both Divine and Human, under which, yet, I will rather perish, than complain to those, who want nothing to complete their mirth, and triumph, but such music.

In point of true conscientious tenderness (attended with humility and meekness, not with proud and arrogant activity, which seeks to hatch every egg of different opinion to a Faction or Schism) I have oft declared, how little I desire My Laws and

---

1 Recklessly wasteful.

Scepter should intrench[1] on God's Sovereignty, which is the only King of men's Consciences; and yet he hath laid such restraints upon men, as commands them to be subject for Conscience sake, giving no men liberty to break the Law established, further than with meekness and patience, they are content to suffer the penalties annexed, rather than perturb the public Peace.

The truth is, some men's thirst after Novelties, others' despair to relieve the necessities of their Fortunes, or satisfy their Ambition, in peaceable times, (distrusting God's providence, as well as their own merits) were the secret (but principal) impulsives to these popular Commotions, by which Subjects have been persuaded to expend much of those plentiful Estates they got, and enjoyed under My Government, in peaceable times; which yet must now be blasted with all the odious reproaches, which impotent malice can invent; and My self exposed to all those contempts, which may most diminish the Majesty of a King, and increase the ungrateful insolencies of My People.

For Mine Honour, I am well assured, that as Mine Innocency is clear before God, in point of any calumnies they object; so My reputation shall like the Sun (after Owls and Bats have had their freedom in the night and darker times) rise and recover it self to such a degree of splendour, as those feral[2] birds shall be grieved to behold, and unable to bear. For never were any Princes more glorious, than those whom God hath suffered to be tried in the furnace of afflictions, by their injurious Subjects.

And who knows but the just and merciful God will do Me good, for some men's hard, false, and evil speeches against Me; wherein they speak rather what they wish, than what they believe, or know.

Nor can I suffer so much in point of Honour, by those rude and scandalous Pamphlets (which like fire in great conflagrations, fly up and down to set all places on like flames) than those men do, who pretending to so much piety, are so forgetful of their duty to God and Me: By no way ever vindicating the Majesty of their KING against any of those, who contrary to the precept of God, and precedent of Angels, *speak evil of dignities, and bring railing accusations against those*, who are honoured with the name of *Gods*.

---

1 Encroach upon.
2 Gloomy; funereal.

But 'tis no wonder if men not fearing GOD, should not Honour their KING.

They will easily contemn[1] such shadows of God, who reverence not that Supreme, and adorable Majesty, in comparison of whom all the glory of Men and Angels is but obscurity; yet hath he graven such Characters of divine Authority, and Sacred power upon Kings, as none may without sin seek to blot them out. Nor shall their black veils be able to hide the shining of My face, while God gives Me a heart frequently and humbly to converse with him, from whom alone are all the traditions of true glory and majesty.

Thou, O Lord, knowest My reproach, and My dishonour, My Adversaries are all before thee.

My Soul is among Lions, among them that are set on fire, even the Sons of Men; whose teeth are spears and arrows; their tongue a sharp sword.[2]

Mine enemies reproach Me all the day long, and those that are mad against Me are sworn together.[3]

O My God, how long shall the sons of men turn My glory into shame? how long shall they love vanity, and seek after lies?[4]

Thou hast heard the reproaches of wicked men on every side. Hold not thy peace, lest My Enemies prevail against me, and lay mine Honour in the dust.[5]

Thou, O Lord, shalt destroy them that speak lies; the Lord will abhor both the blood-thirsty, and deceitful men.

Make my righteousness to appear as the light, and mine innocency to shine forth as the Sun at noonday.[6]

Suffer not my silence to betray mine innocence, nor my displeasure, my patience; That after my Saviour's example, being reviled, I may not revile again; and being cursed by them, I may bless them.

Thou that wouldst not suffer Shimei's *tongue to go unpunished;*[7]

---

1 Treat with contempt.
2 Psalm 57:4.
3 Psalm 102:8.
4 Psalm 4:2.
5 *Hold not thy peace* Psalm 83:1; 109:1; *lay mine ... dust* Psalm 7:5.
6 Psalm 37:6.
7 Shimei, of the house of Saul, cursed and cast stones at King David as he fled Absalom's rebellion. Though David did not retaliate, on his deathbed he instructed his son Solomon to kill Shimei (2 Samuel 16:5-13, 19:16-23; 1 Kings 2:8-9, 36-46).

when by thy judgements on David *he might seem to justify his disdainful reproaches, give me grace to intercede with thy mercy for these my enemies, that the reward of false and lying tongues, even hot burning coals of eternal fire, may not be brought upon them.*

Let my prayers, and patience, be as water to cool and quench their tongues, who are already set on fire with the fire of Hell, and tormented with those malicious flames.[1]

Let me be happy to refute, and put to silence their evil-speaking by well-doing; and let them enjoy not the fruit of their lips, but of my prayer for their repentance, and thy pardon.

Teach me David's *patience and* Hezekiah's *devotion, that I may look to thy mercy through man's malice, and see thy justice in their sin.*[2]

Let Sheba's *seditious speeches,* Rabshakeh's *railing, and* Shimei's *cursing, provoke, as my humble prayer to thee, so thy renewed blessing toward me.*[3]

Though they curse, do thou bless, and I shall be blessed; and made a blessing to my people.

That the stone, which some builders refuse, may become the head stone of the corner.

Look down from heaven, and save me, from the reproach of them that would swallow me up.

Hide me in the secret of thy presence, from the pride of man, and keep me from the strife of tongues.

16. *Upon the Ordinance against the Common-Prayer-Book.*[4]
It is no news to have all Innovations ushered in with the name of Reformations in Church and State, by those, who seeking to gain reputation with the Vulgar for their extraordinary parts, and piety,

---

1 *Water ... flames* Luke 16:24.
2 David's patience is evident in his treatment of Shimei. The pious Hezekiah, king of Judah, opposed idolatry, destroyed sites of pagan worship, and cleansed and opened the Temple (2 Kings 18-20; 2 Chronicles 29-32; Isaiah 36-39).
3 Sheba, son of Bichri, persuaded many to rebel against King David (2 Samuel 20:1-22). The king of Assyria sent Rabshakeh, his field commander, to persuade Hezekiah's subjects to rebel against him (Isaiah 36).
4 In January 1645, Parliament abolished the Book of Common Prayer and substituted the Presbyterian Directory of Worship. *Ordinance* The Acts of the Long Parliament after 1641 were at first called ordinances, as the king did not assent to the legislation.

must needs undo whatever was formerly settled never so well and wisely.

So hardly can the pride of those that study Novelties, allow former times any share or degree of wisdom or godliness.

And because matter of prayer and devotion to God justly bears a great part in Religion, (being the Soul's more immediate converse with the divine Majesty) nothing could be more plausible to the People than to tell them, They served God amiss in that point.

Hence our public Liturgy, or Forms of constant Prayers must be (not amended, in what upon free and public advice might seem to sober men inconvenient for matter or manner, to which I should easily consent, but) wholly cashiered,[1] and abolished, and after many popular contempts offered to the Book, and those that used it according to their Consciences, and the Laws in force, it must be crucified by an Ordinance, the better to please either those men, who gloried in their extemporary vein and fluency: or others, who conscious to their own formality in the use of it, thought they fully expiated their sin of not using it aright, by laying all the blame upon it, and a total rejection of it as a dead letter, thereby to excuse the deadness of their hearts.

As for the matter contained in the Book, sober and learned men have sufficiently vindicated it against the cavils[2] and exceptions of those, who thought it a part of piety to make what profane objections they could against it; especially for Popery and Superstition; whereas no doubt the Liturgy was exactly conformed to the doctrine of the Church of *England*; and this by all Reformed Churches is confessed to be most sound and Orthodox.

For the manner of using Set and prescribed Forms, there is no doubt but that wholesome words, being known and fitted to men's understandings, are soonest received into their hearts, and aptest to excite and carry along with them judicious and fervent affections.

Nor do I see any reason why Christians should be weary of a well-composed Liturgy (as I hold this to be) more than of all other things, wherein the Constancy abates nothing of the excellency and usefulness.

I could never see any Reason, why any Christian should abhor, or be forbidden to use the same Forms of prayer, since he prays to the same God, believes in the same Saviour, professeth the

---

1 Discarded.
2 Frivolous objections.

same Truths, reads the same Scriptures, hath the same duties upon him, and feels the same daily wants for the most part, both inward and outward, which are common to the whole Church.

Sure we may as well before-hand know what we pray, as to whom we pray; and in what words, as to what sense; when we desire the same things, what hinders we may not use the same words? our appetite and digestion too may be good when we use, as we pray for, *our daily bread*.[1]

Some men, I hear, are so impatient not to use in all their devotions their own invention, and gifts, that they not only disuse (as too many) but wholly cast away and contemn the *Lord's Prayer*; whose great guilt is, that it is the warrant and original pattern of all set Liturgies, in the Christian Church.

I ever thought that the proud ostentation of men's abilities for invention, and the vain affectations of variety for expressions, in Public prayer, or any sacred administrations, merits a greater brand of sin, than that which they call Coldness and Barrenness: Nor are men in those novelties less subject to formal and superficial tempers (as to their hearts) than in the use of constant Forms, where not the words, but men's hearts, are to blame.

I make no doubt but a man may be very formal in the most extemporary variety; and very fervently devout in the most wonted expressions: Nor is God more a God of variety, than of constancy: Nor are constant Forms of Prayers more likely to flat,[2] and hinder the Spirit of prayer, and devotion, than un-premeditated and confused variety to distract, and lose it.

Though I am not against a grave, modest, discreet, and humble use of Ministers' gifts, even in public, the better to fit, and excite their own, and the People's affections to the present occasions; yet I know no necessity why private and single abilities should quite justle out, and deprive the Church of the joint abilities and concurrent gifts of many learned and godly men; such as the Composers of the Service-Book were; who may in all reason be thought to have more of gifts and graces enabling them to compose with serious deliberation and concurrent advice, such Forms of prayers, as may best fit the Church's common wants, inform the Hearers' understanding, and stir up that fiduciary and fervent application of their spirits (wherein consists the very life and soul of prayer, and that so much pretended Spirit of prayer)

---

1 A phrase from the Lord's Prayer (Matthew 6:11; Luke 11:3).
2 Dull; deaden.

than any private man by his solitary abilities can be presumed to have; which, what they are many times (even there, where they make a great noise and show) the affectations, emptiness, impertinency, rudeness, confusions, flatness, levity, obscurity, vain, and ridiculous repetitions, the senseless, and oft-times blasphemous expressions; all these burdened with a most tedious and intolerable length, do sufficiently convince all men, but those who glory in that Pharisaic way.

Wherein men must be strangely impudent, and flatterers of themselves, not to have an infinite shame of what they so do and say, in things of so sacred a nature, before God and the Church, after so ridiculous, and indeed, profane a manner.

Nor can it be expected, but that in duties of frequent performance, as Sacramental administrations, and the like, which are still the same; Ministers must either come to use their own Forms constantly, which are not like to be so sound, or comprehensive of the nature of the duty, as Forms of Public composure; or else they must every time affect new expressions when the subject is the same; which can hardly be presumed in any man's greatest sufficiencies not to want (many times) much of that completeness, order, and gravity, becoming those duties; which by this means are exposed at every celebration to every Minister's private infirmities, indispositions, errors, disorders, and defects, both for judgement and expression.

A serious sense of which inconvenience in the Church unavoidably following every man's several[1] manner of officiating, no doubt, first occasioned the wisdom and piety of the Ancient Churches, to remedy those mischiefs, by the use of constant Liturgies of Public composure.

The want of which I believe this Church will sufficiently feel, when the unhappy fruits of many men's ungoverned ignorance, and confident defects, shall be discovered in more errors, schisms, disorders, and uncharitable distractions in Religion, which are already but too many, the more is the pity.

However, if violence must needs bring in, and abet those innovations, (that men may not seem to have nothing to do) which Law, Reason, and Religion forbids, at least to be so obtruded, as wholly to justle out the public Liturgy.

Yet nothing can excuse that most unjust and partial severity of

---

1 Separate; distinct.

those men, who either lately had subscribed to, used and maintained the Service-book; or refused to use it, cried out of the rigour of Laws and Bishops, which suffered them not to use the liberty of their Consciences, in not using it.

That these men (I say) should so suddenly change the Liturgy into a Directory, as if the Spirit needed help for invention, though not for expressions; or as if matter prescribed did not as much stint and obstruct the Spirit, as if it were clothed in, and confined to, fit words: (So slight and easy is that Legerdemain[1] which will serve to delude the vulgar.)

That further, they should use such severity as not to suffer without penalty, any to use the Common-prayer-Book publicly, although their Consciences bind them to it, as a duty of Piety to God, and Obedience to the Laws.

Thus I see no men are prone to be greater Tyrants, and more rigorous exacters[2] upon others to conform to their illegal novelties, than such, whose pride was formerly least disposed to the obedience of lawful Constitutions; and whose licentious humours most pretended Conscientious liberties, which freedom, with much regret they now allow to Me, and My Chaplains, when they may have leave to serve Me, whose abilities, even in their extemporary way comes not short of the others, but their modesty and learning far exceeds the most of them.

But this matter is of so popular a nature, as some men knew it would not bear learned and sober debates, lest being convinced by the evidence of Reason, as well as Laws, they should have been driven either to sin more against their knowledge, by taking away the Liturgy; or to displease some faction of the people by continuing the use of it.

Though I believe they have offended more considerable men, not only for their numbers and estates, but for their weighty and judicious piety, than those are, whose weakness or giddiness they sought to gratify by taking it away.

One of the greatest faults some men found with the Common-Prayer-Book, I believe, was this, That it taught them to pray so oft for Me; to which Petitions they had not Loyalty enough to say *Amen*, nor yet Charity enough to forbear Reproaches, and even Cursings of Me in their own forms, instead of praying for Me.

---

1 Sleight of hand; trickery.
2 Ones who insist (usually excessively) upon something as a matter of right.

I wish their Repentance may be their only punishment; that seeing the mischiefs which the disuse of public Liturgies hath already produced, they may restore that credit, use, and reverence to them, which by the ancient Churches were given to Set Forms of sound and wholesome words.

And thou, O Lord, which art the same God, blessed forever: whose mercies are full of variety, and yet of constancy; Thou deniest us not a new and fresh sense of our old and daily wants, nor despisest renewed affections joined to constant expressions.

Let us not want the benefit of thy Church's united and well-advised Devotions.

Let the matters of our prayers be agreeable to thy will, which is always the same, and the fervency of our spirits to the motions of thy holy Spirit in us.

And then we doubt not, but thy spiritual perfections are such, as thou art neither to be pleased with affected Novelties for matter or manner, nor offended with the pious constancy of our petitions in them both.

Whose variety or constancy thou hast no where either forbidden or commanded, but left them to the piety and prudence of thy Church, that both may be used, neither despised.

Keep men in that pious moderation of their judgements in matters of Religion; that their ignorance may not offend others, nor their opinion of their own abilities tempt them to deprive others of what they may lawfully and devoutly use, to help their infirmities.

And since the advantage of Error consists in novelty and variety, as Truths in unity and constancy: Suffer not thy Church to be pestered with errors, and deformed with undecencies in thy service, under the pretence of variety and novelty. Nor to be deprived of truth, unity, and order, under this fallacy, That constancy is the cause of formality.

Lord keep us from formal Hypocrisy in our own hearts, and then we know that praying to thee, or praising of thee (with David, and other holy men) in the same forms cannot hurt us.

Give us wisdom to amend what is amiss within us, and there will be less to mend without us.

Evermore defend and deliver thy Church from the effects of blind Zeal, and over-bold devotion.

17. *Of the differences between the* KING *and the two Houses, in point of Church-Government.*

Touching the GOVERNMENT of the Church by Bishops, the common Jealousy hath been, that I am earnest and resolute to maintain it, not so much out of piety, as policy, and reason of State.

Wherein so far indeed reason of State doth induce Me to approve that Government above any other, as I find it impossible for a Prince to preserve the State in quiet, unless he hath such an influence upon Church-men; and they such a dependence on Him, as may best restrain the seditious exorbitancies of Ministers' tongues; who with the Keys of Heaven have so far the Keys of the People's hearts, as they prevail much by their Oratory to let in, or shut out, both Peace and Loyalty.

So that I being (as KING) entrusted by God, and the Laws, with the good both of Church and State; I see no Reason I should give up, or weaken by any change, that power and influence which in right and reason I ought to have over both.

The moving Bishops out of the House of Peers (of which I have elsewhere given an account)[1] was sufficient to take off any suspicion, that I incline to them for any use to be made of their Votes in State affairs: Though indeed I never thought any Bishop worthy to sit in that House, who would not Vote according to his Conscience.

I must now in Charity be thought desirous to preserve that Government in its right constitution, as a matter of Religion; wherein both My judgement is fully satisfied, that it hath of all other the fullest Scripture grounds, and also the constant practice of all Christian Churches; till of late years, the tumultuariness of People, or the factiousness and pride of Presbyters, or the covetousness of some States and Princes, gave occasion to some men's wits to invent new models, and propose them under specious titles of *Christ's Government, Scepter, and Kingdom*; the better to serve their turns, to whom the change was beneficial.

They must give Me leave, having none of their temptations to invite Me to alter the Government of Bishops, (that I may have a title to their Estates) not to believe their pretended grounds to any new ways: contrary to the full, and constant testimony of all Histories, sufficiently convincing unbiased men; that as the Primitive Churches were undoubtedly governed by the Apostles and their immediate Successors the first and best Bishops; so it cannot in reason or charity be supposed, that all Churches in the world should either be ignorant of the rule by them prescribed, or

---

1 In Chapter 9, Charles recounts the passing of the Bishops' Exclusion Bill in February 1642.

so soon deviate from their divine and holy pattern: That since the first Age, for 1500 years not one Example can be produced of any settled Church, wherein were many Ministers and Congregations, which had not some Bishop above them, under whose jurisdiction and government they were.

Whose constant and universal practice agreeing with so large, and evident Scripture-directions, and examples, are set down in the Epistles to *Timothy* and *Titus*, for the settling of that Government, not in the persons only of *Timothy* and *Titus*,[1] but in the succession; (the want of Government being that, which the Church can no more dispense with, in point of well-being, than the want of the word and Sacraments, in point of being.)

I wonder how men came to look with so envious an eye upon Bishops' power and authority, as to oversee both the Ecclesiastical use of them, and Apostolical constitution; which to Me seems no less evidently set forth as to the main scope and design of those Epistles, for the settling of a peculiar Office, Power, and Authority in them as President-Bishops above others, in point of Ordination, Censures, and other acts of Ecclesiastical discipline; than those shorter characters of the qualities and duties of Presbyter-Bishops, and Deacons, are described in some parts of the same Epistles; who in the latitude and community of the name were then, and may now not improperly be called *Bishops*; as to the oversight and care of single Congregations, committed to them by the Apostles, or those Apostolical Bishops, who (as *Timothy* and *Titus*) succeeded them in that ordinary power, there assigned over larger divisions, in which were many Presbyters.

The humility of those first Bishops avoiding the eminent title of Apostles, as a name in the Church's style appropriated from its common notion (*of a Messenger, or one sent*) to that special dignity which had extraordinary call, mission, gifts, and power immediately from Christ: they contented themselves with the ordinary titles of Bishops and Presbyters, until use, (the great arbitrator of words, and master of language) finding reason to distinguish by a peculiar name those persons, whose power and office were indeed distinct from, and above all other in the Church, as succeeding the Apostles in the ordinary and constant power of governing the

---

1   The position and function of Timothy and Titus, viewed as apostle-bishops, were often cited as evidence of the biblical nature of episcopacy. The apostles ordained, through the laying on of hands, and appointed church elders (Acts 6:6, 14:23; 1 Timothy 4:14).

Churches, the honour of (whose name they moderately, yet commendably declined) all Christian Churches (submitting to that special authority) appropriated also the name of *Bishop*, without any suspicion or reproach of arrogancy, to those, who were by Apostolical propagation rightly descended and invested into that highest and largest power of governing even the most pure and Primitive Churches: which, without all doubt had many such holy Bishops, after the pattern of *Timothy* and *Titus*; whose special power is not more clearly set down in those Epistles (the chief grounds and limits of all Episcopal claim, as from divine right) than are the characters of these perilous times, and those men that make them such; who not enduring sound doctrine, and clear testimonies of all Churches' practice, are most perverse Disputers, and proud Usurpers, against true Episcopacy: who, if they be not Traitors and Boasters, yet they seem to be very covetous, heady, high-minded; inordinate and fierce, lovers of themselves, having much of the form, little of the power of godliness.[1]

Who, by popular heaps of weak, light, and unlearned Teachers, seek to over-lay and smother the pregnancy and authority of that power of Episcopal Government, which, beyond all equivocation and vulgar fallacy of names, is most convincingly set forth, both by Scripture, and all after Histories of the Church.

This I write rather like a Divine, than a Prince, that Posterity may see (if ever these Papers be public) that I had fair grounds both from Scripture-Canons, and Ecclesiastical examples, whereon My judgement was stated for Episcopal Government.

Nor was it any policy of State, or obstinacy of will, or partiality of affection, either to the men, or their Function which fixed Me: who cannot in point of worldly respects be so considerable to Me as to recompence the injuries and losses I, and My dearest relations with My Kingdoms have sustained, and hazarded, chiefly at first upon this quarrel.

And not only in Religion, of which, Scripture is the best rule, and the Church's Universal practice the best commentary, but also in right reason, and the true nature of Government, it cannot be thought that an orderly Subordination among Presbyters, or Ministers, should be any more against Christianity, than it is in all secular and civil Governments, where parity breeds Confusion and Faction.

---

1   2 Timothy 3:3-5.

I can no more believe, that such order is inconsistent with true Religion, than good features are with beauty, or numbers[1] with harmony.

Nor is it likely that God, who appointed several orders, and a Prelacy, in the Government of his Church, among the Jewish Priests, should abhor or forbid them among Christian Ministers;[2] who have as much of the principles of schism and division as other men; for preventing and suppressing of which, the Apostolical wisdom (which was divine) after that Christians were multiplied so many Congregations, and Presbyters with them, appointed this way of Government, which might best preserve order and union with Authority.

So that I conceive it was not the favour of Princes, or ambition of Presbyters, but the wisdom and piety of the Apostles, that first settled Bishops in the Church; which Authority they constantly used, and enjoyed in those times, which were purest for Religion, though sharpest for Persecution.

Not that I am against the managing of this Presidency and Authority in one man, by the joint Counsel and consent of many Presbyters: I have offered to restore that, as a fit means to avoid those Errors, Corruptions, and Partialities, which are incident to any one man; Also to avoid Tyranny, which becomes no Christians, least of all Church-men; besides, it will be a means to take away that burden, and *odium* of affairs, which may lie too heavy on one man's shoulders, as indeed I think it formerly did on the Bishops here.

Nor can I see what can be more agreeable both to Reason and Religion, than such a frame of Government which is paternal, not Magisterial; and wherein not only the necessity of avoiding Faction and Confusion, Emulations and Contempts, which are prone to arise among equals in power and function; but also the differences of some Ministers' gifts, and aptitudes for Government above others, doth invite to employ them, in reference to those Abilities, wherein they are Eminent.

Nor is this judgement of Mine touching Episcopacy, any pre-

---

1 Metrical periods or feet; that is, lines or verses.
2 In the Old Testament, the tribe of Levi was divided into high priests (largely the descendants of Aaron) and Levitical priests in general. By the second century BCE, there was generally one high priest who served as president of the Sanhedrin, composed of former high priests and priests of elevated social standing.

occupation of opinion, which will not admit any oppositions against it: It is well known I have endeavoured to satisfy My self in what the chief Patrons for other ways can say against this, or for theirs: And I find they have, as far less of Scripture grounds, and of Reason; so for examples, and practice of the Church, or testimonies of Histories, they are wholly destitute, wherein the whole stream runs so for Episcopacy, that there is not the least rivulet for any others.

As for those obtruded examples of some late reformed Churches, (for many retain Bishops still) whom necessity of times and affairs rather excuseth, than commendeth for their inconformity to all Antiquity; I could never see any reason why Churches orderly reformed and governed by Bishops should be forced to conform to those few, rather than to the Catholic example of all Ancient Churches, which needed no Reformation: And to those Churches at this day, who Governed by Bishops in all the Christian world, are many more than Presbyterians or Independents[1] can pretend to be; All whom the Churches in My three Kingdoms lately Governed by Bishops, would equalize (I think) if not exceed.

Nor is it any point of wisdom or charity, where Christians differ, (as many do in some points) there to widen the differences, and at once to give all the Christian world (except a handful of some Protestants) so great a scandal in point of Church-government; whom, though you may convince of their Errors in some points of Doctrine, yet you shall never persuade them, that to complete their Reformation, they must necessarily desert, and wholly cast off that Government, which they, and all before them have ever owned as Catholic, Primitive, and Apostolical: So far, that never Schismatics, nor Heretics (except those Arians[2]) have strayed from the Unity, and Conformity of the Church in that point; ever having Bishops above Presbyters.

Besides, the late general approbation and submission to this

---

1 The Independents believed that the congregation was the body which should lead the church, stressing the priesthood of all believers. The local congregation, therefore, was not subject to episcopal or presbyterial control.

2 Followers of Arius, a fourth-century priest excommunicated for heresy for claiming that Jesus was neither consubstantial with, nor equal to, God the Father, but was the first-born of creation. John Milton defends Arianism in *De Doctrina Christiana* (Chapters 5 and 6).

Government of Bishops, by the Clergy, as well as the Laity of these Kingdoms, is a great confirmation of My Judgement; and their inconstancy is a great prejudice against their novelty; I cannot in charity so far doubt of their learning or integrity, as if they understood not what heretofore they did; or that they did conform contrary to their Consciences; So that their facility and levity is never to be excused, who, before ever the point of Church-government had any free and impartial debate, contrary to their former Oaths and practice, against their obedience to the Laws in force, and against My consent, have not only quite cried down the Government by Bishops; but have approved and encouraged the violent and most illegal stripping all the Bishops, and many other Church-men, of all their due Authority and Revenues, even to the selling away, and utter alienation of those Church-lands from any Ecclesiastical uses: So great a power hath the stream of times, and the prevalency of parties over some men's judgements; of whose so sudden and so total change, little reason can be given, besides the *Scots'* Army coming into *England.*

But the folly of these men will at last punish itself, and the Deserters of Episcopacy will appear the greatest Enemies to, and Betrayers of their own interest: for Presbytery is never so considerable or effectual, as when it is joined to, and crowned with Episcopacy.[1] All Ministers will find as great a difference in point of thriving, between the favour of the People, and of Princes, as plants do between being watered by hand, or by the sweet and liberal dews of Heaven.

The tenuity[2] and contempt of Clegy-men will soon let them see, what a poor carcass they are, when parted from the influence of that Head, to whose Supremacy they have been sworn.

A little moderation might have prevented great mischiefs; I am firm to Primitive Episcopacy, not to have it extirpated, (if I can hinder it.) Discretion without passion might easily reform, whatever the rust of times, or indulgence of Laws, or corruption of manners have brought upon it. It being a gross vulgar error to impute to, or revenge upon the Function, the faults of times, or persons; which seditious and popular principle, and practice, all wise men abhor.

---

1 Episcopacy contains within it features of Presbyterianism; it finds a place for presbyters (an assembly of priests), for example, in synods.
2 Meagreness.

For those secular additaments[1] and ornaments of Authority, Civil Honour and Estate, which My Predecessors, and Christian Princes in all Countries have annexed to Bishops and Churchmen; I look upon them, but as just rewards of their learning, and piety, who are fit to be in any degree of Church-Government; also enablements to works of Charity, and Hospitality, meet strengthenings of their Authority in point of respect, and observance; which in peaceful times is hardly paid to any Governors by the measure of their virtues, so much, as by that of their Estates; Poverty and meanness exposing them and their Authority to the contempt of licentious minds, and manners, which persecuting Times much restrained.

I would have such men Bishops, as are most worthy of those encouragements, and best able to use them: if at any time My judgement of men failed My good intention made My error venial: And some Bishops, I am sure, I had, whose learning, gravity, and piety, no men of any worth or forehead[2] can deny: But, of all men, I would have Church-men, especially the Governors to be redeemed from that vulgar neglect; which (besides an innate principle of vicious opposition, which is in all men against those that seem to reprove, or restrain them) will necessarily follow both the Presbyterian parity, which makes all Ministers equal; and the Independent inferiority, which sets their Pastors below the People.

This for My judgement touching Episcopacy, wherein (God knows) I do not gratify any design or passion with the least perverting of Truth.

And now I appeal to God above, and all the Christian world, whether it be just for Subjects, or pious for Christians, by violence, and infinite indignities, with servile restraints to seek to force Me their KING and Sovereign, as some men have endeavoured to do, against all these grounds of My Judgement, to consent to their weak and divided novelties.

The greatest Pretender of them desires not more than I do, That the Church should be governed, as Christ hath appointed, in true Reason, and in Scripture; of which, I could never see any probable show for any other ways: who either content themselves with the examples of some Churches in their infancy and soli-

1   Additions.
2   Decency.

tude; when one Presbyter might serve one Congregation, in a City or Country; or else they deny these most evident Truths, That the Apostles were Bishops over those Presbyters they ordained, as well as over the Churches they planted; and that, Government being necessary for the Church's well-being, when multiplied and sociated,[1] must also necessarily descend from the Apostles to others, after the example of that power and superiority, they had above others; which could not end with their persons; since the use and ends of such Government still continue.

It is most sure, that the purest Primitive and best Churches flourished under Episcopacy; and may so still, if ignorance, superstition, avarice, revenge, and other disorderly and disloyal passions had not so blown up some men's minds against it, that what they want of Reasons or Primitive Patterns, they supply with violence and oppression; wherein some men's zeal for Bishops' Lands, Houses, and Revenues hath set them on work to eat up Episcopacy: which (however other men esteem) to Me is no less sin, than Sacrilege; or a robbery of GOD (the giver of all we have) of that portion which devout minds have thankfully given again to him, in giving it to his Church and Prophets; through whose hands he graciously accepts even a cup of cold water, as a libation offered to himself.[2]

Furthermore, as to My particular engagement above other men, by an Oath agreeable to My judgement, I am solemnly obliged to preserve that Government, and the Rights of the Church.

Were I convinced of the unlawfulness of the Function, as Antichristian, (which some men boldly, but weakly calumniate) I could soon, with Judgement, break that Oath, which erroneously was taken by Me.

But being daily by the best disquisition[3] of truth, more confirmed in the Reason and Religion of that, to which I am Sworn; How can any man that wisheth not My damnation, persuade Me at once to so notorious and combined sins, of Sacrilege and Perjury? besides the many personal Injustices I must do to many worthy men, who are as legally invested in their Estates, as any, who seek to deprive them; and they have by no Law, been convicted of those crimes, which might forfeit their Estates and Livelihoods.

---

1 United together.
2 Matthew 10:42.
3 Investigation; examination.

I have oft wondered how men pretending to tenderness of Conscience, and Reformation, can at once tell Me, that My Coronation Oath binds Me to Consent to whatsoever they shall propound to Me, (which they urge with such violence) though contrary to all that Rational and Religious freedom which every man ought to preserve; and of which they seem so tender in their own Votes; yet at the same time these men will needs persuade Me, That I must, and ought to dispense with, and roundly break that part of My Oath, which binds Me (agreeable to the best light of Reason and Religion I have) to maintain the Government, and legal Rights of the Church. 'Tis strange My lot should be valid in that part, which both My self, and all men in their own case, esteem injurious and unreasonable, as being against the very natural and essential liberty of our souls; yet it should be invalid, and to be broken in another clause, wherein I think My self justly obliged, both to God and Man.

Yet upon this Rack chiefly have I been held so long, by some men's ambitious Covetousness, and sacrilegious Cruelty; torturing (with Me) both Church and State, in Civil dissentions; till I shall be forced to consent, and declare that I do approve, what (God knows) I utterly dislike, and in My Soul abhor; as many ways highly against Reason, Justice, and Religion: and whereto, if I should shamefully, and dishonourably give My consent; yet should I not by so doing, satisfy the divided Interests and Opinions of those Parties, which contend with each other, as well as both against Me and Episcopacy.

Nor can My late condescending to the *Scots* in point of Church-government, be rightly objected against Me, as an inducement for Me, to consent to the like in My other Kingdoms, For it should be considered that Episcopacy was not so rooted and settled there, as 'tis here; nor I (in that respect) so strictly bound to continue it in that Kingdom as in this; for what I think in My judgement best, I may not think so absolutely necessary for all places, and at all times.

If any shall impute My yielding to them, as My failing and sin, I can easily acknowledge it; but that is no argument to do so again, or much worse; I being now more convinced in that point: nor indeed hath My yielding to them been so happy and successful as to encourage Me to grant the like to others.

Did I see any thing more of Christ, as to Meekness, Justice, Order, Charity, and Loyalty in those that pretend to other modes of Government, I might suspect My judgement to be biased, or fore-stalled with some prejudice and wontedness[1] of opinion; but I have hitherto so much cause to suspect the contrary in the manners of many of those men, that I cannot from them gain the least reputation for their new ways of Government.

Nor can I find that in any Reformed Churches (whose patterns are so cried up, and obtruded upon the Churches under My Dominion) that either Learning, or Religion, works of Piety or Charity, have so flourished beyond what they have done in My Kingdoms (by God's blessing) which might make Me believe either Presbytery or Independency have a more benign influence upon the Church and men's hearts and lives, than Episcopacy in its right constitution.

The abuses of which, deserve to be extirpated, as much as the use retained; for I think it far better to hold to primitive and uniform Antiquity, than to comply with divided novelty.

A right Episcopacy would at once satisfy all just desires and interests of good Bishops, humble Presbyters, and sober People; so as Church affairs should be managed neither with tyranny, parity, nor popularity; neither Bishops ejected, nor Presbyters despised, nor People oppressed.

And in this integrity both of My Judgement and Conscience, I hope God will preserve Me.

For Thou, O Lord, knowst my uprightness, and tenderness, as thou hast set me to be a Defender of the Faith, and a Protector of thy Church,[2] so suffer me not by any violence, to be overborne against my Conscience.

Arise, O Lord, maintain thine own Cause, let not thy Church be deformed, as to that Government, which derived from thy Apostles, hath been retained in purest and primitive times, till the Revenues of the Church became the object of secular envy; which seeks to rob it of all the encouragements of Learning and Religion.

Make me, as the good Samaritan, compassionate, and helpful to thy afflicted Church; which some men have wounded and robbed; others pass by without regard, either to pity, or relieve.[3]

---

1 Habituation.

2 In 1521, Pope Leo X conferred on Henry VIII the title *Fidei Defensor* (Defender of the Faith) for attacking Lutheran ideas in *Assertio Septem Sacramentorum*; the title was retained by his successors.

3 In Luke 10:25-37, Jesus tells the parable of the Good Samaritan in which a priest and Levite ignore a badly beaten man on the road, while a Samaritan (considered a foreigner and moral inferior) cares for him. The parable serves to illustrate the principle: love thy neighbour as thyself.

As my power is from thee, so give me grace to use it for thee.

And though I am not suffered to be Master of my other Rights as a KING, *yet preserve me in that liberty of Reason, love of Religion, and thy Church's welfare, which are fixed in my Conscience as a Christian.*

Preserve, from Sacrilegious invasions, those temporal blessings, which thy providence hath bestowed on thy Church for thy glory.

Forgive their sins and errors, who have deserved thy just permission, thus to let in the wild Boar, and subtle Foxes, to waste and deform thy Vineyard, which thy right hand hath planted, and the dew of Heaven so long watered to a happy and flourishing estate.[1]

O let me not bear the infamous brand to all Posterity of being the first Christian KING *in this Kingdom, who should consent to the oppression of thy Church, and the Fathers of it; whose errors I would rather, with* Constantine, *cover with silence, and reform with meekness,*[2] *than expose their persons, and sacred Functions, to vulgar contempt.*

Thou, O Lord, seest how much I have suffered with, and for thy Church; make no long tarrying O my God, to deliver both me, and it, from unreasonable men; whose counsels have brought forth, and continue such violent confusions, by a precipitant destroying the ancient boundaries of thy Church's peace; thereby letting in all manner of errors, schisms, and disorders.

O thou God, of order, and of truth, in thy good time, abate the malice, assuage the rage, and confound all the mischievous devices of thine, mine, and thy Church's enemies.

That I, and all that love thy Church, may sing praises to thee, and ever magnify thy salvation, even before the sons of men.

18. *Upon* Uxbridge-*Treaty, and other Offers made by the* KING.[3]

I look upon the way of Treaties, as a retiring from fighting like

---

1 Psalm 80:13-15; *dew of heaven* A common Old Testament phrase, esp. in Genesis and Daniel.

2 In 325 CE, the Emperor Constantine called the Council of Nicaea to deal with heresy in the Church, particularly that of Arius and his followers. Constantine eventually allowed the re-admission of Arius into the Church (335 CE).

3 In January 1645, the Uxbridge peace negotiations began between agents of the King, Parliament and the Scots. Charles was asked to sign the Solemn League and Covenant and to pass legislation to reform religion in accordance with the Covenant; to prosecute Catholics; to punish named Royalists by death, sequestration of property, or exclusion from

Beasts, to arguing like Men; whose strength should be more in their understandings, than in their limbs.

And though I could seldom get opportunities to Treat,[1] yet I never wanted either desire or disposition to it; having greater confidence of My Reason, than My Sword: I was so wholly resolved to yield to the first, that I thought neither My self, nor others, should need to use the second, if once we rightly understood each other.

Nor did I ever think it a diminution of Me, to prevent them with Expresses of My desires, and even importunities to Treat: It being an office, not only of humanity, rather to use Reason, than Force; but also of Christianity to *seek peace and ensue*[2] *it.*

As I am very unwillinglly compelled to defend My self with Arms, so I very willingly embraced any thing tending to Peace.

The events of all War by the Sword being very dubious, and of a Civil War uncomfortable; the end hardly recompencing, and late repairing the mischief of the means.

Nor did any success I had ever enhance with Me the price of Peace, as earnestly desired by Me as any man; though I was like to pay dearer for it than any man: All that I sought to reserve was, Mine Honour, and My Conscience; the one I could not part with as a KING, the other as a Christian.

The Treaty at *Uxbridge* gave the fairst hopes of an happy composure; had others applied themselves to it with the same moderation, as I did, I am confident the War had then ended.

I was willing to condescend, as far as Reason, Honour, and Conscience, would give Me leave; nor were the remaining differences so essential to My People's happiness; or of such consequence; as in the least kind to have hindered My Subjects' either security, or prosperity; for they better enjoyed both, many years, before ever those demands were made, some of which, to

---

public office; to grant Parliament control of the military; and to allow Parliament to oversee the education of his children. Charles refused to make these concessions and his counter-proposals (that the military be restored to him; that laws derogatory to him be recalled; that persons exercising "illegal power" over his subjects be discharged; that a Bill be passed to preserve the Book of Common Prayer; that all persons be tried according to the law of the land) were rejected. Negotiations ended on 2 February 1645.

1 Carry on negotiations.

2 *ensue* Pursue; *seek ... ensue it* Psalm 34:14.

deny, I think the greatest Justice to My self, and favour to My Subjects.

I see, Jealousies are not so easily allayed, as they are raised: Some men are more afraid to retreat from violent Engagements, than to Engage: what is wanting in equity, must be made up in pertinacy. Such as had little to enjoy in peace, or to lose in war, studied to render the very name of *Peace* odious and suspected.

In Church affairs, where I had least liberty of prudence, having so many strict ties of Conscience upon Me; yet I was willing to condescend so far to the settling of them, as might have given fair satisfaction to all men, whom faction, covetousness, or superstition had not engaged more, than any true zeal, charity, or love of Reformation.

I was content to yield to all that might seem to advance true piety; I only sought to continue what was necessary in point of Order, Maintenance, and Authority to the Church's Government; and what I am persuaded (as I have elsewhere set down My thoughts more fully) is most agreeable to the true Principles of all Government, raised to its full stature and perfection, as also to the primitive Apostolical pattern, and the practice of the Universal Church conform thereto.

From which wholly to recede, without any probable reason urged or answered, only to satisfy some men's wills and fantasies (which yet agree not among themselves in any point, but that of extirpating Episcopacy, and fighting against Me) must needs argue such a softness, and infirmity of mind in Me, as will rather part with God's Truth, than Man's Peace, and rather lose the Church's honour, than cross some men's Factious humours.

God knows, and time will discover, who were most to blame for the un-succesfulness of that Treaty, and who must bear the guilt of after-calamities. I believe, I am very excusable both before God, and all unpassionate men, who have seriously weighed those transactions, wherein I endeavoured no less the restoration of Peace to My people, than the preservation of my own Crowns to my Posterity.

Some men have that height, as to interpret all fair Condescendings, as Arguments of feebleness, and glory most in an unflexible stiffness, when they see others most supple and inclinable to them.

A grand Maxim with them was always to ask something, which in reason and honour must be denied, that they might have some colour to refuse all that was in other things granted; setting Peace at as high a rate, as the worst effects of War; endeavouring first to make Me destroy My self by dishonourable Concessions, that so they might have the less to do.

This was all which that Treaty, or any other produced, to let the world see, how little I would deny, or they grant, in order to the Public peace. That it gave occasion to some men's further restiveness,[1] is imputable to their own depraved tempers, not to any Concessions or Negations of Mine: I have always the content of what I offered, and they the regret, and blame, for what they refused.

The highest tide of success set me not above a Treaty, nor the lowest ebb below a Fight: Though I never thought it any sign of true valour, to be prodigal of men's lives, rather than to be drawn to produce our own reasons, or subscribe to other men's.

That which made Me for the most part presage the unsuccesfulness of any Treaty, was, some men's unwillingness to Treat: which implied some things were to be gained by the Sword, whose unreasonableness they were loath to have fairly scanned, being more proper to be acted by Soldiers, than by Counsellors.

I pray God forgive them that were guilty of that Treaty's breaking; and give them grace to make their advantages gotten by the Sword a better opportunity to use such moderation, as was then wanting; that so though Peace were for our sins justly deferred, yet at last it may be happily obtained; what we could not get by our Treaties, we may gain by our Prayers.[2]

O Thou, that art the God of Reason, and of Peace, who disdainest not to Treat with Sinners, preventing them with offers of atonement, and beseeching them to be reconciled with thy self: who wantest not power, or justice, to destroy them; yet aboundest in mercy to save: soften our hearts by the blood of our Redeemer, and persuade us to accept of Peace with thy self, and both to procure and preserve peace among our selves, as Men and Christians, How oft have I entreated for Peace, but when I speak thereof, they make them ready to War.[3]

Condemn us not to our passions, which are destructive, both of our selves, and of others.

Clear up our understandings, to see thy Truth, both in Reason, as

---

1 Obstinancy in opinion or course of action.
2 An English translation of the Latin tag at the conclusion of the volume.
3 Psalm 120:7.

Men; and in Religion, as Christians: and incline all our hearts to hold the unity of the Spirit, in the bond of Peace.[1]

Take from us that enmity which is now in our hearts against thee: and give us that charity which should be among our selves.

Remove the evils of War we have deserved, and bestow upon us that Peace, which only Christ our great Peace-maker can merit.

19. Upon the various events of the War; Victories, and Defeats.

The various Successes of this unhappy war, have at least, afforded Me variety of good Meditations: sometimes God was pleased to try Me with Victory, by worsting My Enemies, that I might know how with moderation and thanks to own, and use his power, who is only the true *Lord of Hosts*; able when he pleases to repress the confidence of those, that fought against Me, with so great advantages for power and number.

From small beginnings on My part he let Me see, that I was not wholly forsaken by My people's love, or his protection.

Other times God was pleased to exercise My patience, and teach Me not to trust in the arm of Flesh, but in the living God.[2]

My sins sometimes prevailed against the justice of My Cause: and those that were with Me wanted not matter and occasion for his just chastisement both of them, and Me: Nor were My enemies less punished by that prosperity, which hardened them to continue that injustice by open hostility, which was began by most riotous and unparliamentary Tumults.

There is no doubt but personal and private sins may oft-times over-balance the Justice of Public engagements; nor doth God account every gallant Man (in the world's esteem) a fit instrument to assert in the way of War a righteous Cause; The more men are prone to arrogate to their own skill, valour and strength, the less doth God ordinarily work by them for his own glory.

I am sure the event or success can never state the Justice of any Cause, nor the peace of men's Consciences, nor the eternal fate of their Souls.

Those with Me had (I think) clearly and undoubtedly, for their Justification the Word of God, and the Laws of the Land, together with their own Oaths; all requiring obedience to My just Commands; but to none other under Heaven without Me, or against Me, in the point of raising Arms.

---

1 Ephesians 4:3.
2 1 Timothy 4:10.

Those on the other side are forced to fly to the shifts of some pretended Fears, and wild fundamentals of State (as they call them) which actually overthrow the present fabric, both of Church and State; being such imaginary Reasons for self-defence as are most impertinent for those men to allege, who being My Subjects, were manifestly the first assaulters of Me and the Laws: first by unsuppressing the Tumults, after by listed Forces: The same Allegations they use, will fit any Faction that hath but power and confidence enough to second with the Sword, all their demands against the present Laws and Governors; which can never be such as some side or other will not find fault with, so as to urge what they call a Reformation of them to a Rebellion against them, some parasitic Preachers have dared to call those Martyrs, who died fighting against Me, the Laws, their Oaths, and the Religion Established.

But sober Christians know, That glorious Title, can with Truth be applied only to those, who sincerely preferred God's Truth, and their duty in all these particulars before their lives, and all that was dear to them in this world; who having no advantageous designs by any Innovation, were religiously sensible of those ties to God, the Church, and My self, which lay upon their Souls, both for obedience and just assistance.

God could, and I doubt not but he did through his mercy, crown many of them with eternal life, whose lives were lost in so just a Cause; The destruction of their bodies being sanctified, as a means to save their Souls.

Their wounds, and temporal ruin serving as a gracious opportunity for their eternal health and happiness; while the evident approach of death did, through God's grace, effectually dispose their hearts to such Humility, Faith, and Repentance, which together with the Rectitude of their present engagement, would fully prepare them for a better life than that, which their enemy's brutish and disloyal fierceness could deprive them of; or without Repentance hope to enjoy.

They have often indeed, had the better against My side in the Field, but never, I believe, at the bar of God's Tribunal, or their own Consciences; where they are more afraid to encounter those many pregnant Reasons, both from Law, Allegiance, and all true Christian grounds, which conflict *with*, and accuse them *in* their own thoughts, than they oft were in a desperate bravery to fight against those Forces, which sometimes God gave Me.

Whose condition conquered, and dying, I make no question,

but is infinitely more to be chosen by a sober man, (that duly values his duty, his soul, and eternity, beyond the enjoyments of this present life) than the most triumphant glory, wherein their and Mine Enemies supervive;[1] who can hardly avoid to be daily tormented by that horrid guilt, wherewith their suspicious, or now convicted Consciences do pursue them, especially since they and all the world have seen, how false and un-intended those pretensions were, which they first set forth, as the only plausible (though not justifiable) grounds of raising a War, and continuing it thus long against Me, and the Laws established; in whose safety and preservation all honest men think the welfare of their Country doth consist.

For, and with all which, it is far more honourable and comfortable to suffer, than to prosper in their ruin and subversion.

I have often prayed, that all on My side might join true piety with the sense of their Loyalty; and be as faithful to God and their own souls, as they were to Me. That the defects of the one might not blast the endeavours of the other.

Yet I cannot think, that any shows, or truth of piety on the other side were sufficient to dispense with, or expiate the defects of their Duty and Loyalty to Me, which have so pregnant convictions on men's Consciences, that even profaner men are moved by the sense of them to venture their lives for Me.

I never had any victory which was without My sorrow, because it was on Mine own Subjects, who, like *Absalom*, died many of them in their sin:[2] And yet I never suffered any Defeat, which made Me despair of God's mercy and defence.

I never desired such Victories, as might serve to conquer, but only restore the Laws and Liberties of My people; which I saw were extremely oppressed, together with My Rights by those men, who were impatient of any just restraint.

When Providence gave Me, or denied Me Victory, My desire was neither to boast of My power, nor to charge God foolishly; who I believed at last would make all things to work together for My good.

I wished no greater advantages by the War, than to bring My Enemies to moderation, and My Friends to peace.

---

1 Survive, outlive.
2 The third son of King David, Absalom led a rebellion against his father; when his head was caught in the boughs of an oak tree during battle, he was killed by Joab, one of David's soldiers (2 Samuel 13-18).

I was afraid of the temptation of an absolute conquest, and never prayed more for victory over others, than over My self. When the first was denied, the second was granted Me, which God saw best for Me.

The different events were but the methods of divine justice, by contrary winds to winnow us: That, by punishing our sins, he might purge them from us; and by deferring peace, he might prepare us more to prize, and better to use so great a blessing.

My often Messages for Peace showed, that I delighted not in War: as My former Concessions sufficiently testified, how willingly I would have prevented it; and My total unpreparedness for it, how little I intended it.

The conscience of My Innocency forbade Me to fear a War; but the love of My Kingdoms commanded Me (if possible) to avoid it.

I am guilty in this War of nothing, but this, That I gave such advantages to some men, by confirming their power, which they knew not to use with that modesty, and gratitude, which became their Loyalty and My confidence.

Had I yielded less, I had been opposed less; had I denied more, I had been more obeyed.

'Tis now too late to review the occasions of the War; I wish only a happy conclusion, of so unhappy beginnings: The inevitable fate of our sins was (no doubt) such, as would no longer suffer the divine justice to be quiet: we having conquered his patience, are condemned by mutual conquerings, to destroy one another: for, the most prosperous successes on either side, impair the welfare of the whole.

Those Victories are still miserable, that leave our sins un-subdued; flushing our pride, and animating to continue injuries.

Peace it self is not desirable, till repentance have prepared us for it.

When we fight more against our selves, and less against God, we shall cease fighting against one another; I pray God these may all meet in our hearts, and so dispose us to an happy conclusion of these Civil Wars; that I may know better to obey God, and govern My People, and they may learn better to obey both God and Me.

Nor do I desire any man should be further subject to Me, than all of us may be subject to God.

O my God, make me content to be overcome, when thou wilt have it so.

Teach me the noblest victory over my self, and my Enemies by patience; which was Christ's conquest, and may well become a Christian King.

Between both thy hands, the right sometimes supporting, and the left afflicting; fashion us to that frame of piety thou likest best.[1]

Forgive the pride that attends our prosperous, and the repinings, which follow our disastrous events; when going forth in our own strength thou withdrawest thine, and goest not forth with our Armies.

Be thou all, when we are something, and when we are nothing; that thou mayst have the glory, when we are in a victorious, or inglorious condition.

Thou O Lord knowest, how hard it is for me to suffer so much evil from my Subjects, to whom I intend nothing but good; and I cannot but suffer in those evils which they compel me to inflict upon them; punishing my self in their punishments.

Since therefore both in conquering, and being conquered, I am still a Sufferer; I beseech thee to give me a double portion of thy Spirit, and that measure of grace, which only can be sufficient for me.[2]

As I am most afflicted, so make me most reformed: that I may be not only happy to see an end of these civil distractions, but a chief Instrument to restore and establish a firm, and blessed Peace to my Kingdoms.

Stir up all Parties' pious ambitions to overcome each other with reason, moderation, and such self-denial, as becomes those, who consider, that our mutual divisions are our common distractions, and the Union of all is every good man's chiefest interest.

If O Lord, as for the sins of our peace, thou hast brought upon us the miseries of war; so for the sins of war thou shouldst see fit still to deny us the blessing of peace, and so to keep us in a circulation of miseries; yet give me thy Servant, and all Loyal, though afflicted Subjects, to enjoy that peace which the world can neither give to us, nor take from us.

Impute not to me the blood of my Subjects, which with infinite unwillingness and grief, hath been shed by me, in my just and necessary defence; but wash me with that precious blood, which hath been shed for me, by my great Peacemaker, Jesus Christ. Who will, I trust, redeem me shortly out of all my troubles: for, I know the triumphing of the Wicked is but short, and the joy of Hypocrites is but for a moment.[3]

---

1 Job 10:8 and Psalm 119:73.
2 *double portion ... Spirit* 2 Kings 2:9; *grace ... for me* 2 Corinthians 12:9.
3 *redeem me ... my troubles* Psalm 25:22; *the triumphing ... moment* Job 20:5.

20. *Upon the Reformations of the Times.*

No Glory is more to be envied than that, of due Reforming either Church or State, when deformities are such, that the perturbation and novelty are not like to exceed the benefit of Reforming.

Although God should not honour Me so far, as to make Me an Instrument of so good a work,[1] yet I should be glad to see it done.

As I was well pleased with this Parliament's first intentions to reform what the Indulgence of Times, and corruption of manners might have depraved; so I am sorry to see after the freedom of Parliament was by factious Tumults oppressed, how little regard was had to the good Laws established, and the Religion settled; which ought to be the first rule and standard of reforming: with how much partiality, and popular compliance the passions, and opinions of men have been gratified, to the detriment of the Public, and the infinite scandal of the Reformed Religion.

What dissolutions of all Order, and Government, in the Church; what novelties of Schisms, and corrupt opinions; what undecencies and confusions in sacred administrations; what sacrilegious invasions upon the Rights and Revenues of the Church; what contempt and oppressions of the Clergy; what injurious diminutions and persecutings of Me, have followed, (as showers do warm gleams) the talk of Reformation, all sober men are Witnesses, and with My self, sad Spectators hitherto.

The great miscarriage I think is, that popular clamours and fury, have been allowed the reputation of Zeal, and the public sense; so that the study to please some Parties hath indeed injured all.

Freedom, moderation, and impartiality are sure the best tempers of reforming Counsels, and endeavours: what is acted by Factions, cannot but offend more, than it pleaseth.

I have offered to put all differences in Church affairs and Religion to the free consultation of a Synod or Convocation rightly chosen; the results of whose Counsels as they would have included the Votes of all, so it's like they would have given most satisfaction to all.

The Assembly of Divines, whom the two Houses have applied (in an unwonted way) to advise of Church Affairs, I dislike not further, than that they are not legally convened and chosen; nor

---

1 An allusion to St. Francis of Assisi's prayer: "Make me an instrument of thy peace."

Act in the name of all the Clergy of *England*; nor with freedom and impartiality can do any thing, being limited and confined, if not over-awed, to do and declare what they do.

For I cannot think so many men cried up for learning and piety, who formerly allowed the Liturgy and Government of the Church of *England*, as to the main, would have so suddenly agreed quite to abolish both of them, (the last of which, they knew to be of Apostolical institution, at least; as of Primitive and Universal practice) if they had been left to the liberty of their own suffrages, and if the influence of contrary Factions had not by secret encroachments of hopes, and fears, prevailed upon them, to comply with so great and dangerous Innovations in the Church; without any regard to their own former judgement and practice, or to the common interest and honour of all the Clergy, and in them of Order, Learning, and Religion against examples of all Ancient Churches; the Laws in force, and My consent; which is never to be gained, against so pregnant light, as in that point shines on My understanding.

For I conceive, that where the Scripture is not so clear and punctual in precepts, there the constant and Universal practice of the Church, in things not contrary to Reason, Faith, good Manners, or any positive Command, is the best Rule that Christians can follow.

I was willing to grant, or restore to Presbytery, what with Reason or Discretion it can pretend to, in a conjuncture with Episcopacy; but for that wholly to invade the Power, and by the Sword to arrogate, and quite abrogate the Authority of that Ancient Order, I think neither just, as to Episcopacy, nor safe for Presbytery; nor yet any way convenient for this Church or State.

A due reformation had easily followed moderate Counsels; and such (I believe) as would have given more content, even to the most of those Divines, who have been led on with much Gravity and Formality, to carry on other men's designs: which no doubt many of them by this time discover, though they dare not but smother their frustrations, and discontents.

The specious and popular titles, of Christ's Government, Throne, Scepter, and Kingdom (which certainly is not divided, nor hath two faces, as their parties now have, at least) also the noise of a thorough Reformation, these may as easily be fined[1]

---

1 Refined.

on new models, as fair colours may be put to ill-favoured figures.

The breaking of Church-windows, which Time had sufficiently defaced; pulling down of Crosses, which were but civil, not Religious marks; defacing of the Monuments, and Inscriptions of the Dead, which served but to put Posterity in mind, to thank God, for that clearer light, wherein they live; The leaving of all Ministers to their liberties, and private abilities, in the Public service of God, where no Christian can tell to what he may say *Amen*; nor what adventure he may make, of seeming, at least, to consent to the Errors, Blasphemies, and ridiculous Undecencies, which bold and ignorant men list to vent in their Prayers, Preaching, and other Offices. The setting forth also of old Catechisms, and Confessions of Faith new dressed, importing as much, as if there had been no sound or clear Doctrine of Faith in this Church, before some four or five years' consultation had matured their thoughts, touching their first Principles of Religion.

All these, and the like are the effects of popular, specious, and deceitful Reformations, (that they might not seem to have nothing to do) and may give some short flashes of content to the vulgar, (who are taken with novelties, as children with babies,[1] very much, but not very long) But all this amounts not to, nor can in Justice merit the glory of the Church's thorough Reformation; since they leave all things more deformed, disorderly, and discontented, than when they began, in point of Piety, Morality, Charity, and good Order.

Nor can they easily recompense or remedy the inconveniences and mischiefs, which they have purchased so dearly, and which have, and ever will necessarily ensue, till due remedies be applied.

I wish they would at last, make it their Unanimous work, to do God's work, and not their own: Had Religion been first considered (as it merited) much trouble might have been prevented.

But some men thought, that the Government of this Church and State, fixed by so many Laws, and long Customs, would not run into their new moulds, till they had first melted it in the fire of a Civil War; by the advantages of which they resolved, if they prevailed, to make My self and all My Subjects fall down, and worship the Images they should form and set up: If there had been as much of Christ's Spirit, for meekness, wisdom, and char-

---

1 Dolls.

ity, in men's hearts, as there was of his name used in the pretensions, to reform all to Christ's Rule, it would certainly have obtained more of God's blessing, and produced more of Christ's Glory, the Church's good, the Honour of Religion, and the Unity of Christians.

Public Reformers had need first Act in private, and practice that on their own hearts, which they purpose to try on others; for Deformities within, will soon betray the Pretenders of public Reformations, to such private designs as must needs hinder the public good.

I am sure the right Methods of Reforming the Church cannot consist with that of perturbing the Civil State, nor can Religion be justly advanced by depressing Loyalty, which is one of the chiefest Ingredients, and Ornaments of true Religion, for next to *fear God*, is, *Honour the King*.[1]

I doubt not but Christ's Kingdom may be set up without pulling down Mine; nor will any men in impartial times appear good Christians, that approve not themselves good Subjects.

Christ's Government will confirm Mine, not overthrow it, since as I own Mine from Him, so I desire to rule for his Glory, and his Church's good.

Had some men truly intended Christ's Government, or knew what it meant, in their hearts, they could never have been so ill governed in their words, and actions, both against Me, and one another.

As good ends cannot justify evil means, so nor will evil beginnings ever bring forth good conclusions; unless God, by a miracle of Mercy, create Light out of Darkness, order out of our confusions, and peace out of our passions.

Thou, O Lord, who only canst give us beauty for ashes,[2] and Truth for Hypocrisy; suffer us not to be miserably deluded with Pharisaical washings, instead of Christian reformings.

Our greatest deformities are within, make us the severest Censurers, and first Reformers of our own souls.

That we may in clearness of judgement, and uprightness of heart be means to reform what is indeed amiss in Church and State.

Create in us clean hearts, O Lord, and renew right spirits within

---

1   1 Peter 2:17.
2   Isaiah 61:3.

us;[1] *that we may do all by thy directions, to thy glory, and with thy blessing.*

Pity the deformities, which some rash and cruel Reformers have brought upon this Church and State; Quench the fires which Factions have kindled, under the pretence of Reforming.

As thou hast showed the world by their divisions, and confusions, what is the pravity[2] *of some men's intentions, and weakness of their judgements; so bring us at last more refined out of these fires,*[3] *by the methods of Christian and charitable Reformations; wherein nothing of ambition, revenge, covetousness, or sacrilege, may have any influence upon their counsels, whom thy providence in just and lawful ways shall entrust with so great, good, and now most necessary work. That I and my People may be so blest with inward piety, as may best teach us how to use the blessing of outward peace.*

21. *Upon His Majesty's Letters taken and divulged.*[4]

The taking of My Letters was an opportunity, which, as the malice of Mine enemies could hardly have expected; so they know not how with honour and civility to use it: Nor do I think with sober and worthy minds any thing in them, could tend so much to My reproach, as the odious divulging of them did to the infamy of the Divulgers: The greatest experiments of virtue and Nobleness being discovered in the greatest advantages against an enemy, and the greatest obligations being those, which are put upon us by them, from whom we could least have expected them.

And such I should have esteemed the concealing of My Papers; The freedom and secrecy of which, commands a civility from all men, not wholly barbarous; nor is there any thing more inhuman than to expose them to public view.

Yet since providence will have it so, I am content so much of My heart (which I study to approve to God's omniscience) should be discovered to the world, without any of those dresses, or popular captations,[5] which some men use in their Speeches,

---

1 Psalm 51:10.
2 Depravity.
3 Malachi 3:3; Zechariah 13:9.
4 The king's baggage train was overrun at the Battle of Naseby in June 1645. The captured correspondence revealed Charles I's attempts to garner support from continental sources, as well as his negotiations with the Irish. The letters were published shortly thereafter by order of Parliament as the *King's Cabinet Opened.*
5 Artful, rhetorical elements.

and Expresses; I wish My Subjects had yet a clearer sight into My most retired thoughts:

Where they might discover, how they are divided between the love and care I have, not more to preserve My own Rights, than to procure their peace and happiness, and that extreme grief to see them both deceived and destroyed.

Nor can any men's malice be gratified further by My Letters, than to see My constancy to My Wife, the Laws, and Religion. Bees will gather Honey where the Spider sucks Poison.

That I endeavour to avoid the pressures of my Enemies, by all fair and just correspondencies;[1] no man can blame, who loves me, or the Common-wealth, since my Subjects can hardly be happy if I be miserable, or enjoy their peace and liberties while I am oppressed.

The world may see how soon[2] men's design, like *Absalom's*, is by enormous actions to widen differences, and exasperate all sides to such distances, as may make all reconciliation desperate.

Yet I thank God I can not only with patience bear this, as other indignities, but with Charity forgive them.

The integrity of My intentions is not jealous of any injury, My expressions can do them, for although the confidence of privacy may admit greater freedom in writing such Letters, which may be liable to envious exceptions; yet the Innocency of My chief purposes cannot be so obtained, or mis-interpreted by them, as not to let all men see, that I wish nothing more than an happy composure of differences with Justice and Honour, not more to My own, than My people's content, who have any sparks of Love or Loyalty left in them: who, by those My Letters may be convinced, that I can both mind and act My own, and My Kingdoms' Affairs, so as becomes a Prince; which Mine Enemies have always been very loath should be believed of me, as if I were wholly confined to the Dictates and Directions of others; whom they please to brand with the names of Evil Counsellors.

It's probable some men will now look upon me as my own Counsellor, and having none else to quarrel with under that notion, they will hereafter confine their anger to my self: Although I know they are very unwilling I should enjoy the liberty of my own Thoughts, or follow the light of my own Conscience, which

---

1 Correspondence; also, communications.
2 "Soon" is replaced with "some" in several later editions (e.g., 32nd and 36th editions).

they labour to bring into an absolute captivity to themselves; not allowing me to think their Counsels to be other than good for me, which have so long maintained a War against Me.

The Victory they obtained that day, when my Letters became their prize, had been enough to have satiated the most ambitious thirst of popular glory among the Vulgar; with whom prosperity gains the greatest esteem and applause; as adversity exposeth to their greatest slighting and dis-respect: As if good fortune were always the shadow of Virtue and Justice, and did not oftener attend vicious and injurious actions, as to this world.

But I see no secular advantages seem sufficient to that cause, which began with Tumults, and depends chiefly upon the reputation with the vulgar.

They think no Victories so effectual to their designs as those, that most rout and waste my Credit with my People; in whose hearts they seek by all means to smother and extinguish all sparks of Love, Respect, and Loyalty to Me, that they may never kindle again, so as to recover Mine, the Laws', and the Kingdoms' Liberties, which some men seek to overthrow: The taking away of my Credit is but a necessary preparation to the taking away of my Life, and my Kingdoms; First I must seem neither fit to Live, nor worthy to Reign; By exquisite methods of cunning and cruelty, I must be compelled, first to follow the Funerals of my Honour, and then be destroyed: But I know God's un-erring and impartial Justice can, and will overrule the most perverse wills and designs of men; He is able, and (I hope) will turn even the worst of mine Enemies' thoughts and actions to my good.

Nor do I think, that by the surprise of my Letters, I have lost any more than so many papers: How much they have lost of that reputation, for Civility and Humanity (which ought to be paid to all men, and most becomes such as pretend to Religion) besides that of respect and Honour, which they owe to their KING, present, and after-times will judge. And I cannot think that their own consciences are so stupid, as not to inflict upon them some secret impressions of that shame and dishonour, which attends all unworthy actions, have they never so much of public flattery, and popular countenance.

I am sure they can never expect the divine approbation of such indecent actions, if they do but remember how God blessed the modest respect and filial tenderness, which *Noah's* Sons bare to their Father; nor did his open infirmity justify *Cham's* impudency, or exempt him from the curse of being

Servant of Servants;[1] which curse must needs be on them who seek by dishonourable actions to please the Vulgar, and confirm by ignoble acts, their dependence upon the People.

Nor can their malicious intentions be ever either excusable, or prosperous; who thought by this means to expose Me, to the highest reproach and contempt of My People; forgetting that duty of modest concealment, which they owed to the Father of their Country, in case they had discovered any real uncomeliness; which, I thank God they did not; who can, and I believe hath made Me more respected in the hearts of many (as he did *David*) to whom they thought, by publishing My private Letters, to have rendered Me as a Vile Person, not fit to be trusted or considered, under any Notion of Majesty.

But thou, O Lord, whose wise and all-disposing providence, ordereth the greatest contingencies of human affairs; make me to see the constancy of thy mercies to me, in the greatest advantages thou seemest to give the malice of my Enemies against me.

As thou didst blast the counsel of Achitophel, *turning it to* David's *good, and his own ruin:*[2] *so canst thou defeat their design, who intended by publishing my private Letters, nothing else, but to render me more odious and contemptible to My People.*

I must first appeal to thy Omniscience; who canst witness with my integrity, how unjust and false those scandalous misconstructions are, which my enemies endeavour by those Papers of mine to represent to the world.

Make the evil they imagined, and displeasure they intended thereby against me, so to return on their own heads, that they may be ashamed, and covered with their own confusion, as with a Cloak.[3]

Thou seest how mine Enemies use all means to cloud mine Honour, to pervert my purposes, and to slander the footsteps of thine Anointed.[4]

---

1 Ham (Cham), son of Noah, insolently looked upon his drunk and naked father; his son, Canaan, was therefore cursed; Shem and Japheth, in contrast, respectfully covered Noah with a garment, without looking upon his nakedness, and received his blessing (Genesis 9:21-27).

2 Ahithophel (Achitophel), King David's counsellor, was Absalom's co-conspirator. David's prayer that Ahithophel's good counsel be regarded as foolish was fulfilled, and the rejection of Ahithophel's military advice led to Absalom's death and Ahithophel's suicide (2 Samuel 15:12-17:23).

3 *Return ... heads* Ezekiel 11:21; *that they ... Cloak* Psalm 109:29.

4 *Slander ... Anointed* Psalm 89:51.

But give me an heart content to be dishonoured for thy sake, and thy Church's good.

Fix in me a purpose to honour thee, and then I know thou wilt honour me, either by restoring to me the enjoyment of that Power and Majesty, which thou hast suffered some men to seek to deprive me of; or by bestowing on me that crown of Christian patience, which knows how to serve thee in honour, or dishonour, in good report or evil.

Thou, O Lord, art the fountain of goodness, and honour; thou art clothed with excellent Majesty;[1] *make me to partake of thy excellency for wisdom, justice, and mercy, and I shall not want that degree of Honour, and Majesty, which becomes the Place in which thou hast set Me; who art the lifter up of My head,*[2] *and My salvation.*

Lord, by thy Grace, lead Me to thy Glory, which is both true and eternal.

22. *Upon His Majesty's leaving* Oxford, *and going to the* Scots.[3]
Although God hath given Me three Kingdoms, yet in these He hath not now left Me any place, where I may with Safety and Honour rest my Head:[4] Showing me that himself is the safest Refuge, and the strongest Tower of defence,[5] in which I may put my Trust.

In these extremities, I look not to man so much as to God, He will have it thus; that I may wholly cast my self, and my now distressed affairs upon his mercy, who hath both hearts and hands of all men in his dispose.[6]

What Providence denies to Force, it may grant to Prudence: Necessity is now my Counsellor, and commands me to study my safety by a disguised withdrawing from my chiefest strength, and adventuring upon their Loyalty, who first began my Troubles. Happily God may make them a means honourably to compose them.

This my confidence of Them, may disarm and overcome them;

---

1 *thou art ... Majesty* Psalm 104:1.
2 *lifter ... my head* Psalm 3:3.
3 Charles surrendered to the Scottish army at Southwell, near Newark, in May 1646. The Scots demanded the King sign the Covenant and proclaim a Presbyterian settlement for the church.
4 In Matthew 8:20, Jesus says: "... but the son of man hath not where to lay his head" (see also Luke 9:58).
5 2 Samuel 22:3.
6 Control.

my rendering my Person to Them, may engage their affections to me, who have oft professed, *They fought not against Me, but for Me.*

I must now resolve the riddle of their Loyalty: and give them opportunity to let the world see, they mean not what they do, but what they say.

Yet must God be My chiefest Guard; and My Conscience both My Counsellor and My Comforter: Though I put My Body into their hands, yet I shall reserve My Soul to God, and My self; nor shall any necessities compel Me, to desert Mine Honour, or swerve from My Judgement.

What they sought to take by force, shall now be given them in such a way of unusual confidence of them, as may make them ashamed not to be really such, as they ought, and professed to be.

God sees it not enough to desert Me of all Military power to defend My self; but to put Me upon using their power, who seem to fight against Me, yet ought in duty to defend Me.

So various are all human affairs, and so necessitous may the state of Princes be, that their greatest danger may be in their supposed safety, and their safety in their supposed danger.

I must now leave those, that have Adhered to Me, and apply to those that have Opposed Me; this method of Peace may be more prosperous, than that of War, both to stop the effusion of blood, and to close those wounds already made: and in it I am no less solicitous for My Friends' safety, than Mine own; choosing to venture My self upon further hazards, rather than expose their resolute Loyalty to all extremities.

It is some skill in play to know when a game is lost; better fairly to go over, than to contest in vain.

I must now study to re-inforce My judgement, and fortify My mind with Reason and Religion; that I may not seem to offer up My Soul's liberty, or make My Conscience their Captive; who ought at first to have used Arguments, not Arms, to have persuaded My consent to their new demands.

I thank God no success, darkens or disguises Truth to me; and I shall no less conform my words to my inward dictates now, than if they had been, as the words of a KING ought to be among loyal Subjects, *full of power.*

Reason is the divinest power. I shall never think my self weakened while I may make full and free use of that. No eclipse of outward fortune shall rob me of that light; what God hath denied of outward strength, his grace, I hope, will supply with inward resolutions; not morosity to deny, what is fit to be granted; but not to grant any thing, which Reason and Religion bids me deny.

I shall never think my self less than my self while I am able thus to preserve the Integrity of my Conscience, the only Jewel now left me, which is worth keeping.

O thou Sovereign of our Souls, the only Commander of our Consciences; though I know not what to do, yet mine eyes are toward thee: To the protection of thy mercy I still commend my self.

As thou hast preserved me in the day of Battle, so thou canst still show me thy strength in my weakness.[1]

Be thou unto me in my darkest night, a pillar of fire, to enlighten and direct me; in the day of my hottest affliction, be also a pillar of cloud to overshadow and protect me; be to me, both a Sun and a Shield.[2]

Thou knowest, that it is not any perverseness of will, but just persuasions of Honour, Reason, and Religion, which have made me thus far to hazard my Person, Peace, and Safety, against those, that by force have sought to wrest them from Me.

Suffer not my just resolutions to abate with my outward Forces; let a good Conscience always accompany Me, in My solitude and desertions.

Suffer me not to betray the powers of Reason, and that fortress of My Soul, which I am entrusted to keep for thee.

Lead Me in the paths of thy righteousness,[3] *and show me thy salvation.*

Make my ways to please thee, and then thou wilt make Mine Enemies to be at peace with Me.[4]

23. *Upon the* Scots *delivering the* KING *to the* English; *and His Captivity at* Holmeby.[5]

Yet may I justify those *Scots* to all the world in this, that they have not deceived me; for I never trusted to them further, than to men:

---

1 *preserved ... Battle* Psalm 140:7; *thy strength ... weakness* 2 Corinthians 12:9.

2 *a pillar ... protect me* Wandering in the wilderness, the Israelites were protected by God who "went before them by day in a pillar of a cloud ... and by night in a pillar of fire ..." (Exodus 13:21); *Sun ... Shield* Psalm 84:11.

3 Psalm 23:3.

4 Proverbs 16:7.

5 In January 1647, the Scots handed Charles I over to Parliament in return for their army's arrears of pay. Soon after, he was moved to Holmeby (Holdenby House).

if I am sold by them, I am only sorry they should do it; and that my price should be so much above my Saviour's.[1]

These are but further Essays, which God will have me make of man's uncertainty, the more to fix me on himself; who never faileth them that trust in him; Though the Reeds of *Egypt* break under the hand of him that leans on them: yet the Rock of *Israel* will be an everlasting stay and defence.[2]

God's providence commands me to retire from all to himself, that in him I may enjoy my self, which I lose, while I let out my hopes to others.

The solitude and captivity, to which I am now reduced, gives me leisure enough to study the world's vanity, and inconstancy.

God sees 'tis fit to deprive me of Wife, Children, Army, Friends, and Freedom, that I may be wholly his, who alone is all.

I care not much to be reckoned among the Unfortunate, if I be not in the black List of irreligious, and sacrilegious Princes.

No Restraint shall ensnare my Soul in sin; nor gain that of me, which may make my Enemies more insolent, my Friends ashamed, or my Name accursed.

They have no great cause to triumph, that they have got my Person into their power; since my Soul is still my own: nor shall they ever gain my Consent against my Conscience.

What they call obstinacy, I know God accounts honest constancy, from which Reason and Religion, as well as Honour, forbid me to recede.

'Tis evident now, that it was not Evil Counsellors with me, but a good Conscience in me, which hath been fought against; nor did they ever intend to bring me to my Parliament, till they had brought my mind to their obedience.

Should I grant what some men desire, I should be such as they wish me; not more a King, and far less both Man and Christian.

What Tumults and Armies could not obtain, neither shall Restraint; which though it have as little of safety to a Prince, yet it hath not more of danger.

The fear of men shall never be my snare; nor shall the love of any liberty entangle my soul: Better others betray me, than my self: and that the price of my liberty should be my Conscience;

---

1 Judas betrayed Jesus for thirty pieces of silver (Matthew 26:14-16, 27:3-9). Royalist crowds berated the Scots' army with cries of "Judas" as they withdrew from Newcastle for Scotland.

2 *Though the Reeds ... on them* 2 Kings 18:21; *Rock of Israel* 2 Samuel 23:3.

the greatest injuries my Enemies seek to inflict upon me, cannot be without my own consent.

While I can deny with Reason, I shall defeat the greatest impressions[1] of their malice, who neither know how to use worthily, what I have already granted; nor what to require more of me but this, That I would seem willing to help them to destroy My self and Mine.

Although they should destroy me, yet they shall have no cause to despise me.

Neither liberty nor life are so dear to me, as the peace of my Conscience, the Honour of my Crowns, and the welfare of my People; which my Word may injure more than any War can do; while I gratify a few to oppress all.

The Laws will, by God's blessing, revive, with the love and Loyalty of my Subjects; if I bury them not by my Consent, and cover them in that grave of dishonour, and injustice, which some men's violence hath digged for them.

If my Captivity or death must be the price of their redemption, I grudge not to pay it.

No condition can make a King miserable, which carries not with it, his Soul's, his People's, and Posterity's thralldom.

After-times may see, what the blindness of this Age will not; and God may at length show my Subjects, that I choose rather to suffer for them, than with them; happily I might redeem my self to some show of liberty, if I would consent to enslave them: I had rather hazard the ruin of one King, than to confirm many Tyrants over them; from whom I pray God deliver them, whatever becomes of Me, whose solitude hath not left Me alone.

For thou, O God, infinitely good, and great, art with Me, whose presence is better than life;[2] and whose service is perfect freedom.

Own Me for thy Servant, and I shall never have cause to complain for want of that liberty, which becomes a Man, a Christian, and a King.

Bless Me still with Reason, as a Man; with Religion, as a Christian; and with Constancy in Justice, as a King.

Though thou sufferest Me to be stripped of all outward ornaments,[3]

---

1 Charges, attacks.
2 Psalm 63:3.
3 Accessories, trappings.

yet preserve Me ever in those enjoyments, wherein I may enjoy thy self; and which, cannot be taken from Me against my will.

Let no fire of affliction boil over My passion to any impatience, or sordid fears.

There be many say of Me, There is no help for Me: do thou lift up the light of thy Countenance, upon Me,[1] *and I shall neither want safety, liberty, nor Majesty.*

Give Me that measure of patience and Constancy, which my condition now requires.

My strength is scattered, My expectation from Men defeated, My Person restrained: O be not thou far from Me, lest My Enemies prevail too much against Me.[2]

I am become a wonder, and a scorn to many: O be thou my Helper and Defender.

Show some token upon me for good, that they that hate me may be ashamed, because thou Lord hast holpen and comforted me: establish me with thy free Spirit, that I may do, and suffer thy will, as thou wouldst have me.[3]

Be merciful to me, O Lord, for my Soul trusteth in thee: yea and in the shadow of thy wings will I make my refuge until these calamities be overpast.[4]

Arise to deliver me, make no long tarrying, O my God. Though thou killest me, yet will I trust in thy mercy, and my Saviour's merit.[5]

I know that my Redeemer liveth; though thou leadest me through the veil and shadow of death, yet shall I fear none ill.[6]

24. *Upon their denying His Majesty the Attendance of His Chaplains.*
When Providence was pleased to deprive Me of all other civil comforts and secular attendants, I thought the absence of them all might best be supplied by the attendance of some of My Chaplains; whom for their Function I reverence, and for their Fidelity I have cause to love. By their learning, piety, and prayers, I hoped to be either better enabled to sustain the want of all other enjoy-

---

1 *There be many ... for Me* Psalm 3:2; *do thou lift ... upon Me* Psalm 4:6.
2 Psalm 22:19.
3 *Show some ... comforted me* Psalm 86:17; *establish ... Spirit* Psalm 51:12; *that I ... have me* Echoes the words of Jesus on the Mount of Olives (Luke 22:42).
4 Psalm 57:1.
5 *make ... tarrying* Psalms 40:17, 70:5; *Though thou ... trust* Job 13:15.
6 *I know ... liveth* Job 19:25; *though thou ... none ill* Psalm 23:4.

ments, or better fitted for the recovery and use of them in God's good time: so reaping by their pious help a spiritual harvest of grace amidst the thorns, and after the ploughings of temporal crosses.

The truth is, I never needed or desired more the service and assistance of men judiciously pious, and soberly devout.

The solitude they have confined Me unto, adds the Wilderness to my temptations;[1] For the company they obtrude upon Me, is more sad than any solitude can be.

If I had asked My Revenues, My Power of the *Militia*, or any one of My Kingdoms, it had been no wonder to have been denied in those things, where the evil policy of men forbids all just restitution, lest they should confess an injurious usurpation: But to deny Me the Ghostly[2] comfort of My Chaplains seems a greater rigour and barbarity, than is ever used by Christians to the meanest Prisoners, and greatest Malefactors; whom though the Justice of the Law deprive of worldly comforts, yet the mercy of Religion allows them the benefit of their Clergy, as not aiming at once to destroy their Bodies, and to damn their Souls.

But My Agony must not be relieved with the presence of any one good Angel; for such I account a Learned, Godly, and discreet Divine: and such I would have all Mine to be.

They that envy My being a King, are loath I should be a Christian; while they seek to deprive Me of all things else, They are afraid I should save my Soul.

Other sense, Charity it self can hardly pick out of those many harsh Repulses I received, as to that Request so often made for the attendance of some of My Chaplains.

I have sometime thought the Unchristianness of those denials might arise from a displeasure some men had to see me prefer my own Divines before their Ministers: whom, though I respect for that worth and piety which may be in them; yet I cannot think them so proper for any present comforters or Physicians; Who have (some of them at least) had so great an influence in occasioning these calamities, and inflicting these wounds upon Me.

Nor are the soberest of them so apt for that devotional compliance, and juncture of hearts, which I desire to bear in those

---

1   *Wilderness ... temptations* The suffering of Charles is compared to that of Jesus, who was tempted by Satan in the wilderness (Matthew 4:1-13; Luke 4:1-13).

2   Pertaining to the soul.

holy Offices, to be performed with Me, and for Me; since their judgements standing at a distance from me, or in jealousy of me, or in opposition against me, their Spirits cannot so harmoniously accord with mine, or mine with theirs, either in Prayer, or other holy duties, as is meet, and most comfortable; whose golden Rule, and bond of Perfection consists in that of mutual Love and Charity.

Some remedies are worse than the disease, and some comforters more miserable than misery it self; when like *Job's* friends, they seek not to fortify one's mind with patience; but persuade a man by betraying his own Innocency, to despair of God's mercy;[1] and by Justifying their injuries, to strengthen the hands, and harden the hearts of Insolent Enemies.

I am so much a friend to all Church-men, that have any thing in them beseeming that sacred function, that I have hazarded my own Interests, chiefly upon Conscience and Constancy to maintain their Rights; whom the more I looked upon as Orphans, and under the sacrilegious eyes of many cruel and rapacious Reformers; so I thought it my duty the more to appear as a Father, and a Patron for them and the Church. Although I am very unhandsomely[2] requited by some of them; who may live to repent no less for My sufferings, than their own ungrateful errors, and that injurious contempt and meanness, which they have brought upon their Calling and Persons.

I pity all of them, I despise none: only I thought I might have leave to make choice of some for My special Attendants, who were best approved in My Judgement, and most suitable to My affection. For, I held it better to seem undevout, and to hear no men's prayers, than to be forced, or seem to comply with those petitions, to which the heart cannot consent, nor the tongue say *Amen*, without contradicting a man's own understanding, or belying his own soul.

In Devotions, I love neither profane boldness, nor pious nonsense, but such an humble and judicious gravity as shows the Speaker to be at once considerate both of God's Majesty, the Church's honour, and his own Vileness; both knowing what

---

1 Bereft of family, assets and health, Job was visited by three would-be-comforters, who soon insist that he deserves his misfortune; Job responds: "miserable comforters are ye all" (Job 16:2).
2 Unfittingly, discourteously.

things God allows him to ask, and in what manner it becomes a Sinner to supplicate the divine Mercy for himself, and others.

I am equally scandalized with all prayers, that sound either imperiously,[1] or rudely, and passionately; as either wanting humility to God, or charity to men, or respect to the duty.

I confess I am better pleased, as with studied and premeditated Sermons, so with such public Forms of Prayer, as are fitted to the Church's and every Christian's daily and common necessities; because I am by them better assured, what I may join My heart unto, than I can be of any man's extemporary sufficiency; which as I do not wholly exclude from public occasions, so I allow its just liberty and use in private and devout retirements; where neither the solemnity of the duty, nor the modest regard to others, do require so great exactness as to the outward manner of performance. Though the light of understanding, and the fervency of affection, I hold the main and most necessary requisites both in constant, and occasional, solitary, and social Devotions.

So that I must needs seem to all equal minds with as much Reason to prefer the service of My own Chaplains before that of their Ministers, as I do the Liturgy before their Directory.

In the one, I have been always educated and exercised;[2] In the other, I am not yet Catechized, nor acquainted: And if I were, yet should I not by that, as by any certain rule and Canon of devotion, be able to follow or find out the indirect extravagancies of most of those men, who highly cry up that as a piece of rare composure and use; which is already as much despised and disused by many of them, as the Common-prayer sometimes was by those men; a great part of whose piety hung upon that popular pin[3] of railing against, and contemning the Government, and Liturgy of this Church. But, I had rather be condemned to the woe of *Vae soli*, than to that of *Vae vobis Hypocritis*, by seeming to pray what I do not approve.[4]

It may be, I am esteemed by My Deniers sufficient of My self

---

1 Arrogantly.
2 Practised.
3 That on which something depends.
4 *Vae soli* "Woe to the one who is alone" (Ecclesiastes 4:10: "but woe to him that is alone when he falleth: for he hath not another to help him up"); *Vae vobis Hypocritis* "Woe to you, hypocrites" (Matthew 23:13ff: "But woe unto you, Scribes and Pharisees, hypocrites": see also Luke 11:44).

to discharge My duty to GOD as a Priest, though not to Men as a Prince.

Indeed, I think both Offices, Regal and Sacerdotal,[1] might well become the same Person; as anciently they were under one name, and the united rights of primogeniture: Nor could I follow better precedents, if I were able, than those two eminent Kings, *David*, and *Solomon*; not more famous for their Sceptres and Crowns, than one was for devout Psalms and Prayers; the other for his divine Parables and Preaching: whence the one merited and assumed the name of a Prophet, the other of a Preacher.[2] Titles indeed of greater honour where rightly placed, than any of those the Roman Emperors affected[3] from the Nations they subdued: it being infinitely more glorious to convert Souls to God's Church by the Word, than to conquer men to a subjection by the Sword.

Yet since the order of God's wisdom and providence hath, for the most part, always distinguished the gifts and offices of Kings, of Priests, of Princes and Preachers; both in the Jewish and Christian Churches: I am sorry to find My self reduced to the necessity of being both, or enjoying neither.

For such as seek to deprive Me of Kingly Power and Sovereignty; would no less enforce Me to live many Months without all Prayers, Sacraments, and Sermons, unless I become My own Chaplain.

As I owe the Clergy the protection of a Christian KING, so I desire to enjoy from them the benefit of their gifts and prayers which I look upon as more prevalent[4] than My own, or other men's; by how much they flow from minds more enlightened, and affections less distracted, than those, which are encumbered with secular affairs: besides, I think a greater blessing and acceptableness attends those duties, which are rightly performed, as proper to, and within the limits of that calling, to which God and the Church have specially designed and consecrated some men: And

---

1 Pertaining to the priesthood.

2 Applied to David, *propheta* customarily signifies his role as inspired poet and chief spokesman of God. Solomon, renowned for his wisdom, was credited with writing many works of a homiletic nature, including Proverbs and Ecclesiastes. The Song of Songs and other works on magic, medicine and natural philosophy have also been attributed to him.

3 Assumed.

4 Powerful, forceful.

however, as to that Spiritual Government, by which the devout Soul is subject to Christ, and through his merits daily offers it self and its services to GOD, every private believer is a King and Priest, invested with the honour of a Royal Priesthood;[1] yet as to Ecclesiastical order, and the outward polity of the Church, I think confusion in Religion will as certainly follow every man's turning Priest or Preacher, as it will in the State, where every one affects to rule as King.

I was always bred to more modest, and I think more pious Principles: the consciousness to My spiritual defects makes Me more prize and desire those pious assistances, which holy and good Ministers, either Bishops or Presbyters, may afford Me; especially in these extremities, to which God hath been pleased to suffer some of My Subjects to reduce Me; so as to leave them nothing more, but My life to take from Me: and to leave Me nothing to desire, which I thought might less provoke their jealousy and offence to deny Me, than this of having some means afforded Me for My Soul's comfort and support.

To which end I made choice of men, as no way (that I know) scandalous, so every way eminent for their learning and piety, no less than for their Loyalty: nor can I imagine any exceptions to be made against them, but only this, that they may seem too able and too well affected toward Me and My service.

But this is not the first service (as I count it the best) in which they have forced Me to serve My self; though I must confess I bear with more grief and impatience the want of My Chaplains, than of any other My Servants; and next (if not beyond in some things) to the being sequestered from my Wife and Children, since from these indeed more of human and temporary affections, but from those more of heavenly and eternal improvements may be expected.

My comfort is, that in the enforced (not neglected) want of ordinary means, God is wont to afford extraordinary supplies of his gifts and graces.

If his Spirit will teach Me and help My Infirmities in prayer, reading and meditation (as I hope he will) I shall need no other, either Orator or Instructor.[2]

---

1   1 Peter 2:9.
2   Advocate or teacher.

To Thee therefore, O My God, do I direct My now solitary prayers; what I want of others' help, supply with the more immediate assistances of thy Spirit, which alone can both enlighten My darkness, and quicken My dullness.[1]

O thou Sun of righteousness,[2] *thou sacred Fountain of heavenly light and heat, at once clear and warm my heart, both by instructing of me, and interceding for me: In thee is all fulness: From thee all-sufficiency: By thee is all acceptance. Thou art company enough, and comfort enough: Thou art my King, be also my Prophet and my Priest. Rule me, teach me, pray in me, for me; and be thou ever with me.*

The single wrestlings of Jacob prevailed with thee, in that sacred Duel, when he had none to second him but thy self; who didst assist him with power to overcome thee, and by a welcome violence to wrest a blessing from thee.[3]

O look on me thy Servant, in infinite mercy; whom thou didst once bless with the joint and sociated Devotions of others, whose fervency might inflame the coldness of my affections towards thee; when we went to, or met in thy House with the voice of joy and gladness, worshipping thee in the unity of spirits, and with the bond of Peace.[4]

O forgive the neglect, and not improving of those happy opportunities.

It is now thy pleasure that I should be as a Pelican in the wilderness, as a Sparrow on the housetop,[5] *and as a coal scattered from all those pious glowings, and devout reflections, which might best kindle, preserve, and increase the holy fire of thy graces on the Altar of my heart, whence the sacrifice of prayers, and incense of praises, might be duly offered up to thee.*

Yet O thou that breakest not the bruised Reed, nor quenchest the smoking Flax,[6] *do not despise the weakness of my prayers, nor the smotherings of my soul in this uncomfortable loneness; to which I am constrained by some men's uncharitable denials of those helps, which I much want, and no less desire.*

O let the hardness of their hearts occasion the softenings of mine to thee, and for Them. Let their hatred kindle my love, let their unreason-

---

1 *enlighten My darkness* Psalm 18:28; *dullness* Slowness.
2 Malachi 4:2.
3 Jacob wrestled a divine being at Jabbok brook, refusing to let him go until he received a blessing (Genesis 32:24-30).
4 *voice of ... gladness* Jeremiah 33:11; *unity of ... Peace* Ephesians 4:3.
5 *as a Pelican ... housetop* Psalm 102:6-7.
6 *Yet O ... Flax* Isaiah 42:3 and Matthew 12:20.

able denials of my Religious desires the more excite my prayers to thee. Let their inexorable deafness incline thine ear to me; who art a God easy to be entreated; thine ear is not heavy,[1] that it cannot, nor thy heart hard, that it will not hear; nor thy hand shortened, that it cannot help Me thy desolate Suppliant.[2]

Thou permittest men to deprive me of those outward means, which thou hast appointed in thy Church; but they cannot debar me from the communion of that inward grace, which thou alone breathest into humble hearts.

O make me such, and thou wilt teach me; thou wilt hear me, thou wilt help me: The broken and contrite heart I know thou wilt not despise.[3]

Thou, O Lord canst at once make me thy Temple, thy Priest, thy Sacrifice, and thine Altar; while from an humble heart I (alone) daily offer up in holy meditations, fervent prayers, and unfeigned tears my self to thee; who preparest me for thee, dwellest in me, and acceptest of me.

Thou O Lord didst cause by secret[4] supplies and miraculous infusions, that the handful of meal in the vessel should not spend, nor the little oil in the cruse fail the Widow during the time of drought and dearth.[5]

O look on my soul, which as a Widow, is now desolate and forsaken: let not those saving Truths I have formerly learned now fail my memory; nor the sweet effusions of thy Spirit, which I have sometimes felt, now be wanting to my heart in this famine of ordinary and wholesome food for the refreshing of my Soul.

Which yet I had rather choose than to feed from those hands who mingle my bread with ashes, and my wine with gall;[6] rather tormenting, than teaching me; whose mouths are proner to bitter reproaches of me, than to hearty prayers for me.

Thou knowest, O Lord of truth, how oft they wrest thy holy Scriptures to My destruction, (which are clear for their subjection, and my preservation) O let it not be to their damnation.

Thou knowest how some men (under colour of long prayers) have

---

1 Slow of understanding.

2 Isaiah 59:1.

3 Psalms 51:17 (see also Psalm 34:18).

4 Beyond human apprehension.

5 Elijah, the prophet, lodged with a poor widow woman; in the midst of drought, the scarce supplies of the woman miraculously lasted until it rained (1 Kings 17:12).

6 Matthew 27:34.

sought to devour the houses of their Brethren, their King, and their God.

O let not those men's balms break my head, nor their Cordials oppress my heart, I will evermore pray against their wickedness. [1]

From the poison under their tongues, from the snares of their lips, from the fire, and the swords of their words ever deliver Me, O Lord, and all those Loyal and Religious hearts, who desire and delight in the prosperity of my soul, and who seek by their prayers to relieve this sadness, and solitude of thy servant, O my King and my God.

25. Penitential Meditations and Vows in the KING'S solitude at Holmeby.[2]

Give ear to my words O Lord, consider my Meditation, and hearken to the voice of my cry, my King and my God, for unto thee will I pray.

I said in my haste I am cast out of the sight of thine eyes; nevertheless thou hearest the voice of my supplication, when I cry unto thee.

If thou Lord shouldst be extreme to mark what is done amiss, who can abide it? But there is mercy with thee, that thou mayest be feared; therefore shall sinners fly unto thee.

I acknowledge my sins before thee, which have the aggravation of my condition; the eminency of my place adding weight to my offences.

Forgive, I beseech thee, my Personal, and my People's sins; which are so far mine, as I have not improved the power thou gavest me, to thy glory, and my Subjects' good: Thou hast now brought me from the glory and freedom of a King, to be a Prisoner to my own Subjects: Justify, O Lord, as to thy over-ruling hand, because in many things I have rebelled against thee.

Though thou hast restrained my Person, yet enlarge my heart to thee, and thy grace towards Me.

I come far short of David's piety; yet since I may equal David's afflictions, give me also the comforts and the sure mercies of David.

Let the penitent sense I have of my sins, be an evidence to me, that thou hast pardoned them.

Let not the evils, which I and my Kingdoms have suffered, seem little unto thee; though thou hast not punished us according to our sins.

Turn thee (O Lord) unto me; have mercy upon me, for I am desolate and afflicted.

---

1 Psalm 141:5.
2 Chapter 25 seams together the following passages from the Psalms: 5:1-2; 31:22; 130:3-4; 51:3; 25:16-17; 77:9; 25:6; 27:13; 69:30; 66:20; 37:5.

The sorrows of my heart are enlarged; O bring thou me out of my troubles.

Hast thou forgotten to be gracious, and shut up thy loving kindness in displeasure?

O remember thy compassions of old, and thy loving kindness, which have been for many generations.

I had utterly fainted, if I had not believed to see thy goodness in the land of the living.

Let not the sins of our prosperity deprive us of the benefits of thy afflictions.

Let this fiery trial consume the dross, which in long peace and plenty we had contracted.

Though thou continuest miseries, yet withdraw not thy grace; what is wanting of prosperity, make up in patience and repentance.

And if thy anger be not to be yet turned away, but thy hand of justice must be stretched out still; Let it I beseech thee be against me, and my Father's house; as for these sheep, what have they done?[1]

Let my sufferings satiate the malice of mine, and thy Church's Enemies.

But let their cruelty never exceed the measure of my charity.

Banish from me all thoughts of Revenge, that I may not lose the reward, nor thou the glory of my patience.

As thou givest me a heart to forgive them, so I beseech thee do thou forgive what they have done against thee and me.

And now, O Lord, as thou hast given me an heart to pray unto thee; so hear and accept this Vow, which I make before thee.

If thou wilt in mercy remember Me, and my Kingdoms; In continuing the light of thy Gospel, and settling thy true Religion among us.

In restoring to us the benefit of the Laws, and the due execution of Justice.

In suppressing the many Schisms in Church, and Factions in State.

If thou wilt restore me and mine to the Ancient rights and glory of my Predecessors.

If thou wilt turn the hearts of my people to thy self in Piety, to me in Loyalty, and to one another in Charity.

If thou wilt quench the flames, and withdraw the fuel of these Civil Wars.

If thou wilt bless us with the freedom of public Counsels, and deliver the Honour of Parliaments from the insolency of the vulgar.

---

1   2 Samuel 24:17; 1 Chronicles 21:17.

If thou wilt keep me from the great offence of enacting any thing against my Conscience; and especially from consenting to sacrilegious rapines, and spoilings of thy Church.

If thou wilt restore me to a capacity to glorify thee in doing good, both to the Church and State.

Then shall my soul praise thee, and magnify thy name before my People.

Then shall thy glory be dearer to me than my Crowns; and the advancement of true Religion both in purity and power be my chiefest care.

Then will I rule my People with Justice, and my Kingdoms with equity.

To thy more immediate hand shall I ever own as the rightfull succession, so the merciful restoration of My Kingdoms, and the glory of them.

If thou wilt bring Me again with peace, safety, and honour, to My chiefest City, and my Parliament.

If thou wilt again put the Sword of Justice into My hand to punish and protect.

Then will I make all the world to see, and my very Enemies to enjoy the benefit of this Vow and resolution of Christian charity, which I now make unto thee O Lord.

As I do freely pardon for Christ's sake those that have offended me in any kind; so my hand shall never be against any man to revenge what is past, in regard of any particular injury done to me.

We have been mutually punished in our unnatural divisions; for thy sake O Lord, and for the love of my Redeemer, have I purposed this in my heart, That I will use all means in the ways of amnesty, and indemnity, which may most fully remove all fears, and bury all jealousies in forgetfulness.

Let thy mercies be toward me and mine, as my resolutions of Truth and Peace are toward my People.

Hear my prayer O Lord, which goeth not out of feigned lips.

Blessed be God, who hath not turned away my prayer; nor taken his mercy from me.

O my soul, commit thy way to the Lord, trust in him, and he shall bring it to pass.

But if thou wilt not restore me and mine, what am I that I should charge thee foolishly?

Thou O Lord hast given, and thou hast taken; Blessed be thy name.[1]

May my People and thy Church be happy, if not by me, yet without me.

---

1   Job 1:21.

26. *Upon the Army's Surprisal of the* KING *at* Holmeby, *and the ensuing distractions*[1] *in the two Houses, the Army, and the City.*[2]

What part God will have me now to act or suffer in this new and strange scene of affairs, I am not much solicitous; some little practice will serve that man, who only seeks to represent a part of honesty and honour.

This surprize of Me tells the world, that a KING cannot be so low, but He is considerable; adding weight to that Party where he appears.

This motion, like others of the Times, seems eccentric and irregular, yet not well to be resisted or quieted: Better swim down such a stream, than in vain to strive against it.

These are but the strugglings of those twins, which lately one womb enclosed, the younger striving to prevail against the elder;[3] what the Presbyterians have hunted after, the Independents now seek to catch for themselves.

So impossible is it for lines to be drawn from the centre, and not to divide from each other, so much the wider, by how much they go farther from the point of union.

That the Builders of *Babel* should from division fall to confusion, is no wonder;[4] but for those that pretend to build *Jerusalem*, to divide their tongues and hands, is but an ill *omen*; and sounds too like the fury of those Zealots, whose intestine[5] bitterness and divisions were the greatest occasion of the last fatal destruction of that City.[6]

---

1 Disruptions, divisions.

2 In June 1647, Charles I was seized by Cornet George Joyce and 500 troops. He would remain in army custody—excepting his brief escape—until his death. Charles attempted to use the incident to drive a wedge between the army and Parliament.

3 Even in the womb, Rebekah's twins Jacob and Esau "struggled together within her" (Genesis 25:22-24).

4 When the proud unilingual descendants of Noah built a great tower to achieve fame, God diversified language and scattered the people (Genesis 11:1-9). Both the Independents and Presbyterians claimed to be creating the New Jerusalem; the Presbyterians, however, often charged the Independents with building a Tower of Babel.

5 Internal, with regard to a country or people.

6 Jerusalem fell in 70 CE, after a lengthy siege by Titus (39-81 CE), the son of the Roman emperor Vespasian. In book 5 of *The Wars of the Jews*, Flavius Josephus describes three treacherous factions within Jerusalem whose zealotry set in motion the city's destruction.

Well may I change my Keepers and Prison, but not my captive condition, only with this hope of bettering, that those who are so much professed Patrons for the People's Liberties, cannot be utterly against the Liberty of their KING; what they demand for their own Consciences, they cannot in Reason deny to Mine. In this they seem more ingenuous; than the Presbyterian rigour, who, sometimes complaining of exacting[1] their conformity to laws, are become the greatest Exactors of other men's submission to their novel injunctions, before they are stamped with the Authority of Laws, which they cannot well have without My consent.

'Tis a great argument, that the Independents think themselves manumitted[2] from their Rival's service, in that they carry on a business of such consequence, as the assuming My Person into the Army's custody, without any Commission, but that of their own will and power. Such as will thus adventure on a King, must not be thought over-modest, or timorous to carry on any design they have a mind to.

Their next motion menaces, and scares both the two Houses and the City: which soon after acting over again that former part of tumultuary motions, (never questioned, punished, or repented) must now suffer for both; and see their former sin in the glass of the present terrors and distractions.

No man is so blind as not to see herein the hand of divine justice; they that by Tumults first occasioned the raising of Armies, must now be chastened by their own Army for new Tumults.

So hardly can men be content with one sin, but add sin to sin, till the latter punish the former; such as were content to see Me and many Members of both Houses driven away by the first unsuppressed Tumults, are now forced to fly to an Army, or defend themselves against them.

But who can unfold the riddle of some men's justice? the Members of both Houses who at first withdrew, (as My self was forced to do) from the rudeness of the Tumults, were counted Deserters, and outed of their Places in Parliament.

Such as stayed then, and enjoyed the benefit of the Tumults, were asserted for the only Parliament-men: now the Fliers from, and Forsakers of their Places, carry the Parliamentary power along with them; complain highly against the Tumults, and vindi-

---

1 Demanding.
2 Released; set free.

cate themselves by an Army: such as remained and kept their stations, are looked upon as Abettors of tumultuary insolencies, and Betrayers of the freedom and honour of Parliament.

Thus is Power above all Rule, Order, and Law; where men look more to present Advantages than their Consciences, and the unchangeable rules of Justice; while they are Judges of others, they are forced to condemn themselves.

Now the plea against Tumults holds good, the Authors and Abettors of them are guilty of prodigious insolencies; when as before, they were counted as Friends and necessary Assistants.

I see Vengeance pursues and overtakes (as the Mice and Rats are said to have done a Bishop in *Germany*[1]) them that thought to have escaped and fortified themselves most impregnably against it, both by their multitude and compliance.

Whom the Laws cannot, God will punish, by their own crimes and hands.

I cannot but observe this divine Justice, yet with sorrow and pity; for, I always wished so well to Parliament and City, that I was sorry to see them do, or suffer, any thing unworthy such great and considerable bodies in this Kingdom.

I was glad to see them only scared and humbled, not broken by that shaking: I never had so ill a thought of those Cities as to despair of their Loyalty to Me; which mistakes might eclipse, but I never believed malice had quite put out.

I pray God the storm be yet wholly passed over them; upon whom I look, as Christ did sometime over *Jerusalem*, as objects of my prayers and tears, with compassionate grief,[2] foreseeing those severer scatterings which will certainly befall such as wantonly refuse to be gathered to their duty: fatal blindness frequently attending and punishing wilfulness, so that men shall not be able at last to prevent their sorrows who would not timely repent of their sins; nor shall they be suffered to enjoy the comforts, who securely neglect the counsels belonging to their peace. They will find that Brethren in iniquity are not far from becoming insolent enemies, there being nothing harder than to keep ill men long in one mind.

---

1 In *Coryat's Crudities* (1610) a story is told about the wicked Archbishop of Mainz, who assembled and burned to death many of the poor whom he believed were "like to Mice ... good for nothing but to devour corn"; he was thereafter tormented with throngs of mice who eventually devoured him.

2 Luke 19:41-44; see also Matthew 23:37-24:28.

Nor is it possible to gain a fair period for those notions which go rather in a round and circle of fancy, than in a right line of reason tending to the Law, the only centre of public consistency; whither I pray God at last bring all sides.

Which will easily be done, when we shall fully see how much more happy we are, to be subject to the known Laws, than to the various wills of any men, seem they never so plausible at first.

Vulgar compliance with any illegal and extravagant ways, like violent motions in nature, soon grows weary of it self, and ends in a refractory sullenness:[1] People's rebounds are oft in their faces, who first put them upon those violent strokes.

For the Army (which is so far excusable, as they act according to Soldiers' principles, and interests, demanding Pay and Indemnity) I think it necessary, in order to the public peace that they should be satisfied, as far as is just; no man being more prone to consider them than My self: though they have fought against Me, yet I cannot but so far esteem that valour and gallantry they have sometime showed, as to wish I may never want such men to maintain My self, My Laws, and My Kingdoms, in such a peace, as wherein they may enjoy their share and proportion as much as any men.

But thou, O Lord, who art perfect Unity in a sacred Trinity, in mercy behold those, whom thy Justice hath divided.

Deliver Me from the strivings of My People,[2] and make Me to see how much they need My prayers and pity, who agreed to fight against Me, and yet are now ready to fight against one another; to the continuance of My Kingdoms' distractions.

Discover to all sides the ways of peace, from which they have swerved: which consists not in the divided wills of Parties, but in the point and due observation of the Laws.

Make Me willing to go whither thou wilt lead Me by thy providence; and be thou ever with Me, that I may see thy constancy in the world's variety and changes.

Make me even such as thou wouldst have Me, that I may at last enjoy that safety and tranquillity which thou alone canst give Me.

Divert, I pray thee, O Lord, thy heavy wrath justly hanging over those populous Cities, whose plenty is prone to add fuel to their luxury,

---

1 Obstinate; perverse.
2 Psalm 18:43.

their wealth to make them wanton, their multitudes tempting them to security, and their security exposing them to unexpected miseries.

Give them eyes to see, hearts to consider, wills to embrace, and courage to act those things which belong to thy glory and the public peace, lest their calamity come upon them as an armed man.

Teach them, That they cannot want enemies who abound in sin, nor shall they be long un-disarmed and un-destroyed, who with a high hand persisting to fight against thee and the clear convictions of their own consciences, fight more against themselves, than ever they did against Me.

Their sins exposing them to thy Justice, their riches to others' injuries, their number to Tumults, and their Tumults to confusion.

Though they have with much forwardness helped to destroy Me, yet let not my fall be their ruin.

Let Me not so much consider, either what they have done, or I have suffered, (chiefly at first by them) as to forget to imitate My crucified Redeemer, to plead their ignorance for their pardon; and in My dying extremities to pray to thee O Father to forgive them, for they knew not what they did.

The tears they have denied Me in My saddest condition, give them grace to bestow upon themselves, who the less they were for Me, the more cause they have to weep for themselves.

O let not My blood be upon them and their Children, whom the fraud and faction of some, not the malice of all, have excited to crucify Me.

But thou, O Lord, canst, and wilt (as thou didst My Redeemer) both exalt and perfect Me by My sufferings,[1] *which have more in them of thy mercies, than of man's cruelty or thy own justice.*

27. *To the Prince of* Wales.[2]

Son, if these Papers, with some others, wherein I have set down the private reflections of My Conscience, and My most impartial

---

1 Hebrews 2:10.
2 The future Charles II, to whom the chapter is addressed, was appointed nominal commander of the Western Association during the first Civil War. He left England for France in 1646, relocating to Holland in 1648. On 5 February 1649, the Scottish Parliament proclaimed him king of Great Britain, France, and Ireland. In 1650, he landed in Scotland and raised an army, but returned to the Continent until the Restoration when Cromwell defeated his forces. This chapter, the only one to address an individual directly and to exclude a prayer, recalls the book of advice that Charles I's father, James I, wrote for Henry, Prince of Wales (*Basilikon Doron*, 1599).

thoughts, touching the chief passages, which have been most remarkable, or disputed in My late troubles, come to your hands, to whom they are chiefly designed; they may be so far useful to you, as to state your judgement aright in what hath passed; whereof, a pious is the best use can be made; and they may also give you some directions, how to remedy the present distempers, and prevent (if God will) the like for time to come.

It is some kind of deceiving and lessening the injury of My long restraint, when I find My leisure and solitude have produced something worthy of My self, and useful to you; That neither you, nor any other, may hereafter measure My Cause by the Success; nor My Judgement of things by My misfortunes; which I count the greater by far, because they have so far lighted upon you, and some others, whom I have most cause to love as well as My self; and of whose unmerited sufferings I have a greater sense than of Mine own.

But this advantage of wisdom you have above most Princes; that you have begun, and now spent some years of discretion, in the experience of troubles, and exercise of patience, wherein Piety, and all Virtues, both Moral and Political, are commonly better planted to a thriving (as trees set in winter) than in the warmth, and serenity of times; or amidst those delights, which usually attend Princes' Courts in times of peace and plenty; which are prone, either to root up all plants of true Virtue and Honour; or to be contented only with some leaves, and withering formalities of them, without any real fruits, such as tend to the Public good; for which Princes should always remember they are born and by providence designed.

The evidence of which different education the holy Writ affords us in the contemplation of *David* and *Rehoboam*: The one prepared, by many afflictions for a flourishing Kingdom, the other softened by the unparalleled prosperity of *Solomon*'s Court; and so corrupted to the great diminution, both for Peace, Honour, and Kingdom, by those flatteries, which are as unseparable from prosperous Princes, as Flies are from fruit in summer; whom adversity, like cold weather, drives away.[1]

---

1 Forced to live in exile under harsh conditions before becoming King of Israel, David was a godly king who "walked in integrity of heart and in uprightness." King Rehoboam, who lived a life of ease in the court of his father King Solomon, ignored the cries of his people and threatened to "chastise" them "with scorpions," causing his subjects to revolt (1 Samuel 18-31; 2 Samuel 1-5; 1 Kings 12-14; 2 Chronicles 10:6-16).

I had rather you should be *Charles le Bon,* than *le Grand,* good, than great; I hope God hath designed you to be both, having so early put you into that exercise of his Graces, and gifts bestowed upon you, which may best weed out all vicious inclinations, and dispose you to those Princely endowments, and employments, which will most gain the love, and intend the welfare of those, over whom God shall place you.

With God I would have you begin and end, who is King of Kings; the Sovereign disposer of the Kingdoms of the world, who pulleth down one, and setteth up another.[1]

The best Government, and highest Sovereignty you can attain to is, to be subject to him, that the Sceptre of his Word and Spirit may rule in your heart.

The true glory of Princes consists in advancing God's Glory in the maintenance of true Religion, and the Church's good; Also in the dispensation[2] of civil Power, with Justice and Honour to the public Peace.

Piety will make you prosperous; at least it will keep you from being miserable; nor is he much a loser, that loseth all, yet saveth his own soul at last.[3]

To which Centre of true Happiness God, I trust, hath and will graciously direct all these black lines of Affliction, which he hath been pleased to draw on me, and by which he hath (I hope) drawn me nearer to himself. You have already tasted of that cup whereof I have liberally drank,[4] which I look upon as God's Physic, having that in healthfulness which it wants in pleasure.

Above all, I would have you, as I hope you are already; well-grounded and settled in your Religion: The best profession of which, I have ever esteemed that of the Church of *England,* in which you have been educated; yet I would have your own Judgement and Reason now seal to that sacred bond which education hath written, that it may be judiciously your own Religion, and not other men's custom or tradition, which you profess.

In this I charge you to persevere, as coming nearest to God's Word for Doctrine, and to the primitive examples for Government, with some little amendment, which I have otherwise

---

1 Psalm 75:7.
2 Ordering, administering.
3 Matthew 16:26; Mark 8:36.
4 Matthew 20:23; Mark 10:39.

expressed, and often offered, though in vain. Your fixation[1] in matters of Religion will not be more necessary[2] for your soul's than your Kingdoms' peace, when God shall bring you to them.

For I have observed, that the Devil of Rebellion, doth commonly turn himself into an Angel of Reformation; and the old Serpent can pretend new Lights:[3] When some men's Consciences accuse them for Sedition and Faction, they stop its mouth with the name and noise of Religion; when Piety pleads for peace and patience, they cry out Zeal.

So that, unless in this point You be well settled, you shall never want temptations to destroy you and yours, under pretensions of reforming matters of Religion; for that seems, even to worst men, as the best and most auspicious beginning of their worst designs.

Where, besides the Novelty which is taking enough with the Vulgar, every one hath an affectation, by seeming forward to an outward Reformation of Religion, to be thought zealous; hoping to cover those irreligious deformities, whereto they are conscious by a severity of censuring other men's opinions or actions.

Take heed of abetting any Factions, or applying to any public Discriminations in matters of Religion, contrary to what is in your Judgement, and the Church well settled; your partial adhering, as head, to any one side, gains you not so great advantages in some men's hearts (who are prone to be of their King's Religion) as it loseth you in others; who think themselves, and their profession first despised, then persecuted by you: Take such a course as may either with calmness and charity quite remove the seeming differences and offences by impartiality, or so order affairs in point of Power that you shall not need to fear or flatter any Faction. For if ever you stand in need of them, or must stand to their courtesy, you are undone: The Serpent will devour the Dove: you may never expect less of loyalty, justice, or humanity, than from those, who engage into religious Rebellion; Their interest is always made God's; under the colours of Piety, ambitious policies march, not only with greatest security, but applause, as to the populacy; you may hear from them *Jacob's* voice, but you shall feel they have *Esau's* hands.[4]

---

1 Steadfastness.

2 Emended from "will not be not."

3 Revelation 12:9, 20:2.

4 In order to receive the blessing due the eldest son, Jacob covered his hands with goatskins to make them as rough as Esau's. His blind father, Isaac, blessed Jacob by mistake, denying Esau (the eldest son) his birthright (Genesis 27:18-23).

Nothing seemed less considerable than the Presbyterian Faction in *England*, for many years; so compliant they were to public order: nor indeed was their Party great either in Church, or State, as to men's judgements: But as soon as discontents drove men into Sidings[1] (as ill humours fall to the disaffected part,[2] which causes inflammations) so did all, at first, who affected any novelties, adhere to that Side, as the most remarkable and specious note of difference (then) in point of Religion.

All the lesser Factions at first were officious Servants to Presbytery their great Master: till time and military success discovering to each their peculiar advantages, invited them to part stakes, and leaving the joint stock of uniform Religion, pretended each to drive for their Party the trade of profits and preferments, to the breaking and undoing not only of the Church and State, but even of Presbytery it self, which seemed and hoped at first to have engrossed[3] all.

Let nothing seem little or despicable to you in matters which concern Religion and the Church's peace, so as to neglect a speedy reforming and effectual suppressing Errors and Schisms, which seem at first but as a handbreadth, by seditious Spirits, as by strong winds are soon made to cover and darken the whole Heaven.

When you have done justice to God, your own soul and his Church, in the profession and preservation both of truth and unity in Religion: the next main hinge on which your prosperity will depend, and move, is, that of civil Justice, wherein the settled Laws of these Kingdoms, to which you are rightly Heir, are the most excellent rules you can govern by; which by an admirable temperament give very much to Subjects' industry, liberty, and happiness; and yet reserve enough to the Majesty and prerogative of any King, who owns his People as Subjects, not as Slaves; whose subjection, as it preserves their property, peace, and safety, so it will never diminish your Rights, nor their ingenuous[4] Liberties; which consists in the enjoyment of the fruits of their industry, and the benefit of those Laws to which themselves have consented.

---

1   Factions.
2   Emended from "mart."
3   Absorbed; also, monopolized.
4   Befitting a free-born person.

Never charge[1] your Head with such a Crown, as shall by its heaviness oppress the whole body, the weakness of whose parts cannot return any thing of strength, honour, or safety, to the Head, but a necessary debilitation and ruin.

Your Prerogative is best showed, and exercised in remitting, rather than exacting the rigour of the Laws; there being nothing worse than legal Tyranny.

In these two points, the preservation of established Religion, and Laws, I may (without vanity) turn the reproach of My sufferings, as to the world's censure, into the honour of a kind of Martyrdom, as to the testimony of My own Conscience; The Troublers of My Kingdoms having nothing else to object against Me but this, That I prefer Religion, and Laws established before those alterations they propounded.

And so indeed I do, and ever shall, till I am convinced by better Arguments, than what hitherto have been chiefly used towards Me, Tumults, Armies, and Prisons.

I cannot yet learn that lesson, nor I hope ever will you, That it is safe for a King to gratify any Faction with the perturbation[2] of the Laws, in which is wrapped up the public Interest, and the good of the Community.

How God will deal with Me, as to the removal of these pressures, and indignities, which his justice by the very unjust hands of some of My Subjects, hath been pleased to lay upon Me, I cannot tell: nor am I much solicitous what wrong I suffer from men, while I retain in My soul, what I believe is right before God.

I have offered all for Reformation and Safety, that in Reason, Honour, and Conscience I can; reserving only what I cannot consent unto, without an irreparable injury to My own Soul, the Church, and My People, and to You also, as the next and undoubted Heir of My Kingdoms.

To which if the divine Providence, to whom no difficulties are insuperable, shall in his due time after My decease bring You, as I hope he will; My counsel and charge to You, is, That You seriously consider the former, real, or objected miscarriages, which might occasion My troubles, that You may avoid them.

Never repose so much upon any man's single counsel, fidelity, and discretion, in managing affairs of the first magnitude, (that is,

---

1 Burden.
2 Change, leading to disorder.

matters of Religion and Justice) as to create in Your self, or others, a diffidence of Your own judgement, which is likely to be always more constant and impartial to the interests of Your Crown and Kingdom than any man's.

Next, beware of exasperating any Factions by the crossness, and asperity[1] of some men's passions, humours, or private opinions, employed by You, grounded only upon the differences in lesser matters, which are but the skirts and suburbs[2] of Religion.

Wherein a charitable connivance[3] and Christian toleration often dissipates their strength, whom rougher opposition fortifies; and puts the despised and oppressed Party, into such Combinations, as may most enable them to get a full revenge on those they count their Persecutors, who are commonly assisted by that vulgar commiseration, which attends all, that are said to suffer under the notion of Religion.

Provided the differences amount not to an insolent opposition of Laws, and Government, or Religion established, as to the essentials of them, such motions and minings[4] are intolerable.

Always keep up solid piety, and those fundamental Truths (which mend both hearts and lives of men) with impartial favour and justice.

Take heed that outward circumstances and formalities of Religion devour not all, or the best encouragements of learning, industry, and piety; but with an equal eye, and impartial hand, distribute favours and rewards to all men, as you find them for their real goodness both in abilities and fidelity worthy and capable of them.

This will be sure to gain You the hearts of the best, and the most too; who, though they be not good themselves, yet are glad to see the severer ways of virtue at any time sweetened by temporal rewards.

I have, You see, conflicted with different and opposite Factions; (for so I must needs call and count all those, that act not in any conformity to the Laws established, in Church and State) no sooner have they by force subdued what they counted their Common Enemy, (that is, all those that adhered to the Laws, and to Me) and are secured from that fear, but they are divided to so

---

1 *crossness* Perverse disposition; *asperity* Harshness, severity.
2 The edges or margins.
3 Overlooking, often implying secret sympathy or approval.
4 That which undermines.

high a rivalry, as sets them more at defiance against each other, than against their first Antagonists.

Time will dissipate all factions, when once the rough horns of private men's covetous and ambitious designs, shall discover themselves; which were at first wrapped up and hidden under the soft and smooth pretensions of Religion, Reformation, and Liberty: As the Wolf is not less cruel, so he will be more justly hated, when he shall appear no better than a Wolf under Sheep's clothing.[1]

But as for the seduced Train of the Vulgar, who in their simplicity follow those disguises; My charge and counsel to You, is, That as You need no palliations for any designs, (as other men) so that you study really to exceed (in true and constant demonstrations of goodness, piety, and virtue, towards the People) even all those men, that make the greatest noise and ostentations of Religion; so You shall neither fear any detection, (as they do, who have but the face and mask of goodness) nor shall You frustrate the just expectations of Your People; who cannot in Reason promise themselves so much good from any Subject's novelties, as from the virtuous constancy of their King.

When these mountains of congealed factions shall by the sunshine of God's mercy, and the splendour of Your virtues be thawed and dissipated; and the abused Vulgar shall have learned, that none are greater Oppressors of their Estates, Liberties, and Consciences, than those men, that entitle themselves, The Patrons and Vindicators of them, only to usurp power over them; Let then no passion betray You to any study of revenge upon those, whose own sin and folly will sufficiently punish them in due time.

But as soon as the forked arrow of factious emulations[2] is drawn out, use all princely arts, and clemency to heal the wounds; that the smart of the cure may not equal the anguish of the hurt.

I have offered Acts of Indemnity, and Oblivion, to so great a latitude, as may include all, that can but suspect themselves to be any way obnoxious to the Laws; and which might serve to exclude all future Jealousies and insecurities.

I would have You always propense[3] to the same way, when ever it shall be desired and accepted, let it be granted, not only as an Act of State-policy and necessity, but of Christian charity and choice.

---

1 Matthew 7:15.
2 Ambitious rivalries.
3 Incline.

It is all I have now left Me, a power to forgive those, that have deprived Me of all; and I thank God, I have a heart to do it; and joy as much in this grace, which God hath given Me, as in all My former enjoyments; for this is a greater argument of God's love to Me, than any prosperity can be.

Be confident (as I am) that the most of all sides, who have done amiss, have done so, not out of malice, but mis-information, or mis-apprehension of things.

None will be more loyal and faithful to Me and You, than those Subjects, who sensible of their Errors, and our Injuries, will feel in their own Souls most vehement motives to repentance; and earnest desires to make some reparations for their former defects.

As Your quality sets You beyond any Duel with any Subject; so the nobleness of Your mind must raise You above the meditating any revenge, or executing Your anger upon the many.

The more conscious You shall be to Your own merits, upon Your People, the more prone You will be to expect all love and loyalty from them; and to inflict no punishment upon them for former miscarriages: You will have more inward complacency in pardoning one, than in punishing a thousand.

This I write to you, not despairing of God's mercy, and my Subjects' affections towards You; both which, I hope You will study to deserve, yet We cannot merit of God, but by his own mercy.

If God shall see fit to restore Me, and You after Me, to those enjoyments, which the Laws have assigned to Us; and no Subjects without an high degree of guilt and sin can divest Us of; then may I have better opportunity, when I shall be so happy to see You in peace, to let You more fully understand the things that belong to God's glory, Your own honour, and the Kingdoms' peace.

But if You never see My face again, and God will have Me buried in such a barbarous Imprisonment and obscurity, (which the perfecting some men's designs require) wherein few hearts that love me are permitted to exchange a word, or a look with Me; I do require and entreat You as your Father, and your KING, that You never suffer Your heart to receive the least check against, or disaffection from the true Religion established in the Church of *England*.

I tell You I have tried it, and after much search, and many dis-putes, have concluded it to be the best in the world; not only in the Community, as Christian, but also in the special notion, as

Reformed; keeping the middle way between the pomp of super-stitious Tyranny, and the meanness[1] of fantastic Anarchy.

Not but that (the draught being excellent as to the main, both for Doctrine and Government, in the Church of *England*) some lines, as in very good figures, may happily need some sweetening, or polishing; which might here have easily been done by a safe and gentle hand; if some men's precipitancy had not violently demanded such rude alterations, as would have quite destroyed all the beauty and proportions of the whole.

The scandal of the late Troubles, which some may object, and urge to You against the Protestant Religion established in *England*, is easily answered to them, or Your own thoughts in this, That scarce any one who hath been a Beginner, or an active Prosecutor of this late War against the Church, the Laws, and Me, either was, or is a true Lover, Embracer, or Practiser of the Protestant Religion, established in *England*: which neither gives such rules, nor ever before set such examples.

'Tis true, some heretofore had the boldness to present threatening Petitions to their Princes and Parliaments, which others of the same Faction (but of worse Spirits) have now put in execution: but let not counterfeit and disorderly Zeal abate Your value and esteem of true piety, both of them are to be known by their fruits; the sweetness of the Wine and Fig-tree is not to be despised, though the Brambles and Thorns should pretend to bear Figs and Grapes, thereby to rule over the Trees.[2]

Nor would I have You to entertain any aversation,[3] or dislike of Parliaments; which in their right constitution with Freedom and Honour, will never injure or diminish Your greatness, but will rather be as interchangings of love, loyalty, and confidence, between a Prince, and his People.

Nor would the events of this black Parliament have been other than such (however much biased by Factions in the Elections) if it had been preserved from the insolencies of popular dictates, and tumultuary impressions: The sad effects of which will no doubt, make all Parliaments after this more cautious to preserve that Freedom, and Honour, which belongs to such Assemblies (when once they have fully shaken off this yoke of Vulgar

---

1 Baseness.
2 Matthew 7:16-20; Luke 6:43-44.
3 Aversion to.

encroachment) since the public interest consists in the mutual and common good both of Prince and People.

Nothing can be more happy for all, than in fair, grave, and Honourable ways to contribute their Counsels in Common, enacting all things by public consent; without tyranny or Tumults. We must not starve our selves, because some men have surfeited of wholesome food.

And if neither I, nor You, be ever restored to Our Rights, but God in his severest justice, will punish My Subjects with continuance in their sin, and suffer them to be deluded with the prosperity of their wickedness; I hope God will give Me, and You, that grace, which will teach and enable Us, to want, as well as to wear a Crown, which is not worth taking up, or enjoying upon sordid, dishonourable, and irreligious terms.

Keep You to true principles of piety, virtue, and honour, You shall never want a Kingdom.

A principal point of Your honour will consist in Your deferring all respect, love, and protection to Your Mother, My Wife; who hath many ways deserved well of Me, and chiefly in this, that (having been a means to bless Me with so many hopeful Children; (all which, with their Mother, I recommend to Your love, and care) She hath been content with incomparable magnanimity and patience to suffer both for, and with Me, and You.[1]

My prayer to God Almighty is, (whatever becomes of Me, who am, I thank God, wrapped up and fortified in My own Innocency, and his Grace) that he would be pleased to make You an Anchor, or Harbour rather, to these tossed and weather-beaten Kingdoms; a Repairer by Your wisdom, justice, piety, and valour, of what, the folly and wickedness of some men have so far ruined, as to leave nothing entire in Church or State; to the Crown, the Nobility, the Clergy, or the Commons; either as to Laws, Liberties, Estates, Order, Honour, Conscience, or lives.

When they have destroyed Me, (for I know not how far God may permit the malice and cruelty of My Enemies to proceed, and such apprehensions some men's words and actions have already given Me) as I doubt not but My blood will cry aloud for vengeance to heaven; so I beseech God not to pour out his wrath upon the generality of the People, who have either deserted Me,

---

1 Charles I and Henrietta Maria's surviving children were: Charles, Prince of Wales; James, Duke of York; Henry, Duke of Gloucester; Mary; Elizabeth; and Henrietta Anne.

or engaged against Me, through the artifice and hypocrisy of their Leaders, whose inward horror will be their first Tormentor, nor will they escape exemplary judgements.

For those that loved Me, I pray God, they may have no miss of Me, when I am gone; so much I wish and hope, that all good Subjects may be satisfied with the blessings of Your presence and virtues.

For those that repent of any defects in their duty toward Me, as I freely forgive them in the word of a Christian KING, so I believe You will find them truly Zealous, to repay with interest that loyalty and love to You, which was due to Me.

In sum, what good I intended, do You perform; when God shall give You power: much good I have offered, more I purposed to Church and State, if times had been capable of it.

The deception will soon vanish, and the Vizards[1] will fall off apace; This mask of Religion on the face of Rebellion (for so it now plainly appears, since My Restraint and cruel usage, that they sought not for Me, as was pretended) will not long serve to hide some men's deformities.

Happy times, I hope, attend You, wherein Your Subjects (by their miseries) will have learned, That Religion to their God, and Loyalty to their King, cannot be parted without both their sin and their infelicity.

I pray God bless You, and establish Your Kingdoms in righteousness, Your Soul in true Religion, and Your honour in the love of God and Your people.

And if God will have disloyalty perfected by My destruction; let My memory ever, with My name, live in you; as of Your Father, that loves You: and once a KING of three flourishing Kingdoms; whom God thought fit to honour, not only with the Sceptre and Government of them, but also with the suffering many indignities, and an untimely death for them; while I studied to preserve the rights of the Church, the power of the Laws, the honour of My Crown, the privilege of Parliaments, the liberties of My People, and My own Conscience, which, I thank God, is dearer to Me than a thousand Kingdoms.

I know God can, I hope he yet will restore Me to My Rights. I cannot despair either of his mercy, or of My People's love and pity.

---

1 Masks, disguises.

At worst, I trust I shall but go before You to a better Kingdom, which God hath prepared for Me, and Me for it, through My Saviour Jesus Christ, to whose mercies I commend You and all Mine. Farewell, till We meet, if not on Earth, yet in Heaven.

28. *Meditations upon Death, after the Votes of Non-Addresses, and* HIS MAJESTY'S *closer Imprisonment in* Carisbrooke-Castle.[1]

As I have leisure enough, so I have cause more than enough, to meditate upon, and prepare for My Death: for I know, there are but few steps between the Prisons and Graves of Princes.

It is God's indulgence, which gives Me the space, but Man's cruelty, that gives Me the sad occasions for these thoughts.

For, besides the common burden of mortality, which lies upon Me, as a Man; I now bear the heavy load of other men's ambitions, fears, jealousies, and cruel passions, whose envy or enmity against Me makes their own lives' seem deadly to them, while I enjoy any part of Mine.

I thank God, My prosperity made Me not wholly a Stranger to the contemplations of mortality:

Those are never unseasonable, since this is always uncertain: Death being an eclipse, which oft happeneth as well in clear, as cloudy days.

But My now long and sharp adversity hath so reconciled in Me those natural Antipathies between Life and Death, which are in all men, that I thank God, the common terrors of it are dispelled; and the special horror of it, as to My particular, much allayed: for, although My death at present may justly be represented to Me with all those terrible aggravations, which the policy of cruel and implacable enemies can put upon it, (affairs being drawn to the very dregs of malice) yet I bless God, I can look upon all those stings, as unpoisonous, though sharp; since My Redeemer hath either pulled them out, or given Me the antidote of his Death against them; which as to the immaturity, unjustice, shame, scorn, and cruelty of it exceeded, whatever I can fear.

Indeed, I never did find so much, the life of Religion, the feast of a good Conscience, and the brazen[2] wall of judicious integrity

---

1 On 3 January 1648, the Commons determined to halt negotiations with the king as he had rejected their latest proposals. On 15 January 1648, the House of Lords agreed. On 11 November 1647, the king had escaped from Hampton Court, and sought refuge on the Isle of Wight, where he was siezed and imprisoned in Carisbrooke Castle.

2 Strong as brass.

and constancy, as since I came to these closer conflicts with the thoughts of Death.

I am not so old, as to be weary of life; nor (I hope) so bad, as to be either afraid to die, or ashamed to live: true, I am so afflicted, as might make Me sometime even desire to die; if I did not consider, That it is the greatest glory of a Christian's life to *die daily*,[1] in conquering by a lively faith, and patient hopes of a better life, those partial and quotidian deaths, which kill us (as it were) by piece-meals, and make us overlive our own fates; while We are deprived of health, honour, liberty, power, credit, safety, or estate; and those other comforts of dearest relations, which are as the life of our lives.

Though, as a KING, I think My self to live in nothing temporal so much, as in the love and good-will of My People; for which, as I have suffered many deaths, so I hope I am not in that point as yet wholly dead: notwithstanding, My Enemies have used all the poison of falsity and violence of hostility to destroy, first the love and Loyalty, which is in My Subjects; and then all that content of life in Me, which from these I chiefly enjoyed.

Indeed, they have left Me but little of life, and only the husk and shell (as it were) which their further malice and cruelty can take from Me; having bereaved Me of all those worldly comforts, for which life it self seems desirable to men.

But, O My Soul! think not that life too long, or tedious, wherein God gives thee any opportunities, if not to do, yet to suffer with such Christian patience and magnanimity in a good Cause, as are the greatest honour of our lives, and the best improvement of our deaths.

I know that in point of true Christian valour, it argues pusillanimity to desire to die out of weariness of life; and a want of that heroic greatness of spirit which becomes a Christian in the patient and generous sustaining those afflictions, which as shadows necessarily attend us, while we are in this body; and which are lessened or enlarged as the Sun of our prosperity moves higher, or lower: whose total absence is best recompensed with the Dew of Heaven.

The assaults of affliction may be terrible, like *Samson's* Lion,[2] but they yield much sweetness to those, that dare to encounter

---

1   1 Corinthians 15:31.
2   Strengthened by "the spirit of the Lord," Samson ripped apart with his bare hands a lion that threatened him (Judges 14:5-9).

and overcome them; who know how to overlive the witherings of their Gourds without discontent or peevishness, while they may yet converse with God.

That I must die as a Man, is certain; that I may die a King, by the hands of My own Subjects, a violent, sudden, and barbarous death; in the strength of My years; in the midst of My Kingdoms; My Friends and loving Subjects being helpless Spectators; My Enemies insolent Revilers and Triumphers over Me, living, dying, and dead, is so probable in human reason, that God hath taught me not to hope otherwise, as to man's cruelty; however, I despair not of God's infinite mercy.

I know My Life is the object of the Devil's and wicked men's malice; but yet under God's sole custody and disposal: Whom I do not think to flatter for longer life by seeming prepared to die; but I humbly desire to depend upon him, and to submit to his will both in life and death, in what order soever he is pleased to lay them out to Me. I confess it is not easy for Me to contend with those many horrors of death, wherewith God suffers Me to be tempted; which are equally horrid, either in the suddenness of a barbarous Assassination; or in those greater formalities, whereby My Enemies (being more solemnly cruel) will, it may be, seek to add (as those did, who Crucified Christ) the mockery of Justice, to the cruelty of Malice: That I may be destroyed, as with greater pomp and artifice, so with less pity, it will be but a necessary policy to make My death appear as an act of Justice, done by Subjects upon their Sovereign; who know that no Law of God or Man invests them with any power of Judicature without Me, much less against Me: and who, being sworn and bound by all that is sacred before God and Man, to endeavour My preservation, must pretend Justice to cover their Perjury.

It is, indeed, a sad fate for any man to have his Enemies to be Accusers, Parties, and Judges; but most desperate, when this is acted by the insolence of Subjects against their Sovereign; wherein those, who have had the chiefest hand, and are most guilty of contriving the public Troubles, must by shedding My blood seem to wash their own hands of that innocent blood,[1] whereof they are now most evidently guilty before God and man; and I believe

---

1 As the Roman governor Pilate washed his hands before permitting Jesus' crucifixion: "Pilate ... took water, and washed his hands before the multitude, saying, I am innocent of the blood of this just person" (Matthew 27:24).

in their own consciences too, while they carried on unreasonable demands, first by Tumults, after by Armies. Nothing makes mean spirits more cowardly-cruel in managing their usurped power against their lawful Superiors, than this, the *Guilt of their unjust Usurpation*; notwithstanding, those specious and popular pretensions of Justice against Delinquents, applied only to disguise at first the monstrousness of their designs, who despaired, indeed, of possessing the power and profits of the Vineyard, till the Heir, whose right it is, be cast out and slain.[1]

With them, My greatest fault must be, that I would not either destroy My self with the Church and State by My Word, or not suffer them to do it unresisted by the Sword; whose covetous ambition no Concessions of Mine could ever yet, either satisfy, or abate.

Nor is it likely they will ever think, that Kingdom of brambles, which some men seek to erect (at once, weak, sharp, and fruitless, either to God or man) is like to thrive till watered with the Royal blood of those, whose right the Kingdom is.

Well, God's will be done, I doubt not but My Innocency will find him both My Protector, and My Advocate, who is My only Judge, whom I own as King of Kings, not only for the eminency of his power and majesty above them;[2] but also for that singular care and protection, which he hath over them: who knows them to be exposed to as many dangers (being the greatest Patrons of Law, Justice, Order, and Religion on earth) as there be either Men or Devils, which love confusion.

Nor will he suffer those men long to prosper in their *Babel*, who build it with the bones and cement it with the blood of their Kings.

I am confident they will find Avengers of My death among themselves: the injuries I have sustained from them shall be first punished by them, who agreed in nothing so much as in opposing Me.

Their impatience to bear the loud cry of My blood, shall make them think no way better to expiate it, than by shedding theirs, who with them, most thirsted after Mine.[3]

---

1 In Matthew 21:33-40, Jesus narrates a parable in which tenants murder the son of the landowner (after killing his servants) in order to "seize on his inheritance" (see also Mark 12:1-9; Luke 20:9-16).

2 *God's ... done* Matthew 6:10, 26:42; Luke 11:2; *Advocate* 1 John 2:1; *King of Kings* 1 Timothy 6:15; Revelation 17:14, 19:16.

3 Genesis 4:10.

The sad confusions following My destruction, are already presaged and confirmed to Me by those I have lived to see since My troubles; in which, God alone (who only could) hath many ways pleaded My cause;[1] not suffering them to go unpunished, whose confederacy in sin was their only security; who have cause to fear that God will both further divide, and by mutual vengeance, afterward destroy them.

My greatest conquest of Death is from the power and love of Christ, who hath swallowed up death in the victory of his Resurrection, and the glory of his Ascension.[2]

My next comfort is, that he gives Me not only the honour to imitate his example in suffering for righteousness sake, (though obscured by the foulest charges of Tyranny and Injustice) but also, that charity, which is the noblest revenge upon, and victory over My Destroyers:[3] By which, I thank God, I can both forgive them, and pray for them, that God would not impute My blood to them further than to convince them, what need they have of Christ's blood to wash their souls from the guilt of shedding Mine.

At present, the will of My Enemies seems to be their only rule, their power the measure, and their success the Exactor, of what they please to call Justice; while they flatter themselves with the fancy of their own safety by My danger, and the security of their lives' designs by My Death: forgetting, that as the greatest temptations to sin are wrapped up in seeming prosperities, so the severest vengeances of God are then most accomplished, when men are suffered to complete their wicked purposes.

I bless God, I pray not so much, that this bitter cup of a violent death may pass from Me, as that of his wrath may pass from all those, whose hands by deserting Me, are sprinkled, or by acting and consenting to My death are embrued with My blood.

The will of God hath confined, and concluded Mine; I shall have the pleasure of dying, without any pleasure of desired vengeance.

This I think becomes a Christian toward his Enemies, and a King toward his Subjects.

They cannot deprive Me of more than I am content to lose, when God sees fit by their hands to take it from me; whose mercy

---

1   Psalm 35:1, 43:1, 119:154; 1 Samuel 24:15.
2   1 Corinthians 15:54; Isaiah 25:8.
3   Matthew 5:10; 1 Peter 3:14.

I believe, will more than infinitely recompense what ever by man's injustice he is pleased to deprive me of.

The glory attending my death will far surpass all I could enjoy, or conceive in life.

I shall not want the heavy and envied Crowns of this world, when my God hath mercifully crowned and consummated his graces with glory; and exchanged the shadows of my earthly Kingdoms among men, for the substance of that heavenly kingdom with himself.

For the censures of the world; I know the sharp and necessary tyranny of my Destroyers will sufficiently confute the calumnies of tyranny against me; I am persuaded I am happy in the judicious love of the ablest and best of my Subjects, who do not only pity and pray for me, but would be content even to die with me, or for me.

These know, how to excuse my failings, as a man, and yet to retain, and pay their duty to me as their King; there being no religious necessity binding any Subjects by pretending to punish, infinitely to exceed, the faults and errors of their Princes; especially there, where more than sufficient satisfaction hath been made to the public; the enjoyment of which, private ambitions have hitherto frustrated.

Others, I believe, of softer tempers, and less advantaged by my ruin, do already feel sharp convictions, and some remorse in their consciences; where they cannot but see the proportions of their evil dealings against me in the measure of God's retaliations upon them, who cannot hope long to enjoy their own thumbs and toes, having under pretence of paring others' nails been so cruel as to cut off their chiefest strength.

The punishment of the more insolent and obstinate may be like that of *Korah* and his Complices (at once mutinying against both Prince and Priest) in such a method of divine justice, as is not ordinary; the earth of the lowest and meanest people opening upon them, and swallowing them up in a just disdain of their ill-gotten worse-used Authority:[1] upon whose support and strength they chiefly depended for their building and establishing their designs against Me, the Church, and State.

My chiefest comfort in death consists in my peace, which I

---

1 Korah and his confederates led a revolt against Moses and Aaron; they were swallowed up in an earthquake and 14,700 of their allies died of the plague (Numbers 16).

trust, is made with God; before whose exact Tribunal I shall not fear to appear, as to the Cause so long disputed by the Sword, between me and my causeless Enemies: where I doubt not, but his righteous judgement will confute their fallacy, who from worldly success (rather like Sophisters, than sound Christians) draw those popular conclusions for God's approbation of their actions; whose wise providence (we know) oft permits many events, which his revealed Word (the only clear, safe and fixed rule of good actions and good consciences) in no sort approves.

I am confident the Justice of my Cause, and clearness of My Conscience before God and toward my people will carry me, as much above them in God's decision, as their successes have lifted them above me in the Vulgar opinion: who consider not, that many times those undertakings of men are lifted up to Heaven in the prosperity and applause of the world, whose rise is from Hell, as to the injuriousness and oppression of the design. The prosperous winds which oft fill the sails of Pirates, doth not justify their piracy and rapine.

I look upon it with infinite more content and quiet of Soul, to have been worsted in my enforced contestation[1] for, and vindication of the Laws of the Land, the freedom and honour of Parliaments, the rights of my Crown, the just liberty of my Subjects, and the true Christian Religion in its Doctrine, Government and due encouragements, than if I had, with the greatest advantages of success, overborne them all; as some men have now evidently done, whatever designs they at first pretended.

The prayers and patience of my Friends and loving Subjects will contribute much to the sweetening of this bitter cup, which I doubt not but I shall more cheerfully take, and drink as from God's hand (if it must be so) than they can give it to me, whose hands are unjustly and barbarously lifted up against me.

And, as to the last event, I may seem to owe more to my Enemies, than my Friends; while those will put a period to the sins and sorrows attending this miserable life; wherewith these desire, I might still contend.

I shall be more than Conqueror through Christ enabling me;[2] for whom I have hitherto suffered: as he is the Author of Truth, Order, and Peace; for all which, I have been forced to contend against Error, Faction, and confusion.

---

1 Struggle.
2 Romans 8:37; cited on the title page of *Eikon Basilike*.

If I must suffer a violent death, with my Saviour, it is but mortality crowned with martyrdom: where the debt of death, which I owe for sin to nature, shall be raised, as a gift of faith and patience offered to God.

Which I humbly beseech him mercifully to accept; and although death be the wages of my own sin, as from God, and the effect of others' sins, as men, both against God and me; yet as I hope my own sins are so remitted, that they shall be no ingredients to imbitter the cup of my death, so I desire God to pardon their sins, who are most guilty of my destruction.

The Trophies[1] of my charity will be more glorious and durable over them, than their ill-managed victories over me.

Though their sin be prosperous, yet they had need to be penitent, that they may be pardoned: Both which, I pray God they may obtain; that my temporal death unjustly inflicted by them, may not be revenged by God's just inflicting eternal death upon them: for I look upon the temporal destruction of the greatest King, as far less deprecable, than the eternal damnation of the meanest Subject.

Nor do I wish other, than the safe bringing of the ship to shore, when they have cast me overboard; though it be very strange, that Mariners can find no other means to appease the storm, themselves have raised, but by drowning their Pilot.

I thank God, my Enemies' cruelty cannot prevent my preparation; whose malice in this I shall defeat, that they shall not have the satisfaction to have destroyed my Soul with my Body; of whose salvation, while some of them have themselves seemed, and taught others to despair, they have only discovered this, that they do not much desire it.

Whose uncharitable and cruel Restraints, denying me even the assistance of any of my Chaplains, hath rather enlarged, than any way obstructed my access to the Throne of Heaven.

Where thou dwellest, O King of Kings; who fillest Heaven and Earth, who art the fountain of eternal life, in whom is no shadow of death.[2]

Thou O God art both the just Afflicter of death upon us, and the merciful Saviour of us in it, and from it.

---

1 Monuments; evidence of victory.
2 *Fillest ... Earth* Jeremiah 23:24; *fountain ... life* Psalm 36:9; Revelation 21:6; *shadow ... death* A familiar biblical phrase, frequently invoked by the afflicted, especially David and Job (e.g., Job 12:22, Psalm 23:4).

Yea, it is better for us to be dead to our selves, and live in thee;[1] *than by living in our selves to be deprived of thee.*

O make the many bitter aggravations of My death as a Man, and a King, the opportunities and advantages of thy special graces and comforts in My Soul, as a Christian.

If thou Lord wilt be with Me, I shall neither fear nor feel any evil, though I walk through the valley of the shadow of death.

To contend with death is the work of a weak and mortal man; to overcome it, is the grace of thee alone, who art the Almighty and immortal God.

O My Saviour, who knowst what it is to die with Me, as a Man; make Me to know what it is to pass through death to life with thee My God.[2]

Though I die, yet I know, that thou my Redeemer livest for ever: though thou slayest Me, yet thou hast encouraged me to trust in thee for eternal life.[3]

O withdraw not thy favour from me, which is better than life.[4]

O be not far from me,[5] *for I know not how near a violent and cruel death is to me.*

As thy Omniscience, O God, discovers, so thy Omnipotence can defeat the designs of those, who have, or shall conspire my destruction.

O show me the goodness of thy will, through the wickedness of theirs.

Thou givest me leave as a man to pray, that this cup may pass from me; but thou hast taught Me as a Christian by the example of Christ to add, not My will, but thine be done.[6]

Yea Lord, let our wills be one, by wholly resolving mine into thine: let not the desire of life in me be so great, as that of doing or suffering thy will in either life or death.

As I believe thou hast forgiven all the errors of my life, so I hope thou wilt save me from the terrors of my death.

Make me content to leave the world's nothing, that I may come really to enjoy all in thee, who hast made Christ unto me in life, gain; and in death, advantage.[7]

Though my Destroyers forget their duty to thee and me, yet do not thou, O Lord, forget to be merciful to them.

---

1   Galatians 2:19-20 (see also Romans 6:8-11).
2   John 5:24.
3   *my Redeemer livest* Job 19:25; *though thou ... in thee* Job 13:15.
4   Psalm 63:3.
5   Psalms 22:11, 35:22, 38:21, 71:12.
6   Luke 22:42.
7   Philippians 1:21.

For, what profit is there in my blood, or in their gaining my King-doms, if they lose their own Souls?[1]

Such as have not only resisted my just Power, but wholly usurped and turned it against my self, though they may deserve, yet let them not receive to themselves damnation.

Thou madest thy Son a Saviour to many, that Crucified Him, while at once he suffered violently by them, and yet willingly for them.

O let the voice of his blood be heard for My Murderers, louder than the cry of mine against them.

Prepare them for thy mercy by due convictions of their sin, and let them not at once deceive and damn their own Souls by fallacious pretensions of Justice in destroying me, while the conscience of their unjust usurpation of power against me, chiefly tempts them to use all extremities against me.

O Lord, thou knowst I have found their mercies to me as very false, so very cruel; who pretending to preserve me, have meditated nothing but my ruin.

O deal not with them as blood-thirsty and deceitful men; but over-come their cruelty with thy compassion and my charity.

And when thou makest inquisition for My blood, O sprinkle their polluted, yet penitent Souls with the blood of thy Son, that thy destroy-ing Angel may pass over them.[2]

Though they think my Kingdoms on earth too little to entertain at once both them and me, yet let the capacious Kingdom of thy infinite mercy at last receive both me and my enemies.

When being reconciled to thee in the blood of the same Redeemer,[3] *we shall live far above these ambitious desires, which beget such mortal enmities.*

When their hands shall be heaviest, and cruellest upon me, O let me fall into the arms of thy tender and eternal mercies.

That what is cut off of my life in this miserable moment, may be repaid in thy ever-blessed eternity.

Lord, let thy Servant depart in peace, for my eyes have seen thy salvation.

Vota dabunt, quae bella negârunt.[4]

FINIS.

---

1 Matthew 16:26; Mark 8:36.

2 When Pharoah refused to free the Israelites, he was punished with plagues. The final plague caused the death of all the first-born in the land of Egypt. The Israelite children were protected, however, when their parents sprinkled the blood of lambs on their doorposts (Exodus 12).

3 Romans 5:10; 2 Corinthians 5:18.

4 "What we could not get by our treaties, we may gain by our prayers."

PRAYERS, Used by His Majesty in the time of His SUFFER-INGS. Delivered to Doctor *Juxon* bishop of LONDON immediately before His Death. Also a Letter from the PRINCE.[1]

A *Prayer* in time of Captivity.[2]

O Powerful and Eternal God! to whom nothing is so great, that it may resist; or so small, that it is contemned;[3] look upon My Misery with Thine eye of Mercy, and let Thine infinite power vouchsafe to limit out some proportion of deliverance unto Me, as to Thee shall seem most convenient; let not Injury, O Lord, triumph over Me; and let My faults by Thy hand be corrected; and make not My unjust Enemies the ministers of Thy Justice: But yet, My God, if in Thy wisdom this be the aptest chastisement for My unexcusable trans-gressions; if this ingrateful bondage be fittest for My over-high desires; if the pride of My (not enough humble) heart be thus to be broken; O Lord, I yield unto Thy will, and cheerfully embrace what sorrow Thou wilt have Me suffer: Only thus much let Me crave of Thee, (Let My craving, O Lord, be accepted of, since it even pro-ceeds from Thee) that, by Thy goodness, which is Thy self, Thou wilt suffer some beam of Thy Majesty so to shine in My mind, that I, who acknowledge it My Noblest Title to be Thy Creature, may still, in My greatest Afflictions, depend confidently on Thee. Let Calami-ty be the exercise, but not the overthrow of My Virtue. O let not their prevailing power be to My destruction. And if it be Thy will that they more and more vex Me with punishment; yet, O Lord, never let their wickedness have such a hand, but that I may still carry a pure mind, and steadfast resolution ever to serve Thee, without fear or

---

1   This supplementary material first appeared in William Dugard's edition of *Eikon Basilike*, published on or about 15 March 1649 (Madan 22). The *Apophthegmata* published with this supplementary matter has been omitted. *Doctor Juxon* William Juxon (1582-1663), appointed Bishop of London (1633-49), Lord High Treasurer (1636-41), and a Privy Coun-cillor, was voluntarily imprisoned with the king, served as his chaplain, attended him during his trial and accompanied him to the scaffold. At the Restoration, he was appointed Archbishop of Canterbury.

2   John Milton first noted that this prayer was derived from the prayer of Princess Pamela in Book Three, Chapter Six of *The Countess of Pem-broke's Arcadia* (1638). Milton was charged with inserting the prayer into Dugard's edition to defame the king's memory. Madan proves such a claim false.

3   Treated with contempt; despised.

presumption; yet with that humble Confidence which may best please Thee: so that at the last I may come to Thy eternal Kingdom through the Merits of Thy Son our alone Saviour Jesus Christ. Amen.

Another PRAYER.[1]

Almighty and most merciful Father, look down upon Me Thy unworthy Servant who here prostate My self at the Foot-stool of Thy Throne of Grace;[2] but look upon Me, O Father, through the Mediation and in the Merits of Jesus Christ, in whom Thou art only well-pleased;[3] for, of My self I am not worthy to stand before Thee, or to speak with My unclean lips to Thee, most holy and Eternal God;[4] for as in sin I was conceived and born;[5] so likewise I have broken all Thy Commandments by My sinful motions, unclean thoughts, evil words, and wicked works; omitting many duties I ought to do, and committing many vices which Thou hast forbidden under pain of Thy heavy displeasure: as for My sins, O Lord, they are innumerable; wherefore I stand here liable to all the Miseries in this life, and everlasting Torments in that to come; if Thou should'st deal with Me according to My deserts. I confess, O Lord, that it is Thy Mercy (which endureth for ever) and Thy compassion (which never fails,)[6] which is the cause that I have not been long ago consumed: but with Thee there is Mercy and plenteous Redemption; in the multitude therefore of Thy Mercies, and by the Merits of Jesus Christ, I entreat Thy Divine Majesty, That Thou would'st not enter into judgment with Thy servant, nor be extreme to mark what is done amiss, but be Thou merciful unto Me, and wash away all My sins with that precious blood that My Saviour shed for Me.[7] And I beseech Thee, O

---

1 This prayer is based upon Bishop Lewis Bayly's "A Prayer for the Morning" in *Practice of Piety* (1612). However, it is "the best authenticated" of the prayers, as "a slightly altered copy, in the King's own hand and dating from about 1632, exists in the Public Record Office" (Madan 14).

2 Psalm 99:5, 132:7.

3 Matthew 3:17, 12:18, 17:5; Mark 1:11; 2 Peter 1:17.

4 Isaiah 6:5.

5 Psalm 51:5.

6 *Thy Mercy ... for ever* A common biblical phrase, esp. in the Psalms; *compassion ... fails* Lamentations 3:22.

7 *the multitude ... Thy Mercies* another common biblical expression (see, for example, Psalm 51:1, 69:16, 106:7, 45); *wash ... sins* Acts 22:16 *precious blood ... for Me* 1 Peter 1:19; Matthew 26:28; Mark 14:24; Luke 22:20.

Lord, not only to wash away all My sins, but also to purge My heart by Thy holy Spirit, from the dross of My natural corruption; and as Thou do'st add days to My life, so, good Lord, I beseech Thee, to add repentance to My days, that when I have passed this mortal life, I may be partaker of Thy everlasting Kingdom, through the Merits of Jesus Christ our Lord. Amen.

A *Prayer* and *Confession*, made in, and for the times of Affliction.

Almighty and most merciful Father, as it is only Thy goodness that admits of Our imperfect Prayers, and the knowledge that Thy Mercies are infinite, which can give Us any hope of Thy accepting or granting them; so it is Our bounden and necessary duty to confess our sins freely unto Thee;[1] *and, of all men living, I have most need, most reason, so to do, no man having been so much obliged by Thee; no man more grievously offending Thee; that degree of knowledge which Thou hast given Me, adding likewise to the guilt of My transgressions. For was it through ignorance, that I suffered innocent blood to be shed by a false-pretended way of Justice? or that I permitted a wrong way of Thy Worship to be set up in* Scotland? *and injured the Bishops in* England? *O no; but with shame and grief I confess, that I therein followed the persuasions of worldly wisdom, forsaking the Dictates of a right informed Conscience: Wherefore, O Lord, I have no excuse to make, no hope left, but in the multitude of Thy Mercies; for I know My repentance weak, and My prayers faulty: Grant therefore, merciful Father, so to strengthen My repentance, and amend My prayers, that Thou may'st clear the way for Thine own Mercies, to which, O let Thy Justice at last give place, putting a speedy end to My deserved Afflictions. In the mean time give Me Patience to endure, Constancy against Temptations, and a discerning Spirit to choose, what is best for Thy Church and People which Thou hast committed to My Charge. Grant this, O most merciful Father, for Thy Son Jesus Christ's sake, our only Saviour.* Amen.

---

1 In both the Old and New Testaments, confession of sin is necessary for divine forgiveness (see, for example, Leviticus 5:5; Psalm 32:5; 1 John 1:9).

A *Prayer* in time of imminent danger.

O *Most merciful Father, though My sins are so many and grievous, that I may rather expect the effects of Thy anger, than so great a deliverance, as to free Me from My present great danger; yet, O Lord, since Thy Mercies are over all Thy works, and Thou never failest to relieve all those who with humble and unfeigned repentance come to Thee for succour, it were to multiply, not diminish My transgressions, to despair of Thy heavenly favour: wherefore I humbly desire Thy Divine Majesty, that Thou wilt not only pardon all My sins, but also free Me out of the hands, and protect Me from the malice of My cruel Enemies. But if Thy wrath against My heinous offenses will not otherways be satisfied, than by suffering Me to fall under My present afflictions, Thy will be done; yet, with humble Importunity, I do, and shall never leave to implore the assistance of Thy heavenly Spirit, that My Cause, as I am Thy Vicegerent, may not suffer through My weakness or want of courage. O Lord, so strengthen and enlighten all the faculties of My mind, that with clearness I may show forth Thy Truth, and manfully endure this bloody Trial, that so My sufferings here may not only glorify Thee, but likewise be a furtherance to My salvation hereafter. Grant this, O merciful Father, for his sake, who suffered for Me, even Jesus Christ the Righteous.* Amen.

FINIS

*His Majesty's Reasons against the pretended Jurisdiction of the
High Court of Justice, which He
intended to deliver in Writing*
on Monday
January 22.1648[1]

Having already made My protestations not only against the illegality of this pretended Court, but also that no Earthly Power can justly call Me (who am your King) in question as a Delinquent; I would not any more open My mouth upon this occasion, more than to refer My self to what I have spoken, were I alone in this case concerned. But the duty I owe to God, in the preservation of

---

1 *His Majesty's Reasons*, published initially as a broadside, was received on
5 February 1649 by George Thomason (d. 1666), the London bookseller, publisher, and collector of political manuscripts, newspapers, books, and pamphlets.

the true liberty of My People, will not suffer Me at this time to be silent: For how can any free-born Subject of *England* call Life, or any thing he possesseth his own, if Power without Right daily make new, and abrogate the old fundamental Law of the Land? which I now take to be the present case. Wherefore when I came hither, I expected that you would have endeavoured to have satisfied Me concerning these grounds which hinder Me to Answer to your pretended Impeachment; but since I see that nothing I can say will move you to it (though Negatives are not so naturally proved as Affirmatives) yet I will show you the Reason why I am confident you cannot judge Me, nor indeed the meanest man in *England*; for, I will not (like you) without showing a reason, seek to impose a belief upon My Subjects.

*There is no proceeding just against any man, but what is warranted either by God's Laws, or the municipal Laws of the Country where he lives. Now I am most confident, that this day's proceeding cannot be warranted by God's Law; for on the contrary the authority of obedience unto Kings is clearly warranted and strictly commanded both in the Old and New Testament; which if denied, I am ready instantly to prove: and for the question now in hand, there it is said, That *where the word of a King is, there is Power, and who may say unto him, what doest thou? Eccles. 8.4.* Then for the Laws of this Land, I am no less confident, that no learned Lawyer will affirm that an Impeachment can lie against the *King*, they all going in His Name; and one of their Maxims is, *That the King can do no wrong.*[1] Besides, the Law upon which you ground your proceedings, must either be old, or new; if old, show it; if new, tell what authority warranted by the fundamental Laws of the Land hath made it, and when. But how the House of

---

* "Hereabout I was stopped, and not suffered to speak any more concerning Reasons." [Original marginalia.] During his trial (January 20 to 27, 1649), Charles was often interrupted by John Bradshaw, Lord President of the High Court of Justice, who demanded that Charles answer the charges against him. Insisting the proceedings were illegal, the king refused to plead to the charges (see Appendix B).

---

1 "Rex non potest peccare," the principal legal maxim related to the crown, prevented lawsuits from being brought against the sovereign. See Francis Bacon, *Collection of Some Principal Rules and Maxims of the Common Law* (1630) and William Noy, *Treatise of the principal Grounds and Maxims of the Law of England* (1641).

Commons can erect a Court of Judicature, which was never one it self (as is well known to all Lawyers) I leave to God and the world to judge: And it were full as strange, that they should pretend to make Laws without KING or Lords-House, to any that have heard speak of the Laws of *England*.

And admitting, but not granting, that the People of *England's* Commission could grant your pretended power, I see nothing you can show for that; for certainly you never asked the question of the tenth man of the Kingdom, and in this way you manifestly wrong even the poorest Plough-man, if you demand not his free consent; nor can you pretend any colour for this your pretended Commission without the consent at least of the major part of every man in *England*, of whatsoever quality or condition, which I am sure you never went about to seek; so far are you from having it. Thus you see that I speak not for My own right alone, as I am your KING; but also for the true Liberty of all My Subjects, which consists not in sharing the power of Government, but in living under such Laws, such a Government as may give themselves the best assurance of their lives and property of their goods. Nor in this must or do I forget the Privileges of both Houses of Parliament, which this day's proceeding doth not only violate, but likewise occasion the greatest breach of their Public Faith that (I believe) ever was heard of, with which I am far from charging the two Houses: for all the pretended Crimes laid against Me, bear date long before this late Treaty at *Newport*, in which I having concluded as much as in Me lay, and hopefully expecting the two Houses' agreement thereunto, I was suddenly surprised, and hurried from thence as a Prisoner,[1] upon which account I am against My will brought hither, where since I am come, I cannot but to My power defend the ancient Laws and Liberties of this Kingdom, together with My own just right; then for any thing I can see the higher House is totally excluded.

And for the House of Commons, it is too well known that the major part of them are detained or deterred from sitting, so as if I had no other, this were sufficient for Me to protest against the

---

1 Imprisoned on the Isle of Wight, Charles negotiated with the Presbyterian Members of Parliament at Newport in September and October, 1648. On 2 December, Charles was moved to Hurst Castle, and later to Windsor Castle. On 6 December, Colonel Thomas Pride barred many MPs from Parliament ("Pride's Purge") and the remaining members (the Rump Parliament) annulled the Newport Proposals.

lawfulness of your pretended Court. Besides all this, the Peace of the Kingdom is not the least in My thoughts, and what hopes of settlement is there so long as Power reigns without rule of Law, changing the whole frame of that Government under which this Kingdom hath flourished for many hundred years? (nor will I say what will fall out in case this lawless unjust proceeding against Me do go on) and believe it, the Commons of *England* will not thank you for this change, for they will remember how happy they have been of late years under the Reign of *Q. Elizabeth*, the KING My Father, and My self, until the beginning of these unhappy Troubles; and will have cause to doubt that they shall never be so happy under any new. And by this time it will be too sensibly evident, that the Arms I took up were only to defend the fundamental Laws of this Kingdom, against those who have supposed My power hath totally changed the ancient Government.

Thus having showed you briefly the Reasons, why I cannot submit to your pretended Authority without violating the trust which I have from God, for the welfare and liberty of My People: I expect from you either clear Reasons to convince My judgment, showing Me that I am in an Error, (and then truly I will readily Answer) or that you will withdraw your proceedings.

This I intended to speak in Westminster-hall *on* Monday, 22 January; *but against reason was hindered to show My Reasons.*

A Copy of a Letter which was sent
from the PRINCE to the KING;
Dated from the *Hague,*
Jan. 23. 1648.

SIR!

Having no means to come to the knowledge of Your Majesty's present condition, but such as I receive from the Prints,[1] *or (which is as uncertain) Report, I have sent this Bearer* Seymour *to wait upon Your Majesty;*[2] *and to bring Me an account of it: that I may withal assure Your Majesty, I do not only pray for Your Majesty, according to My*

---

1 Printed newssheets.
2 Henry Seymour, formerly a page and courtier to King Charles I.

Duty; but shall always be ready to do all which shall be in My power,
to deserve that blessing which I now humbly beg of Your Majesty upon,
SIR,
Hague, *Jan*.23.
1648.   *Your* MAJESTY'S
                             most humble and most
                             obedient Son and Servant,
                             CHARLES.

The Superscription was thus,
[For the King.]

Monday 29th. *January*, 1648.
A true Relation of the KING'S *Speech to the*
Lady Elisabeth, *and the Duke of* Gloucester, *the*
day before His death.[1]

His Children being come to meet Him, He first gave His blessing to the Lady *Elisabeth*; and bade her remember to tell her
Brother *James*, when ever she should see him, That it was his
Father's last desire, that he should no more look upon *Charles* as
his eldest Brother only, but be obedient unto him, as his Sovereign; and that they should love one another, and forgive their
Father's Enemies. Then said the *King* to her, Sweet-heart, you'll
forget this: No (said she) I shall never forget it while I live: and,
pouring forth abundance of tears, promised Him to write down
the particulars.

Then the *King* taking the Duke of *Gloucester* upon His Knee,
said, Sweet-heart, Now they will cut off thy Father's Head; (upon
which words the Child looked very steadfastly on Him) Mark
Child what I say, They will cut off My Head, and perhaps make
thee a King: But mark what I say, You must not be a King, so long
as your Brothers, *Charles* and *James*, do live; For they will cut off
your Brothers' Heads (when they can catch them) and cut off thy
Head too at the last: and therefore I charge you, do not be made
a King by them. At which the Child sighing, said, I will be torn

---

1 Princess Elizabeth (1635-50), held by Parliament from the age of seven,
   died at Carisbrooke Castle at fourteen. Henry, Duke of Gloucester
   (1640-60), eight in this final meeting with his father, was permitted to
   reunite with his mother in 1652.

in pieces first. Which falling[1] so unexpectedly from one so young, it made the *King* rejoice exceedingly.

Another Relation from the Lady Elisabeth's
own Hand.

What the *King* said to Me the nine and twentieth of *Jan.*1648. being the last time I had the happiness to see Him; He told me, He was glad I was come, and although He had not time to say much, yet somewhat He had to say to Me, which He had not to another, or leave in writing; because He feared their Cruelty was such, as that they would not have permitted Him to write to me. He wished me not to grieve and torment my self for Him; for that would be a glorious death that He should die; it being for the Laws and Liberties of this Land, and for maintaining the true Protestant Religion. He bid me read Bishop *Andrewes'* Sermons, *Hooker's Ecclesiastical Polity*, and Bishop *Laud's* book against *Fisher*, which would ground me against Popery.[2] He told me, He had forgiven all His Enemies, and hoped God would forgive them also; and commanded Us, and all the rest of my Brothers and Sisters to forgive them. He bid me tell my Mother, That His thoughts had never strayed from Her, and that His Love should be the same to the last. Withal, He commanded me and my Brother to be obedient to Her. And bid me send His Blessing to the rest of my Brothers and Sisters, with Commendation to all His Friends. So after He had given me His Blessing, I took my leave.

Further, He commanded Us all to forgive those people, but never to trust them; for they had been most false to Him, and to those that gave them power, and He feared also to their own souls: And desired me not to grieve for Him, for He should die a *Martyr*, and that He doubted not but the Lord would settle His Throne upon His Son, and that We should be all happier, than We

---

1 Issuing; proceeding.
2 Lancelot Andrewes, *XCVI Sermons* (London, 1629); Richard Hooker, *Of the Laws of Ecclesiastical Polity* (London, 1594-97); William Laud, *A relation of the conference between William Laud, then, Lord Bishop of St. Davids: now, Lord Arch-Bishop of Canterbury: and Mr. Fisher the Jesuit* (London, 1639).

could have expected to have been, if He had lived: With many other things, which at present I cannot remember. *Elisabeth*

Another Relation from the Lady Elisabeth.

The *King* said to the Duke of *Gloucester*, that He would say nothing to him but what was for the good of his soul: He told him, that He heard the Army intended to make him King; but it was a thing not for him to take upon him, if he regarded the welfare of his Soul; for he had two Brothers before him; and therefore commanded him upon His Blessing, never to accept of it, unless it redounded lawfully upon him: And commanded him to fear the Lord, and He would provide for him.

"An *Epitaph* upon King CHARLES"[1]

So falls that stately Cedar: while it stood,
That was the only Glory of the Wood:
Great CHARLES, *Thou earthly God, Celestial Man,*
Whose life, like others, though it were a Span:
Yet in that Span, was comprehended more
Than Earth hath waters, or the Ocean shore.
Thy heavenly Virtues Angels should rehearse;
It is a theme too high for human Verse.
He that would know Thee right then, let him look
Upon Thy rare-incomparable Book,
And read it o'er and o'er; which if he do,
He'll find thee King, *and* Priest, *and* Prophet *too:*
And sadly see our loss; and, though in vain,
With fruitless wishes call Thee back again.
Nor shall Oblivion sit upon Thy Hearse,
Though there were neither Monument, nor Verse.
　　Thy Sufferings *and Thy* Death *let no man name;*
　　It was Thy Glory, *but the Kingdom's* Shame.
　　　　　　　　　　J.H.

1　This epitaph has been attributed both to James Howell and John Hewett.

"*Upon His Sacred Majesty's incomparable* EIKON BASILIKE"[1]

Dread Sir!
Couldst thou before thy death have *giv'n*, what we
Might *ask*, Thy *Book* had been the *Legacy*.
Thy *Will* can make but *Heirs* of *Monarchy*;
But This doth make each man an Heir of *Thee*.
Blest Soul! *Thou* art now mounted up on High,
Beyond our *Reach*, yet not above our *Eye*.
Lo here Thy *other-Self*: Thus Thou canst be
In Heav'n and Earth, without *Ubiquity*.
Like This Thou hast no *Picture*: So Divine,
Might any *Image* be ador'd, 'twere *Thine*.
So curious is this Work; 'tis easily known,
'Twas drawn by no man's *Pencil*, but Thine own.
None could express a *King*, but Thou: We see,
Men cannot, *Gods* may limn[2] a *Deity*.
The *Style* betrays a *King*, the *Art* a *Man*,
The high *Devotion* speaks a *Christian*.
These meet in CHARLES alone; but *He*, there's none
So fully *All*, as if He were but *One*:[3]
How short of Thee is *Balzac's* Prince;[4] He knew
Not how to *think*, what Thou knew'st how to *do*:
Thou art the *Copy*[5] for our Kings: and He
Shall still be best, that frames Himself by *Thee*:
Thy Work's a Practic *Pattern* for Thy *Son*,
Who, having this, shall need no *Xenophon*.[6]
They that would know thy Parts, must read *Thee*: Look,

---

1 This poem is located in the prefatory matter of the twenty-second edition of *Eikon Basilike*. Its author—F.N.G[entleman]—has not been identified.
2 Paint.
3 Charles is here associated with God, identified as the "All in All" and
the "One" throughout the Bible (e.g., "But to us there is but one God,
the Father, of whom are all things, and we in him; and one Lord Jesus
Christ, by whom are all things, and we by him"—1 Corinthians 8:6).
4 Jean Louis Guez de Balzac published a eulogy to Louis XIII entitled *Le
Prince* (Paris, 1631).
5 The original, from which a copy is made.
6 The Greek historian (c. 431-352 BCE); that is, Charles II need not look
to history for models of good kingship as he need only imitate his father.

You'll find each *Line* a *Page*, each *Page* a *Book*:
Each *Comma* is so full, each *Colon* good,
'Tis Pity, death did put a *Period*.
Great *Tully*[1] had been silenc'd amongst men,
Had but Thy *Tongue* been equal to Thy *Pen*:
But this *Defect* doth prove Thy skill more choice,
That makes the *Echo* sweeter than the *voice*:
Our *Bodley's* shelves[2] will now be full; No man
Will want more Books; This one's a *Vatican*.
Yet 'tis but CHARLES contracted: Since His fall
Heav'n hath the *Volume*, Earth the *Manual*.

F.N.G.

---

1 Marcus Tullius Cicero (106-43 BCE), the renowned Roman rhetorician.
2 The shelves of the Bodleian library.

SELECTIONS FROM
EIKONOKLASTES

ΕΙΚΟΝΟΚΛΑΣΤΗΣ

IN

Answer

To a Book Intitl'd

ΕΙΚΩΝ ΒΑΣΙΛΙΚΗ,

THE

PORTRATURE of his Sacred MAJESTY

in his *Solitudes* and *Sufferings.*

The Author   *I.M.*

PROV. 28. 15,16,17.

15. *As a roaring Lyon, and a ranging Beare, so is a wicked Ruler over the poor people.*

16. *The Prince that wanteth understanding, is also a great oppressor; but he that hateth covetousnesse shall prolong his dayes.*

17. *A man that doth violence to the blood of any person, shall fly to the pit, let no man stay him.*

Salust. Conjurat. Catilin.

Regium imperium, quod initio conservandæ libertatis, atque augendæ reipub. causâ fuerat, in superbiam, dominationemque se convertit.

Regibus boni, quam mali, suspetiores sunt; semperque his aliena virtus formidolosa est.

Quidlibet impunè facere, hoc scilicet regium est.

Published by Authority.

London, Printed by *Matthew Simmons,* next dore to the gilded Lyon in Aldersgate Street.   1649.

THE PREFACE.

To descant[1] on the misfortunes of a Person fallen from so high a dignity, who hath also paid his final debt both to Nature and his Faults, is neither of it self a thing commendable, nor the intention of this discourse. Neither was it fond ambition, or the vanity to get a Name, present, or with Posterity, by writing against a King: I never was so thirsty after Fame, nor so destitute of other hopes and means, better and more certain to attain it. For Kings have gained glorious Titles from their Favourers by writing against private men, as *Henry* the 8th did against *Luther*; but no man ever gained much honour by writing against a King, as not usually meeting with that force of Argument in such Courtly *Antagonists*, which to convince might add to his reputation. Kings most commonly, though strong in Legions, are but weak at Arguments; as they who ever have accustomed from the Cradle to use their will only as their right hand, their reason always as their left. Whence unexpectedly constrained to that kind of combat, they prove but weak and puny Adversaries. Nevertheless for their sakes who through custom, simplicity, or want of better teaching, have not more seriously considered Kings, than in the gaudy name of Majesty, and admire them and their doings, as if they breathed not the same breath with other mortal men, I shall make no scruple to take up (for it seems to be the challenge both of him and all his party) to take up this Gauntlet, though a King's, in the behalf of Liberty, and the Common-wealth.

And further, since it appears manifestly the cunning drift of a factious and defeated Party, to make the same advantage of his Book, which they did before of his Regal Name and Authority, and intend it not so much the defence of his former actions, as the promoting of their own future designs; making thereby the Book their own rather than the King's, as the benefit now must be their own more than his, now the third time to corrupt and disorder the minds of weaker men, by new suggestions and narrations, either falsely or fallaciously representing the state of things, to the dishonour of this present Government, and the retarding of a general peace, so needful to this afflicted Nation, and so nigh obtained, I suppose it no injury to the dead, but a good deed rather to the living, if by better information given

---

1 Make remarks, observations.

them, or, which is enough, by only remembering[1] them the truth of what they themselves know to be here misaffirmed, they may be kept from entering the third time unadvisedly into War and bloodshed.[2] For as to any moment of solidity[3] in the Book it self, stuffed with naught else but the common grounds of Tyranny and Popery, sugared a little over; or any need of answering, in respect of staid and well-principled men, I take it on me as a work assigned rather, than by me chosen or affected. Which was the cause both of beginning it so late, and finishing it so leisurely, in the midst of other employments and diversions.[4] And if the late King had thought sufficient those Answers and Defences made for him in his life time, they who on the other side accused his evil Government, judging that on their behalf enough also hath been replied, the heat of this controversy was in likelihood drawing to an end; and the further mention of his deeds, not so much unfortunate as faulty, had in tenderness to his late sufferings, been willingly forborne; and perhaps for the present age might have slept with him unrepeated; while his Adversaries, calmed and assuaged with the success of their cause, had been the less unfavourable to his memory. But since he himself, making new appeal to Truth and the World, hath left behind him this Book as the best advocate and interpreter of his own actions, and that his Friends by publishing, dispersing, commending, and almost adoring it, seem to place therein the chief strength and nerves of their cause, it would argue doubtless in the other party great deficience and distrust of themselves, not to meet the force of his reason in any field whatsoever, the force and equipage of whose Arms they have so often met victoriously. And he who at the Bar stood excepting[5] against the form and manner of his Judicature, and complained that he was not heard, neither he nor his Friends shall have that cause now to find fault; being met and debated with in this open

---

1 Reminding.
2 Two civil wars had already been fought (1642 to 1646, and 1648).
3 Smallest particle of substance.
4 Milton's comment here is suggestive of an order by the Council of State that he respond to *Eikon Basilike*. He had been appointed Secretary for Foreign Tongues to the Council on 15 March 1649 (incidentally, the date of Dugard's first printing of the King's Book). However, no order is extant. Oliver Cromwell had first unsuccessfully attempted to enlist John Selden to write a reply.
5 Objecting.

and monumental Court of his own erecting; and not only heard uttering his whole mind at large, but answered. Which to do effectually, if it be necessary that to his Book nothing the more respect be had for being his, they of his own Party can have no just reason to exclaim.[1] For it were too unreasonable that he, because dead, should have the liberty in his Book to speak all evil of the Parliament; and they, because living, should be expected to have less freedom, or any for them, to speak home the plain truth of a full and pertinent reply. As he, to acquit himself, hath not spared his Adversaries, to load them with all sorts of blame and accusation, so to him, as in his Book alive, there will be used no more Courtship than he uses; but what is properly his own guilt, not imputed any more to his evil Counsellors (a Ceremony used longer by the Parliament than he himself desired)[2] shall be laid here without circumlocutions at his own door. That they who from the first beginning, or but now of late, by what unhappiness I know not, are so much affatuated,[3] not with his person only, but with his palpable faults, and dote upon his deformities, may have none to blame but their own folly, if they live and die in such a stricken blindness, as next to that of *Sodom* hath not happened to any sort of men more gross, or more misleading.[4]

First then that some men (whether this were by him intended or by his Friends) have by policy accomplished after death that revenge upon their Enemies, which in life they were not able, hath been oft related. And among other examples we find that the last Will of *Caesar* being read to the people,[5] and what bounteous Legacies he had bequeathed them, wrought more in that Vulgar audience to the avenging of his death, than all the art he could ever use, to win their favour in his life-time. And how much their intent, who published these overlate Apologies and Meditations of

---

1 Complain.

2 In the early years of the conflict, Charles I was seen as redeemable if his "evil counsellors" could be removed from influence. The point is central to the Grand Remonstrance (November 1641) and the Nineteen Propositions (June 1642).

3 Infatuated.

4 In Genesis 19, God destroyed the cities of Sodom and Gomorrah with fire and brimstone because of the depravity and spiritual blindness of their citizens.

5 See Suetonius' *Life of Caesar* and Plutarch's *Caesar*; see also Shakespeare's treatment of Caesar's will in Act 3, Scene 2 of *Julius Caesar*.

the dead King, drives to the same end of stirring up the people to bring him that honour, that affection, and by consequence, that revenge to his dead Corpse, which he himself living could never gain to his Person, it appears both by the conceited[1] portraiture before his Book, drawn out to the full measure of a Masquing Scene, and set there to catch fools and silly gazers, and by those Latin words after the end, *Vota dabunt quae Bella negarunt*,[2] intimating, that what he could not compass by War, he should achieve by his Meditations. For in words which admit of various sense, the liberty is ours to choose that interpretation which may best mind[3] us of what our restless enemies endeavour, and what we are timely to prevent. And here may be well observed the loose and negligent curiosity of those who took upon them to adorn the setting out of this Book: for though the Picture set in Front would Martyr him and Saint him to befool the people, yet the Latin Motto in the end, which they understand not, leaves him, as it were, a politic contriver to bring about that interest by fair and plausible words, which the force of Arms denied him. But quaint Emblems and devices begged[4] from the old Pageantry of some Twelfth-night's entertainment at *Whitehall*, will do but ill to make a Saint or Martyr: and if the People resolve to take him Sainted at the rate of such a Canonising, I shall suspect their Calendar more than the *Gregorian*.[5] In one thing I must commend his openness who gave the Title to this Book, *Eikon Basilike*, that is to say, The King's Image; and by the Shrine he dresses out for him, certainly, would have the people come and worship him. For which reason this Answer also is entitled *Iconoclastes*, the famous Surname of many Greek Emperors, who in their zeal to the command of God, after long tradition of Idolatry in the Church, took courage and broke all superstitious Images to pieces.[6] But the people, exorbitant and

---

1 Fanciful.
2 The closing epigraph of *Eikon Basilike*; Milton's translation follows.
3 Remind.
4 Taken as a matter of course, without warrant.
5 *Twelfth-night's ...Whitehall* Milton alludes here to masques performed in the Banqueting House. They were denounced by Puritan polemicists who saw them as idolatrous (see, for example, William Prynne's *Histriomastix*, 1633). Masques were performed at court on Twelfth Night to mark the end of the Christmas season. *Calendar ... Gregorian* England did not change to what they perceived as the "popish" Gregorian calendar until 1751.
6 Leo III ("the Isaurian"), Emperor of Byzantium from 717 to 741 CE, attempted to suppress devotion to holy images, beginning a lengthy struggle over iconoclasm.

excessive in all their motions, are prone ofttimes not to a religious only, but to a civil kind of Idolatry in Idolising their Kings; though never more mistaken in the object of their worship; heretofore being wont to repute for Saints, those faithful and courageous Barons, who lost their lives in the Field, making glorious War against Tyrants for the common Liberty; as *Simon de Momfort*, Earl of *Leicester*, against *Henry* the third; *Thomas Plantagenet* Earl of *Lancaster*, against *Edward* the second.[1] But now with a besotted and degenerate baseness of spirit, except some few, who yet retain in them the old English fortitude and love of freedom, and have testified it by their matchless deeds, the rest embastardized[2] from the ancient nobleness of their Ancestors, are ready to fall flat and give adoration to the Image and memory of this Man, who hath offered at more cunning fetches[3] to undermine our Liberties and put Tyranny into an Art, than any British King before him. Which low dejection and debasement of mind in the people, I must confess I cannot willingly ascribe to the natural disposition of an Englishman, but rather to two other causes. First to the Prelates and their fellow-teachers, though of another Name and Sect,[4] whose Pulpit-stuff, both first and last, hath been the Doctrine and perpetual infusion of servility and wretchedness to all their hearers; and their lives the type of worldliness and hypocrisy, without the least true pattern of virtue, righteousness, or self-denial in their whole practice. I attribute it next to the factious inclination of most men divided from the public by several ends and humours of their own. At first no man less beloved, no man more generally condemned than was the King; from the time that it became his custom to break Parliaments at home, and either wilfully or weakly to betray Protestants abroad,[5] to the beginning of these Combustions. All men inveighed against him, all men, except Court-vassals,

---

1 Simon de Montfort forced the Provisions of Oxford on his brother-in-law Henry III, which limited royal power and called for a representative body; he later overthrew Henry III, who failed to abide by those provisions. Thomas Plantagenet supported ordinances which restricted the power of Edward II.

2 Rendered bastard or degenerate.

3 Dodges, stratagems, or tricks.

4 Milton is alluding to the Presbyterians and their insistence that the trial and execution of the king went against the Solemn League and Covenant.

5 The allusion is primarily to Ireland, but the La Rochelle expedition (treated in Chapter 2) is also relevant.

opposed him and his Tyrannical proceedings; the cry was universal; and this full Parliament was at first unanimous in their dislike and Protestation against his evil Government. But when they who sought themselves and not the Public, began to doubt that all of them could not by one and the same way attain to their ambitious purposes, then was the King, or his Name at least, as a fit property, first made use of, his doings made the best of, and by degrees justified: Which begot him such a party, as after many wiles and strugglings with his inward fears, emboldened him at length to set up his Standard against the Parliament.[1] When as before that time, all his adherents, consisting most of dissolute swordmen and Suburb roisters,[2] hardly amounted to the making up of one ragged regiment strong enough to assault the unarmed house of Commons. After which attempt seconded by a tedious and bloody war on his subjects, wherein he hath so far exceeded those his arbitrary violences in time of peace, they who before hated him for his high misgovernment, nay, fought against him with displayed banners in the field, now applaud him and extol him for the wisest and most religious Prince that lived. By so strange a method amongst the mad multitude is a sudden reputation won, of wisdom by wilfulness and subtle shifts, of goodness by multiplying evil, of piety by endeavouring to root out true religion.

But it is evident that the chief of his adherents never loved him, never honoured either him or his cause, but as they took him to set a face upon their own malignant designs, nor bemoan his loss at all, but the loss of their own aspiring hopes: Like those captive women whom the Poet notes in his *Iliad*, to have bewailed the death of *Patroclus* in outward show, but indeed their own condition.

Πάτροκλον πρόφασιν, σφῶν δ' αὐτῶν κήδε' ἑκάστη.
Hom. *Iliad. τ.*[3]

And it needs must be ridiculous to any judgement unenthralled, that they who in other matters express so little fear either of God or man, should in this one particular outstrip all pre-

---

1 Charles I raised his standard at Nottingham on 22 August 1642.
2 Swaggering bullies.
3 George Chapman translates these lines from *The Iliad* (Book 19): "Thus spake she weeping, and with her did th'other ladies moan / Patroclus' fortunes in pretext, but in sad truth their own."

cisianism[1] with their scruples and cases, and fill men's ears continually with the noise of their conscientious Loyalty and Allegiance to the King, Rebels in the mean while to God in all their actions beside: much less that they whose professed Loyalty and Allegiance led them to direct Arms against the King's Person, and thought him nothing violated by the Sword of Hostility drawn by them against him, should now in earnest think him violated by the unsparing Sword of Justice, which undoubtedly so much the less in vain she bears among Men, by how much greater and in highest place the offender. Else Justice, whether moral or political, were not Justice, but a false counterfeit of that impartial and Godlike virtue. The only grief is, that the head was not strook off to the best advantage and commodity[2] of them that held it by the hair: Which observation, though made by a Common Enemy, may for the truth of it hereafter become a Proverb. But as to the Author of these Soliloquies, whether it were the late King, as is Vulgarly believed, or any secret *Coadjutor*,[3] and some stick[4] not to name him, it can add nothing, nor shall take from the weight, if any be, of reason which he brings. But allegations, not reasons are the main Contents of this Book; and need no more than other contrary allegations to lay the question before all Men in an even balance; though it were supposed that the Testimony of one man in his own cause affirming, could be of any moment to bring in doubt the authority of a Parliament denying. But if these his fair spoken words shall be here fairly confronted and laid parallel to his own far differing deeds, manifest and visible to the whole Nation, then surely we may look on them who notwithstanding shall persist to give to bare words more credit than to open deeds, as men whose judgement was not rationally evinced[5] and persuaded, but fatally stupefied and bewitched, into such a blind and obstinate belief. For whose cure it may be doubted, not whether any charm, though never so wisely murmured, but whether any prayer can be available.

---

1 Rigid precision in religious observance. The term was originally applied to the Puritans.
2 Benefit.
3 Assistant; the word carries ecclesiastical implications, suggesting a clerical co-author.
4 Hesitate, scruple.
5 Convinced, proved by argument.

EIKONOKLASTES

1. *Upon the King's calling this last Parliament.*
THAT which the King lays down here as his first foundation, and as it were the head stone of his whole Structure, that *He called this last Parliament not more by others' advice and the necessity of his affairs, than by his own choice and inclination,* is to all knowing men so apparently not true, that a more unlucky and inauspicious sentence, and more betokening the downfall of his whole Fabric,[1] hardly could have come into his mind. For who knows not that the inclination of a Prince is best known either by those next about him, and most in favour with him, or by the current of his own actions. Those nearest to this King and most his Favourites, were Courtiers and Prelates; men whose chief study was to find out which way the King inclined, and to imitate him exactly. How these men stood affected to Parliaments, cannot be forgotten. No man but may remember it was their continual exercise to dispute and Preach against them; and in their common discourse nothing was more frequent, than that *they hoped the King should now have no need of Parliaments any more.* And this was but the copy which his Parasites had industriously taken from his own words and actions, who never called a Parliament but to supply his necessities; and having supplied those, as suddenly and ignominiously dissolved it, without redressing any one grievance of the people. Sometimes choosing rather to miss of his Subsidies, or to raise them by illegal courses, than that the people should not still miss of their hopes, to be relieved by Parliaments.

The first he broke off at his coming to the Crown; for no other cause than to protect the Duke of *Buckingham* against them who had accused him, besides other heinous crimes, of no less than poisoning the deceased King his Father.[2] And still the latter breaking was with more affront and indignity put upon the House

---

1 Edifice.
2 Charles I's first parliament sat from 18 June to 11 July 1625; it was then adjourned to Oxford, where it sat for only a few weeks. Charles abruptly dissolved his second parliament, assembled in February 1626, to halt the impeachment proceedings against Buckingham, which included the charge of poisoning James I. George Villiers (1592-1628), the last favourite of James I, was granted the title Duke of Buckingham (1623) after a meteoric rise in the Jacobean court. He continued to have significant influence with Charles I before his assassination.

and her worthiest Members, than the former:[1] Insomuch that in the fifth year of his Reign, in a Proclamation he seems offended at the very rumour of a Parliament divulged among the people: as if he had taken it for a kind of slander, that men should think him that way exorable,[2] much less inclined: and forbids it as a presumption to prescribe him any time for Parliaments; that is to say, either by persuasion or Petition, or so much as the reporting of such a rumour; for other manner of prescribing was at that time not suspected. By which fierce Edict, the people, forbidden to complain, as well as forced to suffer, began from thenceforth to despair of Parliaments. Whereupon such illegal actions, and especially to get vast sums of Money, were put in practice by the King and his new Officers, as Monopolies, compulsive Knighthoods, Cote, Conduct and Ship-money, the seizing not of one *Naboth's* Vineyard, but of whole Inheritances under the pretence of Forest, or Crown-Lands, corruption and Bribery compounded for, with impunities granted for the future, as gave evident proof that the King never meant, nor could it stand with the reason of his affairs, ever to recall Parliaments; having brought by these irregular courses the people's interest, and his own to so direct an opposition, that he might foresee plainly, if nothing but a Parliament could save the people, it must necessarily be his undoing.

Till eight or nine years after, proceeding with a high hand in these enormities, and having the second time levied an injurious War against his native Country *Scotland*,[3] and finding all those other shifts of raising Money, which bore out his first expedition, now to fail him, not *of his own choice and inclination*, as any Child may see, but urged by strong necessities, and the very pangs of

---

1   The third parliament (the "latter"), first assembled on 17 March 1628, compelled Charles I to agree to the Petition of Right. It was dissolved on 4 March 1629, two days after Sir John Eliot vociferously protested royal policy in the chamber of the House of Commons while the Speaker of the House was prevented from reading the royal order to adjourn parliament.

2   Accessible to entreaty.

3   *injurious War ... Scotland* The first of the two Bishops' Wars ended with the Treaty of Berwick (18 June 1639) and the second with the Treaty of Ripon (21 October 1640); *first in Ireland ... afterwards* Strafford called an Irish parliament in March 1640 which granted four subsidies to the king for the Second Bishops' War. Both the Short Parliament (summoned in April 1640) and the city of London refused him subsidies and loans.

State which his own violent proceedings had brought him to, he calls a Parliament; first in *Ireland*, which only was to give him four Subsidies, and so to expire; then in *England*, where his first demand was but twelve Subsidies, to maintain a Scotch War, condemned and abominated by the whole Kingdom; promising their grievances should be considered afterwards. Which when the Parliament, who judged that War it self one of their main grievances, made no haste to grant, not enduring the delay of his impatient will, or else fearing the conditions of their grant, he breaks off the whole Session, and dismisses them and their grievances with scorn and frustration.[1]

Much less therefore did he call this last Parliament by his own choice and inclination; but having first tried in vain all undue ways to procure Money, his Army of their own accord being beaten in the North, the Lords' Petitioning, and the general voice of the people, almost hissing him and his ill-acted regality off the Stage, compelled at length both by his wants, and by his fears, upon mere extremity he summoned this last Parliament. And how is it possible that he should willingly incline to Parliaments, who never was perceived to call them but for the greedy hope of a whole National Bribe, his Subsidies, and never loved, never fulfilled, never promoted the true end of Parliaments, the redress of grievances, but still put them off, and prolonged[2] them, whether gratified or not gratified; and was indeed the Author of all those grievances. To say therefore that he called this Parliament of his own choice and inclination, argues how little truth we can expect from the sequel[3] of this Book, which ventures in the very first period to affront more than one Nation with an untruth so remarkable; and presumes a more implicit Faith in the people of *England*, than the Pope ever commanded from the Romish Laity; or else a natural sottishness fit to be abused and ridden.[4] While in the judgement of wise Men, by laying the foundation of his defence on the avouchment[5] of that which is so manifestly untrue, he hath given a worse foil[6] to his own cause, than when his whole Forces were at any time overthrown. They therefore

---

1 Charles dissolved the Short Parliament on 5 May 1640.
2 Prorogued; adjourned.
3 The following chapters.
4 Taken advantage of.
5 Declaration.
6 Injury.

who think such great Service done to the King's affairs in publishing this Book, will find themselves in the end mistaken: if sense and right mind, or but any mediocrity[1] of knowledge and remembrance, hath not quite forsaken men.

But to prove his inclination to Parliaments, he affirms here *To have always thought the right way of them, most safe for his Crown, and best pleasing to his People.* What he thought we know not; but that he ever took the contrary way we saw; and from his own actions we felt long ago what he thought of Parliaments or of pleasing his People: a surer evidence than what we hear now too late in words.

He alleges, that *the cause of forbearing to convene Parliaments was the sparks which some men's distempers there studied to kindle.* They were indeed not tempered to his temper; for it neither was the Law, nor the rule by which all other tempers were to be tried; but they were esteemed and chosen for the fittest men in their several Counties, to allay and quench those distempers which his own inordinate doings had inflamed. And if that were his refusing to *convene*, till those men had been qualified[2] to his temper, that is to say, his will, we may easily conjecture what hope there was of Parliaments, had not fear and his insatiate poverty in the midst of his excessive wealth constrained him.

He hoped by his freedom, and their moderation to prevent misunderstandings. And wherefore not by their freedom and his moderation? But freedom he thought too high a word for them; and moderation too mean a word for himself: this was not the way to prevent misunderstandings. He still *feared passion and prejudice in other men*; not in himself: *and doubted not by the weight of his* own *reason, to counterpoise any Faction*; it being so easy for him, and so frequent, to call his obstinacy reason, and other men's reason, Faction. We in the mean while must believe, that wisdom and all reason came to him, by Title, with his Crown; passion, prejudice, and Faction, came to others by being Subjects.

He was sorry to hear with what popular heat Elections were carried in many places. Sorry rather that Court Letters, and intimations prevailed no more, to divert, or to deter the people from their free Election of those men, whom they thought best affected to Religion, and their Country's Liberty, both at that time in danger to be lost. And such men they were as by the Kingdom were sent to

---

1 Proportion.
2 Reduced.

advise him, not sent to be cavilled at,[1] because Elected, or to be entertained by him with an undervalue and misprision[2] of their temper, judgement, or affection. In vain was a Parliament thought fittest by the known Laws of our Nation, to advise and regulate unruly Kings, if they, in stead of hearkening to advice, should be permitted to turn it off, and refuse it by vilifying and traducing their advisers, or by accusing of a popular heat those that lawfully elected them.

His own and his Children's interest obliged him to seek and to preserve the love and welfare of his Subjects. Who doubts it? But the same interest, common to all Kings, was never yet available to make them all seek that, which was indeed best for themselves and their Posterity. All men by their own and their Children's interest are obliged to honesty and justice: but how little that consideration works in private men, how much less in Kings, their deeds declare best.

He intended to oblige both Friends and Enemies, and to exceed their desires, did they but pretend to any modest and sober sense; mistaking the whole business of a Parliament. Which met not to receive from him obligations, but Justice; nor he to expect from them their modesty, but their grave advice, uttered with freedom in the public cause. His talk of modesty in their desires of the common welfare, argues him not much to have understood what he had to grant, who misconceived so much the nature of what they had to desire. And for *sober sense* the expression was too mean; and recoils with as much dishonour upon himself, to be a King where sober sense could possibly be so wanting in a Parliament.

The odium and offences which some men's rigour, or remissness in Church and State had contracted upon his Government, he resolved to have expiated with better Laws and regulations, And yet the worst of misdemeanours committed by the worst of all his favourites, in the height of their dominion, whether acts of rigour or remissness, he hath from time to time continued, owned, and taken upon himself by public Declarations, as often as the Clergy, or any other of his Instruments felt themselves over-burdened with the people's hatred. And who knows not the superstitious rigour of his Sunday's Chapel, and the licentious remissness of his Sunday's Theatre; accompanied with that reverend Statute for

---

1 Frivolously objected to.
2 Failure to appreciate or recognize the value.

Dominical[1] Jigs and Maypoles, published in his own Name, and derived from the example of his Father *James*.[2] Which testifies all that rigour in superstition, all that remissness in Religion to have issued out originally from his own House, and from his own Authority. Much rather then may those general miscarriages in State, his proper Sphere, be imputed to no other person chiefly than to himself. And which of all those oppressive Acts, or Impositions did he ever disclaim or disavow, till the fatal awe of this Parliament hung ominously over him. Yet here he smoothly seeks to wipe off all the envy of his evil Government upon his Substitutes, and under-Officers: and promises, though much too late, what wonders he purposed to have done in the reforming of Religion; a work wherein all his undertakings heretofore declare him to have had little or no judgement. Neither could his Breeding, or his course of life acquaint him with a thing so Spiritual. Which may well assure us what kind of Reformation we could expect from him; either some politic form of an imposed Religion, or else perpetual vexation, and persecution to all those that complied not with such a form. The like amendment he promises in State; not a step further *than his Reason and Conscience told him was fit to be desired;* wishing *he had kept within those bounds, and not suffered his own judgement to have been over-borne in some things,* of which things one was the Earl of *Strafford's* execution. And what signifies all this, but that still his resolution was the same, to set up an arbitrary Government of his own;[3] and that all Britain was to be tied and chained to the conscience, judgement, and reason, of one Man; as if those gifts had been only his peculiar and Prerogative, entailed[4] upon him with his fortune to be a King. When as doubtless no man so obstinate, or so much a Tyrant, but professes to be guided by that which he calls his Reason, and his Judgement, though never so corrupted; and pretends also his conscience. In the mean while, for any Parliament or the whole Nation to have either reason, judgement, or conscience, by this rule was altogether in vain, if it thwarted the King's will; which

---

1 Pertaining to Sunday.
2 Charles I's *Declaration of Sports* (1633) was a formal reassertion of James I's declaration of 1618.
3 The familiar charge of absolutism, closely tied in many minds, including Milton's, with Catholicism.
4 *peculiar* An exclusive privilege; *entailed* Transmitted as an inalienable inheritance.

was easy for him to call by any other more plausible name. And thus we find these fair and specious promises, made upon the experience of many hard sufferings, and his most mortified retirements, being thoroughly sifted, to contain nothing in them much different from his former practices, so cross, and so averse to all his Parliaments, and both the Nations of this Island. What fruits they could in likelihood have produced in his restorement, is obvious to any prudent foresight.

And this is the substance of his first Section, till we come to the devout of it, modelled into the form of a private Psalter. Which they who so much admire either for the matter or the manner, may as well admire the Arch-Bishop's late Breviary,[1] and many other as good *Manuals*, and *Handmaids of Devotion*, the lip-work of every Prelatical Liturgist, clapped together, and quilted[2] out of Scripture phrase, with as much ease, and as little need of Christian diligence, or judgement, as belongs to the compiling of any ordinary and saleable piece of English Divinity, that the Shops value. But he who from such a kind of Psalmistry, or any other verbal Devotion, without the pledge and earnest of suitable deeds, can be persuaded of a zeal, and true righteousness in the person, hath much yet to learn; and knows not that the deepest policy of a Tyrant hath been ever to counterfeit Religious. And *Aristotle* in his Politics, hath mentioned that special craft among twelve other tyrannical *Sophisms*.[3] Neither want we examples. *Andronicus Comnenus* the *Byzantine* Emperor, though a most cruel Tyrant, is reported by *Nicetas* to have been a constant reader of Saint *Paul's* Epistles;[4] and by continual study had so incorporated the phrase and style of that transcendent Apostle into all his familiar Letters, that the imitation seemed to vie with the Original. Yet this availed not to deceive the people of that Empire; who notwithstanding his Saint's vizard, tore him to pieces for his Tyranny. From Stories of this nature both Ancient and Modern

---

1 The Roman Catholic book containing the "Divine Office" for each day, here associated with the Laudian Prayer Book.

2 *clapped together* Hastily and carelessly put together. The term can also mean "to imprison," again demonstrating Milton's view of episcopacy; *quilted* Pieced or joined together.

3 See Book 5, Chapter 9 of Aristotle's *Politics*.

4 Andronicus I ruled the Byzantine Empire from 1183 to 1185 CE. Nicetas Akominatos (or Choniates) (d. 1206) describes his reign in *O City of Byzantium. The Annals of Niketas Choniates.*

which abound, the Poets also, and some English, have been in this point so mindful of *Decorum*, as to put never more pious words in the mouth of any person, than of a Tyrant. I shall not instance an abstruse Author, wherein the King might be less conversant, but one whom we well know was the Closet[1] Companion of these his solitudes, *William Shakespeare*;[2] who introduces the Person of *Richard* the third, speaking in as high a strain of piety, and mortification, as is uttered in any passage of this Book; and sometimes to the same sense and purpose with some words in this place, *I intended*, saith he, *not only to oblige my Friends, but mine Enemies*. The like saith *Richard, Act. 2. Scen. I.*

I do not know that Englishman alive,
With whom my soul is any jot at odds,
More than the Infant that is born tonight;
I thank my God for my humility.[3]

Other stuff of this sort may be read throughout the whole Tragedy, wherein the Poet used not much licence in departing from the truth of History, which delivers him a deep dissembler, not of his affections only, but of Religion.

In Praying therefore, and in the outward work of Devotion, this King we see hath not at all exceeded the worst of Kings before him. But herein the worst of Kings, professing Christianism, have by far exceeded him. They, for ought we know, have still prayed their own, or at least borrowed from fit Authors. But this King, not content with that which, although in a thing holy, is no holy theft, to attribute to his own making other men's whole Prayers, hath as it were unhallowed, and unchristianed the very duty of Prayer it self, by borrowing to a Christian use Prayers offered to a Heathen God. Who would have imagined so little fear in him of the true all-seeing Deity, so little reverence of the Holy Ghost, whose office is to dictate and present our Christian Prayers, so little care of truth in his last words, or honour to himself, or to his Friends, or sense of his afflictions, or of that sad hour which was upon him, as immediately before his death to pop

---

1 Private chamber; the private apartment of a monarch, used for household or private devotions.
2 Charles I had the second Folio in his possession during his captivity—ironically containing Milton's epitaph on Shakespeare.
3 *Richard III* 2.1.70-3.

into the hand of that grave Bishop who attended him,[1] for a special Relic of his Saintly exercises, a Prayer stolen word for word from the mouth of a Heathen Woman praying to a Heathen God; and that in no serious Book, but in the vain amatorious Poem[2] of Sir *Philip Sidney's Arcadia*; a Book in that kind full of worth and wit, but among religious thoughts, and duties not worthy to be named; nor to be read at any time without good caution; much less in time of trouble and affliction to be a Christian's Prayer-Book. It hardly can be thought upon without some laughter, that he who had acted over us so stately and so Tragically, should leave the World at last with such a ridiculous exit, as to bequeath among his deifying friends that stood about him, such a piece of mockery to be published by them, as must needs cover both his and their heads with shame and confusion. And sure it was the hand of God that let them fall and be taken in such a foolish Trap, as hath exposed them to all derision, if for nothing else, to throw contempt and disgrace in the sight of all Men upon this his Idolised Book, and the whole rosary of his Prayers; thereby testifying how little he accepted them from those who thought no better of the living God, than of a Buzzard[3] Idol, that would be served and worshipped with the polluted trash of Romances and *Arcadias*, without discerning the affront so irreligiously and so boldly offered him to his face.

Thus much be said in general to his Prayers; and in special to that Arcadian Prayer used in his Captivity; enough to undeceive us what esteem we are to set upon the rest.

And thus far in the whole Chapter we have seen and considered, and it cannot but be clear to all men, how, and for what ends, what concernments, and necessities the late King was no way induced, but every way constrained to call this last Parliament; yet here in his first Prayer he trembles not to avouch[4] as in the ears of God, *That he did it with an upright intention, to his glory, and his people's good*: Of which dreadful attestation how sincerely meant, God, to whom it was avowed, can only judge; and he hath judged already; and hath written his impartial Sentence in Characters legible to all Christendom; and besides hath taught us, that there be some, whom he hath given over to delusion; whose very

---

1 William Juxon, Bishop of London.
2 Trivial love poem.
3 Senseless, stupid.
4 Declare.

mind and conscience is defiled;[1] of whom Saint *Paul* to *Titus* makes mention.

2. *Upon the Earl of Strafford's Death.*

THIS next Chapter is a penitent confession of the King, and the strangest, if it be well weighed, that ever was Auricular.[2] For he repents here of giving his consent, though most unwillingly, to the most seasonable[3] and solemn piece of Justice, that had been done of many years in the Land: But his sole conscience thought the contrary. And thus was the welfare, the safety, and within a little, the unanimous demand of three populous Nations to have attended still on the singularity of one Man's opinionated conscience; if men had always been so tame and spiritless; and had not unexpectedly found the grace to understand, that if his conscience were so narrow and peculiar to it self, it was not fit his Authority should be so ample and Universal over others. For certainly a private conscience sorts not with a public Calling; but declares that Person rather meant by nature for a private fortune. And this also we may take for truth, that he whose conscience thinks it sin to put to death a capital Offender, will as oft think it meritorious to kill a righteous Person. But let us hear what the sin was that lay so sore upon him, and, as his Prayer given to Dr. *Juxon* testifies, to the very day of his death; it was his signing the Bill of *Strafford's* execution: a man whom all men looked upon as one of the boldest and most impetuous instruments that the King had to advance any violent or illegal design. He had ruled *Ireland*, and some parts of *England* in an Arbitrary manner, had endeavoured to subvert fundamental Laws, to subvert Parliaments, and to incense the King against them; he had also endeavoured to make Hostility between *England* and *Scotland*: He had counselled the King to call over that Irish Army of Papists, which he had cunningly raised, to reduce *England,* as appeared by good Testimony then present at the Consultation. For which, and many other crimes alleged and proved against him in 28. Articles, he was condemned of high Treason by the Parliament. The Commons by far the greater number cast[4] him; the Lords, after they

---

1 Titus 1:15.

2 Addressed to the ear, with an added sense of affecting the ear to the exclusion of mental apprehension.

3 Opportune; timely.

4 Condemned. In the House of Commons on 21 April 1641, the vote for the Bill of Attainder was 204 in favour, 59 opposed; of the 45 Lords to vote on the Bill on May 8th, a slim majority voted in its favour.

had been satisfied in a full discourse by the King's Solicitor, and the opinions of many Judges delivered in their House, agreed likewise to the Sentence of Treason. The People universally cried out for Justice. None were his Friends but Courtiers, and Clergymen, the worst at that time, and most corrupted sort of men; and Court Ladies, not the best of Women; who when they grow to that insolence as to appear active in State affairs, are the certain sign of a dissolute, degenerate, and pusillanimous Common-wealth. Last of all the King, or rather first, for these were but his Apes,[1] was not satisfied in conscience to condemn him of High Treason; and declared to both Houses, *That no fears or respects whatsoever should make him alter that resolution founded upon his conscience.* Either then his resolution was indeed not founded upon his conscience, or his conscience received better information, or else both his conscience and this his strong resolution strook sail, notwithstanding these glorious words, to his stronger fear. For within a few days after, when the Judges at a privy Council, and four of his elected Bishops had picked the thorn out of his conscience,[2] he was at length persuaded to sign the Bill for *Strafford's* Execution. And yet perhaps that it wrung his conscience to condemn the *Earl* of high Treason is not unlikely: not because he thought him guiltless of highest Treason, had half those crimes been committed against his own private Interest or Person, as appeared plainly by his charge against the six Members, but because he knew himself a Principal in what the *Earl* was but his accessory, and thought nothing Treason against the Common-wealth, but against himself only.

Had he really scrupled to sentence that for Treason which he thought not Treasonable, why did he seem resolved by the Judges and the Bishops? And if by them resolved, how comes the scruple here again? It was not then, as he now pretends, *The importunities of some and the fear of many* which made him sign, but the satisfaction given him by those Judges and Ghostly Fathers of his own choosing. Which of him shall we believe? For he seems not one, but double; either here we must not believe him professing that his satisfaction was but seemingly received, and out of fear, or else we may as well believe that the scruple was no real scruple, as we can believe him here against himself before, that the satisfaction then received was no real satisfaction: of such a variable and fleeting conscience what hold can be taken? But that

---

1 Irrational or absurd imitators.
2 The bishops of Carlisle, Durham, Lincoln, and London.

indeed it was a facile conscience, and could dissemble satisfaction when it pleased, his own ensuing actions declared: being soon after found to have the chief hand in a most detested conspiracy against the Parliament and Kingdom, as by Letters and examinations of *Percy, Goring*,[1] and other Conspirators came to light; that his intention was to rescue the Earl of *Strafford*, by seizing on the Tower of *London*; to bring up the English Army out of the North, joined with eight thousand Irish Papists raised by *Strafford*, and a French Army to be landed at *Portsmouth* against the Parliament and their Friends. For which purpose the King, though requested by both Houses to disband those Irish Papists, refused to do it, and kept them still in Arms to his own purposes. No marvel then, if being as deeply criminous as the Earl himself, it stung his conscience to adjudge to death those misdeeds whereof himself had been the chief Author: no marvel though in stead of blaming and detesting his ambition, his evil Counsel, his violence and oppression of the people, he fall to praise his great *Abilities*; and with Scholastic[2] flourishes beneath the decency of a King, compares him to *the Sun*,[3] which in all figurative use, and significance bears allusion to a King, not to a Subject: No marvel though he knit contradictions as close as words can lie together, *not approving in his judgement*, and yet approving in his subsequent reason all that *Strafford* did, as *driven by the necessity of times and the temper of that people*; for this excuses all his misdemeanours: Lastly, no marvel that he goes on building many fair and pious conclusions upon false and wicked premises, which deceive the common Reader not well discerning the antipathy of such connections: but this is the marvel, and may be the astonishment of all that have a conscience, how he durst in the sight of God (and with the same words of contrition wherewith *David* repents the murdering of *Uriah*)[4] repent his lawful compliance to that just act

---

1 Henry Percy, brother of the tenth Earl of Northumberland, and Lord George Goring were the leaders of the "First Army Plot" in March 1641.
2 Characteristic of the scholar, as distinguished from the man of affairs; pedantic.
3 Solar imagery had long been associated with monarchs.
4 David arranged the death of Uriah the Hittite in battle in order to protect his adulterous relationship with Bathsheba, Uriah's wife (2 Samuel 11; 1 Kings 15:5). For David's supposed confession of this sin, see Psalm 51:4.

of not saving him, whom he ought to have delivered up to speedy punishment; though himself the guiltier of the two. If the deed were so sinful to have put to death so great a Malefactor, it would have taken much doubtless from the heaviness of his sin, to have told God in his confession, how he laboured, what dark plots he had contrived, into what a league entered, and with what Conspirators against his Parliament and Kingdoms, to have rescued from the claim of Justice so notable and so dear an Instrument of Tyranny, Which would have been a story, no doubt as pleasing in the ears of Heaven, as all these equivocal repentances. For it was fear, and nothing else which made him feign before both the scruple and the satisfaction of his conscience, that is to say, of his mind: his first fear pretended conscience that he might be borne with to refuse signing; his latter fear being more urgent made him find a conscience both to sign and to be satisfied. As for repentance it came not on him till a long time after; when he saw *he could have suffered nothing more, though he had denied that Bill.* For how could he understandingly repent of letting that be Treason which the Parliament and whole Nation so judged? This was that which repented him, to have given up to just punishment so stout a Champion of his designs, who might have been so useful to him in his following civil Broils. It was a worldly repentance not a conscientious; or else it was a strange Tyranny which his conscience had got over him, to vex him like an evil spirit for doing one act of Justice, and by that means to *fortify his resolution* from ever doing so any more. That mind must needs be irrecoverably depraved, which either by chance or importunity tasting but once of one just deed, spatters[1] at it, and abhors the relish[2] ever after. To the Scribes and Pharisees, woe was denounced by our Saviour, for straining at a Gnat and swallowing a Camel; though a Gnat were to be strained at: But to a conscience with whom one good deed is so hard to pass down, as to endanger almost a choking, and bad deeds without number though as big and bulky as the ruin of three Kingdoms, go down currently without straining, certainly a far greater woe appertains. If his conscience were come to that unnatural *dyscrasy*,[3] as to digest poison and to keck[4] at wholesome food, it was not for the Parliament, or any of his

---

1 Ejects particles of food from the mouth while speaking.
2 Taste.
3 Distemper; disorder.
4 Retch or vomit.

Kingdoms to feed with him any longer. Which to conceal he would persuade us that the Parliament also in their conscience escaped not *some touches of remorse* for putting *Strafford* to death, in forbidding it by an *after act* to be a precedent for the future. But in a fairer construction, that act implied rather a desire in them to pacify the King's mind, whom they perceived by this means quite alienated: in the mean while not imagining that this after act should be retorted on them to tie up Justice for the time to come upon like occasion, whether this were made a precedent or not, no more than the want of such a precedent, if it had been wanting, had been available to hinder this.

But how likely is it that this after act argued in the Parliament their least repenting for the death of *Strafford*, when it argued so little in the King himself: who notwithstanding this after act which had his own hand and concurrence, if not his own instigation, within the same year accused of high Treason no less than six Members at once for the same pretended crimes which his conscience would not yield to think treasonable in the Earl. So that this his subtle Argument to fasten a repenting, and by that means a guiltiness of *Strafford's* death upon the Parliament, concludes upon his own head; and shows us plainly that either nothing in his judgement was Treason against the Common-wealth, but only against the King's Person, a tyrannical Principle, or that his conscience was a perverse and prevaricating conscience, to scruple that the Common-wealth should punish for Treasonous in one eminent offender, that which he himself sought so vehemently to have punished in six guiltless persons. If this were *that touch of conscience which he bore with greater regret,* than for any other sin committed in his life, whether it were that proditory[1] Aid sent to *Rochelle*[2] and Religion abroad, or that prodigality of shedding blood at home, to a million of his Subjects' lives not valued in comparison of one *Strafford,* we may consider yet at last what true sense and feeling could be in that conscience, and what fitness to be the master conscience of three Kingdoms.

But the reason why he labours that we should take notice of so much *tenderness and regret in his soul* for *having any hand in*

---

1 Traitorous, treacherous.
2 Ostensibly meant to aid the French Protestants (the Huguenots), the
   mission to La Rochelle resulted in Buckingham handing over seven
   ships to the King of France. The event figured in the attempt to
   impeach Buckingham.

Strafford's death, is worth the marking[1] ere we conclude. *He hoped it would be some evidence before God and Man to all posterity that he was far from bearing that vast load and guilt of blood* laid upon him by others. Which hath the likeness of a subtle dissimulation; bewailing the blood of one man, his commodious[2] Instrument, put to death most justly, though by him unwillingly, that we might think him too tender to shed willingly the blood of those thousands, whom he counted Rebels. And thus by dipping voluntarily his finger's end, yet with show of great remorse in the blood of *Strafford*, whereof all men clear him, he thinks to scape that Sea of innocent blood wherein his own guilt inevitably hath plunged him all over. And we may well perceive to what easy satisfactions and purgations he had inured his secret conscience, who thinks, by such weak policies and ostentations[3] as these, to gain belief and absolution from understanding Men.

★ ★ ★

7. *Upon the Queen's departure.*

TO this Argument we shall soon have said; for what concerns it us to hear a Husband divulge his Household privacies, extolling to others the virtues of his Wife; an infirmity not seldom incident to those who have least cause. But how good she was a Wife, was to himself, and be it left to his own fancy; how bad a Subject, is not much disputed. And being such, it need be made no wonder, though she left a Protestant Kingdom with as little honour as her Mother left a Popish.[4]

That this *Is the first example of any Protestant Subjects that have taken up Arms against their King a Protestant*, can be to Protestants no dishonour; when it shall be heard that he first levied War on them, and to the interest of Papists more than of Protestants. He might have given yet the precedence of making War upon him to the Subjects of his own Nation; who had twice opposed him in

---

1 Considering, remarking upon.
2 Accommodating.
3 Conspicuous claims meant to attract admiration.
4 Unsuccessful in her attempt to overthrow Cardinal Richelieu, Marie de' Medici (1573-1642), widow of Henri IV of France and mother of Henrietta Maria, fled France for Brussels in 1631. She resided in England from October 1638 until August 1641.

the open Field,[1] long ere the English found it necessary to do the like. And how groundless, how dissembled is that fear, lest she, who for so many years had been averse from the Religion of her Husband, and every year more and more, before these disturbances broke out, should for them be now the more alienated from that to which we never heard she was inclined. But if the fear of her Delinquency and that Justice which the Protestants demanded on her,[2] was any cause of her alienating the more, to have gained her by indirect means had been no advantage to Religion; much less than was the detriment to lose her further off. It had been happy if his own actions had not given cause of more scandal to the Protestants, than what they did against her could justly scandalise any Papist.

Them who accused her, well enough known to be the Parliament, he censures for *Men yet to seek their Religion, whether Doctrine, Discipline, or good manners*; the rest he soothes with the name of true English Protestants, a mere schismatical name, yet he so great an enemy of Schism.

He ascribes *Rudeness and barbarity worse than Indian* to the English Parliament: and *all virtue* to his Wife, in strains that come almost to Sonnetting: How fit to govern men, undervaluing and aspersing the great Council of his Kingdom, in comparison of one Woman. Examples are not far to seek, how great mischief and dishonour hath befallen to Nations under the Government of effeminate and Uxorious[3] Magistrates. Who being themselves governed and overswayed at home under a Feminine usurpation, cannot but be far short of spirit and authority without doors, to govern a whole Nation.

Her tarrying here he could not think safe among them who were shaking hands with Allegiance to lay faster hold on Religion; and taxes them of a duty rather than a crime, it being just to obey God rather than Man, and impossible to serve two Masters.[4] I would they had quite shaken off what they stood shaking hands with; the fault was in their courage, not in their cause.

In his Prayer he prays that *The disloyalty of his Protestant Sub-*

---

1 In the two Bishops' Wars.
2 The House of Commons voted to impeach Henrietta Maria on a charge of high treason in May 1643; the impeachment was passed by the House of Lords later that year.
3 Submissively fond of, or devotedly attached to, a wife.
4 *just to … than Man* Acts 5:29; *impossible … Masters* Matthew 6:24.

jects may not be a hindrance to her love of the true Religion; and never prays that the dissoluteness of his Court, the scandals of his Clergy, the unsoundness of his own judgement, the lukewarmness of his life, his Letter of compliance to the Pope, his permitting Agents at *Rome*, the Pope's *Nuncio* here,[1] may not be found in the sight of God far greater hindrances to her conversion.

But this had been a subtle Prayer indeed, and well prayed, though as duly as a *Pater-noster*, if it could have charmed us to sit still, and have Religion and our Liberties one by one snatched from us, for fear least rising to defend our selves, we should fright the Queen a stiff Papist from turning Protestant. As if the way to make his Queen a Protestant had been to make his Subjects more than half way Papists.

He prays next *That his constancy may be an antidote against the poison of other men's example.* His constancy in what? Not in Religion, for it is openly known that her Religion wrought more upon him, than his Religion upon her, and his open favouring of Papists, and his hatred of them called Puritans, made most men suspect she had quite perverted him. But what is it that the blindness of hypocrisy dares not do? It dares pray, and thinks to hide that from the eyes of God, which it cannot hide from the open view of man.

★ ★ ★

12. *Upon the Rebellion in* Ireland.

The Rebellion and horrid massacre of English Protestants in *Ireland*, to the number of 154000 by their own computation,[2]

---

1 *his Letter ... to the Pope* In his letter to Pope Gregory XV, published by William Prynne in *The Popish Royal Favourite* (1643), Charles I claimed not "to be a partisan of any Faction against the Catholic, Apostolic Roman Religion"; *Agents at Rome* Sir Kenelm Digby, one such agent, attempted to raise money in Rome for Henrietta Maria and the Royalist war effort as well as for the Irish rebels (see chapter 12); *the Pope's Nuncio* Count Rossetti, the papal envoy sent in August 1639 to replace the ailing George Con.

2 This figure is just one example of exaggerated accounts of Irish atrocities (see, for example, Milton's *Observations Upon the Articles of Peace*). In the 1650 revised edition of *Eikonoklastes*, Milton adds that 154,000 were massacred "in the Province of Ulster only," a figure, which added to those of other counties, "makes up the total sum of that slaughter in all likelihood four times as great."

although *so sudden, and so violent*, as at first to amaze all men that were not accessory, yet from whom, and from what counsels it first sprung; neither was, nor could be possibly so secret, as the contrivers thereof blinded with vain hope, or the despair that other plots would succeed, supposed. For it cannot be imaginable that the Irish guided by so many subtle and *Italian* heads of the Romish party, should so far have lost the use of reason, and indeed of common Sense, as not supported with other strength than their own, to begin a War so desperate and irreconcilable against both England and Scotland at once. All other Nations, from whom they could expect aid, were busied to the utmost in their own most necessary concernments. It remains then that either some authority or some great assistance promised them from England, was that whereon they chiefly trusted. And as it is not difficult to discern from what inducing cause this insurrection first arose, so neither was it *hard at first to have applied* some effectual *remedy*, though not prevention. But the assurance which they had in private, that no remedy should be applied, was, it seems, one of the chief reasons that drew on their undertaking.

Seeing then the main incitement and authority for this Rebellion must be needs derived from *England*, it will be next inquired who was the prime Author. The King here denounces a malediction temporal and eternal, not simply to the Author, but to the *malicious Author* of this blood-shed; and by that limitation may exempt, not himself only, but perhaps the Irish Rebels themselves; who never will confess to God or Man that any blood was shed by them maliciously; but either in the Catholic cause, or common Liberty, or some other specious Plea, which the conscience from grounds both good and evil usually suggests to it self: thereby thinking to elude the direct force of that imputation which lies upon them.

Yet he acknowledges *It fell out as a most unhappy advantage of some men's malice against him*: but indeed of most men's just suspicion, by finding in it no such wide departure or disagreement from the scope of his former Counsels and proceedings. And that he himself was the Author of that Rebellion, he denies both here and elsewhere, with many imprecations, but no solid evidence: What on the other side against his denial hath been affirmed in three Kingdoms being here briefly set in view, the Reader may so judge as he finds cause.

This is most certain, that the King was ever friendly to the Irish Papists, and in his third year, against the plain advice of Parliament, like a kind of Pope, sold them many indulgences for Money; and upon all occasions advancing the Popish party, and negotiating under hand by Priests who were made his Agents, engaged the Irish Papists in a War against the Scotch Protestants.[1] To that end he furnished them, and had them trained in Arms; and kept them up the only Army in his three Kingdoms, till the very burst of that Rebellion. The Summer before that dismal *October*, a Committee of most active Papists, all since in the head of that Rebellion, were in great favour at *White-Hall*; and admitted to many private consultations with the King and Queen.[2] And to make it evident that no mean matters were the subject of those Conferences, at their request he gave away his peculiar right to more than five Irish Counties, for the payment of an inconsiderable Rent. They departed not home till within two Months before the Rebellion; and were either from the first breaking out, or soon after, found to be the chief Rebels themselves. But what should move the King, besides his own inclination to Popery, and the prevalence of his Queen over him, to hold such frequent and close meetings with a Committee of Irish Papists in his own House, while the Parliament of *England* sat unadvised with, is declared by a Scotch Author,[3] and of it self is clear enough. The Parliament at the beginning of that Summer, having put *Strafford* to death, imprisoned others his chief Favourites,[4] and driven the rest to fly, the King, who had in vain tempted both the Scotch and the English Army to come up against the Parliament and City, finding no compliance answerable to his hope from the Protestant Armies, betakes himself last to the Irish; who had in readiness an Army of eight thousand Papists, and a Committee here of the same Religion. And with them who thought the time now come to do eminent service for the Church of *Rome* against a Puritan Parliament, he concludes that so soon as both Armies in *England* were disbanded, the Irish should appear in Arms, master all the

---

1 In 1628, Charles I granted a number of concessions to Irish Catholics, recalled here by Milton in relation to the events of 1638-41.

2 In the summer of 1641, five representatives of the Irish Parliament met privately with the king. They would later play significant roles in the rebellion.

3 Edward Bowles, the author of *The Mystery of Iniquity Yet Working in the Kingdoms of England, Scotland, and Ireland, for the Destruction of Religion Truly Protestant* (1643).

4 Most notably, William Laud, Archbishop of Canterbury.

Protestants, and help the King against his Parliament. And we need not doubt that those five Counties were given to the Irish for other reason than the four Northern Counties had been a little before offered to the Scots.[1] The King in *August* takes a journey into *Scotland*; and overtaking the Scotch Army then on their way home, attempts the second time to pervert them, but without success. No sooner come into *Scotland*, but he lays a plot, so saith the Scotch Author, to remove out of the way such of the Nobility there, as were most likely to withstand, or not to further his designs. This being discovered, he sends from his side one *Dillon* a Papist Lord,[2] soon after a chief Rebel, with Letters into *Ireland*; and dispatches a Commission under the great Seal of *Scotland* at that time in his own custody, commanding that they should forthwith, as had been formerly agreed, cause all the Irish to rise in Arms. Who no sooner had received such command, but obeyed; and began in Massacre, for they knew no other way to make sure the Protestants, which was commanded them expressly; and the way, it seems, left to their discretion. He who hath a mind to read the Commission it self, and sound reason added why it was not likely to be forged, besides the attestation of so many Irish themselves, may have recourse to a Book entitled *The Mystery of Iniquity.*

After the Rebellion [had] broken out, which in words only he detested, but under hand favoured and promoted by all the offices of friendship, correspondence, and what possible aid he could afford them, the particulars whereof are too many to be inserted here, I suppose no understanding Man could longer doubt who was *Author or Instigator* of that Rebellion. If there be who yet doubt, I refer them especially to that Declaration of *July* 1643. concerning this matter.[3] Against which testimonies, likelihoods, evidences, and apparent actions of his own, being so

---

1 The four northern counties of England are those that border Scotland: Northumberland, Cumberland, Westmorland, and Durham. Charles I supposedly proposed this offer in 1641 in order to gain the Scots' support for his cause.

2 Thomas Dillon, fourth Viscount Dillon, Lord of the Privy Council of Ireland and joint governor of Mayo in 1641, served under Charles I in 1642, and participated in the rising of James Butler, Duke of Ormonde, in 1649. He was made Master of the Rolls in 1662.

3 *A Declaration of the Commons, Concerning the Rebellion In Ireland, with Some Papers of the Earl of Antrim.*

abundant, the bare denial of one man, though with imprecation,[1] cannot in any reason countervail.

As for the Commission granted them, he thinks to evade that by retorting, that *some in England fight against him* and yet *pretend his authority*. But though a Parliament by the known Laws may affirm justly to have the King's authority, inseparable from that Court, though divided from his Person, it is not credible that the Irish Rebels who so much tendered[2] his Person above his Authority, and were by him so well received at *Oxford*, would be so far from all humanity as to slander him with a particular Commission signed and sent them by his own hand.

And of his good affection to the Rebels this Chapter it self is not without witness. He holds them less in fault than the *Scots*, as from whom they might *allege* to have fetched *their imitation*; making no difference between men that rose necessarily to defend themselves, which no Protestant Doctrine ever disallowed, against them who threatened War, and those who began a voluntary and causeless Rebellion with the Massacre of so many thousands who never meant them harm.

He falls next to flashes,[3] and a multitude of words, in all which is contained no more, than what might be the Plea of any guiltiest Offender, He was not the Author because *he hath the greatest share of loss and dishonour by what is committed*. Who is there that offends God or his Neighbour, on whom the greatest share of loss and dishonour lights not in the end? But in the act of doing evil, men use not to consider the event of their evil doing: or if they do, have then no power to curb the sway of their own wickedness. So that the greatest share of loss and dishonour to happen upon themselves, is no argument that they were not guilty. This other is as weak, that *a King's interest* above that of any other man, *lies chiefly in the common welfare of his Subjects*; therefore no King will do aught against the Common welfare. For by this evasion any Tyrant might as well purge himself from the guilt of raising troubles or commotions among the people, because undoubtedly his chief Interest lies in their sitting still.

I said but now that even this Chapter, if nothing else, might suffice to discover his good affection to the Rebels; which in this

---

1   A prayer or entreaty.
2   Had a tender regard for.
3   Superficial brilliancy; vain empty phrases.

that follows too notoriously appears; imputing this insurrection to *the preposterous rigour, and unreasonable severity, the covetous zeal and uncharitable fury of some men* (these *some men* by his continual paraphrase are meant the Parliament) and lastly, *to the fear of utter extirpation*. If the whole Irishry of Rebels had feed[1] some advocate to speak partially and sophistically in their defence, he could have hardly dazzled better: Yet never the less would have proved himself no other than a plausible deceiver. And perhaps those feigned terrors and jealousies were either by the King himself, or the Popish Priests which were sent by him, put into the head of that inquisitive people, on set purpose to engage them. For who had power *to oppress* them, or to relieve them being oppressed, but the King or his immediate Deputy? This rather should have made them rise against the King than against the Parliament. Who threatened or ever thought of their extirpation, till they themselves had begun it to the English? As for *preposterous rigour, covetous zeal, and uncharitable fury*; they had more reason to suspect those evils first from his own commands, whom they saw using daily no *greater argument* to prove *the truth* of his Religion than by *enduring no other but his own* Prelatical; and to force it upon others, made Episcopal, Ceremonial, and Common-Prayer-Book Wars. But the Papists understood him better than by the outside; and knew that those Wars were their Wars. Although if the Common-wealth should be afraid to suppress open Idolatry, lest the Papists thereupon should grow desperate, this were to let them grow and become our persecutors, while we neglected what we might have done Evangelically, to be their Reformers. Or to do as his Father *James* did, who in stead of taking heart and putting confidence in God by such a deliverance as from the Powder Plot, though it went not off, yet with the mere conceit of it, as some observe, was hit into such a *Hectic* trembling between Protestant and Papist all his life after, that he never durst from that time do otherwise than equivocate or collogue[2] with the Pope and his adherents.[3]

He would be thought to commiserate the sad effects of that Rebellion, and to lament that *the tears and blood spilt there did not*

---

1 Hired; paid by fees.
2 Employ feigned flattery in order to curry favour.
3 Following the discovery of the Gunpowder Plot of 1605, many Protestants (like Milton, in hindsight) felt that James I should have more strictly enforced anti-Catholic legislation.

quench the sparks of our civil discord here. But who began these dissentions, and what can be more openly known than those retardings and delays which by himself were continually devised, to hinder and put back the relief of those distressed Protestants, whom he seems here to compassionate. The particulars are too well known to be recited, and too many.[1]

But *he offered to go himself in person upon that expedition*; and reckons up many surmises why he thinks they would not suffer him. But mentions not that by his underdealing to debauch[2] Armies here at home, and by his secret intercourse with the chief Rebels, long ere that time every where known, he had brought the Parliament into so just a diffidence of him, as that they durst not leave the Public Arms to his disposal, much less an Army to his conduct.

He concludes *That next the sin of those who began that Rebellion theirs must needs be who hindered the suppressing, or diverted the aids.* But judgement rashly given ofttimes involves the Judge himself. He finds fault with those *who threatened all extremity to the Rebels*, and pleads much that mercy should be shown them. It seems he found himself not so much concerned as those who had lost Fathers, Brothers, Wives and Children, by their cruelty; whom in justice to retaliate is not as he supposes *unevangelical*; so long as Magistracy and War is not laid down under the Gospel. If this his Sermon of affected mercy were not too Pharisaical, how could he permit himself to cause the slaughter of so many thousands here in *England* for mere Prerogatives, the Toys and Gewgaws[3] of his Crown, for Copes and Surplices, the Trinkets of his Priests, and not perceive his own zeal, while he taxes others, to be most preposterous and unevangelical. Neither is there the same cause to destroy a whole City for the ravishing of a Sister, not done out of Villainy, and recompense offered by Marriage; nor the same case for those Disciples to summon fire from Heaven upon the whole City where they were denied lodging, and for a Nation by just War and execution to slay whole Families of them who so bar-

---

1 An English response to the Irish Rebellion was delayed by debates on whether the king or parliament would have command of a military force to quell the rebellion. Only after the Civil Wars and the execution of the king did an organized military body, under Cromwell, take the field in Ireland.

2 Entice, seduce away from allegiance.

3 Gaudy trifles, ornaments.

barously had slain whole Families before. Did not all *Israel* do as much against the *Benjamites* for one Rape committed by a few, and defended by the whole Tribe, and did they not the same to *Jabesh-Gilead* for not assisting them in that revenge?[1] I speak not this that such measure should be meted rigorously to all the Irish, or as remembering that the Parliament ever so Decreed, but to show that this his Homily[2] hath more of craft and affectation in it, than of sound Doctrine.

But it was happy that his going into *Ireland* was not consented to: For either he had certainly turned his raised Forces against the Parliament it self, or not gone at all; or had he gone, what work he would have made there, his own following words declare.

He would have punished some; no question; for some perhaps who were of least use, must of necessity have been sacrificed to his reputation, *and the conveniencie of his affairs.* Others he *would have disarmed,* that is to say in his own time: but *all of them he would have protected from the fury of those that would have drowned them, if they had refused to swim down the popular stream.* These expressions are too often met, and too well understood for any man to doubt his meaning. By the *fury of those*, he means no other than the Justice of Parliament, to whom yet he had committed the whole business. Those who would have refused to swim down the popular stream, our constant key tells us to be Papists, Prelates, and their Faction: these, by his own confession here, he would have protected against his Puritan Parliament: And by this who sees not that he and the Irish Rebels had but one aim, one and the same drift, and would have forthwith joined in one body against us.

He goes on still in his tenderness of the Irish Rebels fearing lest *our zeal should be more greedy to kill the Bear for his skin than for any harm he hath done.* This either justifies the Rebels to have done no harm at all, or infers his opinion that the Parliament is more bloody and rapacious in the prosecution of their Justice, than those Rebels were in the execution of their barbarous cruelty. Let men doubt now and dispute to whom the King was a Friend most, to his English Parliament, or to his Irish Rebels.

With whom, that we may yet see further how much he was their Friend, after that the Parliament had brought them every where either to Famine, or a low condition, he, to give them all

---

1 Judges 19-21.
2 Discourse, with a view to spiritual edification.

the respite and advantages they could desire, without advice of Parliament, to whom he himself had committed the managing of that War, makes a Cessation;[1] in pretence to relieve the Protestants, *overborne there with numbers*, but as the event proved, to support the Papists, by diverting and drawing over the English Army there, to his own service here against the Parliament. For that the Protestants were then on the winning hand, it must needs be plain; who notwithstanding the miss[2] of those Forces which, at their landing here, mastered without difficulty great part of Wales and Cheshire, yet made a shift to keep their own in *Ireland*.[3] But the plot of this Irish Truce is in good part discovered in that Declaration of *September* 30th. 1643.[4] And if the Protestants were but *handfuls* there, as he calls them, why did he stop and waylay both by Land and Sea, to his utmost power, those Provisions and Supplies which were sent by the Parliament? How were so many *handfuls* called over, as for a while stood him in no small stead, and against our main Forces here in *England*?

Since therefore all the reasons that can be given of this Cessation appear so false and frivolous, it may be justly feared that the design it self was most wicked and pernicious. What remains then? He *appeals to God*, and is cast; likening his punishments to *Job's* trials, before he saw them to have *Job's* ending.[5] He cannot stand *to make prolix*[6] *Apologies*. Then surely those long Pamphlets set out for Declarations and Remonstrances in his Name, were none of his; and how they should be his indeed, being so repugnant to the whole course of his actions, augments the difficulty.

But he usurps a common saying, *That it is Kingly to do well and hear ill*. That may be sometimes true: but far more frequently, to do ill and hear well; so great is the multitude of Flatterers, and them that deify the name of King.

Yet not content with these neighbours, we have him still a per-

---

1 The cessation of arms was negotiated by Charles I's Lord Deputy of Ireland, the Duke of Ormonde, with the Catholic Confederacy at Kilkenny on 15 September 1643.
2 Loss.
3 Managed to secure their position without the troops sent to England.
4 The Declaration denounced the cessation of arms of September 15th, suggesting that it sought merely to protect the Irish Rebels.
5 Unlike Job, Charles I did not enjoy a full restoration of that which he had lost.
6 Lengthy.

petual Preacher of his own virtues, and of that especially which who knows not to be *Patience* perforce.[1]

He *believes it will at last appear that they who first began to embroil his other Kingdoms, are also guilty of the blood of Ireland.* And we believe so too; for now the Cessation is become a Peace by published Articles, and Commission to bring them over against *England*, first only ten thousand by the Earl of *Glamorgan*, next all of them, if possible, under *Ormond*, which was the last of all his transactions done as a public Person.[2] And no wonder; for he looked upon the blood spilt, whether of Subjects or of Rebels with an indifferent eye, *as exhausted out of his own veins*; without distinguishing as he ought, which was good blood and which corrupt; the not letting out whereof endangers the whole body.

And what the Doctrine is ye may perceive also by the Prayer, which after a short ejaculation[3] for the *poor Protestants*, prays at large for the Irish Rebels, that God would not give them over, *or their Children to the covetousness, cruelty, fierce and cursed anger* of the Parliament.

He finishes with a deliberate and solemn curse *upon himself and his Father's House.* Which how far God hath already brought to pass, is to the end that men by so eminent an example should learn to tremble at his judgements; and not play with Imprecations.

13. *Upon the calling in of the* Scots *and their coming.*
It must needs seem strange to Men who accustom themselves to ponder and contemplate things in their first original and institution, that Kings, who, as all other Officers of the Public, were at first chosen and installed only by consent and suffrage of the People, to govern them as Freemen by Laws of their own framing, and to be, in consideration of that dignity and riches bestowed upon them, the entrusted Servants of the Common-wealth, should notwithstanding grow up to that dishonest encroachment, as to esteem themselves Masters, both of that great trust which

---

1 Of necessity.
2 The Articles of Peace were proclaimed on 17 January 1649. Milton was commissioned by the Council of State to respond to these (see his *Observations Upon the Articles of Peace*); Earl of Glamorgan Edward Somerset (1601-67), Marquis of Worcester and Earl of Glamorgan, was sent by the king to Ireland in 1645 to raise Royalist troops.
3 A hasty, emotional utterance; a short prayer in time of emergency.

they serve, and of the People that betrusted them: counting what they ought to do both in discharge of their public duty, and for the great reward of honour and revenue which they receive, as done all of mere grace and favour; as if their power over us were by nature, and from themselves, or that God had sold us into their hands.[1] This ignorance or wilful mistake of the whole matter, had taken so deep root in the imagination of this King, that whether to the English or to the Scot, mentioning what acts of his Regal Office, though God knows how unwillingly, he had passed, he calls them, as in other places, Acts of grace and bounty; so here *special obligations, favours, to gratify active spirits, and the desires of that party.* Words not only sounding pride and Lordly usurpation, but Injustice, Partiality, and Corruption. For to the Irish he so far condescended, as first to tolerate in private, then to covenant openly the tolerating of Popery: So far to the Scot, as to remove Bishops, establish Presbytery, and the *Militia* in their own hands; *preferring, as some thought, the desires of Scotland before his own Interest and Honour.* But being once on this side *Tweed,*[2] his reason, his conscience, and his honour became so straightened with a kind of false Virginity, that to the English neither one nor other of the same demands could be granted, wherewith the Scots were gratified; as if our air and climate on a sudden had changed the property and the nature both of Conscience, Honour, and Reason, or that he found none so fit as English to be the subjects of his arbitrary power. *Ireland* was as *Ephraim*, the strength of his head, *Scotland*, as *Judah*, was his Law-giver; but over *England* as over *Edom* he meant to cast his Shoe;[3] and yet so many sober Englishmen not sufficiently awake to consider this, like men enchanted with the *Circaean* cup of servitude,[4] will not be held back from running their own heads into the Yoke of Bondage.

The sum of his discourse is against *settling of Religion by violent means;* which whether it were the Scots' design upon *England,* they are best able to clear themselves.[5] But this of all may seem strangest, that the King who, while it was permitted him, never

---

1 Milton had developed such arguments at length in *The Tenure of Kings and Magistrates.*
2 The river Tweed in Scotland.
3 Psalm 60:7-8.
4 In Homer's *Odyssey* (Book 10), the goddess Circe gives Odysseus's men drugged wine, which turns them into swine.
5 To free themselves from fault or guilt.

did thing more eagerly than to molest and persecute the consciences of most Religious men, he who had made a War and lost all, rather than not uphold a Hierarchy of persecuting Bishops, should have the confidence here to profess himself so much an Enemy of those that force the conscience. For was it not he, who upon the English obtruded new Ceremonies, upon the Scots a new Liturgy, and with his Sword went about to engrave a bloody *Rubric*[1] on their backs? Did he not forbid and hinder all effectual search of Truth, nay like a besieging Enemy stopped all her passages both by Word and Writing? Yet here can talk of *fair and equal disputations*: Where notwithstanding, if all submit not to his judgement as not being *rationally convicted*, they must submit (and he conceals it not) to his *penalty* as counted *obstinate*. But what if he himself and those his *learned Churchmen*, were the convicted or the obstinate part long ago; should Reformation suffer them to sit Lording over the Church in their fat Bishoprics and Pluralities, like the great Whore that sitteth upon many Waters,[2] till they would vouchsafe to be disputed out? Or should we sit disputing while they sat plotting and persecuting? Those Clergymen were not *to be driven into the fold like Sheep*, as his Simile runs, but to be driven out of the Fold like Wolves, or Thieves, where they sat *Fleecing* those Flocks which they never fed.

He believes *that Presbytery though proved to be the only Institution of Jesus Christ were not by the Sword to be set up without his consent*; which is contrary both to the Doctrine, and the known practice of all Protestant Churches; if his Sword threaten those who of their own accord embrace it.

And although *Christ* and his Apostles, being to civil affairs but private men, contended not with Magistrates,[3] yet when Magistrates themselves and especially Parliaments, who have greatest right to dispose of the civil Sword, come to know Religion, they ought in conscience to defend all those who receive it willingly, against the violence of any King or Tyrant whatsoever. Neither is it therefore true; *That Christianity is planted or watered with Christian blood*; for there is a large difference between forcing men by

---

1 A direction for the conduct of divine service inserted in liturgical books, properly written or printed in red.

2 Revelation 17:1, 15; many Reformed commentators interpreted the "great Whore" or the "whore of Babylon" as the Papacy or the Roman Catholic Church.

3 On Caesar's authority, see Mark 12:17 and Luke 20:25.

the Sword to turn *Presbyterians,* and defending those who willingly are so, from a furious inroad of bloody Bishops, armed with the *Militia* of a King their Pupil. And if *covetousness and ambition be an argument that Presbytery hath not much of Christ,* it argues more strongly against Episcopacy; which from the time of her first mounting to an order above the Presbyters, had no other Parents than Covetousness and Ambition. And those *Sects, Schisms, and Heresies,* which he speaks of, *if they get but strength and numbers,* need no other *pattern* than Episcopacy and himself, to *set up their ways by the like method of violence.* Nor is there any thing that hath more marks of Schism and Sectarism than English Episcopacy; whether we look at Apostolic times or at reformed Churches; for the *universal way of Church-government before,* may as soon lead us into gross error, as their universally corrupted Doctrine. And Government by reason of ambition was likeliest to be corrupted much the sooner of the two. However nothing can be to us Catholic or universal in Religion, but what the Scripture teaches; whatsoever without Scripture pleads to be universal in the Church, in being universal is but the more Schismatical. Much less can *particular Laws and Constitutions* impart to the Church of *England,* any power of consistory[1] or tribunal above other Churches, to be the sole Judge of what is Sect or Schism, as with much rigour, and without Scripture they took upon them. Yet these the King resolves here to defend and maintain to his last, pretending, after all those conferences offered, or had with him, *not to see more rational and religious motives than Soldiers carry in their Knapsacks*; with one thus resolved it was but folly to stand disputing.

He imagines *his own judicious zeal to be most concerned in his tuition of the Church.* So thought *Saul* when he presumed to offer Sacrifice; for which he lost his Kingdom; So thought *Uzziah* when he went into the Temple; but was thrust out with a Leprosy for his opinioned zeal, which he thought *judicious.*[2] It is not the part of a King, because he ought to defend the Church, therefore to set himself supreme head over the Church, or to meddle with Ecclesial Government, or to defend the Church otherwise than the Church would be defended; for such defence is bondage; nor to defend abuses, and stop all Reformation under the name of *New moulds fancied and fashioned to private designs.* The holy things

---

1 Courts that heard cases dealing with ecclesiastical law.
2 1 Samuel 15:13 and 2 Chronicles 26:16-19.

of Church are in the power of other keys than were delivered to his keeping.[1] Christian liberty purchased with the death of our Redeemer, and established by the sending of his free spirit to inhabit in us, is not now to depend upon the doubtful consent of any earthly Monarch; nor to be again fettered with a presumptuous negative voice, tyrannical to the Parliament, but much more Tyrannical to the Church of God: which was compelled to implore the aid of Parliament, to remove his force and heavy hands from off our consciences, who therefore complains now of that most just defensive force, because only it removed his violence and persecution. If this be a violation to his conscience, that it was hindered by the Parliament from violating the more tender consciences of so many thousand good Christians, let the usurping conscience of all Tyrants be ever so violated.

He wonders, Fox wonder,[2] how we could so much *distrust God's assistance*, as to call in the Protestant aid of our Brethren in *Scotland*; why then did he, if his trust were in God and the justice of his Cause, not scruple to solicit and invite earnestly the assistance both of Papists and of Irish Rebels? If the Scots were by us at length sent home, they were not called in to stay here always; neither was it for the people's ease to feed so many Legions, longer than their help was needful.

The Government of their Kirk we despised not, but their imposing of that Government upon us; not Presbytery but Arch-Presbytery, *Classical, Provincial, and Diocesan* Presbytery, claiming to it self a Lordly power and Superintendency both over Flocks and Pastors, over Persons and Congregations no way their own. But these debates in his judgement would have been ended better *by the best Divines in Christendom in a full and free Synod.* A most improbable way, and such as never yet was used, at least with good success, by any Protestant Kingdom or State since the Reformation: Every true Church having wherewithal from Heaven, and the assisting Spirit of Christ implored to be complete and perfect within it self. And the whole Nation is not easily to be thought so raw, and so perpetually a novice after all this light, as to need the help and direction of other Nations, more than what they write in public of their opinion, in a matter so familiar as Church Government.

---

1 The keys to the kingdom of heaven (see Matthew 16:19).
2 Fox-like cunning.

In fine[1] he accuses *Piety* with the want of *Loyalty* and *Religion* with the breach of *Allegiance*, as if God and he were one Master, whose commands were so often contrary to the commands of God. He would persuade the Scots that their *chief Interest consists in their fidelity to the Crown*. But true policy will teach them to find a safer interest in the common friendship of *England*, than in the ruins of one ejected Family.

★ ★ ★

21. *Upon His Letters taken and divulged.*

THE King's Letters taken at the Battle of *Naseby*, being of greatest importance to let the people see what Faith there was in all his promises and solemn protestations, were transmitted to public view by special Order of the Parliament. They discovered his good affection to Papists and Irish Rebels, the straight intelligence he held, the pernicious and dishonourable Peace he made with them, not solicited but rather soliciting, which by all invocations that were holy he had in public abjured. They revealed his endeavours to bring in foreign Forces, Irish, French, Dutch, Lorrainers, and our old Invaders the Danes upon us, besides his subtleties and mysterious arts in treating: to sum up all, they showed him governed by a Woman. All which though suspected vehemently before, and from good grounds believed, yet by him and his adherents peremptorily denied, were, by the opening of that Cabinet, visible to all men under his own hand.

The Parliament therefore to clear themselves of aspersing him without cause, and that the people might no longer be abused and cajoled, as they call it, by falsities and Court impudence, in matters of so high concernment, to let them know on what terms their duty stood, and the Kingdom's peace, conceived it most expedient and necessary, that those Letters should be made public. This the King affirms was by them done without *honour and civility*: words, which if they contain not in them, as in the language of a Courtier most commonly they do not, more of substance and reality than compliment, Ceremony, Court fawning and dissembling, enter not I suppose further than the ear into any wise man's consideration. Matters were not then between the Parliament and a King their enemy in that State of trifling, as to

---

1 In conclusion.

observe those superficial vanities. But if honour and civility mean, as they did of old, discretion, honesty, prudence, and plain truth, it will be then maintained against any Sect of those *Cabalists*,[1] that the Parliament in doing what they did with those Letters, could suffer in their honour and civility no diminution. The reasons are already heard.

And that it is with none more familiar than with Kings, to transgress the bounds of all honour and civility, there should not want examples good store, if brevity would permit; In point of Letters this one shall suffice. The *Duchess* of *Burgundy* and heir of *Duke Charles*, had promised to her Subjects that she intended no otherwise to Govern, than by advice of the three Estates; but to *Louis* the French King had written Letters, that she had resolved to commit wholly the managing of her affairs to four Persons, whom she named. The three Estates not doubting the sincerity of her Princely word, send Ambassadors to *Louis*, who then besieged *Arras* belonging to the Duke of *Burgundy*. The King taking hold of this occasion to set them at division among themselves, questioned their Credence; which when they offered to produce with their instructions, he not only shows them the private Letter of their Duchess, but gives it them to carry home, wherewith to affront her; which they did, she denying it stoutly; till they, spreading it before her face in a full assembly, convicted her of an open lie. Which although *Commines*[2] the historian much blames, as a deed too harsh and dishonourable in them who were Subjects, and not at War with their Princess, yet to his Master *Louis*, who first divulged those Letters, to the open shaming of that young Governess, he imputes no incivility or dishonour at all, although betraying a certain confidence reposed by that Letter in his royal secrecy.

With much more reason then may letters not intercepted only, but won in battle from an enemy, be made public to the best advantages of them that win them, to the discovery of such important truth or falsehood. Was it not more dishonourable in himself to feign suspicions and jealousies, which we first found among those Letters, touching the chastity of his Mother, thereby to gain assistance from the King of *Denmark*, as in vindication

---

1 Secret intriguers or plotters.
2 Philippe de Commines's account of Marie of Burgundy is included in his memoirs published in Paris in 1552.

of his Sister?[1] The Damsel of *Burgundy*, at sight of her own letter, was soon blank, and more ingenuous than to stand outfacing;[2] but this man whom nothing will convince, thinks by talking world without end, to make good his integrity and fair dealing contradicted by his own hand and seal. They who can pick nothing out of them but phrases shall be counted *Bees*: they that discern further both there and here, that *constancy to his Wife* is set in place before Laws and Religion, are in his naturalities[3] no better than *Spiders*.

He would work the people to a persuasion, that *if he be miserable they cannot be happy*. What should hinder them? Were they all born Twins of *Hippocrates* with him and his fortune, one birth one burial?[4] It were a Nation miserable indeed, not worth the name of a Nation, but a race of Idiots, whose happiness and welfare depended upon one Man. The happiness of a Nation consists in true Religion, Piety, Justice, Prudence, Temperance, Fortitude, and the contempt of Avarice and Ambition. They in whomsoever these virtues dwell eminently, need not Kings to make them happy, but are the architects of their own happiness; and whether to themselves or others are not less than Kings. But in him, which of these virtues were to be found, that might extend to the making happy, or the well-governing of so much as his own household, which was the most licentious and ill-governed in the whole Land.

But the opening of his Letters was designed by the Parliament to make *all reconciliation desperate*. Are the lives of so many good and faithful men, that died for the freedom of their Country, to be so slighted, as to be forgotten in a stupid reconcilement without Justice done them? What he fears not by War and slaughter, should we fear *to make desperate* by opening his Letters? Which fact he would parallel with *Cham's* revealing of his Father's

---

1 A letter from Charles I to Colonel Cochrane accuses Parliament of attempting "to lay a great blemish upon his Royal Family" (*King's Cabinet Opened*) by defaming his mother, Anne of Denmark.

2 Maintaining a stance with boldness or effrontery.

3 Illustrations drawn from natural things.

4 In *City of God*, Augustine writes: "Cicero tells us that Hippocrates, the most famous of all doctors, left it on record that in a case where two brothers fell ill at the same time and their illness grew worse simultaneously, and began to subside at the same moment, he suspected that they were twins" (Book 4, Chapter 2).

nakedness: When he at that time could be no way esteemed *the Father of his Country*, but the destroyer; nor had he ever before merited that former title.

He thanks God he cannot only bear this with patience, but with charity forgive the doers. Is not this mere mockery to thank God for what he can do, but will not? For is it patience to impute *Barbarism and inhumanity* to the opening of an Enemy's Letter, or is it Charity to clothe them with curses in his Prayer, whom he hath forgiven in his Discourse? In which Prayer to show how readily he can return good for evil to the Parliament, and that if they take away his Coat, he can let them have his Cloak also, for the dismantling of his Letters he wishes *They may be covered with the Cloak of confusion.* Which I suppose they do resign with much willingness, both Livery, Badge, and Cognisance,[1] to them who chose rather to be his Servants and Vassals, than to stand against him for the Liberty of their Country.

★ ★ ★

27. *Entitled to the Prince of Wales.*
WHAT the King wrote to his Son, as a Father, concerns not us; what he wrote to him, as a King of *England*, concerns not him; God and the Parliament having now otherwise disposed of *England*. But because I see it done with some artifice and labour, to possess the people that they might amend their present condition, by his or by his Son's restorement,[2] I shall show point by point, that although the King had been reinstalled to his desire, or that his Son admitted, should observe exactly all his Father's precepts, yet that this would be so far from conducing to our happiness, either as a *remedy to the present distempers, or a prevention of the like to come*, that it would inevitably throw us back again into all our past and fulfilled[3] miseries; would force us to fight over again all our tedious Wars, and put us to another fatal struggling for Liberty and life, more dubious than the former. In which as our suc-

---

1 Heraldic bearing, coat of arms.
2 Immediately upon his father's execution, Charles II was proclaimed king by Ormonde in Ireland. On 5 February 1649, he was proclaimed king of Great Britain, France, and Ireland by the Scottish Parliament.
   Though the English Parliament abolished the monarchy on 17 March 1649, Charles II returned to England as king in May 1660.
3 Completed.

cess hath been no other than our cause; so it will be evident to all posterity, that his *misfortunes* were the mere consequence of his perverse *judgement.*

First he argues from *the experience of those troubles* which both he and his Son have had, to the improvement of their *piety and patience*: and by the way bears witness in his own words, that the corrupt education of his youth, which was but glanced at only in some former passages of this answer, was a thing neither of mean consideration, nor untruly charged upon him or his Son: himself confessing here that *Court delights are prone either to root up all true virtue and honour, or to be contented only with some leaves and withering formalities of them, without any real fruits tending to the public good*: Which presents him still in his own words another *Rehoboam, softened* by a far worse Court than *Solomon's, and so corrupted* by *flatteries,* which he affirms to be *unseparable,* to the overturning of all *peace,* and the loss of his own honour and Kingdoms. That he came therefore thus bred up and nurtured to the Throne, far worse than *Rehoboam,* unless he be of those who equalised his Father to King *Solomon,*[1] we have here his own confession. And how voluptuously, how idly reigning in the hands of other men, he either tyrannised or trifled away those seventeen years of peace, without care, or thought, as if to be a King had been nothing else in his apprehension, but to eat and drink, and have his will, and take his pleasure, though there be who can relate his domestic life to the exactness of a diary, there shall be here no mention made. This yet we might have then foreseen, that he who spent his leisure so remissly and so corruptly to his own pleasing, would one day or other be worse busied and employed to our sorrow. And that he acted in good earnest what *Rehoboam* did but threaten, to make his little finger heavier than his Father's loins, and to whip us with his two twisted Scorpions, both temporal and spiritual Tyranny, all his Kingdoms have felt.[2] What good use he made afterward of his adversity, both his impenitence and obstinacy to the end (for he was no *Manasseh*)[3] and the sequel of these his meditated resolutions, abundantly express;

---

1 James I was frequently referred to as the "British Solomon."

2 1 Kings 12:10-14 and 2 Chronicles 10:10-14.

3 After Manasseh, king of Judah, was captured by the Babylonians, he repented of his idolatry, "humbled himself" before God and "took away the strange gods, and the idol out of the house of the Lord" (2 Chronicles 33:9-16).

retaining, commending, teaching to his Son all those putrid and pernicious documents both of State and of Religion, instilled by wicked Doctors, and received by him as in a Vessel nothing better seasoned, which were the first occasion both of his own and all our miseries. And if he in the best maturity of his years and understanding made no better use to himself or others of his so long and manifold afflictions, either looking up to God, or looking down upon the reason of his own affairs, there can be no probability that his Son, bred up, not in the soft effeminacies of Court only, but in the rugged and more boisterous licence of undisciplined Camps and Garrisons, for years unable to reflect with judgement upon his own condition, and thus ill instructed by his Father, should give his mind to walk by any other rules than these bequeathed him as on the death bed of his Father, and as the choicest of all that experience, which his most serious observation and retirement in good or evil days had taught him. *David* indeed by suffering without just cause, learnt that meekness and that wisdom by adversity, which made him much the fitter man to reign. But they who suffer as oppressors, Tyrants, violators of Law, and persecutors of Reformation, without appearance of repenting, if they once get hold again of that dignity and power which they had lost, are but whetted and enraged by what they suffered, against those whom they look upon as them that caused their sufferings.

How he hath been *subject to the sceptre of God's word and spirit*, though acknowledged to be the *best Government*, and what his *dispensation of civil power* hath been, with what *Justice*, and what *honour to the public peace*, it is but looking back upon the whole catalogue of his deeds, and that will be sufficient to remember us. *The Cup of God's physic*, as he calls it, what alteration it wrought in him to a firm *healthfulness* from any surfeit, or excess whereof the people generally thought him sick, if any man would go about to prove, we have his own testimony following here, that it wrought none at all.

First, he hath the same fixed opinion and esteem of his old *Ephesian* Goddess,[1] called the *Church of England*, as he had ever; and charges strictly his Son after him to persevere in that Anti-Papal Schism (for it is not much better) as that *which will be necessary both for his soul's, and the Kingdom's Peace*. But if this can be

---

1 The goddess Diana was worshipped by the Ephesians (Acts 19:28).

any foundation of the Kingdom's peace, which was the first cause of our distractions, let common sense be Judge. It is a rule and principle worthy to be known by Christians, that no Scripture, no nor so much as any ancient Creed, binds our Faith, or our obedience to any Church whatsoever, denominated by a particular name; far less, if it be distinguished by a several Government from that which is indeed Catholic. No man was ever bid be subject to the Church of *Corinth, Rome*, or *Asia*, but to the Church without addition, as it held faithful to the rules of Scripture, and the Government established in all places by the Apostles; which at first was universally the same in all Churches and Congregations; not differing or distinguished by the diversity of Countries, Territories, or civil bounds. That Church that from the name of a distinct place takes authority to set up a distinct Faith or Government, is a Schism and Faction, not a Church. It were an injury to condemn the Papist of absurdity and contradiction, for adhering to his Catholic Romish Religion, if we, for the pleasure of a King and his politic considerations, shall adhere to a Catholic English.

But suppose the Church of *England* were as it ought to be, how is it to us the safer by being so named and established, when as that very name and establishment, by his contriving, or approbation, served for nothing else but to delude us and amuse us, while the Church of *England* was almost changed into the Church of *Rome*. Which as every Man knows in general to be true, so the particular Treaties and Transactions tending to that conclusion, are at large discovered in a Book entitled the *English Pope*. But when the people, discerning these abuses, began to call for Reformation, in order to which the Parliament demanded of the King to unestablish that Prelatical Government, which without Scripture had usurped over us, straight, as *Pharaoh* accused of Idleness the *Israelites* that sought leave to go and sacrifice to God, he lays faction to their charge.[1] And that we may not hope to have ever any thing reformed in the Church either by him or his Son, he forewarns him, *That the Devil of Rebellion doth most commonly turn himself into an Angel of Reformation*: and says enough to make him hate it, as the worst of Evils, and the bane of his Crown: nay he counsels him to *let nothing seem little or despicable to him, so as not speedily and effectually to suppress errors and Schisms*. Whereby we

---

1 Exodus 5:8.

may perceive plainly that our consciences were destined to the same servitude and persecution, if not worse than before, whether under him, or if it should so happen, under his Son; who count all Protestant Churches erroneous and schismatical, which are not Episcopal. His next precept is concerning our civil Liberties; which by his sole voice and predominant will must be circumscribed, and not permitted to extend a hand's breadth further than his interpretation of *the Laws already settled*. And although all human Laws are but the offspring of that frailty, that fallibility, and imperfection which was in their Authors, whereby many Laws, in the change of ignorant and obscure Ages, may be found both scandalous, and full of grievance to their Posterity that made them, and no Law is further good, than mutable upon just occasion, yet if the removing of an old Law, or the making of a new would save the Kingdom, we shall not have it unless his arbitrary voice will so far slacken the stiff curb of his Prerogative, as to grant it us; who are as free born to make our own Laws, as our Fathers were who made these we have. Where are then the English Liberties which we boast to have been left us by our Progenitors? To that he answers, that *Our Liberties consist in the enjoyment of the fruits of our industry, and the benefit of those Laws to which we our selves have consented.* First, for the enjoyment of those fruits, which our industry and labours have made our own upon our own, what privilege is that, above what the *Turks, Jews,* and *Moors* enjoy under the Turkish Monarchy? For without that kind of Justice, which is also in *Argiers,*[1] among Thieves and Pirates between themselves, no kind of Government, no Society, just or unjust could stand; no combination or conspiracy could stick together. Which he also acknowledges in these words: *That if the Crown upon his head be so heavy as to oppress the whole body, the weakness of inferior members cannot return any thing of strength, honour, or safety to the head; but that a necessary debilitation* must follow. So that this Liberty of the Subject concerns himself and the subsistence of his own regal power in the first place, and before the consideration of any right belonging to the Subject. We expect therefore something more, that must distinguish free Government from slavish. But in stead of that, this King, though ever talking and protesting as smooth as now, suffered it in his own

---

1   Algiers, the capital of Algeria, North Africa, was the chief seat of the Barbary pirates from the late sixteenth to the early nineteenth century.

hearing to be Preached and pleaded without control, or check, by them whom he most favoured and upheld, that the Subject had no property of his own Goods, but that all was the King's right.

Next for the *benefit of those Laws to which we our selves have consented*, we never had it under him; for not to speak of Laws ill executed, when the Parliament, and in them the People have consented to divers Laws, and, according to our ancient Rights, demanded them, he took upon him to have a negative will, as the transcendent and ultimate Law above all our Laws; and to rule us forcibly by Laws to which we our selves did not consent, but complained of. Thus these two heads wherein the utmost of his allowance here will give our Liberties leave to consist, the one of them shall be so far only made good to us, as may support his own interest, and Crown, from *ruin* or *debilitation*; and so far Turkish Vassals enjoy as much liberty under *Mahomet* and the Grand Signor:[1] the other we neither yet have enjoyed under him, nor were ever like to do under the Tyranny of a negative voice, which he claims above the unanimous consent and power of a whole Nation virtually[2] in the Parliament.

In which negative voice to have been cast by the doom of War, and put to death by those who vanquished him in their own defence, he reckons to himself more than a negative *Martyrdom*. But Martyrs bear witness to the truth, not to themselves. If I bear witness of my self, saith *Christ*, my witness is not true.[3] He who writes himself *Martyr* by his own inscription, is like an ill Painter, who, by writing on the shapeless Picture which he hath drawn, is fain to tell passengers what shape it is; which else no man could imagine: no more than how a Martyrdom can belong to him, who therefore dies for his Religion because it is *established*. Certainly if *Agrippa* had turned Christian, as he was once turning, and had put to death Scribes and Pharisees for observing the Law of *Moses*, and refusing Christianity, they had died a truer Martyrdom.[4] For those Laws were established by God and *Moses*, these by no warrantable authors of religion, whose Laws in all other best reformed Churches are rejected. And if to die for an estab-

---

1 The Sultan of Turkey.
2 To all intents; in essential qualities.
3 John 5:31.
4 In Acts 26:28, Agrippa said to Paul: "Almost thou persuadest me to be a Christian."

lishment of Religion be Martyrdom, then Romish Priests executed for that, which had so many hundred years been established in this Land, are no worse Martyrs than he. Lastly, if to die for *the testimony of his own conscience*, be enough to make him Martyr, what Heretic dying for direct blasphemy, as some have done constantly,[1] may not boast a martyrdom? As for the constitution or repeal of civil Laws, that power lying only in the Parliament, which he by the very Law of his Coronation was to grant them, not to debar them, nor to preserve a lesser Law with the contempt and violation of a greater, it will conclude him not so much as in a civil and metaphorical sense to have died a Martyr of our Laws, but a plain transgressor of them. And should the Parliament, endued with Legislative power, make our Laws, and be after to dispute them piece-meal with the reason, conscience, humour, passion, fancy, folly, obstinacy, or other ends of one man, whose sole word and will shall baffle and unmake what all the wisdom of a Parliament hath been deliberately framing, what a ridiculous and contemptible thing a Parliament would soon be, and what a base unworthy Nation we, who boast our freedom, and send them with the manifest peril of their lives to preserve it, they who are not marked by destiny for Slaves, may apprehend. In this servile condition to have kept us still under hatches, he both resolves here to the last, and so instructs his Son.

As to those offered condescensions[2] of *Charitable connivance, or toleration*, if we consider what went before, and what follows, they moulder into nothing. For what with not suffering *ever so little* to *seem a despicable* schism, without effectual suppression, as he warned him before, and what with *no opposition of Law, Government, or established Religion* to be permitted, which is his following proviso, and wholly within his own construction, what a miserable and suspected toleration, under Spies and haunting Promoters[3] we should enjoy, is apparent. Besides that it is so far beneath the honour of a Parliament and free Nation, to beg and supplicate the Godship of one frail Man, for the bare and simple toleration of what they all consent to be both just, pious, and best pleasing to God, while that which is erroneous, unjust, and mischievous in the Church or State, shall by him alone against them

---

1 Steadfastly, in the sense of obstinately.
2 Concessions.
3 Professional accusers or informers.

all, be kept up and established; and they censured the while for a *covetous, ambitious, and sacrilegious Faction.*

Another bait to allure the people, is the charge he lays upon his Son, to be tender of them. Which if we should believe in part, because they are his Herd, his Cattle, the Stock upon his ground, as he accounts them, whom to waste and destroy would undo himself, yet the inducement which he brings to move him, renders the motion it self something suspicious. For if Princes *need no Palliations*, as he tells his Son, wherefore is it that he himself hath so often used them? Princes, of all other men, have not more change of Raiment in their Wardrobes, than variety of Shifts and *palliations* in their solemn actings and pretences to the People.

To try next if he can ensnare the prime Men of those who have opposed him, whom, more truly than his meaning was, he calls the *Patrons and vindicators of the People*, he gives out *Indemnity*, and offers *Acts of Oblivion*. But they who with a good conscience and upright heart, did their civil duties in the sight of God, and in their several places, to resist Tyranny, and the violence of Superstition banded both against them, he may be sure will never seek to be forgiven that, which may be justly attributed to their immortal praise; nor will assent ever to the guilty blotting out of those actions before men, by which their Faith assures them they chiefly stand approved, and are had in remembrance before the throne of God.

He exhorts his Son *not to study revenge.* But how far he, or at least they about him, intend to follow that exhortation, was seen lately at the *Hague*;[1] and by what attempts were likewise made in other places. How implacable they would be, it will be wisdom and our safety to believe rather, and prevent, than to make trial. And it will concern the multitude, though courted here, to take heed how they seek to hide or colour their own fickleness and instability with a bad repentance of their well-doing, and their fidelity to the better cause; to which at first so cheerfully and conscientiously they joined themselves.

He returns again to extol *the Church of England*, and again requires his Son by the joint authority of *a Father and a King, not to let his heart receive the least check, or disaffection against it.* And not without cause, for by that means having sole influence upon

---

1 Dr. Isaac Dorislaus, assassinated by Royalists at The Hague on 12 May 1649, had composed, with John Cook, the official charges against Charles I.

the Clergy, and they upon the people, *after long search and many disputes*, he could not possibly find a more compendious[1] and politic way to uphold and settle Tyranny, than by subduing first the Consciences of Vulgar men, with the insensible poison of their slavish Doctrine: for then the body and besotted[2] mind without much Reluctancy was likeliest to admit the Yoke.

He commends also *Parliaments held with freedom and* with *Honour*. But I would ask how that can be, while he only must be the sole free Person in that number; and would have the power with his unaccountable denial, to dishonour them by rejecting all their Counsels, to confine their Law-giving power, which is the Foundation of our freedom, and to change at his pleasure the very name of a Parliament into the name of a Faction.

The conclusion therefore must needs be quite contrary to what he concludes; that nothing can be more *unhappy*, more dishonourable, more unsafe *for all*, than when a wise, *grave, and honourable Parliament* shall have laboured, debated, argued, consulted, and, as he himself speaks, *contributed* for the public good *all their Counsels in common*, to be then frustrated, disappointed, denied and repulsed by the single whiff of a negative, from the mouth of one wilful man; nay to be blasted, to be struck as mute and motionless as a Parliament of Tapestry in the Hangings; or else after all their pains and travail to be dissolved, and cast away like so many Naughts in Arithmetic, unless it be to turn the 0 of their insignificance into a lamentation with the people, who had so vainly sent them. For this is not to *enact all things by public consent*, as he would have us be persuaded, this is to enact nothing but by the private consent and leave of one not negative tyrant; this is mischief without remedy, a stifling and obstructing evil that hath no vent, no outlet, no passage through: Grant him this, and the Parliament hath no more freedom than if it sat in his Noose, which when he pleases to draw together with one twitch of his Negative, shall throttle a whole Nation, to the wish of *Caligula* in one neck.[3] This with the power of the Militia in his own hands over our bodies and estates, and the Prelates to enthral our con-

---

1 Profitable.
2 Intellectually or morally stupefied.
3 The Roman Emperor Caligula wished that his people had one neck, so that he might behead them all in a single stroke; the same allusion is made by John Bradshaw, President of the High Court of Justice, shortly before sentencing Charles I.

sciences either by fraud or force, is the sum of that happiness and liberty we were to look for, whether in his own restitution, or in these precepts given to his Son. Which unavoidably would have set us in the same state of misery, wherein we were before; and have either compelled us to submit like bond-slaves, or put us back to a second wandering over that horrid Wilderness of distraction and civil slaughter, which, not without the strong and miraculous hand of God assisting us, we have measured out; and survived. And who knows, if we make so slight of this incomparable deliverance, which God hath bestowed upon us, but that we shall like those foolish *Israelites*, who deposed God and *Samuel* to set up a King, *Cry out* one day *because of our King*, which we have been mad upon; and then God, as he foretold them, will no more deliver us.[1]

There remains now but little more of his discourse, whereof yet to take a short view will not be amiss. His words make semblance[2] as if he were magnanimously exercising himself, and so teaching his Son, *To want as well as to wear a Crown*; and would seem to account it *not worth taking up or enjoying upon sordid, dishonourable, and irreligious terms*; and yet to his very last did nothing more industriously than strive to take up and enjoy again his sequestered[3] Crown, upon the most sordid, disloyal, dishonourable, and irreligious terms, not of making peace only, but of joining and incorporating with the murderous Irish, formerly by himself declared against, for *wicked and detestable Rebels, odious to God and all good Men*. And who but those Rebels now, are the chief strength and confidence of his Son; while the Presbyter Scot that woos and solicits him, is neglected and put off, as if no terms were to him sordid, irreligious and dishonourable, but the Scottish and Presbyterian.[4]

He bids his Son *Keep to the true principles of piety, virtue, and honour, and he shall never want a Kingdom*. And I say, People of *England*, keep ye to those principles, and ye shall never want a King. Nay after such a fair deliverance as this, with so much fortitude and valour shown against a Tyrant, that people that should

---

1 1 Samuel 8:1-18.
2 Give the outward appearance.
3 Seized; confiscated by authority.
4 Charles II's negotiations with the Scots concluded with the treaty of Heligoland on 11 June 1650, preparing the way for his landing in Scotland.

seek a King, claiming what this Man claims, would show themselves to be by nature slaves, and arrant beasts; not fit for that liberty which they cried out and bellowed for, but fitter to be led back again into their old bondage, like a sort of clamouring and fighting brutes, broke loose, that know not how to use or possess the liberty which they fought for.

The last sentence, whereon he seems to venture the whole weight of all his former reasons and argumentations, *That Religion to their God, and loyalty to their King cannot be parted, without the sin and infelicity of a People*, is contrary to the plain teaching of Christ, that *No man can serve two Masters*, but, if he hold to the one, he must reject and forsake the other. If God then, and earthly Kings be for the most part not several only but opposite Masters, it will as oft happen, that they who will serve their King must forsake their God; and they who will serve God, must forsake their King; which then will neither be their sin, nor their infelicity; but their wisdom, their piety, and their true happiness: as to be deluded by these unsound and subtle ostentations here, would be their misery.

28. *Entitled Meditations upon Death.*

It might be well thought by him who reads no further than the Title of this last Essay, that it required no Answer. For all other human things are disputed, and will be variously thought of to the World's end. But this business of Death is a plain case, and admits no controversy: In that centre all Opinions meet. Nevertheless, since out of those few mortifying hours that should have been entirest to themselves, and most at peace from all passion, and disquiet, he can afford spare time to inveigh bitterly against that Justice which was done upon him, it will be needful to say something in defence of those proceedings; though briefly, in regard so much on this Subject hath been Written lately.

It happened once, as we find in *Esdras*, and *Josephus*,[1] Authors not less believed than any under sacred, to be a great and solemn debate in the Court of *Darius*, what thing was to be counted strongest of all other. He that could resolve this, in reward of his excelling wisdom, should be clad in Purple, drink in Gold, sleep on a Bed of Gold, and sit next *Darius*. None but they doubtless

---

1   1 Esdras 3-4 and Josephus's *Antiquities of the Jews* (Book 11, Chapters 3-4).

who were reputed wise, had the Question propounded[1] to them. Who after some respite given them by the King to consider, in full Assembly of all his Lords and gravest Counsellors, returned severally what they thought. The first held that Wine was strongest; another that the King was strongest. But *Zorobabel* Prince of the Captive Jews, and Heir to the Crown of Judah, being one of them, proved Women to be stronger than the King, for that he himself had seen a Concubine take his Crown from off his head to set it upon her own: And others besides him have lately seen the like Feat done, and not in jest. Yet he proved on, and it was so yielded by the King himself, and all his sages, that neither Wine nor Women, nor the King, but Truth, of all other things was the strongest. For me, though neither asked, nor in a Nation that gives such rewards to wisdom, I shall pronounce my sentence somewhat different from *Zorobabel*; and shall defend, that either Truth and Justice are all one, for Truth is but Justice in our knowledge, and Justice is but Truth in our practice, and he indeed so explains himself in saying that with Truth is no accepting of Persons, which is the property of Justice; or else, if there be any odds, that Justice, though not stronger than Truth, yet by her office is to put forth and exhibit more strength in the affairs of mankind. For Truth is properly no more than Contemplation; and her utmost efficiency[2] is but teaching: but Justice in her very essence is all strength and activity; and hath a Sword put into her hand, to use against all violence and oppression on the earth. She it is most truly, who accepts no Person, and exempts none from the severity of her stroke. She never suffers injury to prevail, but when falsehood first prevails over Truth; and that also is a kind of Justice done on them who are so deluded. Though wicked Kings and Tyrants counterfeit her Sword, as some did that Buckler, fabled to fall from Heaven into the Capitol,[3] yet she communicates her power to none but such as like her self are just, or at least will do Justice. For it were extreme partiality and injustice, the flat denial and overthrow of her self, to put her own authentic Sword into the hand of an unjust and wicked Man, or so far

---

1 Asked.
2 Ability to accomplish.
3 In Book 3 of Ovid's *Fasti*, Jupiter drops a buckler (a shield) from heaven into the hands of Numa Pompilius, the second king of Rome, a shield that guarantees Rome's safety as long as it is preserved. Numa places the original buckler, and eleven copies, in the charge of the Salian priests.

to accept and exalt one mortal Person above his equals, that he alone shall have the punishing of all other men transgressing, and not receive like punishment from men, when he himself shall be found the highest transgressor.

We may conclude therefore that Justice, above all other things, is and ought to be the strongest: She is the strength, the Kingdom, the power and majesty of all Ages. Truth her self would subscribe to this, though *Darius* and all the Monarchs of the World should deny. And if by sentence thus written it were my happiness to set free the minds of English men from longing to return poorly under that Captivity of Kings, from which the strength and supreme Sword of Justice hath delivered them, I shall have done a work not much inferior to that of *Zorobabel*: who by well praising and extolling the force of Truth, in that contemplative strength conquered *Darius*; and freed his Country, and the people of God from the Captivity of *Babylon*.[1] Which I shall yet not despair to do, if they in this Land whose minds are yet Captive, be but as ingenuous to acknowledge the strength and supremacy of Justice, as that Heathen King was, to confess the strength of Truth: or let them but as he did, grant that, and they will soon perceive that Truth resigns all her outward strength to Justice: Justice therefore must needs be strongest, both in her own and in the strength of Truth. But if a King may do among men whatsoever is his will and pleasure, and notwithstanding be unaccountable to men, then contrary to this magnified wisdom of *Zorobabel*, neither Truth nor Justice, but the King is strongest of all other things: which that Persian Monarch himself in the midst of all his pride and glory durst not assume.

Let us see therefore what this King hath to affirm, why the sentence of Justice and the weight of that Sword which she delivers into the hands of men, should be more partial to him offending, than to all others of human race. First he pleads that *No Law of God or man gives to subjects any power of judicature without or against him*. Which assertion shall be proved in every part to be most untrue. The first express Law of God given to mankind, was that to *Noah*, as a Law in general to all the sons of men. And by that most ancient and universal Law, *Whosoever sheddeth man's blood, by man shall his blood be shed*; we find here no exception.[2] If a King therefore do this, to a King, and that by men also, the same shall

---

1   1 Esdras 4:13-63.
2   Genesis 9:6.

be done. This in the Law of *Moses*, which came next, several times is repeated, and in one place remarkably, *Numb*. 35. *Ye shall take no satisfaction for the life of a murderer, but he shall surely be put to death: the Land cannot be cleansed of the blood that is shed therein*, but by the blood of him that shed it. This is so spoken, as that which concerned all *Israel*, not one man alone to see performed; and if no satisfaction were to be taken, then certainly no exception. Nay the King, when they should set up any, was to observe the whole Law, and not only to see it done, but to *do it; that his heart might not be lifted up above his Brethren*, to dream of vain and reasonless prerogatives or exemptions, whereby the Law it self must needs be founded in unrighteousness.

And were that true, which is most false, that all Kings are the Lord's Anointed, it were yet absurd to think that the Anointment of God, should be as it were a charm against Law; and give them privilege who punish others, to sin themselves unpunishably. The high Priest was the Lord's anointed as well as any King, and with the same consecrated oil: yet *Solomon* had put to death *Abiathar*, had it not been for other respects than that anointment.[1] If God himself say to Kings, *Touch not mine anointed*,[2] meaning his chosen people, as is evident in that Psalm, yet no man will argue thence, that he protects them from Civil Laws if they offend, then certainly, though *David* as a private man, and in his own cause, feared to lift his hand against the Lord's Anointed, much less can this forbid the Law, or disarm justice from having legal power against any King.[3] No other supreme Magistrate in what kind of Government soever lays claim to any such enormous Privilege; wherefore then should any King who is but one kind of Magistrate, and set over the People for no other end than they?

Next in order of time to the Laws of *Moses*, are those of Christ, who declares professedly his judicature to be spiritual, abstract[4]

---

1 Though Abiathar the priest conspired against King Solomon, the king spared him, saying: "Get thee to Anathoth, unto thine own fields; for thou art worthy of death: but I will not at this time put thee to death, because thou barest the ark of the Lord GOD before David my father, and because thou hast been afflicted in all wherein my father was afflicted" (1 Kings 2:26).

2 Psalm 105:15.

3 David prevented his men from killing King Saul, "the Lord's anointed," though Saul had sought to slay him (1 Samuel 24:6-10).

4 Separate.

from civil managements, and therefore leaves all Nations to their own particular Laws, and way of Government. Yet because the Church hath a kind of Jurisdiction within her own bounds, and that also, though in process of time much corrupted and plainly turned into a corporal judicature, yet much approved by this King, it will be firm enough and valid against him, if subjects, by the Laws of Church also, be *invested with a power of judicature* both without and against their King, though pretending, and by them acknowledged *next and immediately under Christ supreme head and Governor.* *Theodosius* the Emperor having made a slaughter of the *Thessalonians* for sedition, but too cruelly, was excommunicated to his face by Saint *Ambrose,* who was his subject:[1] and excommunion is the utmost of Ecclesiastical Judicature, a spiritual putting to death. But this, ye will say, was only an example. Read then the Story; and it will appear, both that *Ambrose* avouched it for the Law of God, and *Theodosius* confessed it of his own accord to be so; *and that the Law of God was not to be made void in him, for any reverence to his Imperial power.* From hence, not to be tedious, I shall pass into our own Land of *Britain*; and show that Subjects here have exercised the utmost of spiritual Judicature and more than spiritual against their Kings, his Predecessors. *Vortiger* for committing incest with his Daughter, was by *Saint German,* at that time his Subject, cursed and condemned in a British Council about the year 448;[2] and thereupon soon after was deposed. *Mauricus* a King in *Wales,* for breach of Oath, and the murder of *Cynetus* was excommunicated, and cursed with all his offspring, by *Oudoceus* Bishop of *Landaff* in full Synod, about the year 560; and not restored, till he had repented.[3] *Morcant* another King in *Wales* having slain *Frioc* his Uncle, was fain to come in Person and receive judgement from the same Bishop and his

---

1 After Theodosius I (b. 346 CE) ordered the massacre of the Thessalonians to avenge the murder of his officials, Ambrose (c. 340-397), Bishop of Milan, refused him communion until he publicly repented of his crime (Augustine, *City of God,* Book 5, Chapter 26). Anthony Van Dyck (1599-1661) painted a portrait ("The Emperor Theodosius is forbidden by Saint Ambrose to enter Milan Cathedral") on the subject.

2 The charge against Vortigern (fl. 425-450) is related by Nennius in the *History of the Britons* and described in detail by Milton in the *History of Britain* (1670).

3 A story recorded in the *Book of Llan Dav,* as is the following account of Morcant.

Clergy; who upon his penitence acquitted him, for no other cause than lest the Kingdom should be destitute of a Successor in the Royal Line. These examples are of the Primitive, British, and Episcopal Church; long ere they had any commerce or communion with the Church of *Rome*. What power afterward of deposing Kings, and so consequently of putting them to death, was assumed and practised by the Canon Law, I omit as a thing generally known. Certainly if whole Councils of the Romish Church have in the midst of their dimness discerned so much of Truth, as to Decree at *Constance*, and at *Basil*, and many of them to avouch at *Trent* also, that a Council is above the Pope, and may judge him, though by them not denied to be the Vicar of Christ,[1] we in our clearer light may be ashamed not to discern further, that a Parliament is, by all equity, and right, above a King, and may judge him, whose reasons and pretensions to hold of God only, as his immediate Vicegerent, we know how far fetched they are, and insufficient.

As for the Laws of man, it would ask a Volume to repeat all that might be cited in this point against him from all Antiquity. In Greece, *Orestes* the Son of *Agamemnon*, and by succession King of *Argos*, was in that Country judged and condemned to death for killing his Mother: whence escaping, he was judged again, though a Stranger, before the great Council of *Areopagus* in *Athens*. And this memorable act of Judicature, was the first that brought the Justice of that grave Senate into fame and high estimation over all *Greece* for many ages after.[2] And in the same City Tyrants were to undergo Legal sentence by the Laws of *Solon*.[3] The Kings of *Sparta*, though descended lineally from *Hercules* esteemed a God among them, were often judged and sometimes put to death by the most just and renowned Laws of *Lycurgus*;[4] who, though a

---

1 The three great Councils of the Roman Catholic Church: Constance (1414-18), Basle (1431-49), and Trent (1545-63).
2 Though Orestes murdered his mother Clytemnestra (Euripides, *Orestes*), he is acquitted by the Athenian Areopagus (Aeschylus, *Eumenides*).
3 Athenian statesman and poet, Solon established a legal code which released peasants from serfdom and slavery and cancelled debts secured by land or liberty. His constitutional reforms resulted in the popular assembly (Plutarch, *Life of Solon*).
4 The founder of the Spartan constitution, Lycurgus established a senate, "a power equal to the king's in matters of great consequence," to give "steadiness and safety to the commonwealth" (Plutarch, *Life of Lycurgus*).

King, thought it most unequal to bind his Subjects by any Law, to which he bound not himself. In *Rome* the Laws made by *Valerius Publicola*, and what the Senate decreed against *Nero*, that he should be judged and punished according to the Laws of their Ancestors, and what in like manner was decreed against other Emperors, is vulgarly known.[1] And that the Civil Law warrants like power of Judicature to Subjects against Tyrants, is written clearly by the best and famousest Civilians. For if it was decreed by *Theodosius*, and stands yet firm in the Code of *Justinian*,[2] that the Law is above the Emperor, then certainly the Emperor being under Law, the Law may judge him, and if judge him, may punish him proving tyrannous: how else is the Law above him, or to what purpose. These are necessary deductions; and thereafter hath been done in all Ages and Kingdoms, oftener than to be here recited.

But what need we any further search after the Laws of other Lands, for that which is so fully and so plainly set down lawful in our own. Where ancient Books tell us, *Bracton*, *Fleta*, and others, that the King is under Law, and inferior to his Court of Parliament;[3] that although his place *to do Justice* be highest, yet that he stands as liable *to receive Justice*, as the meanest of his Kingdom. Nay *Alfred* the most worthy King, and by some accounted first absolute Monarch of the Saxons here, so ordained; as is cited out

---

1   *Valerius Publicola* The Roman consul Publius Valerius (later Publicola— "people cherisher") "emphasized the majesty of democracy" and "enacted a law by which any one who sought to make himself tyrant might be slain without trial" (Plutarch, *Life of Publicola*); *Senate ... against Nero* For his tyrannical rule, the Roman Emperor Nero Claudius Caesar was declared a public enemy by the Senate and condemned to die according to the "ancient style." Afraid to be stripped naked, fastened by the neck in a wooden fork, and flogged to death, Nero committed suicide (Suetonius, *Lives of the Caesars*).
2   The Emperor Justinian codified Roman civil law (Codex Justinianus). He nowhere explicitly states "the Law is above the Emperor." To the contrary, in his *Institutes* he asserts "Again, what the Emperor determines has the force of a statute, the people having conferred on him all their authority and power by the *lex regia*, which was passed concerning his office and authority" (*The Institutes*, Book 1, Chapter 2).
3   In *De Legibus*, Henry of Bracton (c. 1210-68) argued for the subjection of the monarch to the law. The anonymous *Fleta*, purportedly co-authored by judges imprisoned during the reign of Edward I, also argued for restrictions upon monarchical authority.

of an ancient Law Book called the *Mirror;* in *Rights of the King-dom*, p. 31.[1] where it is complained on, *As the sovereign abuse of all,* that *the King should be deemed above the Law, whereas he ought be subject to it by his Oath*: Of which Oath anciently it was the last clause, that the King *should be as liable, and obedient to suffer right, as others of his people.* And indeed it were but fond and senseless, that the King should be accountable to every petty suit in lesser Courts, as we all know he was, and not be subject to the Judica-ture of Parliament in the main matters of our common safety or destruction; that he should be answerable in the ordinary course of Law for any wrong done to a private Person, and not answer-able in Court of Parliament for destroying the whole Kingdom. By all this, and much more that might be added as in an argu-ment overcopious rather than barren, we see it manifest that all Laws both of God and Man are made without exemption of any person whomsoever; and that if Kings presume to overtop the Law by which they reign for the public good, they are by Law to be reduced into order: and that can no way be more justly, than by those who exalted them to that high place. For who should better understand their own Laws, and when they are trans-gressed, than they who are governed by them, and whose consent first made them: and who can have more right to take knowledge of things done within a free Nation than they within themselves?[2]

Those objected Oaths of Allegiance and Supremacy we swore, not to his Person, but as it was invested with his Authority; and his authority was by the People first given him conditionally, in Law and under Law and under Oath also for the Kingdom's good, and not otherwise: the Oaths then were interchanged, and mutual; stood and fell together; he swore fidelity to his trust; not as a deluding ceremony, but as a real condition of their admitting him for King; and the Conqueror himself swore it ofter than at his Crowning: they swore Homage, and Fealty to his Person in that trust. There was no reason why the Kingdom should be further bound by Oaths to him, than he by his Coronation Oath to us, which he hath every way broken: and having broken, the ancient Crown-Oath of *Alfred* above mentioned, conceals not his penalty.

As for the Covenant, if that be meant, certainly no discreet Person can imagine it should bind us to him in any stricter sense

---

1 Authored by John Sadlar, *Rights of the Kingdom* was published in 1649.
2 At his trial, Charles I, questioning the court's authority, stated that he knew "as much law as any gentleman in England" (see Appendix B).

than those Oaths formerly. The acts of Hostility which we received from him, were no such dear obligements that we should owe him more fealty and defence for being our Enemy, than we could before when we took him only for a King. They were accused by him and his Party to pretend Liberty and Reformation, but to have no other end than to make themselves great, and to destroy the King's Person and Authority. For which reason they added that third Article, testifying to the World, that as they were resolved to endeavour first a Reformation in the Church, to extirpate Prelacy, to preserve the Rights of Parliament, and the Liberties of the Kingdom, so they intended, so far as it might consist with the preservation and defence of these, to preserve the King's Person and Authority; but not otherwise. As far as this comes to, they Covenant and Swear in the sixth Article to preserve and defend the persons and authority of one another, and all those that enter into that League; so that this Covenant gives no unlimitable exemption to the King's Person, but gives to all as much defence and preservation as to him, and to him as much as to their own Persons, and no more; that is to say, in order and subordination to those main ends for which we live and are a Nation of men joined in society either Christian or at least human. But if the Covenant were made absolute, to preserve and defend any one whomsoever, without respect had, either to the true Religion, or those other Superior things to be defended and preserved however, it cannot then be doubted, but that the Covenant was rather a most foolish, hasty, and unlawful Vow, than a deliberate and well-weighed Covenant; swearing us into labyrinths, and repugnances,[1] no way to be solved or reconciled, and therefore no way to be kept: as first offending against the Law of God, to Vow the absolute preservation, defence, and maintaining of one Man though in his sins and offences never so great and heinous against God or his Neighbour; and to except a Person from Justice, whereas his Law excepts none. Secondly, it offends against the Law of this Nation, wherein, as hath been proved, Kings in receiving Justice, and undergoing due trial, are not differenced from the meanest Subject. Lastly, it contradicts and offends against the Covenant it self, which vows in the fourth Article to bring to open trial and condign[2] punishment all those that shall be found guilty of such crimes and Delinquencies,

1 Contradictions.
2 Fitting; adequate.

whereof the King by his own Letters and other undeniable testimonies not brought to light till afterward, was found and convicted to be the chief actor in what they thought him at the time of taking that Covenant, to be overruled only by evil Counsellors; and those, or whomsoever they should discover to be principal, they vowed to try, *either by their own supreme Judicatories*, for so even then they called them, *or by others having power from them to that effect*. So that to have brought the King to condign punishment hath not broke the Covenant, but it would have broke the Covenant to have saved him from those Judicatories, which both Nations declared in that Covenant to be *Supreme* against any person whatsoever. And if the Covenant swore otherwise to preserve him than in the preservation of true Religion and our Liberties, against which he fought, if not in Arms, yet in Resolution to his dying day, and now after death still fights against, in this his Book, the Covenant was better broken, than he saved. And God hath testified by all propitious and evident signs, whereby in these latter times he is wont to testify what pleases him; that such a solemn, and for many Ages unexampled act of due punishment, was no *mockery of Justice*, but a most grateful and well-pleasing Sacrifice. Neither was it *to cover their perjury* as he accuses, but to uncover his perjury to the Oath of his Coronation.

The rest of his discourse quite forgets the Title; and turns his Meditations upon death into obloquy and bitter vehemence against his *Judges and Accusers*; imitating therein, not our Saviour, but his Grand-mother *Mary* Queen of Scots, as also in the most of his other scruples, exceptions and evasions:[1] and from whom he seems to have learnt, as it were by heart, or else by kind, that which is thought by his admirers to be the most virtuous, most manly, most Christian, and most Martyr-like both of his words and speeches here, and of his answers and behaviour at his Trial.[2]

---

1 In May 1568, Mary, Queen of Scots, fled to England where she was soon imprisoned; implicated in a number of Catholic plots against Elizabeth I, she was executed in February 1587. During her trial she declared: "As an absolute Queen, I cannot submit to orders, nor can I submit to the laws of the land without injury to myself, the King my son and all other sovereign princes.... For myself I do not recognize the laws of England.... I do not desire vengeance. I leave it to Him who is the just Avenger of the innocent and of those who suffer for His Name under whose power I will take shelter."

2 See Appendix B: The Trial of Charles I.

It is a sad fate, he saith, *to have his Enemies both Accusers, Parties, and Judges.* Sad indeed, but no sufficient Plea to acquit him from being so judged. For what Malefactor might not sometimes plead the like? If his own crimes have made all men his Enemies, who else can judge him? They of the Powder-plot against his Father might as well have pleaded the same. Nay at the Resurrection it may as well be pleaded, that the Saints who then shall judge the World, are *both Enemies, Judges, Parties, and Accusers.*

So much he thinks to abound in his own defence, that he undertakes an unmeasurable task; to bespeak[1] *the singular care and protection of God over all Kings, as being the greatest Patrons of Law, Justice, Order, and Religion on Earth.* But what Patrons they be, God in the Scripture oft enough hath expressed; and the earth it self hath too long groaned under the burden of their injustice, disorder, and irreligion. Therefore *To bind their Kings in chains, and their Nobles with links of Iron,*[2] is an honour belonging to his Saints; not to build *Babel,* which was *Nimrod's* work, the first King, *and the beginning of his Kingdom was Babel,*[3] but to destroy it, especially that spiritual *Babel:* and first to overcome those European Kings, which receive their power; not from God, but from the beast; and are counted no better than his ten horns. *These shall hate the great Whore,* and yet *shall give their Kingdoms to the Beast that carries her; they shall commit Fornication with her,* and yet *shall burn her with fire,* and yet *shall lament the fall of Babylon,* where they fornicated with her.[4]

Thus shall they be too and fro, doubtful and ambiguous in all their doings, until at last, *joining their Armies with the Beast,* whose power first raised them, they shall perish with him by the *King of Kings* against whom they have rebelled; and *the Fowls shall eat their flesh.*[5] This is their doom written, and the utmost that we find concerning them in these latter days; which we have much more cause to believe, than his unwarranted Revelation here, proph-

---

1 Exclaim.

2 Psalm 149:8.

3 Genesis 10:10.

4 *and first … fornicated with her* Here Milton associates early-modern European kings with the "ten horns" of the seven-headed beast upon which the whore of Babylon sits (Revelation 17:1-5); *These shall hate … with fire* Revelation 17:16; 18:9-10.

5 *joining their Armies … have rebelled* Revelation 17:13-14; *the Fowls … their flesh* Revelation 19:18, 21.

esying what shall follow after his death, with the spirit of Enmity, not of Saint *John*.

He would fain bring us out of conceit with the good *success* which God hath vouchsafed us. We measure not our Cause by our success, but our success by our Cause. Yet certainly in a good Cause success is a good confirmation; for God hath promised it to good men almost in every leaf of Scripture. If it argue not for us, we are sure it argues not against us; but as much or more for us, than ill success argues for them; for to the wicked, God hath denounced[1] ill success in all that they take in hand.[2]

He hopes much of those *softer tempers*, as he calls them, and *less advantaged by his ruin, that their consciences do already* gripe them. 'Tis true, there be a sort of moody, hot-brained, and always unedified consciences; apt to engage their Leaders into great and dangerous affairs past retirement, and then, upon a sudden qualm and swimming of their conscience, to betray them basely in the midst of what was chiefly undertaken for their sakes. Let such men never meet with any faithful Parliament to hazard for them; never with any noble Spirit to conduct and lead them out; but let them live and die in servile condition and their scrupulous queasiness, if no instruction will confirm them. Others there be in whose consciences the loss of gain, and those advantages they hoped for, hath sprung a sudden leak. These are they that cry out the Covenant broken, and to keep it better slide back into neutrality, or join actually with Incendiaries and Malignants.[3] But God hath eminently begun to punish those, first in *Scotland*, then in *Ulster*, who have provoked him with the most hateful kind of mockery, to break his Covenant under pretence of strictest keeping it; and hath subjected them to those Malignants, with whom they scrupled not to be associates. In God therefore we shall not fear what their false fraternity can do against us.

He seeks again with cunning words to turn our success into our sin. But might call to mind, that the Scripture speaks of those also, who *when God slew them, then sought him;* yet did but *flatter him with their mouth, and lied to him with their tongues; for their heart*

---

1 Announced, proclaimed.
2 See, for example, Psalm 1:6.
3 Those disposed to rebel against God or constituted authority. Like *Delinquent*, the term was a commonplace used by Parliamentarians or Royalists.

was not right with him.[1] And there was one, who in the time of his affliction trespassed more against God; *This was that King Ahaz.*[2] He glories much in the forgiveness of his Enemies; so did his Grandmother at her death. Wise men would sooner have believed him had he not so often told us so. But he hopes to erect *the Trophies of his charity over us.* And Trophies of Charity no doubt will be as *glorious* as Trumpets before the alms of Hypocrites; and more especially the Trophies of such an aspiring charity as offers in his Prayer to share Victory with God's *compassion,* which is over all his Works. Such Prayers as these may perhaps catch the people, as was intended: but how they please God, is to be much doubted, though prayed in secret, much less written to be divulged. Which perhaps may gain him after death a short, contemptible, and soon fading reward; not what he aims at, to stir the constancy and solid firmness of any wise Man, or to unsettle the conscience of any knowing Christian, if he could ever aim at a thing so hopeless, and above the genius of his *Cleric* elocution, but to catch the worthless approbation of an inconstant, irrational, and Image-doting rabble. The rest, whom perhaps ignorance without malice, or some error, less than fatal, hath for the time misled, on this side Sorcery or obduration, may find the grace and good guidance to bethink[3] themselves, and recover.

---

1 Psalm 78:34, 36-37.

2 Ahaz, the king of Judah, worshipped idols and failed to rely on God for deliverance from his enemies. His people were, therefore, slaughtered and enslaved during his reign. He is generally viewed as a figure of reckless apostasy (2 Kings 16; 2 Chronicles 28; Isaiah 1-10).

3 Recollect, remember.

Appendix A: Other Contemporary Responses to Eikon Basilike

1. From *EIKON ALETHINE*.[1] *The Portraiture of Truth's most sacred Majesty truly suffering, though not solely. Wherein the false colours are washed off, wherewith the Painter-stainer had bedaubed Truth, the late King and the Parliament, in his counterfeit Piece entitled Eikon Basilike. Published to undeceive the World.* London: Printed by Thomas Paine, 1649

> The Curtain's drawn; All may perceive the plot,
> And Him who truly the black Babe begot:
> Whose sable mantle makes me bold to say
> A Phaeton Sol's chariot[2] ruled that day.
> Presumptuous Priest to skip into the throne,
> And make his King his Bastard Issue own.
> The Author therefore hath conceived it meet,
> The Doctor should do penance in this sheet.[3]

* * *

13. *Upon the calling in of the* Scots, *and their coming.*
Here the Doctor plays above board again, showing that nothing troubled his Worship so much as the fear of the *Scots* settling Presbytery.

---

1 *Eikon Alethine*, or "The True Image," was published several months before *Eikonoklastes*. It also responded to *Eikon Basilike* chapter by chapter.

2 In Greek mythology, Phaeton, the son of Helios, takes his father's solar chariot; unable to control the immortal horses, he is killed by a thunderbolt sent by Zeus to prevent him from setting the world on fire.

3 This dedicatory poem accompanies an illustration in which a curtain is lifted to reveal the priestly author of *Eikon Basilike*; above the illustration is a line from Horace's *Ars Poetica*: "Spectatum admissi risum teneatis" [Admitted to the sight, would you not laugh?]; *in this sheet* in these papers (the book). Doing penance in a sheet was prescribed for adultery; hence, this phrase refers to begetting "the black Babe" and the "Bastard Issue."

The defence of the Hierarchy, and Liturgy are the pricks[1] he most levels at, though now and then he shoots at Rovers[2] in other Chapters.

His bow was bent for to gall Episcopacy's enemies, and though he seems to march against other foes, yet still Parthian like he will now and then shoot backward at them.[3]

And now he thinks he hath gotten a good ground to play his prize on, and a handsome[4] occasion to cry up his *Diana*.

The other causes that moved the *Scots* nothing concerned his particular but by the by, liberty and freedom in the state he could willingly allow, would they but suffer slavery in the Church.

And therefore like a *Goliath* with his Weaver's beam, nay and his whole Woof too, falls upon those that dare refuse to worship his *Dagon*;[5] laying at the *Scots* for coming in to aid the *English*, and ever and anon putting in a thrust at the *English*, who have quitted Episcopacy.

But his whole discourse being made up rather of affirming than proving his own to be the only good Government, it will be but folly to spend time, Ink, and Paper in answering him, I shall therefore only hint some of his redoubted arguments.

1. *Wise and learned men think, that nothing hath more marks of Schism and Sectarism than this Presbyterian way, both as to the ancient, and still most universal way of Church-Government.* Well argued Doctor; Universality then is a mark of infallibility, stick close to this, and thy square Cap[6] may perhaps be changed into

---

1 Fixed targets.
2 Targets chosen at random, often for long-distance shooting. Like "pricks," the terms is from archery.
3 The Parthian cavalry shot when retreating (or pretending to retreat); in the current context, a verbal parting shot.
4 Convenient.
5 *like a Goliath ... his Dagon* According to 2 Samuel 21:19, "the brother of Goliath the Gittite" had a staff "whose spear was like a weaver's beam." However, the phrase "the brother of" does not appear in the Hebrew text and the staff is most commonly associated with Goliath. See Falstaff's line in Shakespeare's *The Merry Wives of Windsor*: "in the shape of a man, Master Brook, I fear not Goliath with a weaver's beam" (Act 5, Scene 1); *Woof* The threads that cross from side to side of a weaver's web; *Dagon* A Philistine fertility god (1 Samuel 5:2-7); Milton makes Dagon a fallen angel in *Paradise Lost* (1.457-66).
6 An academic cap; hence, a university man.

a Cardinal's Hat: yet let me tell you, that Christ teaches, that we should not be led by a multitude.

2. *But that Christ and his Apostles ever commanded to set such a parity of Presbyters, and in such a way as those Scots endeavour; I think is not very disputable.* As he thinks, the Bell tinks, *Ergo*, rare I profess;[1] yet Doctor, by your leave, I am certain it is so disputable, that all the brains and stairs[2] in your party, to the third degree of a Doctor, nay, to the very apex of a Bishop, cannot disprove it.

But I will take leave of him in a word or two for this Chapter, thus stuffed with folly and passion.

Surely in matters of Religion, those truths gain most on men's judgements and consciences, which are least urged by secular violence, which weakens Truth with prejudices. If this be true, why did your Metropolitan[3] so set the late King to war against the *Scots* for denying Episcopacy, and a Popish Liturgy; and your whole Tribe (good Doctor) so freely contribute to the maintenance of it? Or why did you imprison, whip, brand, and maim men here, for scrupling at your superstitious ceremonies, and Idolatrous cringings?[4]

But now fearing that his thus speaking truth, will but confound his worship, he will try what he can get by falsehood, and he scorns to steal from Truth, but like a right *Cavalier*, will plunder her openly.

For he saith, *There was never any thing upon the point, which those Scots had by Army, or Commissioners, to move the late King with, by their solemn obtestations,[5] and pious threatenings,* (good Doctor mock not at piety in others, so little of which you show your self) *but only this, To represent to him the wonderful necessity of setting up their Presbytery in England.* Now fie upon thee, art thou one of the sons of *Aaron* (for else how durst thou aim to be an High-priest) which should have *Holiness to the Lord* written on thy forehead, and dost thou thus on thy front so impudently imprint

---

1 An allusion to the proverb "as the fool thinketh, the bell tinketh"; that is, "to the fool the bell seems to say what he wants it to say" (*OED* tink v1).

2 Ascending series, alluding to the hierarchy of the Episcopal church.

3 Belonging to a metropolitan see; here, specifically, the Archbishop of Canterbury.

4 Servile or obsequious bowing.

5 Entreaties.

a falsehood;[1] which all, that ever saw, or shall see, the *Scots'* many Addresses to the late King, will run and read?

But he intends not to leave this good quality so, and therefore will assert, that the Parliament *was more than competently furnished with Arms, Ammunition, Navy, Forts, etc.* when they invited in the *Scots*, and all that he might but infer, *They were as men jealous of the justifiableness of their doings and designs before God, who never think they have human strength enough to carry their work on, seem it ever so plausible to the people.*

Of the truth of this, all men can judge, who know in how low a condition the Parliament was at that time by the treacheries of some revolters, as well as open foes, as easily as of the other by the *Scots'* Declarations, to whom I shall leave both to receive their sentence, which if just, our Author's Clergy will not save him.

* * *

21. *Upon his Majesty's Letters taken and divulged.*
Here our Author supposes that he hath gotten a plausible ground to lay a deep foundation for reproach against the Parliament but the right consideration of the cause of their divulging will easily level this rare Edifice, which will appear but an heap of malicious forgery, and scandalous Sophistry in the Doctor.

The late King's Penmen (with which he was from the first thoroughly stored[2]) did in all their Libellous Pamphlets endeavour to insinuate as well as our Doctor; that many jealousies were raised, and scandals cast upon the late King to stir up the people against him.

Now God having by his providence bestowed so fair an opportunity, and blessed occasion upon the Parliament, they truly judged that they were bound in duty not to put this Candle under a Bushel, which being set in its proper place would enlighten the

---

1 Aaron, the brother of Moses, was divinely called to the priesthood (Exodus 28-30) and served, with his sons, in the Tabernacle. On Mount Sinai, God declared to Moses: "it shall be upon Aaron's forehead, that Aaron may bear the iniquity of the holy things, which the children of Israel shall hallow in all their holy gifts; and it shall be always upon his forehead, that they may be accepted before the LORD" (Exodus 28:38).
2 Supplied.

whole house, and be a means to direct men out of those dungeons of error, which those dark lanterns had led them into.[1]

So that to vindicate truth, and their own innocency from the Cabs'[2] calumnies, and to undeceive the poor seduced people, whom they conceived were most likely to be guided out of that labyrinth, which *Minos*, and his *Dedalian* Artificers had enclosed them in, by this clue of thread,[3] these letters were printed.

Wherein might be discovered under his own hand how the late King was not only led, but had engaged himself so to be by the Queen's evil counsels.

2. That notwithstanding all Vows, and Protestations not unattended with dreadful imprecations, and execrations of the contrary; how he endeavoured to engage *Irish, Dutch, Lorraniers, French,* and *Danish* to an invasion of *England,* not sparing to wound his Mother's honour under a feigned pretence to exasperate the *Dane* against the Parliament.

3. How he juggled in his Treaties, and Concessions, granting one thing publicly, and entering the contrary in the Council-Book, with much more which is summarily presented in that Book, and hath been handled before in this.

And lastly, whereby *his Subjects (as the Doctor is content he should since providence will have it so,* and he cannot hinder it) *having a clearer sight into the King's most retired thoughts, so much of his heart might be discovered to them without any of those dresses, or popular captations,* (which his Pen and Inkhorn officers used to muster in his former Declarations, and expresses) as would exactly demonstrate *how he was divided between the love and care he had, not more to preserve his own Tyranny, than to procure their slavery and misery, and that extreme grief, to see them so able and willing to deceive his hopes, and destroy his endeavours.*

Excellently therefore may we retort these inversions, That Truth and the Parliament's cause could not be more gratified than by the publishing [of] these Letters, whereby the *world might*

---

1 In his Sermon on the Mount, Jesus declared: "Neither do men light a candle, and put it under a bushel, but on a candlestick; and it giveth light unto all that are in the house" (Matthew 5:15; see also Mark 4:21; Luke 8:16).

2 An abridged and corrupted form of cavalier (or the Spanish *caballero*).

3 A ball of thread. In Greek mythology, Dedalus created the maze that housed the Minotaur; after killing this beast, Theseus escaped the labyrinth with the aid of the ball of thread given him by Ariadne.

see the late King's constancy (pardon the abuse of the word) *to his Wife, her Laws, and Religion.*

2. *That Bees neither will nor can gather honey* where only poison is to be sucked, nor could any man find a Cordial prescribed in those receipts by the Physician in ordinary[1] to the Commonwealth; and I may well affirm, that had not the Parliament then accounted but an extraordinary Doctor given it the better Antidotes it had long ere this been buried in bondage.

3. That the late King's endeavouring to force us to undergo his yoke, and bear his pressures by the help of foreign enemies, no man can *call fair and just correspondencies, who loves himself, or his Country*, since an honest man can hardly be happy if it be miserable, or enjoy peace and liberty while it is oppressed.

4. That the world may see how the design here like the *Turkish* Tyrants in *Egypt*, was by foreign force to keep *England* in slavery, though I think it would have proved as fatal to himself, and that these as those *Mammalucks*[2] would have shared his Kingdom among themselves.

But here let the world judge from the Doctor's mouth, with what patience he makes the late King bear this, as he terms it, indignity; and what charity forgive them, when he hath endeavoured to aggravate the fact with whatsoever his wit or malice can suggest; and also what wonderful cause he hath to thank God for these pretended graces.

Surely our Doctor durst not deny that man to be a notorious Hypocrite, who whilst he seemed with cast up eyes to thank God for his grace enabling him to bear, forgive another's injuries (as he conceived them) should discharge his Pistol at the face of his adversary at the very same instant; and yet this is his own case.

5. That multitudes were convinced by those Letters *that the late King did both mind and act such things as ill became a Prince*, which before many of those (the Doctor calls his enemies) had not so little charity to believe, and others out of respect did endeavour to conceal under the name of evil Counsellors.

By which it appears, That the Parliament sought to smother, and extinguish all ill conceit of the late King's Person so long, that

---

1 *receipts* Prescriptions; *Physician in ordinary* An official designation for a doctor in regular attendance.

2 Mamelukes. An Egyptian military body composed of European slaves, who seized the throne in 1254 CE. More broadly, any slaves in an Islamic country.

he and his regiments of Satyrs (those half Goats, half Men, whose feet if tracked close discovered the prints of the Beast, though their upper parts were covered with a Protestant profession) had almost routed and wasted their innocency.

For the Doctor's far fetched argument of *Noah's* Sons' practices, it is little to the purpose;[1] for we are so far from esteeming Kings to be the Fathers of Parliaments, that we affirm them to be theirs, and the people's creatures.

But should we admit it, it is apparent that they went backwards and covered his shame, which too deep a draught of the *Babylonish* Cup made him disclose; and if he would kick off the garment, and curse them for covering him, nay his *Chams* help him so to do, is not the curse come upon them deservedly of being Servants of Servants?[2] though I suppose the Doctor would count it a great blessing to attain to the title of *Servus servarum Gregorius 16ᵗʰ Gregory* the sixteenth Servant of Servants;[3] and would it not be rare to have Episcopacy rooted out of *England* in the time of this, who is as great a *Gregory* as he could be for his heart, in whose Popedom it was planted.

But I am confident I may conclude, *That present, and after times will judge*, that the Parliament is so far from losing the reputation of civility or humanity, that it hath gained much respect and honour by so faithful a discharging their duty and trust, as the publishing of Letters so fraught with traitorous designs, and attempts against the safety of the good people of *England* as those Flyboats[4] were, must, and will appear. [...]

---

1 Genesis 9:21-27.
2 In Genesis 9:25 Noah curses the son of Ham: "And he said, Cursed be Canaan; a servant of servants shall he be unto his brethren."
3 During the reign of James I, Gregory XV (1554-1623) served as Pope. The author suggests that the priestly author of *Eikon Basilike* would like to be styled Gregory XVI given his Catholic sympathies and claims that Charles I allowed a Popish church to be established in England.
4 Fast sailing vessels; in warfare, frigates.

2. From *The Life and Reign of King Charles, Or the Pseudo-Martyr discovered. With a late Reply to an Invective Remonstrance against the Parliament and present Government*. London: Printed for W. Reybold, 1651[1]

[...]

Observations on the King's Portraiture.

The King's Book, which hath flown abroad, and throughout the Kingdom, as it were between the wings of *Mercury*,[2] and hath so much taken in the opinion of the vulgar belief, and esteemed to be such an impregnable rampier,[3] incirculating his innocency, that it hath been thought not assaultable; I confess at the first sight thereof it took for a while, as his protestations formerly had done, in many apprehensions; but on a second consideration of the title (The King's Image) with the dress that is bestowed upon his Effigies in a posture of devotion, in imitation of *David* in his ejaculations to Heaven, surely I could not believe that such a piece of vanity was of the King's designment, but the mere juggling device of some hypocritical or Mahometan Impostor, the better to stir up the People and vain beholders to pity him: But entering into the Body of the Book, and considering the choice of the many Subjects whereof it treats, the whole contexture whereof hath already been sufficiently handled without mittens by a Gentleman of such abilities as gives place to none for his integrity, learning and judgement;[4] yet on re-consideration of the whole (amongst others of his Chapters) coming to that of (listing of Armies) and in that to his Interrogations, *Whose innocent blood hath he shed? what Widows' or Orphans' tears can witness against me?* Doubtless were there no other evidence throughout all the whole book (as God knows every page yields plenty of such impudencies) those two Interrogatories would be sufficient to prove him one of the bloodiest out-facers of truth that ever was known in the world. Passing by his own acknowledgement, that himself first began the late War, and consequently guilty of all the innocent blood spilt throughout the three Kingdoms, it would not be

---

1 This anonymous work has been falsely attributed both to John Milton and to Hamon L'Estrange (1605-60).

2 In Roman mythology, Jove's messenger, associated with the spread of news. Many newsbooks of the period reflect this in their titles; for example, *Mercurius Pragmaticus* or *Mercurius Politicus*.

3 Fortification.

4 John Milton.

amiss to retort his own Interrogatories, and to ask whether there be any one Family or Kindred throughout three Kingdoms, that yields not a Father, Mother, Brother, Sister, or a Kinsman, whose tears have not cried to Heaven for the infinity of blood spilt through his willfulness, or for the wounds, or loss of Limbs of so many throughout the Land we which see daily haulting[1] and crutching it in hospitals, and in every of our streets; and hath there been no Widows' or Orphans' tears shed? or no complaints made to himself for the goods taken violently from them, and firing of numberless habitations by his own merciless Soldiers, Commissioned by himself, yea commanded to be put in execution, as it may be instanced in thousands of sad examples, yea by poor Widows crying and kneeling unto him for the rapines committed either in his own sight, or by his permission, when they received no other answer, but his turning about from their lamentations, and saying that he did it not, when it lay in his power, and by his oath and duty he stood bound to see it redressed, which he never was known to have done, but to slight whatsoever complaints were addressed unto him of that nature? And was he ever known to spare either friend or foe, where money was to be had to prosecute his perfidious[2] and bloody designs, which he took not? Amongst thousands of precedents of this nature, did he spare Mr *Ascham*, a known Royalist, and one that assisted him in his bloody Wars, when he sent *Rupert*,[3] that plundering kinsman of his, to rifle the Gentleman's house at *Layford* in the County of *Berks*, who took from him ten thousand pounds at once in ready money, and out of his bounty (whereof he was very seldom known to be over liberal) sent back the tenths thereof as a dividend between his two unmarried daughters, and that also on great suit made unto him, and the tears of the Gentlewomen themselves that he would be pleased to consider their distressed condition? with what face could he so much as pretend to innocency, or appeal to the witness of any Widows' or Orphans' tears, when 'tis openly known, that he never spared any man's blood in his wrath, who was in arms against him, otherwise than for his own ends, and safety of such of his own side as the Parliament

---

1 Limping or walking lamely.
2 Treacherous.
3 Prince Rupert (1619-82), the second son of King Charles I's sister Elizabeth of Bohemia, by her marriage to Frederick, Elector Palatine. He served as Charles I's General of the Horse during the Civil War.

had in their custody? when he had granted our Commissions of *Oyer* and *Determiner* to his chief Justice *Heath* and others to hang all such as had opposed his Tyranny in taking the Parliament's part, until he was induced to retract those Commissions in regard that two for one of his own might happily by his own Precedent have gone to the Gallows?[1] and do not his own Letters to the Queen confirm his resolution to take money wheresoever he could find it, when he tells her that his only want was money, which good Swords and Pistols would fetch in? and hath not the practice of all his barbarous Wars verified as much as he therein soothes up himself,[2] to be supplied either by hook or crook? If no innocent blood can be found to witness against him, let the ghosts of 200000 poor Innocent souls, barbarously butchered in *Ireland* speak; if no Widows' or Orphans' tears can witness against him, let the dumb stones of those demolished palaces at *Basing*, *Ragland*, *Belvoyer*, and infinite others speak, where those formidable garrisons of his were made to the terror and damage of all men in their vicinity, and whose reducing cost so much innocent blood.[3] Neither let those great Lords and prime Gentlemen of this Kingdom, whose Lands and total Inheritances are lately voted to be sold, in reparation of the public losses, and in defence of the general interest of the Commonwealth (changed) when it could not otherwise subsist, but by rooting up his tyrannous monarchy be silent; And if no other tears of Widows and orphans can be found to accuse him, let his ambition, injustice, oppression, rapine, and bloodshed speak, let that vast number of Gentlemen which have made their compositions (for siding with him in his unjust and destructive Wars) at Goldsmiths' hall, speak or[4] be silent, whose Wives and Children, live in want, and happily[5]

---

1   The Commission of oyer and terminer was a commission directed to the King's Judges, Sergeants, and others of note, empowering them to hear and determine indictments on specified offences, such as treasons or felonies, special commissions being granted on occasions of insurrections.

2   Glosses over his offences to render them less objectionable.

3   All three were sites of extensive sieges of Royalist garrisons by the Parliament's army. Charles I was held responsible for the predatory nature of these garrisons on the surrounding countryside, as well as for civilian casualties and the loss of parliamentary troops.

4   Emended from "of."

5   Perchance; appropriately.

not without tears enough for the indigence whereunto they are reduced through his only means.[1] Now if all these sad instances be the effects and Trophies of his seventeen years' reign, which he boasts that the people enjoyed in such measure of peace, justice and plenty, as all the neighbour Nations have either admired or envied; and if this his Portraiture and Image be that monument which his friends, since his death, or rather before, had prepared in readiness, and stolen the pattern from *Mecha*,[2] and to hang it in that his ayrery Mahometan regality,[3] supported by this their impostured Loadstone, whereby to present his sacred memory, in his Solitudes, to posterity, surely it may be suspected, they were not so exactly their Crafts-masters, or so much his friends as foes, to Saint him before his time, and in such a shrine, as necessarily must render him to future times (infamous) an imparalleled dissembler, and a greater deceiver than *Mahomet* ever was, and of the number of those of whom the Prophet *David* makes mention, which *speak peace to their Neighbours, when mischief was in their hearts*,[4] (as all the world knows he hath too often practised to his people and Parliaments) when as it would have much better became him to have left out his many Pharisaical justifications, and to have remembered, *that he which covereth his sins shall not prosper, but who so confesseth and foresaketh them shall have mercy;*[5] this had been the better way to have invited others to have spoken less and more favourable of him, than now in conscience they ought, having such an artificial and faced[6] piece of impudent justifications, exposed and set forth purposely to deceive the poor people, and to affront truth, and the evident managery[7] of his bloody and licentious reign, which necessarily

---

1 Parliament passed an ordinance sequestering the estates of any that gave assistance to the king's cause on 27 March 1643. The resulting committee met at Goldsmiths' Hall. An ordinance of August 1643 allowed for a wife to request a "fifth" of the sequestered estate to support herself and her children.

2 Mecca.

3 See the note to "*Mahoment's* Tomb" in the sixth chapter of *Eikon Basilike*. The author is making the commonplace association between arbitrary government and "Turkish tyranny."

4 Psalm 28:3.

5 Proverbs 28:13.

6 Bold; shameless.

7 Cunning management.

to the World's end will give an occasion to rip up[1] his life, and show to the present and after ages, what a Tomb these juggling[2] impostors have erected for him; and with what Epitaphs of impiety, injustice, blood and rapine, it will be adorned, instead of that glory wherewith they intended to perpetuate to his memory; though sufficient and enough hath already been written, in discovery of this grand Imposture, and to every piece and parcel thereof so much answered as may satisfy all men in their right wits; as to others that are out of them, and have a desire to be cosened[3] out of their understandings, I think an Asian belief would better fit them than an European Faith, a gallimaufried Alcoran,[4] rather than a true and rational Remonstrance, dressed with no other Rhetoric than the naked truth; and shall men be silent when they see it overborne with the multitudinous denials, flams,[5] and falsehoods of his defeated and malicious parties? [...]

3. From *EIKON AKLASTOS*[6] *The Image Unbroken.* *A Perspective of the Impudence, Falsehood, Vanity, and Prophaneness, Published in a Libel entitled EIKONOKLASTES against EIKON BASILIKE*. Printed 1651

The INTRODUCTION
When the book called *Icon-basilice* was coming forth the Rebels' guilt Suggested Suspicions to them of danger from the memory of his late Majesty as formerly they apprehended from his life, striving, that he might not appear to posterity out of those ignominious Circumstances, which they had contrived in the murder of him, and thence their rigid Inquisition after persons and Presses. Rebels rise by flattery, rule by force, and they, that made so many appeals to the people, forbid them now to know the groans

---

1 To reopen a person's dubious past to discussion.
2 Deceiving.
3 Cheated, deceived.
4 Confusedly jumbled Koran.
5 Fanciful compositions, tricks.
6 Anthony à Wood claimed that this royalist tract, a rebuttal of *Eikonoklastes*, was written by Joseph Jane, a member of the 1643 Oxford Parliament. Royston is known to have sold copies

of a dead Martyr. Upon the coming forth of the book, they found what they feared, that many, whose passion kept them from a right judgement in the heat of Action, saw their own errors in that book, and that the person, and cause of his late Majesty began to be more Generally understood, and being not able to strangle it in the birth, they sought how to cast it forth to be destroyed, raising rumours, that it was not the work of his late Majesty thinking to make men less intent on the book, if the author were suspected, and that they might thereby take off all opinions of piety, and wisdom from his late Majesty which might be collected from his writings, it being the Custom of Rebels to prevail more by Calumnies upon the disposition, than the Actions of Princes. They seek to improve cruelty above nature for having by wicked hands destroyed the Lord's anointed, they would deface the Memory of their own vile Actions against him, hiring false Prophets to curse him, and they grudge at his Crown in heaven, as they usurped that on earth. It's no new thing for persons of most eminent virtue to fall into the obloquy, and suffer by the rage of the misled people, and therefore no wonder if innocence find an orator to accuse it, and Treason an Advocate, to defend it. Rebellion never wanted a Trumpet and though the contrivance of it be in Caves, and vaults, yet success makes it outface the light. His Majesty's book hath passed the censure of the greatest part of the learned world, being translated into the most spread[1] Languages, and strangers honour his Memory, and abhor his murderers, but such, as regard not the all-seeing eye of God beholding their wickedness, despise the judgement of the whole world, and there is a man[2] found out, that will break down the united reason of mankind, and he tells men, they must take his word above their own, and all men's reason, this he undertakes, that looks on kings, as Ants, and the king's book, as wanting all moment of Solidity, and if, as he chose the Title of *Iconoclastes* he had written his book in a Foreign, or learned language, his unfaithfulness, and impudence would be as open, and odious as his vanity is ridiculous.

And though the exceptions against his Majesty's book fall away of themselves, and Traitors' Apologies carry with them their own Confutation, yet indignation at the shameless insolence, and

---

1 Widespread; *Eikon Basilike* was translated into Latin, Dutch, Danish, French, and German.
2 John Milton.

untruth of *Iconoclastes* provokes a just vindication of his late Majesty from the lewd slanders of the answerer. A Dumb child got speech at the apprehension of an Injury to the father, and it's a dead Loyalty, that stands unmoved at the cursing of a Shimei, and those curses of Shimei recorded in Scripture were less virulent, and more excusable, than this Author's language of his late Majesty through his whole Treatise, which is a Treason against God, and Man, Religion, Truth, and Justice.

★ ★ ★

Upon the QUEEN'S DEPARTURE
What concerns it us here to hear a husband divulge his household privacies, extolling to others the virtues of his wife, an infirmity not seldom incident to those, who have least cause, Just Testimony to virtue is never an infirmity, but necessary from the husband, where conjugal affection hath derived the hatred of his Enemies to his wife. If the divulging of household privacies concerned him not, it is his lewdness to take occasions of derision, and base language from it. Treasons to the mind are as pestilence to the body, that turns all diseases into its own malignant humour, for this Libeller cannot forbear despite[1] to the King for speaking that, which he saith doth not concern others, nor to the Queen for being named.

How good a wife she was to himself, how bad a subject is not much disputed, And to whom was she a subject, to the Rebels? Those that acknowledge themselves subjects to the King, will have the Queen esteemed a bad subject for her Zeal to his State, and safety, these evil spirits, that possess the Rebels persuade men, that it is a fault to be bad subjects, and yet will allow none to be subjects, but the King, his wife, and children.

It need be made no wonder, though she left a Protestant Kingdom with as little honour, as her mother left a Popish. This mention of her mother shows the extension of a Traiterous malice, that spares no relations, nor conditions though unconcerned. Those, that compelled the Queen's departure did more contribute to the dishonour of a Protestant Kingdom, and the Protestant Religion, whereof they take the name without the truth, than the greatest Enemy to the Protestant Religion could have effected, what the case of her mother was we enquire not, but the world sees, that these

---

1 Scorn, contempt.

injuries to her Majesty exceeded example, and Rebels' injustice fixes no dishonour, but on themselves.

The king says *this is the first example of any Protestant subjects, that have taken up Arms against their King a Protestant.* The Libeller says *it can be to Protestants no dishonour, when it shall be heard, that he first levied war on them, and to the interest of Papists more than of Protestants.* But then it is dishonour, if he first levied not war upon them? And all that read his book must conclude, that they first levied war upon him, what else doth he mean by defending the Tumults, seizing the forts, and Militia, raising an Army, and upbraiding the king with fears to hazard such a scuffle. But were it otherwise, the Protestants have disclaimed his Traiterous pretence of taking Arms against the King under colour of Religion, or otherwise, and hold it dishonour to their Religion, that such Rebellious principles should be charged upon them, and nothing could be more for the interest of Papists, than that Protestants should maintain, and practise that doctrine of Rebellion. The world is satisfied, how disloyally the King was prosecuted by Arms, and had it been otherwise, subjects ought to petition not return violence, and in all the excuses that these Traitors have used, they never mention any offer of satisfaction to the King, or desire to lay down his Arms, but require his submission, and giving up his rights, or otherwise they would take it by force. The precedence of the Scots' war will not take off the dishonour.

He says, *It's a groundless, and dissembled fear, that she, that was for many years averse to her husband's Religion should be now the more alienated,* and can the Libeller deny, but that the aversion of any may be increased, and confirmed by the wickedness of the persons of the contrary Religion, how groundless then, and shameless is his exception?

If the fear of her delinquency, and Justice demanded on her, was any cause of her alienating the more, to have gained her by indirect means, had been no advantage to Religion. As the King observed, that this was the first example of Protestant subjects, that took Arms against their king: so this of charging the Queen with Delinquency was the first example in that kind, that traitorous impudence had produced, and when it shall be heard, that a company of such vile persons charge the Queen with Crimes for assisting her husband, they will be assured, that not fear of Delinquency, but their barbarous cruelty might more alienate her, and disadvantage Religion. *Them, who accused her* he says *well enough known to be the Parliament,* the King censures, *for men yet to seek their Religion, whether doctrine, discipline, or good manners.* And so doth the whole world, whatever name the Libeller give such men, who are well enough known to be a Traitorous faction.

The name of true English Protestants is a mere schismatical name. And why? Are there not several confessions in the Protestant Churches, and do they hold one another Schismatics for that reason? How often hath this Libeller named the best reformed Churches, is not that as much a name of schism? he is ignorant in the nature of schism, though he be so well practised in it, and it's strange he would observe a Schismatical name from the title of a nation, and not from his title of Independency, that produceth as many titles, and distinctions, as there be Parishes, or Parlours.

The King ascribes rudeness, and barbarity worse than Indian to the English Parliament. To the Libeller's Parliament he very well may. He says *the King ascribes all virtues to his wife undervaluing the great Council of his Kingdom in comparison of one woman.* And not only he, but all good men abominate that wicked Council, which used such rudeness, and barbarity towards her, and from hence the Libeller tells us *there are examples of mischief under uxorious Magistrates, and Feminine usurpation.* And must Magistrates therefore have no wives, or no affections to them? And the examples of feminine usurpation are more frequent in Republican Tribunes than Monarchs.

The king says, *her tarrying here he could not think safe among them who were shaking hands with Allegiance to lay faster hold on Religion.* The Libeller says that *he taxes them of a duty rather than a Crime, it being just to obey God rather than man.* And is perjury, and the breach of Allegiance obedience to God, and do men obey God, that break one Commandment upon pretence to keep another. The Scripture tells us he that breaks one Commandment is guilty of all, but these are they, that say they love God, and yet hate their brother,[1] hate and kill their King God's viceregent.

The libeller says *it was the fault of their courage, that they had not quite shaken off, what they stood shaking hands with.* It's like their conscience, and Religion were not the cause they did not, but the

---

1 *The Scripture ... of all* "For whosoever shall keep the whole law, and yet offend in one point, he is guilty of all" (James 2:10); *say they love ... their brother* "If a man say, I love God, and hateth his brother, he is a liar: for he that loveth not his brother whom he hath seen, how can he love God whom he hath not seen?" (1 John 4:20).

Libeller was not of their Counsel, for the time required they should keep their mask longer.

He is offended at the King's prayer, *that the disloyalty of his protestant subjects may not be a hindrance to her love of the true Religion*, and says that *he never prays, that the dissoluteness of his Court, the Scandals of his Clergy, unsoundness of his own judgement, Lukewarmness of his life, letter of compliance to the Pope, permitting his nuncio here, may not be found far greater hinderances.* All these put together are far short of the scandal of the disloyalty of his subjects. The Court dissoluteness is made a common place of scandal, not verity in respect of the application, there being not such excesses in his Majesty's Court, that deserved a special observation, and the restraint of dissoluteness was more observable, than the Crime. As to the scandals of his Clergy, though we must believe, that offences will come, yet the scandal of the present disloyalty was more offensive to those of different Religion, than any disorders in Civil conversation, and the injustice of the Rebels towards the Clergy, hath showed the untruth of the scandals, that were cast upon them, and though their malice traduced,[1] and persecuted them, their proofs could not convict them of the scandal supposed. His Majesty's own judgement cannot be overcast by a Rebel's malice, and his exemplary life cannot be stained by a Libeller's pen. His letter to the Pope was no compliance, nor could it give offence to protestant or hope to Papist, and these Rebels, that comply with Turks, and infidels least of all think it a compliance. The Libeller well knows there was no nuncio in England, and if the King should have denied the Queen the exercise of her Religion, whereto he was bound by the Articles upon the match, he had given greater scandal by breaking the Articles, than by permitting her the repair of[2] persons in matters of her Religion.[3] But says the Libeller, *they must not sit still*, that is not Rebel, *and see their Religion snatched away*. But they have Rebelled to snatch away Religion. He says, *It's known, that her Religion wrought*

---

1 Misrepresented, vilified.
2 Social intercourse with; association with.
3 The marriage treaty of November 1624 permitted Henrietta Maria freedom of religion; a chapel wherever she resided which was open to all English Catholics; a body of priests, almoners and chaplains to perform religious functions in the chapels; and charge of the religious education of her children until their thirteenth year. It also required the suspension of English recusancy laws.

more upon him, than his upon her, and his favouring of Papists, and hatred of Puritans, made men suspect she had perverted him. No doubt suspicions were industriously raised, and carefully nourished against the King, though they believed them not, that made use of them. The King was not bound to destroy all Papists, and could not deny them the protection of a King, and he had just reason to suspect those bloody Puritans, whose inclinations he discerned to that wickedness they have since avowed.

From his suppositions he ascends to his exclamations. *What is it, that the blindness of hypocrisy dare not do? It dares pray, and think to hide that from the eyes of God, which it cannot from the open view of men.* We find this very frequent in this Author, and in this very Period, that in contempt of God, and men, charges the King with Crimes he not only knew false, but which are so known unto the whole world, and conclude against his own narrations, and others' view. [...]

Appendix B: The Trial and Execution of Charles I

1. Trial of King Charles I

Figure 3: Trial of King Charles I (artist unknown) [17th Century]
National Portrait Gallery, London.

[The material in Appendix B chronicles the final days of Charles I, from his trial to his execution. The trial of the king, which commenced on 20 January 1649, took place in the Great Hall of Westminster Palace. Charles I was impeached as a "Tyrant, Traitor, Murderer, and a Public and implacable Enemy to the Commonwealth of England." As the selections from the trial indicate (B.2), the king rejected the legal authority of the High Court of Justice, refusing to enter a plea. The anonymous seventeenth-century line engraving (B.1) reveals the dramatic shift in power that occurred during the trial: the upper half recalls the enthroned king surrounded by the lords, while the lower half depicts John Bradshaw, the Lord President of the trial, assuming the seat of authority. The king received the sentence of death on 27 January 1649. His scaffold was erected outside the Banqueting Hall of Whitehall Palace. On 30 January 1649, shortly before his execution, Charles I pronounced his final speech, in which he maintained his innocence (B.3).]

2. Selections from *"The Manner of the Trial of Charles Stuart King of England," A True Copy of the Journal of The high Court of Justice, for the Trial of K. Charles I. As it was Read in the House of Commons, and Attested under the hand of Phelps, Clerk to that Infamous Court.* London: Printed by *H.C.* for *Thomas Dring*, 1684

[...]
Westminster-Hall, Jan. 20. 1648.
On *Saturday,* being the 20th. Day of *January,* 1648. the *Lord President* of the *High Court of Justice,* his two Assistants, and the rest of the Commissioners of the said Court, according to the Adjournment of the said Court from the *Painted Chamber,* came to the Bench, or Place prepared for their Sitting, at the West End of the Great Hall at *Westminster;* divers Officers of the said Court, one and twenty Gentlemen with Partizans,[1] and a Sword and Mace marching before them up into the Court, where the *Lord President,* in a crimson Velvet Chair fixed in the midst of the Court, placed himself, having a Desk with a crimson Velvet Cush-

---

1 Long-handled spears borne as halberds by guards.

ion before him:[1] the rest of the Members placing themselves on each side of him, upon several Seats or Benches prepared, and hung with Scarlet for that purpose. The *Lord President*'s two Assistants sitting next of each side of him, and the two Clerks of the Court placed at a Table somewhat lower, and covered with a *Turkey* Carpet;[2] upon which Table was also laid the Sword and Mace, the said Guard of Partizans dividing themselves on each side of the Court before them.

Three Proclamations are made for all persons that were Adjourned over thither,[3] to draw near.

The Court being thus sat, and Silence enjoined, the Great Gate of the Hall was set open, to the intent that all persons (without exception) desirous to see or hear, might come unto it: upon which the Hall was presently filled, and Silence again ordered and proclaimed.

After Silence, proclaimed as aforesaid, the Act of the Commons of *England* Assembled in Parliament, for Erecting of a High Court of Justice for Trying and Judging of *CHARLES STUART* King of *England*, was openly read by one of the Clerks of the Court.[4]

The Act being read, the Court was called, every Commissioner present, thereupon rising to his Name.[5]

This done, the Court command the Sergeant at Arms to send for the Prisoner; and thereupon, Col. *Tomlinson*, who had the Charge of the Prisoner, within a quarter of an hour's space brought him, attended by Col. *Hacker*, and two and thirty Offi-

---

1 John Bradshaw (1602-59), Chief Justice of Chester prior to the king's trial. He was chosen to preside over the trial after the offer was rejected by all of the highest-ranking judges in England. On 30 January 1661, Bradshaw's body, along with those of Oliver Cromwell and Henry Ireton, was exhumed from Westminster Abbey and hanged at Tyburn; their heads were then displayed on poles at Westminster Hall.

2 *two Clerks of the Court* John Phelps and Andrew Broughton. After the Restoration, both men fled to Switzerland; *Turkey Carpet* A carpet imported from Turkey, or an imitation thereof.

3 From the Painted Chamber.

4 The Act had been passed in the Commons on 6 January 1649.

5 The list of those present follows at this point. Of the 135 commissioners appointed for the trial, 68 were present at the opening session. On 22 January, 70 commissioners were present; on the 23rd, 71; on the 27th, 68. Only 59 signed the king's death warrant.

cers with Partizans, guarding him to the Court, his own Servants immediately attending him.[1]

Being thus brought up in the Face of the Court, the Sergeant at Arms with his Mace receives him, and conducts him straight to the Bar, having a crimson Velvet Chair set before him. After a stern looking upon the Court and the People in the Galleries on each side of him, he places himself in the Chair, not at all moving[2] his Hat, or otherwise showing the least respect to the Court; but presently riseth up again, and turns about, looking downwards upon the Guards placed on the left side, and on the multitude of Spectators on the right side of the said great Hall, the Guard that attended him, in the mean time dividing themselves on each side the Court, and his own Servants following him to the Bar, stand on the left hand of the Prisoner.

The Prisoner having again placed himself in his Chair, with his Face towards the Court, and Silence being again ordered and proclaimed, the *Lord President* in the Name of the Court, addressed himself to the Prisoner, acquainting him, *That the Commons of* England *Assembled in Parliament, being deeply sensible of the Evils and Calamities that had been brought upon this Nation, and of the innocent Blood that had been spilled in it, which was fixed upon him as the principal Author of it, had resolved to make Inquisition for this Blood, and according to the Debt they did owe to God, to Justice, the Kingdom, and themselves, and according to that Fundamental Power that rested, and Trust reposed in them by the People, other Means failing through his Default, had resolved to bring him to Trial and Judgement, and had therefore constituted that Court of Justice, before which he was then brought, where he was to*

---

1   *Col. Tomlinson* Matthew Tomlinson, who guarded Charles I at Windsor Castle during the final weeks of his life, commanded the escort that brought the King from Windsor to Westminster on the day of his execution. As he treated Charles I with respect and did not sign his death warrant, he secured at the Restoration a full pardon in exchange for testifying against Colonels Hacker and Axtell; *Col. Hacker* Francis Hacker was in command of the soldiers who guarded Charles I during his trial and execution, and signed, with Colonel Daniel Axtell, the order to the executioner. For their part in the regicide, Hacker and Axtell were hanged and quartered on 19 October 1660.

2   Removing; it had been resolved in the Painted Chamber prior to the first day's sitting, that, "as to the Prisoner's putting off his Hat, the Court will not insist upon it for this day" (Nelson 25).

hear his Charge, upon which the Court would proceed according to Justice.

Hereupon, Mr. *Cook*, Solicitor for the Common-wealth, standing within a Bar, with the rest of the Council for the Commonwealth on the right hand of the Prisoner, offered to speak; but the Prisoner, having a Staff in his hand, held it up, and softly laid it upon the said Mr. *Cook*'s Shoulder two or three times, bidding him hold; nevertheless, the *Lord President* ordering him to go on, Mr. *Cook* did according to the Order of the Court, to him directed, in the Name, and on the behalf of the People of *England*, exhibit a Charge of High Treason, and other high Crimes, and did therewith accuse the said *CHARLES STUART* King of *England*; praying in the Name, and on the behalf aforesaid, that the Charge might be accordingly received and read, and due Proceedings had thereupon; and accordingly preferred a Charge in writing, which being received by the Court, and delivered to the Clerk of the Court, the *Lord President* in the Name of the Court ordered it should be read.

But the King interrupting the reading of it, the Court notwithstanding commanded the Clerk to read it, acquainting the Prisoner that if he had any thing to say after, the Court would hear him; whereupon the Clerk read the Charge, the Tenor whereof is as follows, *viz.*

A Charge of High Treason, and other High Crimes Exhibited to the *High Court of Justice* by *John Cook* Esq;[1] Solicitor General, appointed by the said Court, for, and on the behalf of the People of *England*, against *CHARLES STUART* King of *England*.

That *He the said* CHARLES STUART, *being admitted King of* England, *and therein trusted with a limited Power to govern by, and according to the Laws of the Land, and not otherwise; and by his Trust, Oath and Office, being obliged to use the Power committed to him, for the Good and Benefit of the People, and for the Preservation of their Rights and Liberties; Yet nevertheless, out of a wicked Design to erect*

---

1   Cook, a barrister of Gray's Inn, was initially responsible—along with Isaac Dorislaus, John Aske, and the recently appointed Attorney General, Anthony Steele—for drawing up the charge against Charles I. Cook was not the first choice for prosecuting attorney. He came to it only after Anthony Steele was excused at the last minute due to ill health.

and uphold in himself an unlimited *Tyrannical Power to rule according to his Will, and to overthrow the Rights and Liberties of the People, yea to take away and make void the Foundations thereof, and of all redress and remedy of misgovernment, which by the Fundamental Constitutions of this Kingdom, were reserved on the People's behalf, in the Right and Power of frequent and successive Parliaments or National Meetings in Council, He the said* CHARLES STUART, *for accomplishment of such his Designs, and for the Protecting of himself and his Adherents, in his and their wicked Practices, to the same Ends, hath Traitorously and Maliciously Levied War against the present Parliament, and the People therein represented; Particularly, upon or about the Thirtieth day of* June, *in the Year of our Lord* 1642. *at* Beverely *in the County of* York; *and upon or about the Thirtieth day of* July *in the Year aforesaid, in the County of the City of* York; *and upon or about the four and twentieth day of* August *in the same Year, at the County of the Town of* Nottingham, *where, and when he set up his Standard of War; and also on or about the twenty third day of* Octob. *in the same Year, at* Edge-Hill *and* Keynton *Field, in the County of* Warwick; *and upon or about the thirtieth day of* November *in the same Year, at* Brainford *in the County of* Middlesex; *and upon or about the thirtieth day of* August, *in the Year of our Lord* 1643, *at* Caversham-Bridge *near* Reading *in the County of* Berks; *and upon or about the thirtieth day of* October *in the Year last mentioned, at or near the City of* Gloucester; *and upon or about the thirtieth day of* November *in the Year last mentioned, at* Newbury *in the County of* Berks; *and upon or about the thirty first day of* July *in the Year of our Lord* 1644. *at* Cropredy-Bridge *in the County of* Oxon; *and upon or about the thirtieth day of* September *in the last Year mentioned, at* Bodwyn *and other Places near adjacent, in the County of* Cornwall; *and upon or about the thirtieth day of* November *in the Year last mentioned, at* Newbury *aforesaid; and upon or about the eighth day of* June *in the Year of our Lord* 1645. *at the Town of* Leicester; *and also upon the fourteenth day of the same Month in the same Year, at* Naseby-Field *in the County of* Northampton. *At which several Times and Places, or most of them, and at many other Places in this Land, at several other times within the Years afore-mentioned; and in the Year of our Lord* 1646. *He the said* CHARLES STUART *hath caused and procured many Thousands of the free People of this Nation to be slain, and by Divisions, Parties, and Insurrections within this Land, by Invasions from Foreign Parts, endeavoured and procured by him, and by many other evil ways and means, He the said* CHARLES STUART *hath not only maintained and carried on the said War both by Land and*

Sea, during the Year before mentioned, but also hath renewed or caused to be renewed the said War against the Parliament and good People of this Nation, in this present Year 1648. *in the Counties of* Kent, Essex, Surrey, Sussex, Middlesex, *and many other Counties and Places in* England *and* Wales; *and also by Sea. And particularly He the said* CHARLES STUART *hath for that purpose given Commission to his Son the Prince, and others, whereby, besides multitudes of other Persons, many such as were by the Parliament entrusted and employed for the safety of the Nation (being by him or his Agents[1] corrupted to the betraying of their Trust, and revolting from the Parliament) have had Entertainment[2] and Commission for the continuing and renewing of War and Hostility against the said Parliament and People, as aforesaid; By which cruel and unnatural Wars by him the said* CHARLES STUART *Levied, Continued and Renewed as aforesaid, much innocent Blood of the free People of this Nation hath been spilled, many Families have been undone, the Public Treasury wasted and exhausted, Trade obstructed, and miserably decayed, vast Expense and Damage to the Nation incurred, and many parts of this Land spoiled, some of them even to desolation. And for further Prosecution of his said evil Designs, He the said* CHARLES STUART *doth still continue his Commissions to the said Prince, and other Rebels and Revolters both* English *and Foreigners, and to the* E. *of* Ormond, *and to the* Irish *Rebels and Revolters associated with him; from whom further Invasions upon this Land are threatened, upon the procurement and on the behalf of the said* CHARLES STUART.

All which wicked Designs, Wars, and evil Practices of him the said CHARLES STUART, *have been, and are carried on for the advancement and upholding of a Personal Interest of Will and Power, and pretended Prerogative to himself and his Family, against the Public Interest, Common Right, Liberty, Justice and Peace of the People of this Nation, by and for whom he was entrusted as aforesaid.*

By all which it appeareth, that He the said CHARLES STUART *hath been, and is the Occasioner, Author, and Continuer of the said unnatural, cruel and bloody Wars, and therein guilty of all the Treasons, Murders, Rapines, Burnings, Spoils, Desolations, Damages and Mis-*

---

1   Emended from "Angels," the phrase "being by him or his Agents corrupted" recurring on page 317. ("Angels," denoting "fallen or rebellious spirits" or more generally "messengers," however, is possibly intended here).

2   Maintenance (support) for service.

chiefs to this Nation acted and committed in the said Wars, or occasioned thereby.

And the said *John Cook* by Protestation saving on behalf of the said People of *England*, the liberty of exhibiting at any time hereafter any other Charge against the said *CHARLES STUART*, and also of replying to the Answers which the said *CHARLES STUART* shall make to the Premises,[1] or any of them, or any other Charge that shall be so exhibited, doth for the said Treasons and Crimes, on the behalf of the said People of *England*, impeach the said *CHARLES STUART*, as a Tyrant, Traitor, Murderer, and a Public and implacable Enemy to the Commonwealth of *England*, and pray that the said *CHARLES STUART* King of *England*, may be put to answer all and every the Premises, and that such Proceedings, Examinations, Trials, Sentences and Judgements may be thereupon had, as shall be agreeable to Justice.

Subscribed, *John Cook.*

The Prisoner, while the Charge was reading,[2] sat down in his Chair, looking sometimes on the High Court, and sometimes on the Galleries, and rose again, and turned about to behold the Guards and Spectators, and after sat down looking very sternly, and with a Countenance not at all moved, till these words, *viz. CHARLES STUART to be a Tyrant, Traitor,* etc. were read; at which he laughed as he sat in the face of the Court.

The Charge being read, the *Lord President*, in the Name of the Court, demanded the Prisoner's answer thereto.

But the Prisoner declining that, fell into a Discourse of the late Treaty in the Isle of *Wight*, and demanded, *By what lawful Authority he was brought from the Isle thither?* upbraiding the Court with the many unlawful Authorities in the World, instancing in Robbers and takers of Purses, pleading his Kingship, and thereby a Trust committed to him by God, by descent, which he should betray, together with the Liberties of the People, in case he should answer to an unlawful Power, which he charged the Court to be, and that *they were raised by an Usurped Power*; and affirmed, that *He stood more for the Liberties of the People, than any of the Judges there sitting*, and again demanded, *by what Authority he was brought thither?*

To which it was replied by the Court, *That had he been pleased*

---

1 Matters mentioned previously.
2 Was being read aloud.

*to have observed what was declared to him by the Court at his first
coming, and the Charge which he had heard read unto him, he might
have informed himself by what Authority he was brought before them;
namely,* By the Authority of the *Commons of* England *Assembled in*
Parliament, *on the behalf of the People of* England: and did therefore again several times advise him *to consider of a better Answer;*
which he refused to do, but persisted in his Contumacy.[1] Whereupon, the Court at length told him, That, *they did expect from him
a Positive Answer to the Charge;* affirming their Authority, and giving him to understand, that *they were upon God's and the Kingdom's Errand, and that the Peace stood for, would be better had and
kept when Justice was done, and that was their present Work;* advised
him seriously to *consider what he had to do at his next appearance;*
which was declared should be upon *Monday* following, and so
remanded him to his former Custody.

The Prisoner all the time having kept on his Hat, departed,
without showing any the least respect to the Court; but going out
of the Bar, said, *He did not fear that Bill;* pointing to the Table
where the Sword and Charge lay.

The Prisoner being withdrawn, three Proclamations were
made, and the Court Adjourned it self to the *Painted Chamber* on
Monday Morning then next, at Nine of the Clock; declaring, that
from thence they intended to Adjourn to the same Place again.

* * *

Westminster-Hall, Jan. 22. 1648. *Post Merid.*
The Commissioners coming from the *Painted Chamber,* take their
Place in the Public Court in *Westminster Hall,* as on *Saturday*
before; and being sat, and the Hall Doors set open,

Three Proclamations are made, for all Persons that were
Adjourned over to this time, to give their Attendance, and for all
Persons to keep Silence, upon pain of Imprisonment.[2]

---

1 Wilful disobedience to the court.
2 This admonishment occurred because of an outburst on 20 January. As
   Phelps read the roll call of Commissioners on the 20th, a masked lady
   (hearing Lord Fairfax's name) cried out: "He [Fairfax] has more wit
   than to be here." The lady declared that Fairfax "never would sit among
   them and they did wrong to name him." Lady Fairfax is believed to be
   this masked woman.

The Court is thereupon called.[1]

The Court being called, the Sergeant is commanded to fetch his Prisoner.

The King is again brought Prisoner to the Bar, as on *Saturday* before; Proclamation is made for Silence, while Pleas of the Commonwealth were in hand, and Order given to the Captain of the Guard to take into his Custody such as should disturb the Court.

Mr. *Solicitor* moved the Court, that the Prisoner might give a Positive Answer to his Charge, or otherwise that the Court would take the Matter of it *pro Confesso*,[2] and proceed thereupon according to Justice; which being pressed by the Court upon the Prisoner, and their Judgement again made known unto him, That he was to Answer his Charge, otherwise that his Contumacy would be recorded.

The Prisoner, that notwithstanding, still insisted upon his former Plea, and that the Court had no Power, nor the *Commons* of *England*, who had constituted it, to proceed against him; upon which, the Clerk of the Court, by Command, and according to former Order, required his Answer in the Form prescribed: and the Prisoner still refusing to submit thereto, his Default[3] *and Contempt were again Recorded, the Prisoner remanded, and the Court Adjourned it self till the next day, being Tuesday,* at Twelve of the Clock, to the *Painted Chamber*; withal, giving Notice, that from thence they intended to Adjourn to this Place again.

* * *

Westminster-Hall, 23 Jan. 1648.[4] *Post Merid.*

Three Proclamations being made, and Attendance and Silence commanded as formerly,

The Court is thereupon called.[5]

The Court being called, the Sergeant is required to send for the Prisoner, who was accordingly brought to the Bar, where he took his Seat as formerly. Proclamation is thereupon made for

---

1 A list of the Commissioners present follows.
2 Taken as confessed.
3 Failure to answer to the charges, resulting in a court's proceeding upon the defendant's guilt.
4 Emended from "28 Jan. 1648."
5 A list of the Commissioners present follows.

Silence, while the Pleas of the Commonwealth are in hand, and the Captain of the Guard commanded by Proclamation, to take into custody all that shall disturb the Proceedings of the Court.

Mr. Solicitor *Cook* addressing himself to the Court, repeated the former Delays and Contempts of the Prisoner, so as that no more needed on his part, but to demand Judgement; yet offered notwithstanding the Notoriety of the Facts charged, mentioned in the Commons' Act, appointing the Trial, to prove the Truth of the same by Witnesses,[1] if thereto required; and therefore prayed, and yet (he said) not so much he, as the innocent Blood that had been shed, the cry whereof was very great, that a speedy Sentence and Judgement might be pronounced against the Prisoner at the Bar according to Justice.

Hereupon the Court putting the Prisoner in mind of former Proceedings, and that although by the Rules of Justice, if Advantage were taken of his past Contempts, nothing would remain but to pronounce Judgement against him, they had nevertheless determined to give him leave to Answer his Charge; which, as was told him in plain terms (for Justice knew no respect of Persons) to plead *Guilty* or *Not Guilty* thereto.

To which he made Answer as formerly, That he would not acknowledge the Jurisdiction of the Court, and that it was against the Fundamental Laws of the Kingdom; that there was no Law to make a King a Prisoner; that he had done nothing against his Trust; and issued out into such like Discourses.

Upon which, the Court's Resolution was again remembered to him, and he told, That he had now the third time publicly disowned and affronted the Court; That, how good a Preserver he had been of the Fundamental Laws, and Freedoms of the People, his Actions had spoken; that men's Intentions were used to be showed by their Actions, and that he had written his Meaning in bloody Characters throughout the Kingdom, and that he should find at last, though at present he would not understand it, that he was before a Court of Justice.

Hereupon, in the manner appointed, the Clerk in the Name of the Court demanding the Prisoner's Answer to his Charge, and the same refused, the Default was Recorded, the Prisoner remanded, and the Court Adjourned to the *Painted Chamber.*

★ ★ ★

---

1 The court had prepared a dossier of depositions.

27 Jan. 1648. *post Merid.*

Westminster-Hall

The *Lord President,* and the rest of the Commissioners come together from the *Painted Chamber* to *Westminster-Hall,* according to their Adjournment, and take their Seats there, as formerly; and three Proclamations being made for Attendance and Silence,

The Court is called.[1]

The Prisoner is brought to the Bar, and Proclamation is again (as formerly) made for Silence; and the Captain of the Guard ordered to take into his Custody all such as should disturb the Court.

The *President* stood up, with an intention of address to the People, and not to the Prisoner, who had so often declined the Jurisdiction of the Court; which the Prisoner observing, moved he might be heard before Judgement given; whereof he received assurance from the Court, and that he should be heard after he had heard them first.

Whereupon the Court proceeded, and remembered the great Assembly then present, of what had formerly passed betwixt the Court and the Prisoner, the Charge against him in the Name of the People of *England,*[2] exhibited to them, being a Court constituted by the Supreme Authority of *England,* his refusal three several days and times to own them as a Court, or to answer to the Matter of his Charge, his thrice recorded Contumacy, and other his[3] Contempts and Defaults in the precedent Courts; upon which, the Court then declared, that they might not be wanting to themselves, or to the Trust reposed in them, and that no man's Wilfulness ought to serve him to prevent Justice; and that they had therefore thought fit to take the substance of what had passed, into their serious consideration, to wit, the Charge, and the Prisoner's Contumacy, and the Confession which in Law doth arise upon that Contumacy, the Notoriety of the Fact charged, and other the Circumstances material in the Cause; and upon the whole Matter, had resolved and agreed upon a Sentence then ready to be pronounced against the Prisoner: But that in regard of his desire to be further heard, they were ready to hear

---

1 A list of the Commissioners present follows.

2 When Bradshaw made this claim, the masked Lady Fairfax cried, "Not half, not a quarter of the people of England. Oliver Cromwell is a traitor." She was then removed from the Hall.

3 In addition to.

him as to any thing material which he would offer to their consideration before the Sentence given, relating to the Defence of himself concerning the Matter charged; and did then signify so much to the Prisoner; who made use of that leave given, only to protest his respects of the Peace of the Kingdom, and Liberty of the Subject; and to say, That *the same made him at last to desire, That having somewhat to say that concerned both, he might before the Sentence given, be heard in the* Painted Chamber, *before the Lords and Commons;* saying, *it was fit to be heard, if it were Reason which he should offer, whereof they were Judges:* And pressing the Point much, he was forthwith answered by the Court, and told,

That, *that which he had moved was a declining of the Jurisdiction of the Court, whereof he had Caution frequently before given him.*

That, *it sounded to further delay, of which he had been too much guilty.*

That, *the Court being founded (as often had been said) upon the Authority of the* Commons *of* England, *in whom rested the* Supreme Jurisdiction, *the motion tended to set up another, or a co-ordinate Jurisdiction in derogation of the Power whereby the Court sat, and to the manifest delay of their Justice; in which regard,* he was told, *they might forthwith proceed to Sentence; yet for his further satisfaction of the entire Pleasure and Judgement of the Court, upon what he had then said,* he was told, and accordingly it was declared, that *the Court would withdraw half an hour.*

The Prisoner by command being withdrawn, the Court make their recess into the Room called The *Court of Wards,* considered of the Prisoner's Motion, and gave the *President* Direction to declare the Dissent thereto, and to proceed to the Sentence.

The Court being again set, and the Prisoner returned, was according to their Direction, informed, That *he had in effect received his Answer before the Court withdrew, and that their Judgement was (as to his Motion) the same to him before declared;* That, *the Court acted, and were Judges appointed by the Highest Authority, and that Judges were not to delay, no more than to deny Justice;* That, *they were good words in the good old Charter of* England, Nulli negabimus, nulli vendemus, nulli differemus Justitiam vel Rectum.[1] That, *their Duty called upon them to avoid further Delays, and to proceed to Judgement; which was their unanimous Resolution.*

---

1 The Magna Carta (cap. 40) reads "Nulli vendemus, nulli negabimus, aut differemus rectum aut justiciam" [To no one will we sell, to no one deny or delay right or justice].

Unto which, the Prisoner replied, and insisted upon his former Desires, confessing a delay, but that it was important for the Peace of the Kingdom, and therefore pressed again with much earnestness to be heard before the Lords and Commons.

In Answer whereto, he was told by the Court, That *they had fully before considered of his Proposal, and must give him the same Answer to his renewed desires, and that they were ready to proceed to Sentence, if he had nothing more to say.*

Whereunto he subjoined,[1] *He had no more to say*; but desired that might be Entered which he had said.

Hereupon, after some Discourse used by the *President*, for vindicating the Parliament's Justice, explaining the Nature of the Crimes of which the Prisoner stood charged, and for which he was to be condemned; and by way of Exhortation to the Prisoner, to a serious Repentance for his high Transgressions against God and the People, and to prepare for his Eternal Condition;

The Sentence formerly agreed upon, and put down in Parchment-Writing, *O Yes*[2] being first made for Silence, was by the Court's Command, solemnly pronounced and given: the Tenor whereof followeth.

Whereas the Commons *of* England *Assembled in Parliament, have by their late Act, Entitled,* An Act of the *Commons* of *England* Assembled in Parliament, for Erecting of an *High Court of Justice* for the Trying and Judging of *CHARLES STUART* K. *of* England; *Authorized and Constituted us an* High Court of Justice *for the Trying and Judging of the said* CHARLES STUART, *for the Crimes and Treasons in the said Act mentioned; By virtue whereof, the said* CHARLES STUART *hath been three several times convented*[3] *before this High Court, where, the first Day, being* Saturday *the Twentieth of* Jan. *instant, in pursuance of the said Act, a Charge of high Treason and other high Crimes, was in the behalf of the People of* England, *Exhibited against him, and read openly unto him, wherein he was charged, That he the said* CHARLES STUART, *being admitted King of* England, *and therein trusted with a limited Power, to govern by and according to the Law of the Land, and not otherwise; and by his Trust, Oath and Office, being obliged to use the Power committed to him, for the Good and Benefit of the People, and for the preservation of their Rights and Liberties; Yet nevertheless, out of a wicked Design to erect*

---

1 Added at the end of his statement.
2 Calling to order.
3 Summoned.

and uphold in himself an Unlimited and Tyrannical Power to rule according to his Will, and to overthrow the Rights and Liberties of the People, and to take away and make void the Foundations thereof, and of all Redress and Remedy of Misgovernment, which by the Fundamental Constitutions of this Kingdom were reserved on the People's behalf, in the Right and Power of frequent and successive Parliaments, or National Meetings in Council, he, the said CHARLES STUART, *for accomplishment of such his Designs, and for the protecting of himself and his Adherents in his and their wicked Practices, to the same End, hath traitorously and maliciously Levied War against the present Parliament, and People therein represented, as with the Circumstances of Time and Place, is in the said Charge more particularly set forth; And that he had thereby caused and procured many Thousands of the free People of this Nation to be slain; and by Divisions, Parties and Insurrections within this Land, by Invasions from Foreign Parts, endeavoured and procured by him, and by many other evil ways and means, he the said* CHARLES STUART *hath not only maintained and carried on the said War both by Sea and Land, but also hath renewed or caused to be renewed the said War against the Parliament and good People of this Nation in this present Year* 1648. *in several Counties and Places in this Kingdom in the Charge specified; and that he hath for that purpose given his Commission to his Son the Prince, and others, whereby besides multitudes of other persons, many, such as were by the Parliament entrusted and employed, for the Safety of this Nation, being by him or his Agents corrupted, to the betraying of their Trust, and revolting from the Parliament, have had Entertainment and Commission for the continuing and renewing of the War and Hostility against the said Parliament and People; and that by the said cruel and unnatural War so levied, continued and renewed, much innocent Blood of the free People of this Nation hath been spilt, many Families undone, the Public Treasure wasted, Trade obstructed, and miserably decayed, vast expense and damage to the Nation incurred, and many parts of the Land spoiled, some of them even to desolation; and that he still continues his Commission to his said Son, and other Rebels and Revolters, both* English *and* Foreigners, *and to the Earl of* Ormond, *and to the* Irish Rebels *and Revolters associated with him, from whom further Invasions upon this Land are threatened by his Procurement, and on his behalf; And that all the said wicked Designs, Wars and evil Practices of him the said* CHARLES STUART, *were still carried on for the Advancement and Upholding of the Personal Interest of Will, Power and pretended Prerogative to himself and his Family, against the Public Interest, Common Right, Liberty, Justice and Peace of the People of this Nation; And that he thereby hath been and is the Occasioner, Author and Continuer of the said unnatural, cruel and bloody Wars, and therein guilty of all the Treasons, Murders, Rapines, Burnings, Spoils, Desolations, Damage, and Mischief to this Nation, acted and committed in the said Wars, or occasioned thereby: Whereupon, the Proceedings and Judgement of this Court were prayed against him, as a Tyrant, Traitor and Murderer, and public Enemy to the Commonwealth, as by the said Charge more fully appeareth: To which Charge being read unto him as aforesaid, He the said CHARLES STUART was required to give his Answer; but he refused so to do. And upon Monday, the twenty second day of January instant, being again brought before this Court, and there required to answer directly to the said Charge, he still refused so to do; whereupon his Default and Contumacy was Entered: and the next day, being the third time brought before the Court, Judgement was then prayed against him on the behalf of the People of England, for his Contumacy, and for the Matters contained against him in the said Charge, as taking the same for confessed, in regard of his refusing to Answer thereto: Yet notwithstanding, this Court (not willing to take advantage of his Contempt) did once more require him to Answer to the said Charge, but he again refused so to do; Upon which his several Defaults, this Court might justly have proceeded to Judgement against him, both for his Contumacy, and the Matters of the Charge, taking the same for confessed, as aforesaid.*

Yet nevertheless, this Court for their own clearer Information, and further satisfaction, have thought fit to examine Witnesses upon Oath, and take notice of other Evidences touching the Matters contained in the said Charge, which accordingly they have done.[1]

Now therefore upon serious and mature deliberation of the Premises, and consideration had of the Notoriety of the Matters of Fact charged upon him as aforesaid, this Court is in judgement and Conscience satisfied that he the said CHARLES STUART is guilty of Levying War against the said Parliament, and People, and maintaining and continuing the same; for which in the said Charge he stands accused, and by the general course of his Government, Councils and Practices before and since this Parliament began (which have been, and are notorious and public, and the Effects whereof remain abundantly

---

1 The Commissioners appointed a committee to hear in private (on January 24th and 25th) the testimony of thirty-three witnesses, soldiers and civilians who testified the king had personally participated in the wars. Their depositions were then read out to the High Court in the Painted Chamber.

upon Record) this Court is fully satisfied in their Judgements and Consciences, that he hath been and is guilty of the wicked Designs and Endeavours in the said Charge set forth, and that the said War hath been Levied, maintained and continued by him, as aforesaid, in prosecution and for accomplishment of the said Designs; And that he hath been and is the Occasioner, Author and Continuer of the said unnatural, cruel and bloody Wars, and therein guilty of High Treason, and of the Murders, Rapines, Burnings, Spoils, Desolations, Damage and Mischief to this Nation, acted and committed in the said War, and occasioned thereby. For all which Treasons and Crimes, this Court doth adjudge, That he the said CHARLES STUART, as a Tyrant, Traitor, Murderer and Public Enemy to the good People of this Nation, shall be put to Death by the severing of his Head from his Body.

This Sentence being read, the *President* spake as followeth;

The Sentence now Read and Published, is the Act, Sentence, Judgement and Resolution of the whole Court.

Whereupon the whole Court stood up and owned it.

The Prisoner being withdrawn, the Court Adjourned it self forthwith into the *Painted Chamber*. [...]

3. **"King Charles His Speech Made upon the Scaffold at Whitehall-Gate immediately before his Execution."** *King Charles His Trial at the High Court of Justice sitting in Westminster Hall.* **The Second Edition. London: Printed by J.M. for Peter Cole, Francis Tyton, and John Playford, 1650[1]**

Tuesday, January 30.

About ten in the Morning the King was brought from St. *James*'s, walking on foot through the Park, with a *Regiment of Foot*, part before and part behind him, with Colours flying, Drums beating,

---

1 On the morning of the execution, Bishop Juxon prayed with, and administered the Sacrament to, the king. He then read the lesson from the Prayer Book for that day: the Passion of Christ. Charles I, accompanied by Juxon and Sir Thomas Herbert (appointed by Parliament to attend the king during his captivity), then walked with Colonel Tomlinson, from St. James's Palace towards the palace at Whitehall. The king was to be executed on a scaffold erected outside Whitehall's Banqueting House.

his private guard of *Partizans*,[1] with some of his *Gentlemen* before, and some behind bare-headed, Dr. *Juxon* next behind him, and Colonel *Tomlinson* (who had the charge of him) talking with the King bare-headed from the Park, up the stairs into the Gallery, and so into the *Cabinet-Chamber*, where he used to lie, where he continued at his *Devotion*, refusing to dine (having before taken the *Sacrament*) only about an hour before he came forth, he drank a glass of Claret wine, and eat a piece of bread about twelve at noon.

From thence he was accompanied by Dr. *Juxon*, Colonel *Tomlinson*, and other Officers, formerly appointed to attend him, and the private guard of *Partizans*, with *Musketeers* on each side, through the *Banqueting-house* adjoining, to which the Scaffold was erected, between *Whitehall-Gate*, and the *Gate* leading into the Gallery from S. *James's*: The Scaffold was hung round with black,[2] and the floor covered with black, and the Axe and Block laid in the middle of the Scaffold. There were divers Companies of Foot, and Troops of Horse placed on the one side of the Scaffold towards *Kings-street*, and on the other side towards *Charing-Cross*, and the multitudes of people that came to be *Spectators* very great.

The King being come upon the Scaffold, looked very earnestly on the Block, and asked Col. *Hacker* if there were no higher: and then spake thus (directing his Speech chiefly to Col. *Tomlinson*.)

King. *I Shall be very little heard of any body here, I shall therefore speak a word unto you here:*[3] *Indeed I could hold my peace very well, if I did not think that holding my peace would make some men think that I did submit to the guilt, as well as to the punishment: but I think it is my duty to God first, and to my Country, for to clear my self both as an honest man, a good King, and a good Christian. I shall begin*

---

1 Footmen carrying partisans.
2 Parliament had issued a directive instructing that the scaffold be thus covered.
3 Though the area around the Banqueting House at Whitehall (the site of the execution) was packed with spectators, the low scaffold was enclosed by ranks of soldiers. On the scaffold with the king were: Colonel Tomlinson, Bishop Juxon, Colonel Hacker, several soldiers, two disguised headsmen, and two or three shorthand writers. When giving his speech, Charles I referred to notes written on a small piece of paper.

first with my Innocency, *Introth*[1] *I think it not very needful for me to insist long upon this, for all the world knows that I never did begin a War with the two Houses of Parliament, and I call God to witness, to whom I must shortly make an account, That I never did intend for to encroach upon their Privileges, they began upon me, it is the Militia they began upon, they confessed that the Militia was mine, but they thought it fit for to have it from me: and to be short, if any body will look to the dates of Commissions, of their Commissions and mine, and likewise to the Declarations, will see clearly that they began these unhappy Troubles, not I: so that as the guilt of these enormous Crimes that are laid against me, I hope in God that God will clear me of it, I will not, I am in charity: God forbid that I should lay it upon the two Houses of Parliament, there is no necessity of either, I hope that they are free of this guilt: for I do believe that ill Instruments between them and me, has been the chief cause of all this blood-shed: so that by way of speaking, as I find my self clear of this, I hope (and pray God) that they may too: yet for all this, God forbid that I should be so ill a Christian as not to say that God's Judgments are just upon me: Many times he does pay Justice by an unjust Sentence, that is ordinary: I will only say this, That an unjust Sentence* that I suffered for to take effect, is punished now by an unjust Sentence upon me, that is, so far I have said, to show you that I am an innocent man.*

Now for to show you that I am a good Christian: I hope there is† *a good man that will bear me witness, That I have forgiven all the world, and even those in particular that have been the chief causers of my death; who they are, God knows, I do not desire to know, I pray God forgive them. But this is not all, my Charity must go farther. I wish that they may repent, for indeed they have committed a great sin in that particular: I pray God with St. Stephen, That this be not laid to their charge, nay, not only so, but that they may take the right way to the Peace of the Kingdom, for my Charity commands me, not only to forgive particular men, but my Charity commands me to endeavour to the last gasp the Peace of the Kingdom: So (Sirs) I do wish with all my Soul, and I do hope (there is*‡ *some here will carry it further) that they may endeavour the Peace of the KINGDOM.*

---

* Strafford. [Original marginalia.]
† Pointing to Dr. *Juxon.* [Original marginalia.]
‡ Turning to some gentlemen that wrote. [Original marginalia.]

---

1 In truth; truly.

Now (Sirs) I must show you both how you are out of the way, and will put you in a way: First, you are out of the way, for certainly all the way you ever have had yet, as I could find by any thing, is in the way of Conquest; certainly this is an ill way, for Conquest (Sir) in my opinion is never just, except there be a good just Cause, either for matter of Wrong or just Title, and then if you go beyond it, the first quarrel that you have to it, that makes it unjust at the end that was just at the first: But if it be only matter of Conquest, then it is a great Robbery: as a Pirate said to Alexander, *that He was the great Robber, he was but a petty Robber: and so, Sir, I do think the way that you are in, is much out of the way. Now Sir, for to put you in the way, believe it you will never do right, nor God will never prosper you, until you give God his due, the King his due (that is, my Successors) and the People their due: I am as much for them as any of you: You must give God his due, by regulating rightly his Church (according to his Scripture) which is now out of order: For to set you in a way particularly now I cannot, but only this, A National Synod freely called, freely debating among themselves, must settle this, when that every Opinion is freely and clearly heard.*

*For the King, indeed I will not (*then turning to a Gentleman that touched the Axe, said, *Hurt not the Axe, that may hurt me.* * *For the King) the Laws of the Land will clearly instruct you for that; therefore, because it concerns my own particular, I only give you a touch of it.*

For the people: And truly I desire their Liberty and Freedom as much as any body whomsoever, but I must tell you, That their Liberty and their Freedom, consists in having of Government; those Laws, by which their Life and their Goods may be most their own. It is not for having share in Government (Sir) that is nothing pertaining to them; A Subject and a Sovereign are clean different things, and therefore until they do that, I mean, That you do put the People in that Liberty as I say, certainly they will never enjoy themselves.

Sirs, It was for this that now I am come here: If I would have given way to an Arbitrary way, for to have all Laws changed according to the power of the Sword, I needed not to have come here, and therefore I tell you (and I pray God it be not laid to your charge) That I am the Martyr of the People.

Introth Sirs, I shall not hold you much longer, for I will only say this to you, That in truth I could have desired some little time longer, because that I would have put this that I have said in a little more

---

* Meaning if he did blunt the edge. [Original marginalia.]

order, and a little better digested than I have done, and, therefore I hope that you will excuse Me.

I have delivered my Conscience, I pray God that you do take those courses that are best for the good of the kingdom and your own salvations.

Dr. Juxon. Will your Majesty (though it may be very well known Your Majesty's affections to Religion, yet it may be expected that you should) say somewhat for the World's satisfaction.

King. *I thank you very heartily (my Lord) for that I had almost forgotten it. Introth, Sirs, My Conscience in Religion I think is very well known to all the world, and therefore I declare before you all, That I die a Christian, according to the profession of the Church of England, as I found it left me by my Father, and this honest man* I *think will witness it.* Then turning to the Officers, said: *Sirs, excuse me for this same, I have a good cause, and I have a gracious God. I will say no more.* Then turning to Colonel *Hacker,* he said; *Take care they do not put me to pain, and Sir this, and it please you;* But then a Gentleman coming near the Axe, The King said, *Take heed of the Axe. Pray take heed of the Axe,* Then the King speaking to the Executioner, said, *I shall say but very short Prayers, and when I thrust out my hands* ———— Then the King called to Doctor *Juxon* for his *Night-Cap,* and having put it on, he said to the Executioner, *Does my hair trouble you?* who desired him to put it all under his Cap, which the King did accordingly by the help of the Executioner and the Bishop: Then the King turning to Doctor *Juxon,* said, *I have a good Cause and a gracious God on my side.*

Doctor Juxon. There is but one Stage more. This Stage is turbulent and troublesome; it is a short one: But you may consider, it will soon carry you a very great way: it will carry you from earth to heaven; and there you shall find a great deal of cordial joy and comfort.

King. *I go from a corruptible, to an incorruptible Crown;*[1] *where no disturbance can be, no disturbance in the world.*

Doctor Juxon. You are exchanged from a Temporal to an Eternal Crown, a good exchange.

The King then said to the Executioner, is my hair well? Then the King took off His Cloak and His George,[2] giving his George

---

*   Pointing to D. *Juxon.* [Original marginalia.]

---

1   *Crown* 1 Corinthians 9:25.

2   The jewel that forms part of the insignia of the Order of the Garter, of which St. George was the patron saint.

to Doctor *Juxon*, saying, Remember*————Then the King put off his Doublet, and being in his Waistcoat, put his Cloak on again, then looking upon the Block, said to the Executioner, *You must set it fast.*

Executioner. It is fast Sir.

King. *It might have been a little higher.*[1]

Executioner. It can be no higher Sir.

King. *When I put out my hands this way,*† *then*————

After that having said two or three words (as he stood) to himself, with hands and Eyes lift up; Immediately stooping down, laid his neck upon the Block: And then the Executioner again putting his hair under his Cap, the King said (Thinking he had been going to strike) *stay for the sign.*

Executioner. Yes, I will, and it please your Majesty.

And after a very little pause, the King stretching forth his hands, The Executioner at one blow severed his head from his body.

That when the King's head was cut off, the Executioner held it up, and showed it to the Spectators.

And his Body was put in a Coffin covered with black Velvet for that purpose, and conveyed into his Lodgings there: And from thence it was carried to his house at S. *James's*, where his body was put in a Coffin of lead, laid there to be seen by the people;[2] and about a fortnight after it was carried to *Windsor*, accompanied with the Duke of *Lenox*, the Marquess of *Hartford*, and the Earl of *Southampton*, and Doctor *Juxon*, late Bishop of *London*, and others, and Interred in the Chapel-Royal in the Vault with King *Henry* the eight, having only this Inscription upon his Coffin. *Charles, King of England, etc.* 1648.[3]

Sic transit Gloria Mundi.[4]

FINIS

---

* It is thought for to give it to the Prince. [Original marginalia.]

† Stretching them out. [Original marginalia.]

---

1 The block was unusually low, ten inches or less from the ground.

2 Very few individuals were admitted to see the king's body.

3 On 7 February 1649, the body of Charles I was transported by Sir Thomas Herbert and Anthony Mildmay to Windsor. The next day, the duke of Richmond and the earls of Hertford, Lindsey, and Southampton selected a place for burial in St. George's Chapel. Colonel Whichcot, the Governor, refused to allow Bishop Juxon to read the service for the dead from the Prayer Book at the funeral, held on February 9th. The king was, therefore, buried in silence.

4 "Thus passes the glory of the world."

Appendix C: Restoration Revelations and Restraints

[The following documents attest to the struggle, after the Restoration, to control the representation of Charles I and to punish those who endorsed the regicide in print. The Proclamation (C.1) demonstrates the danger that John Milton, and other writers who advocated and defended the execution of the king, faced upon the restoration of Charles II in May 1660. Milton was forced into hiding. Though Parliament called in Milton and John Goodwin, and their books, on 16 June 1660, the Proclamation was not issued until 13 August. While both Milton and Goodwin escaped detainment, the common hangman burned the books in question on 27 August in London. Milton emerged from hiding after the Act of Free and General Pardon, Indemnity and Oblivion was issued on 29 August—though the Act did not exempt Milton from punishment specifically. Sometime between 13 September and 6 November, Milton was apprehended by James Norfolke, sergeant-at-arms of the Commons, who believed that the Proclamation of August 13 was still in effect. Milton was released from custody on 15 December 1660.

The memorandum (C.2) is ascribed to Arthur Annesley (1614–86), created first Earl of Anglesey on 20 April 1661. Between 1660 and 1682, Anglesey held various offices, including vice-treasurer and receiver-general of Ireland, treasurer of the navy, lord privy seal, and privy councillor. He amassed a considerable library and was, incidentally, a friend of John Milton. Upon his death, his son put his library up for sale; Millington, the auctioneer, discovered the handwritten memorandum in the Earl's copy of *Eikon Basilike*, a key document in the authorship controversy. Millington tore out the memorandum and had it delivered to Whitehall, where it was seen by others. Madan offers no explanation for its appearance in copies of *Eikonoklastes* published in Amsterdam in 1690 (Madan 162).]

1. By the King. A Proclamation. London, Printed by *John Bill*, Printer to the King's most Excellent Majesty, 1660

For calling in, and suppressing of two Books written by *John Milton*; the one Entitled, *Johannis Miltoni Angli pro Populo Anglicano*

Defensio, contra Claudii Anonymi, aliàs Salmasii, Defensionem Regiam;[1] and the other in answer to a Book Entitled, *The Portraiture of his Sacred Majesty in his Solitude and Sufferings*. And also a third Book Entitled, *The Obstructors of Justice*, written by *John Goodwin*.[2]

CHARLES R.

Whereas *John Milton*, late of *Westminster* in the County of *Middlesex*, hath published in Print two several Books, The one Entitled, *Johannis Miltoni Angli pro Populo Anglicano Defensio, contra Claudii Anonymi, aliàs Salmasii, Defensionem Regiam*: And the other in Answer to a Book Entitled, *The Portraiture of his Sacred Majesty in his Solitude and Sufferings*. In both which are contained sundry Treasonable Passages against Us and Our Government, and most Impious endeavours to justify the horrid and unmatchable Murder of Our late Dear Father, of Glorious Memory.

And whereas *John Goodwin*, late of *Coleman-Street, London*, Clerk, hath also published in Print, a Book Entitled, *The Obstructors of Justice*, written in defence of the traitorous Sentence against his said late Majesty. And whereas the said *John Milton*, and *John Goodwin*, are both fled, or so obscure themselves, that no endeavours used for their apprehension can take effect, whereby they might be brought to Legal Trial, and deservedly receive condign[3] punishment for their Treasons and Offences.

Now to the end that Our good Subjects may not be corrupted in their Judgements, with such wicked and Traitorous principles, as are dispersed and scattered throughout the beforementioned Books: We, upon the motion of the Commons in Parliament now assembled, do hereby straightly charge and Command all and every Person and Persons whatsoever, who live in any City, Borough, or Town Incorporate, within this Our Kingdom of *England*, the Dominion of *Wales*, and Town of *Berwick* upon *Tweed*, in whose hands any of those Books are, or

---

1 Milton published *The First Defense of the English People* in 1651 in response to Claude De Saumaise's *Defense of the Reign of Charles I* (November 1649), a work commissioned by Charles II.

2 Goodwin (1594?-1665) supported the Independents during the Civil War and wrote a significant number of works until the Restoration. His book was burned by the common hangman, but Goodwin, who went into hiding, was cleared of prosecution some months later by an indemnity.

3 Appropriate.

hereafter shall be, That they upon pain of Our high Displeasure, and the consequence thereof, do forthwith, upon publication of this Our Command, or within Ten days immediately following, deliver, or cause the same to be delivered to the Mayor, Bailiffs, or other chief Officer or Magistrate, in any of the said Cities, Boroughs, or Towns Incorporate, where such person or persons so live; or, if living out of any City, Borough, or Town Incorporate, then to the next Justice of Peace adjoining to his or their dwelling or place of abode; or if living in either of Our Universities, then to the Vice Chancellor of that University where he or they do reside.

And in default of such voluntary delivery, which We do expect in observance of Our said Command, That then and after the time before limited, expired, the said Chief Magistrate of all and every the said Cities, Boroughs, or Towns Incorporate, the Justices of the Peace in their several Counties, and the Vice-Chancellors of Our said Universities respectively, are hereby Commanded to Seize and Take, all and every the Books aforesaid, in whose hands or possession soever they shall be found, and certify the names of the Offenders unto Our Privy Council.

And We do hereby also give special Charge and Command to the said Chief Magistrates, Justices of the Peace, and Vice-Chancellors respectively, That they cause the said Books which shall be so brought unto any of their hands, or seized or taken as aforesaid, by virtue of this Our Proclamation, to be delivered to the respective Sheriffs of those Counties where they respectively live, the first and next Assizes that shall after happen. And the said Sheriffs are hereby also required, in time of holding such Assizes, to cause the same to be publicly burned by the hand of the common Hangman.

And We do further straightly Charge and Command, That no man hereafter presume to Print, Vend, Sell, or Disperse any the aforesaid Books, upon pain of Our heavy Displeasure, and of such further Punishment, as for their presumption in that behalf, may any way be inflicted upon them by the Laws of this Realm.

Given at Our Court at *Whitehall*, the Thirteenth day of *August*, in the Twelfth year of Our Reign, One thousand six hundred and sixty.
GOD SAVE THE KING.

2. The Anglesey Memorandum (1686), added to EIKONOKLASTES In Answer To a Book Intitl'd EIKON BASILIKE. By John Milton. Amsterdam, 1690

An ADVERTISEMENT.

Whereas a Book, called *Eikon Basilike*, or King *Charles* the *First's Meditations*, is most commonly reported and believed by many, especially the Clergy, to be composed by King *Charles* the *First*; the following Insertion of the Noble Lord *Anglesey*, under his own Hand was found by *Edward Millington*, prefixed to one of the Books, reputed to be King *Charles* the *First's*.

Which *Memorandum*, if the *Declaration* of two Kings may be believed, is sufficient to satisfy the World, how much that King was imposed upon by Dr. *Gauden* Bishop of *Exeter*.

MEMORANDUM.

King *Charles* the *Second*, and the Duke of *York*, did both (in the last Session of Parliament, 1675. when I showed them in the Lords' House, the Written Copy of this Book, wherein are some Corrections and Alterations, written with the Late King *Charles* the *First's* own Hand,) assure me that this was none of the said King's compiling, but made by Dr. *Gauden* Bishop of *Exeter*, which I here insert for the undeceiving of others in this Point, by attesting so much under my Hand:

Anglesey

Works Cited and Select Bibliography

Achinstein, Sharon. "Milton Catches the Conscience of the King: *Eikonoklastes* and the Engagement Controversy." *Milton Studies* 29 (1993): 143-63.

Almack, Edward, ed. *Eikon Basilike*. London: De La More Press, 1904.

Anon. *Monumentum Regale: or a Tomb, Erected for that incomparable and Glorious Monarch. Charles the First*. London, 1649.

Aristotle. *The Art of Rhetoric*. Trans. John Henry Freese. Cambridge, MA: Harvard UP; London: William Heinemann, 1975.

Barber, Sarah. "Charles I: Regicide and Republicanism." *History Today* 46.1 (1996): 29-34.

Beecham, Henry. "John Gauden and the Authorship of the *Eikon Basilike*." *The Library: A Quarterly Journal of Bibliography* 20 (1965): 142-44.

Benjamin, Walter. *The Origin of German Tragic Drama*. Trans. John Osborne. London: New Left Books, 1977.

Boehrer, Bruce. "Elementary Structures of Kingship: Milton, Regicide, and the Family." *Milton Studies* 23 (1987): 97-117.

Bourdieu, Pierre. *Language and Symbolic Power*. Ed. John B. Thompson. Trans. Gino Raymond and Matthew Adamson. Cambridge, MA: Harvard UP, 1991.

Brome, Alexander. *Poems*. Ed. Roman R. Dubinski. Toronto: U of Toronto P, 1982.

Burnet, Bishop Gilbert. *History of His Own Times*. London, 1724.

Cable, Lana. "Milton's Iconoclastic Truth." *Politics, Poetics, and Hermeneutics in Milton's Prose*. Ed. David Loewenstein and James Grantham Turner. Cambridge: Cambridge UP, 1990. 135-51. Revised in, "'Unimprisonable Utterance': Imagination and the Attack on *Eikon Basilike*." *Carnal Rhetoric: Milton's Iconoclasm and the Poetics of Desire*. Durham: Duke UP, 1995. 144-70.

Corns, Thomas N. "Imagery in Civil War Polemic: Milton, Overton and the *Eikon Basilike*." *Milton Quarterly* 14.1 (March 1980): 1-6.

———. "Lovelace, Herrick, and the *Eikon Basilike*." *Uncloistered Virtue: English Political Literature, 1640-1660*. Oxford: Clarendon Press; New York: Oxford UP, 80-91.

———, ed. *The Royal Image: Representations of Charles I.* Cambridge: Cambridge UP, 1999.

Daniel, Clay. "*Eikonoklastes* and the Miltonic King." *South Central Review: The Journal of the South Central Modern Language Association* 15.2 (Summer 1998): 34-48.

Delany, Paul. *British Autobiography in the Seventeenth Century.* London: Routledge & Kegan Paul, 1969.

Doble, Charles E. "Notes and Queries on the *Eikon Basilike* I." *The Academy* 575 (12 May 1883): 330-32.

———. "Notes and Queries on the *Eikon Basilike* II." *The Academy* 577 (26 May 1883): 367-68.

———. "Notes and Queries on the *Eikon Basilike* III." *The Academy* 579 (9 June 1883): 402-03.

———. "Notes and Queries on the *Eikon Basilike* IV." *The Academy* 582 (30 June 1883): 457-59.

Dzelzainis, Martin. "Republicanism." *A Companion to Milton.* Ed. Thomas N. Corns. Oxford: Blackwell, 2001. 294-308.

Farrer, J.A. "Political Forgery: The *Eikon Basilike*." *Literary Forgeries.* London: Longmans, Green, and Co., 1907. 98-125.

Filmer, Sir Robert. *Patriarcha and Other Writings.* Ed. Johann P. Sommerville. Cambridge: Cambridge UP, 1991.

Greene, Douglas G. "A Note on *Eikon Basilike*." *Notes and Queries* 19 (1972): 176.

Guibbory, Achsah. "Charles's Prayers, Idolatrous Images, and True Creation in Milton's *Eikonoklastes*." *Of Poetry and Politics: New Essays on Milton and His World.* Ed. P.G. Stanwood. Binghamton, NY: Medieval and Renaissance Texts and Studies, 1995. 283-94.

Helgerson, Richard. "Milton Reads the King's Book: Print, Performance, and the Making of a Bourgeois Idol." *Criticism: A Quarterly for Literature and the Arts* 29.1 (Winter 1987): 1-25.

Hiles, Jane. "Milton's Royalist Reflex: The Failure of Argument and the Role of Dialogics in *Eikonoklastes*." *Spokesperson Milton: Voices in Contemporary Criticism.* Ed. Charles W. Durham and Kristin Pruitt McColgan. Selinsgrove: Susquehanna UP; London; Cranbury, NJ: Associated University Presses, 1994. 87-100.

Hollingworth, Richard. *A Defence of King Charles I. Occasioned by the Lies and Scandals of Many Bad Men of this Age.* London, 1692.

Hughes, Merritt Y. "Milton's *Eikon Basilike*." *Calm of Mind: Tercentenary Essays on Paradise Regained and Samson Agonistes in*

Honor of John S. Diekhoff. Ed. Joseph Anthony Wittreich. Cleveland: The Press of Case Western Reserve University, 1971. 1-24.

——. "New Evidence on the Charge that Milton Forged the Pamela Prayer in the *Eikon Basilike.*" *Review of English Studies* 3.10 (1952): 130-40.

James VI and I. *King James VI and I: Political Writings.* Ed. Johann P. Sommerville. Cambridge: Cambridge UP, 1994.

Kelsey, Sean. "Staging the Trial of Charles I." *The Regicides and the Execution of Charles I.* Ed. J. Peacey. Houndmills: Palgrave, 2001. 71-90.

——. *Inventing a Republic: the Political Culture of the English Commonwealth, 1649-1653.* Manchester: Manchester UP, 1997.

Knachel, Philip. *Eikon Basilike: The Portraiture of His Sacred Majesty in His Solitudes and Sufferings.* Ithaca, NY: Published for The Folger Shakespeare Library by Cornell UP, 1966.

Knoppers, Laura Lunger. *Constructing Cromwell: Ceremony, Portrait and Print, 1645-1661.* Cambridge: Cambridge UP, 2000.

Knott, John R. "'Suffering for Truth's sake': Milton and Martyrdom." *Politics, Poetics, and Hermeneutics in Milton's Prose.* Ed. David Loewenstein and James Grantham Turner. Cambridge: Cambridge UP, 1990. 153-170.

Lacey, Andrew. *The Cult of King Charles the Martyr.* Woodbridge: Boydell, 2003.

Loewenstein, David. "'Casting Down Imaginations': Milton as Iconoclast." *Criticism: A Quarterly for Literature and the Arts* 31.3 (Summer 1989): 253-70. Revised in, "'Casting Down Imaginations': Iconoclasm as History." *Milton and the Drama of History: Historical Vision, Iconoclasm, and the Literary Imagination.* Cambridge: Cambridge UP, 1990. 51-73.

McKnight, Laura Blair. "Crucifixion or Apocalypse? Refiguring the *Eikon Basilike.*" *Religion, Literature and Politics in Post-Reformation England, 1540-1688.* Ed. Donna.B. Hamilton and Richard Strier. Cambridge: Cambridge UP, 1996. 138-60.

MacLean, Gerald M. *Time's Witness: Historical Representation in English Poetry, 1603-1660.* Madison: U of Wisconsin P, 1990.

Madan, Francis Falconer. *A New Bibliography of the Eikon Basilike of King Charles the First; with a Note on the Authorship.* London: B. Quaritch, 1950.

Maddison, R.E. "*The King's Cabinet Opened*: A Case Study in Pamphlet History." *Notes and Queries* 13 (1966): 2-9.

Magnus, Elisabeth M. "Originality and Plagiarism in *Areopagiti-*

ca and *Eikonoklastes.*" *English Literary Renaissance* 21.1 (1991 Winter): 87-101.

Milton, John. *The Complete Prose Works of John Milton.* Ed. Don M. Wolfe, et al. 8 vols. New Haven: Yale UP, 1953-82.

Nalson, J. *A True Copy of the Journal of the High Court of Justice, for the Trial of K. Charles I.* London, 1684.

Nicholson, Oliver. "The Passing of Arthur and *Eikon Basilike.*" *Notes and Queries* 44 (September 1997): 342-44.

Norbrook, David. *Writing the English Republic: Poetry, Rhetoric and Politics, 1627-1660.* Cambridge: Cambridge UP, 1999.

O'Keefe, Timothy J. "The Imaginal Strategy of John Milton's *Eikonoklastes.*" *Ball State University Forum* 11.4 (1971): 33-45.

Peacock, John. "The Politics of Portraiture." *Culture and Politics in Early Stuart England.* Ed. Kevin Sharpe and Peter Lake. Stanford: Stanford UP, 1993. 199-228.

———. "The Visual Image of Charles I." *The Royal Image: Representations of Charles I.* Ed. Thomas N. Corns. Cambridge: Cambridge UP, 1999. 176-239.

Pocock, J.G.A. *The Machiavellian Moment: Florentine Political Thought and the Atlantic Republican Tradition.* 2nd ed. Princeton: Princeton UP, 2003.

Potter, Lois. *Secret Rites and Secret Writings: Royalist Literature 1641-1660.* Cambridge: Cambridge UP, 1989.

Randall, Helen W. "The Rise and Fall of a Martyrology: Sermons on Charles the First." *Huntingdon Library Quarterly* 10 (1946-47): 135-67.

Raymond, Joad. "Popular Representations of Charles I." *The Royal Image: Representations of Charles I.* Ed. Thomas N. Corns. Cambridge: Cambridge UP, 1999. 47-73.

Sandler, Florence. "Icon and Iconoclast." *Achievements of the Left Hand: Essays on the Prose of John Milton.* Ed. Michael Lieb and John T. Shawcross. Amherst: U of Massachusetts P, 1974. 160-84.

Scott, Edward J.L., ed. *Eikon Basilike.* London, 1880.

Sharpe, Kevin. *The Personal Rule of Charles I.* New Haven: Yale UP, 1992.

———. "Private Conscience and Public Duty in the Writings of Charles I." *Historical Journal* 40.3 (1997): 643-65.

———. "The King's Writ: Royal Authors and Royal Authority in Early Modern England." *Culture and Politics in Early Stuart England.* Ed. Kevin Sharpe and Peter Lake. Basingstoke: Macmillan, 1994. 117-38.

——. "'So Hard A Text'?: Images of Charles I, 1612-1700." *Historical Journal* 43.2 (2000): 383-405.

——. "'An Image Doting Rabble': the Failure of Republican Culture in Seventeenth-Century England." *Refiguring Revolutions: Aesthetics and Politics from the English Revolution to the Romantic Revolution.* Ed. Kevin Sharpe and Steven N. Zwicker. Berkeley: U of California P, 1998. 25-56.

Sherwood, Roy. *The Court of Oliver Cromwell.* London: Croom Helm, 1977.

Sirluck, Ernest. "*Eikon Basilike, Eikon Alethine,* and *Eikonoklastes.*" *Modern Language Notes* 69.7 (1954): 497-502.

——. "The *Eikon Basilike*: An Unreported Item in the Contemporary Authorship Controversy." *Modern Language Notes* 70.5 (1955): 331-32.

Skerpan, Elizabeth P. "Rhetorical Genres and the *Eikon Basilike.*" *Explorations in Renaissance Culture* 2 (1985): 99-111.

Stevens, Paul. "Milton's Janus-faced Nationalism: Soliloquy, Subject, and the Modern Nation State." *Journal of English and Germanic Philology* 100:2 (2001): 247-68.

Stewart, Byron S. "The Cult of the Royal Martyr." *Church History* 38.2 (1969): 175-87.

Symmons, Edward. *A Vindication of King Charles: Or, a Loyal Subject's Duty.* London, 1648.

Tomlinson, Howard. "Commemorating Charles I—King and Martyr?" *History Today* 45.2 (1995): 11-18.

Trevor-Roper, Hugh. "'*Eikon Basilike*': The Problem of the King's Book." *Historical Essays.* London: Macmillan; New York: St. Martin's Press, 1957.

Wagstaffe, Thomas. *A Vindication of King Charles the Martyr, Proving that His Majesty was the Author of Eikon Basilike. Against a Memorandum said to be Written by the Earl of Anglesey: and Against the Exceptions of Dr. Walker, and Others.* London, 1697.

Walker, Garthine. *Crime, Gender and Social Order in Early Modern England.* Cambridge: Cambridge UP, 2003.

Wedgwood, C.V. *A Coffin for King Charles: The Trial and Execution of Charles I.* Pleasantville, NY: The Akadine Press, 2001.

Wheeler, Elizabeth Skerpan. "*Eikon Basilike* and the Rhetoric of Self-Representation." *The Royal Image: Representations of Charles I.* Ed. Thomas N. Corns. Cambridge: Cambridge UP, 1999. 122-40.

Wilcher, Robert. "What was the King's Book for?: The Evolution of *Eikon Basilike*." *The Yearbook of English Studies: Politics, Patronage and Literature in England 1558-1658* 21 (1991): 218-28.

——. "Trial and Martyrdom: September 1647-January 1649." *The Writing of Royalism, 1628-1660*. Cambridge: Cambridge UP, 2001. 277-86.

Wordsworth, Christopher. *'Who Wrote* Eikon Basilike?*' Considered and Answered, in Two Letters*. London: John Murray, 1824.

——. *Documentary Supplement to 'Who Wrote* Eikon Basilike?*'* London: John Murray, 1825.

Zaller, Robert. "Breaking the Vessels: The Desacralization of Monarchy in Early Modern England." *Sixteenth Century Journal* 29.3 (1998): 757-78.

Zwicker, Steven N. *Lines of Authority: Politics and English Literary Culture, 1649-1689*. Ithaca: Cornell UP, 1993.